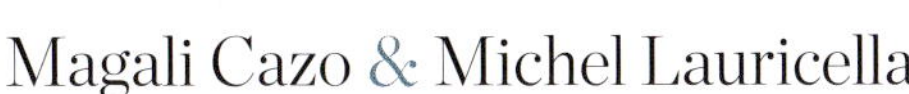
Magali Cazo & Michel Lauricella

The Little Drawing Workshop

52 Weeks of Drawing Lessons and Skill Building

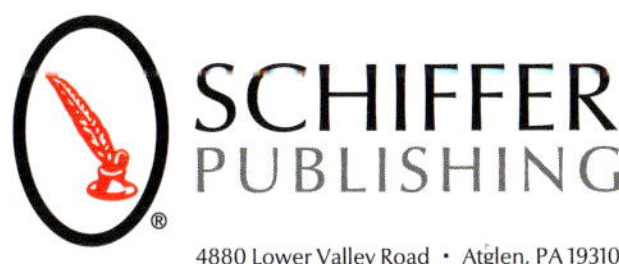

4880 Lower Valley Road • Atglen, PA 19310

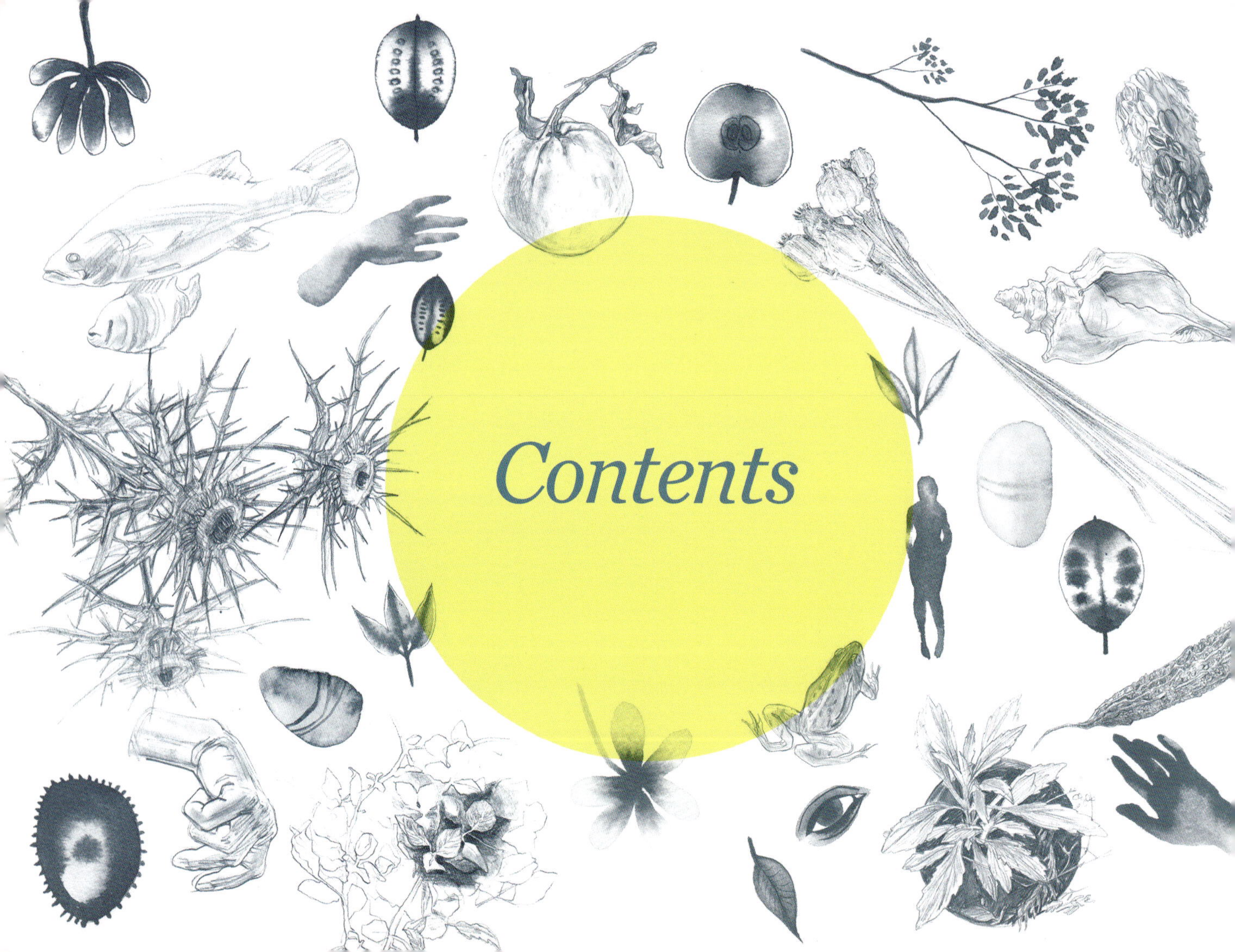

Contents

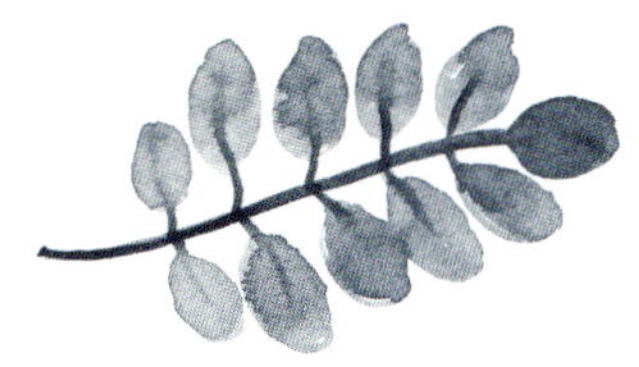

WEEKS

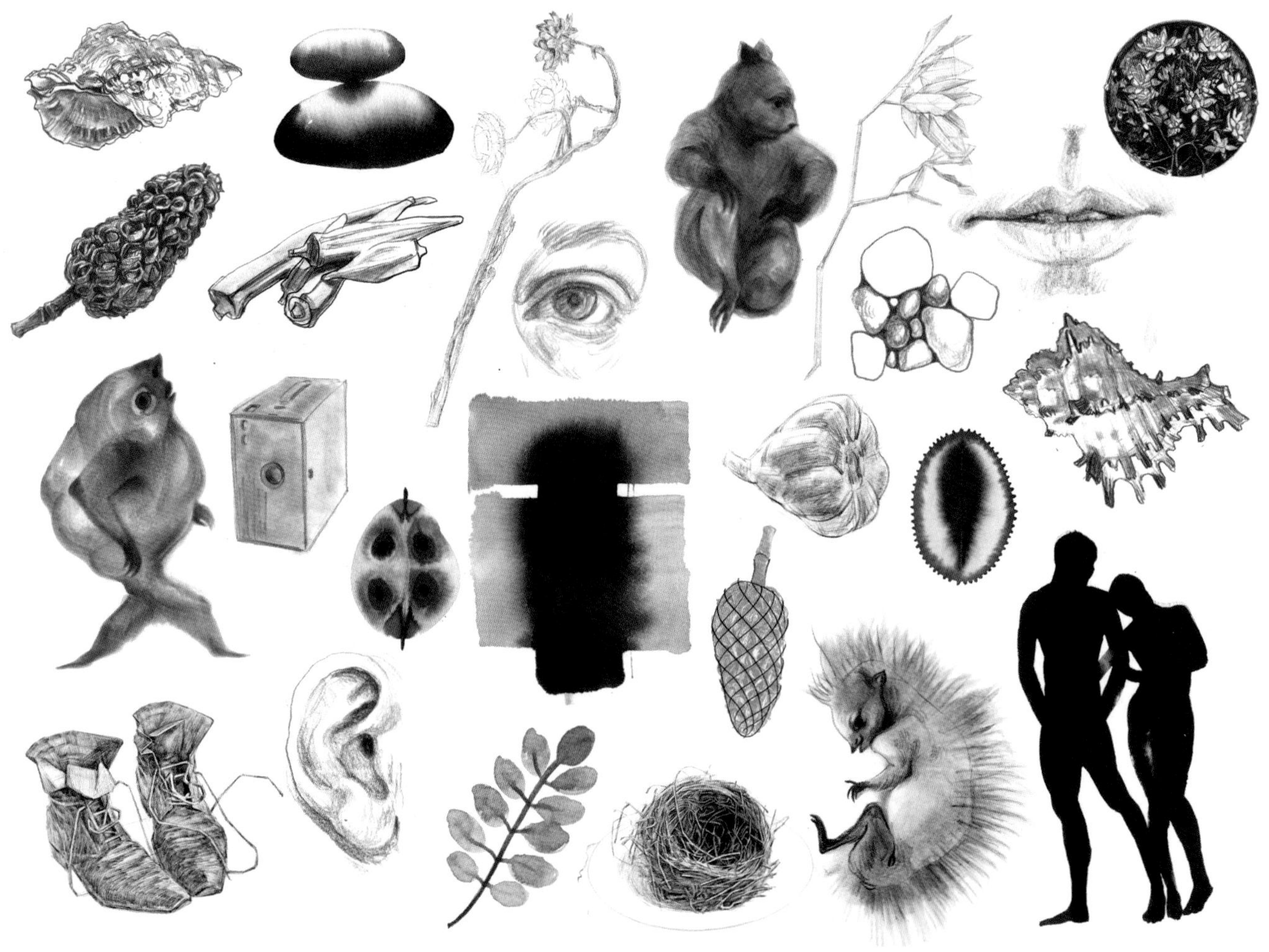

52 weeks, one year of drawing

This book is a collection of 52 exercises, in as many weeks, which alternate technical and expressive approaches, for one year of drawing. It is intended for all those, beginners or advanced, who wish to venture into a regular practice of drawing. Depending on your achievements, you will be able to respond to the proposals with more or less ambition.

We have preferred to divide the year into weeks rather than days in order to let you arrange this learning as you wish, but also and especially so that you can take the time to let your drawing and your ideas mature.

For each week, we propose a main exercise and additional suggestions, to be carried out according to your availability.

Ideally, divide the exercise into as many versions as possible. Regularity, the main key to progress, is preferable to long but scattered working hours. Take the time to give a real place to the practice of drawing in your life.

While the first half of this book is devoted to learning and recalling basic concepts, the second half encourages you to make choices, to question "methods," and to identify your preferences, where the pleasure has been most intense.

We hope that this book will lead you to a better understanding of yourself, in and through creation. Its purpose is to help you identify your interests, desires, and rhythm; familiarize yourself with the creative process; and accept its detours, questions, and infinite, contrary, and complementary possibilities.

The outcome can take the form of a free, realistic, or abstract work, constructed or "thrown away" according to moods or motives, or simply to vary experiences.

If we had the desire to design this book for two, it is because it seemed to us that the union of our two perspectives could open the field of possibilities. By comparing our visions of drawing and its learning, it seemed necessary to us to witness a practice in which one aspect does not exclude the other. There are multiple answers to the question "What is drawing?"; moreover, there are just as many reasons, and these different approaches can coexist peacefully. It will therefore be a question of observational drawing, imagination, figuration, and abstraction.

—Magali Cazo & Michel Lauricella

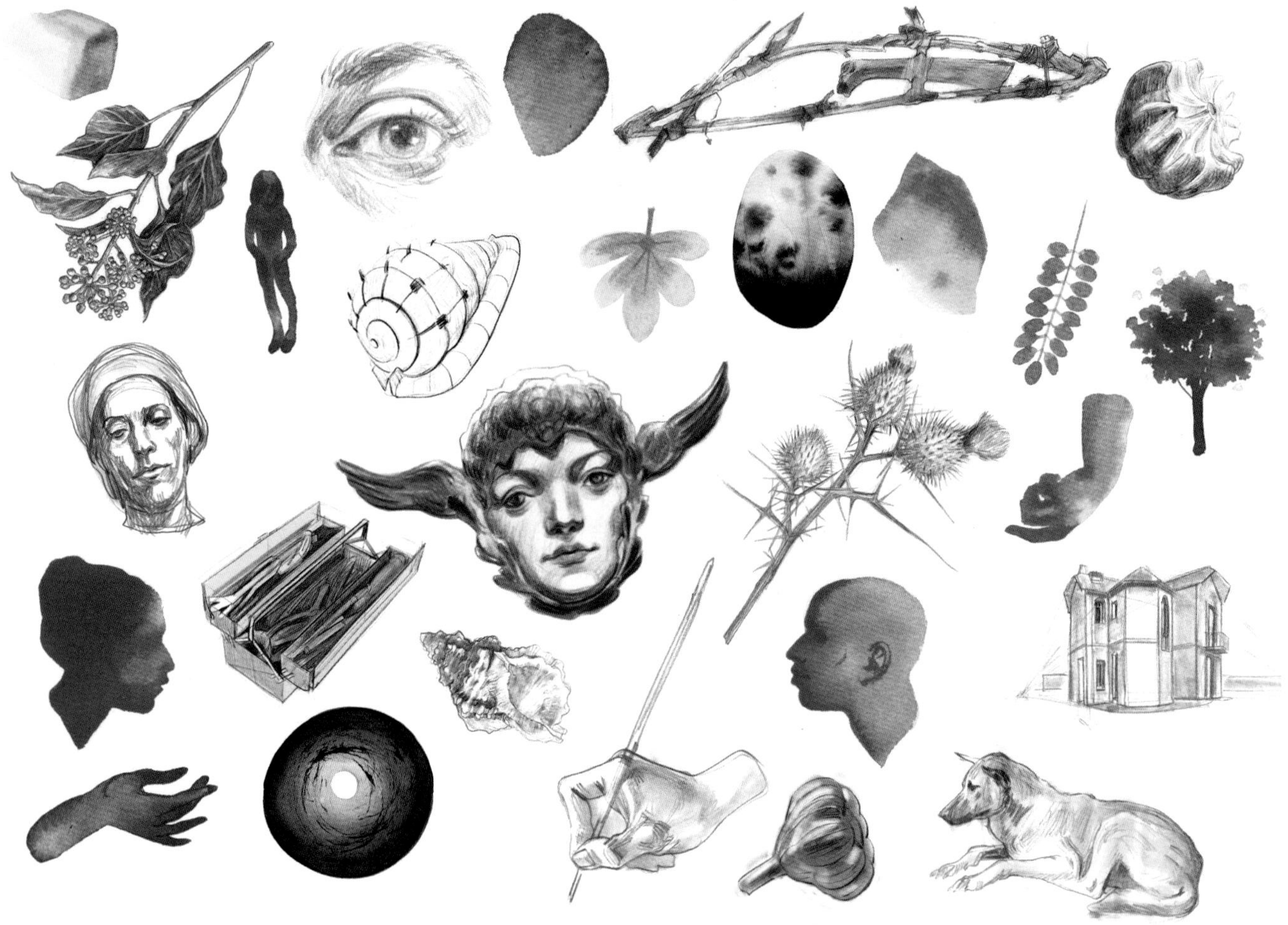

Introduction

Drawing allows us to develop our curiosity, our anchor in life, and our capacity for wonder. In drawing we speak without words; it's a universal language. "If we could say it with words, there would be no reason to paint," observed Edward Hopper.

The image reaches a part of the viewer that he cannot always analyze: beyond the subject represented, the line, contrast, color, framing, and composition also speak for themselves . . .

All these abstract notions silently communicate secret information to the viewer.

Through study and observation, drawing allows us to understand a form, a thing, a being. This practice makes us more and more curious and eager to grasp what surrounds us. When drawing is a means of expression, it offers the opportunity to "digest" our experiences and emotions. It somehow lightens our heads and hearts! It is a vector of sensations because it allows us to perceive things that we did not imagine before picking up a pencil. Moreover, we often notice that we are more successful at what we love: exploring our deepest feelings helps bring a drawing to life. Our motivation is greater when we do a portrait of a loved one.

We like to consider drawing as a mental practice. In reality, it is just as physical: it is often a matter of feeling what you represent in your body. We could even say that it is a question of becoming what we draw, of embodying it in order to reveal our identity. A drawing with perfectly correct proportions, but without feeling, may seem to have less resemblance than a "false" but "authentic" drawing.

For most of us, drawing preceded language—just as it existed in human history before writing. One could say that something very primal in us pushes us to trace and transmit to others what we carry within us and what we see.

But drawing is a victim of its sacralization: as we grow up, many of us no longer see it as a natural and spontaneous practice, but as a mysterious gift that only a few would possess. We are teachers and can testify to the fear that this belief engenders in our beginner students. This is why it is important to us to propose a practice of drawing based on pleasure.

The acquisition of technical skills, such as morphology and perspective, will be a valuable help. They are presented as aspects of the drawing, among others. Some of you will be happy to explore them; others will feel that their sensitivity leads them more towards free expression exercises.

THE EXERCISES

The first week is a starting time, with the development of your own space in which to create. At midterm and during the last week, the time will be reviewed. The rest of the weeks are structured according to this plan:

- a quotation, usually from an artist, always in connection with the proposed exercise
- the objective of the exercise
- "Your turn": the techniques used, the description of the exercise
- "If you have time": suggestions for continuing the exercise
- "Go and see": examples formulated to make your internet searches easier

Each time, we will invite you to look at the images of three artists—painters, sculptors, comic book and fashion designers, illustrators, photographers—who will broaden your field of possibilities.

The work proposals from photos ideally imply that you take these pictures yourself. Be present at all stages of creation. Selection, framing, lighting, color or black and white, etc. Drawing is choosing.

Drawing from your own photos allows you to start a personal vision before the research begins.

1. Woodless graphite pencil

2. India ink and wash brush

3. Colored pencils

4. Charcoals of different diameters

THE MATERIALS

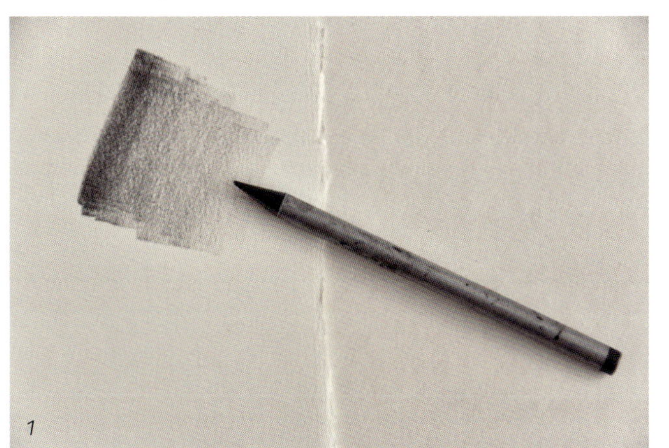

1

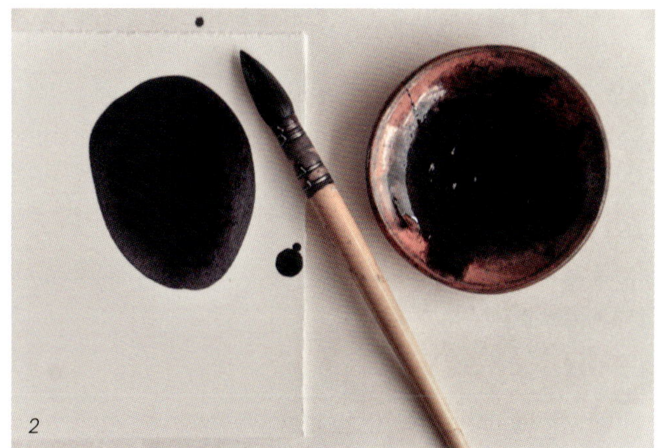

2

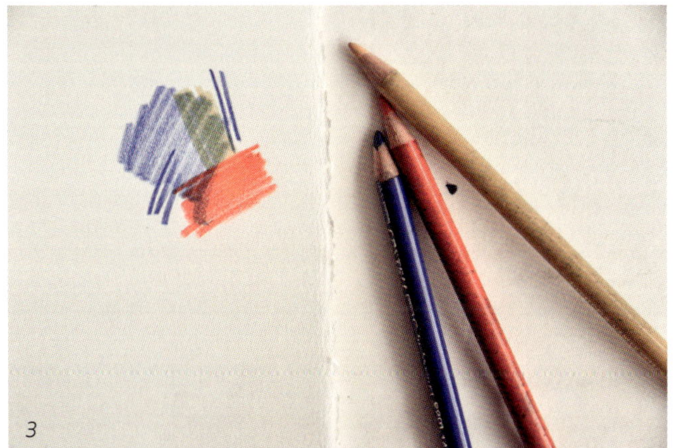

3

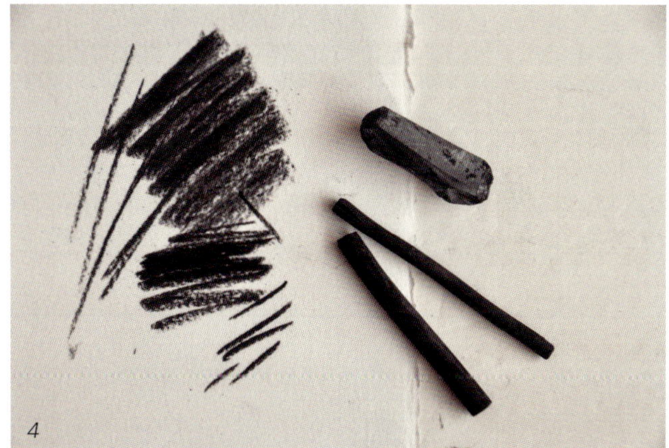

4

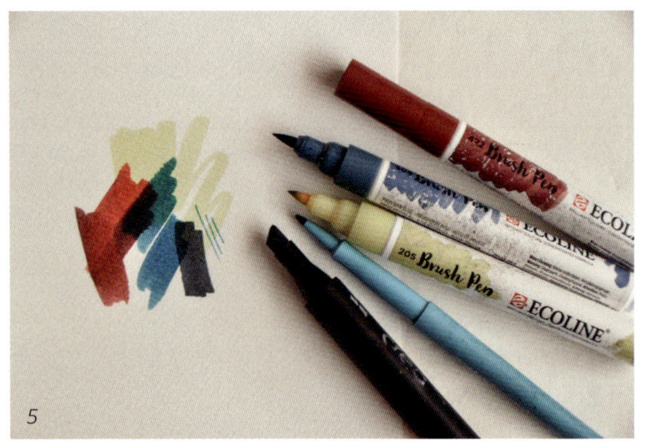

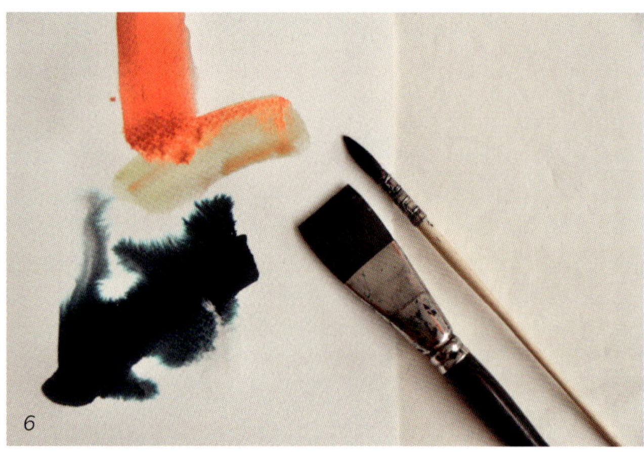

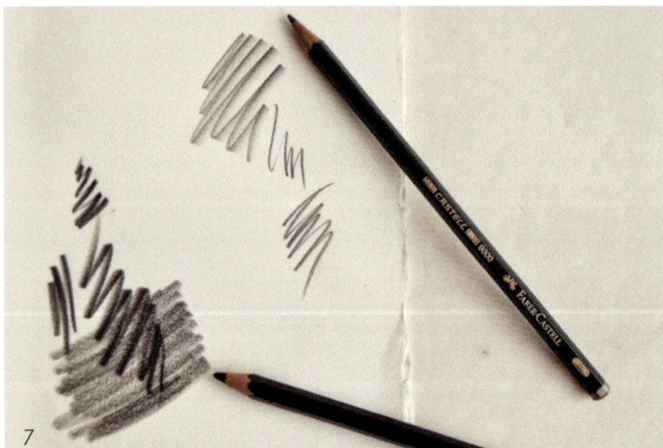

5. Different felt pens

6. Colored inks and wash brushes

7. Plain pencil (graphite lead) at the top and black watercolor pencil at the bottom

The following is a nonexhaustive list of tools and materials. You can adapt it to your budget: for example, colored pencils for children are fine for beginners. Once you have gained experience in the different techniques, you will be able to choose better products according to your preferences. Equipping yourself shouldn't be an obstacle.

- **Graphite lead (ordinary pencil):** An ore, a variety of crystallized carbon. A great classic! The ordinary pencil (HB) is available in all types of hardness. The greasiest (from 2B to 9B) are particularly pleasant and offer beautiful shades of mineral black glossy. The driest (H series) are appreciated for their strength; they are often used in the preparatory stages. Greasy pencils (series B) are always used over dry ones.

- **Charcoal:** Semicarbonized charcoal. Great flexibility of use: it is easily erased with a cloth or a kneaded eraser. Ideal for quick sketches but also for the preparatory stages of construction. It may require a coat of fixative.

- **Black chalk:** Shale. It has a good density and goes very well with charcoal applied as an undercoat.

- **Red chalk:** Iron oxide ore. It differs from black chalk in color but is very similar in texture.

- **Crayons:** Pigment, clay or kaolin, and wax. These tools of our childhood offer a large quantity of nuances. They make it possible to approach color with less apprehension than painting!

- **Felts:** Water-based or alcohol-based. Just like crayons, they are tools much appreciated by professionals. There are many brands, the color ranges are extensive, and different line thicknesses are available. Felt pens do not allow for error, but they can also be worked in successive layers.

- **Ballpoint pen:** A common tool of great interest! It allows many nuances according to the intensity of the pressure of the hand on the support. You can start your drawing with a light hand and press down gradually. The Bic brand offers different tip thicknesses, which allows you to enrich your "palette."

- **India ink:** Black carbon ink. This ink is still highly appreciated for the quality and density of its shade. Diluted in water, it offers an infinite number of shades. On moist paper, it allows all kinds of experiments: diffusion, drops, haloes, etc.

- **Watercolor:** Pigments (mineral or vegetable) and gum arabic (extracted from the acacia). A delicate water technique, which can be worked by superimposing. We like to associate it with high-quality paper and play with the reserve blank (an area of paper left blank).

- **Ecoline and Colorex ink:** Diluted with water, these inks offer intense colors.

- **Gouache:** Pigments, gum arabic, and the addition of a white pigment. This paint is good on paper supports: that is why we will use it in this book dedicated to drawing, especially since it combines very well with dry techniques, such as graphite leads or watercolor pencils. It is very opaque paint with a beautiful matte finish.

- **Dry pastel:** Pigments, gum arabic or tragacanth, and white soil.

This very old tool is still appreciated. It is generally used on high quality-paper that is somewhat eye-catching. It can be used in combination with inks, once dry, and provides a contrast in tone, writing, and texture on the surface.

- **Oil pastel:** With oily or waxy binder. It is more attractive than dry pastel. Once placed on the support, it can be reworked with improvised tools—kitchen knife, etc.—which makes it possible to remove material and engrave it.

- **Typographic ink:** Oil-based ink, soluble or not in water, used for engraving. In this book, we will use this medium to create monotypes. The monotype is the printing of a single print (hence its name) of a drawing made on a sheet of paper affixed to a surface coated with typographic ink (or oil painting).

You will also need:

- brushes (ideally wash brushes, often more expensive, but whose spindle shape leaves a beautiful reserve of ink while allowing both large lines and fine indications to be drawn with the tip)
- tracing paper, in sheets or rolls
- A5, A4, and A3 notebooks, all three sizes in 80 g
- basic white machine paper or recovered paper of all kinds for your tests
- white watercolor paper (preferably in 300 g, to prevent it from curling)
- Digital tools—graphic tablet in Photoshop, Illustrator, Paint, Procreate, etc. If you are already equipped, you can of course use them. But we advise you to vary the pleasures and not to try to transpose the traditional techniques proposed above to these digital tools.

Use a small additional notebook for research and small notes, in order to keep a link with the exercises proposed each week, which can be done on multiple media and formats.

Create a bank of images and references (cut photos, pasted into another notebook, digital files, Pinterest, etc.). The goal is to identify your areas of interest by simply and intuitively grouping images that you like (fashion, architecture, photography, comics, painting, sculpture, etc.).

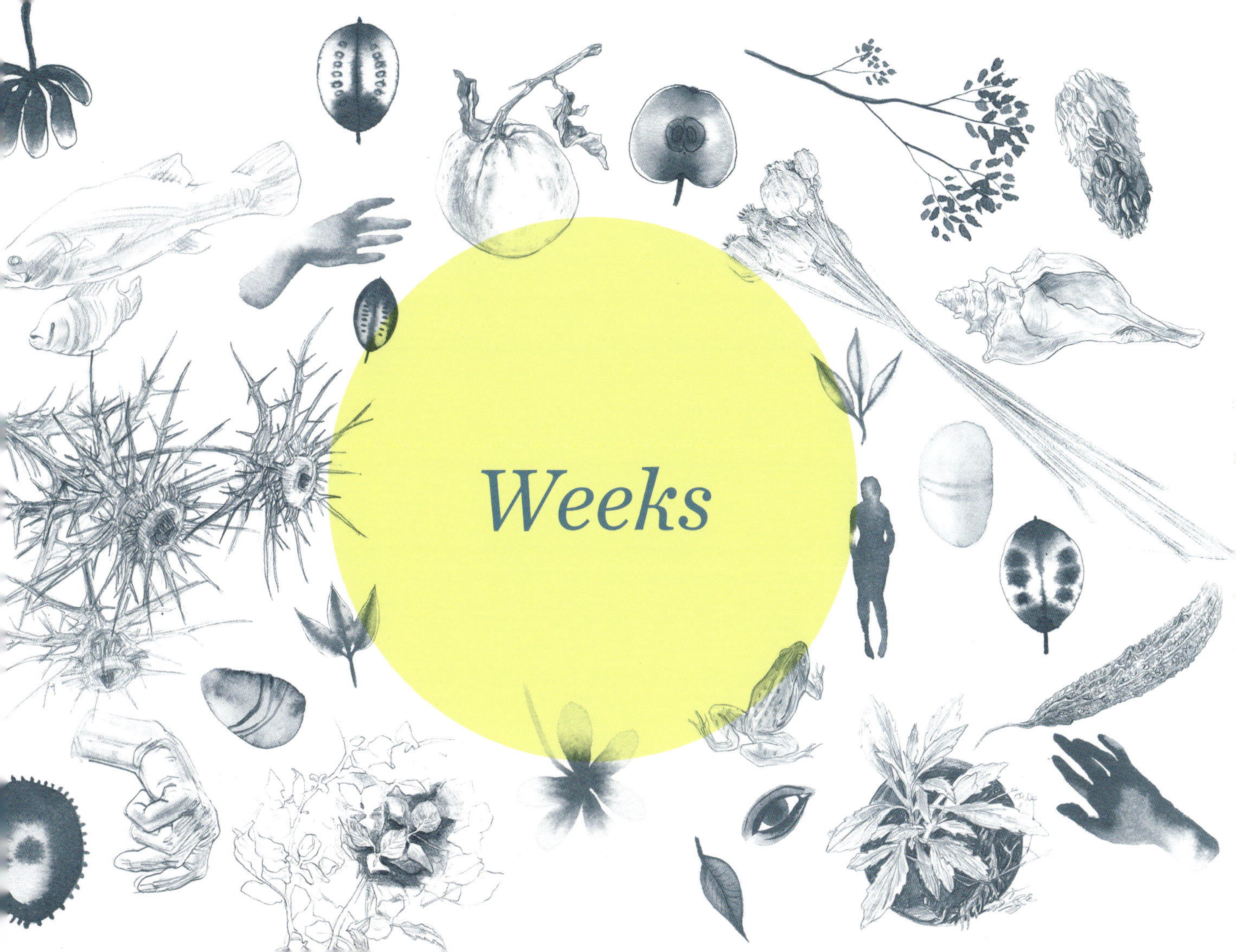

Weeks

A place of one's own

An artist must understand silence.
An artist must create a space for silence to enter his work.
Silence is like an island in the middle of a turbulent ocean.
—Marina Abramovic, *Walk through Walls: Memoir*

Start this year of creation by building your "nest"!

A workshop, a room, a small corner, or even a piece of wall and a desk: the important thing is to have a place of your own. It will house the objects and images that you like, that intrigue and stimulate you. This will help you concentrate. No matter the size of your place: what matters is to feel that it can welcome your experiments with confidence. We need it to create: putting "outside" what we wear "inside" sometimes makes us vulnerable. These moments are small metamorphoses, and no animal molts in plain sight!

The habit of a place helps you get into the right mood more quickly. When we enter our workshop, we know that it is the place of work and introspection. Our brains are used to it; it knows the way! It is more willing to create there than elsewhere—solitude is more fertile and less frightening.

During the week, look for objects, pictures, memories, books, and natural elements that can inspire you. Don't think; follow your intuition. Some of these finds will remain in plain view, on a shelf or a wall—others will be stored but will come to your rescue in case of a mental block. This small imaginary museum can be the gateway to a good working session.

In addition, as already mentioned in the introduction, we strongly advise you to keep your production out of sight throughout this year: it is not so simple to know what you want to express, and external opinions that come too early could take you away from your objective instead of getting closer to it.

Go and see

Brassaï (1899–1984), photos of workshops
Charles Matton (1931–2008), *The Boxes*
Gautier Deblonde (contemporary), the Atelier series

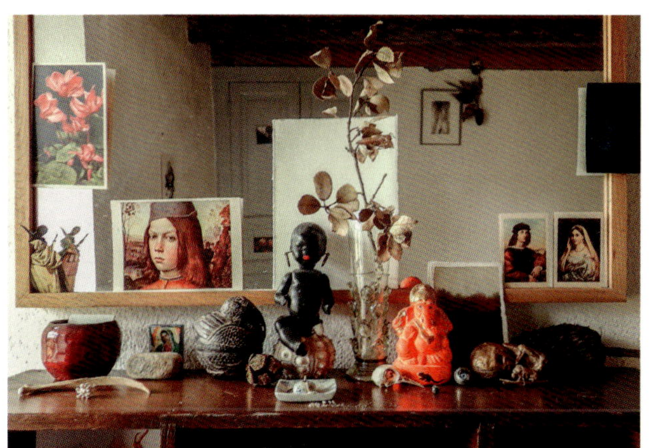

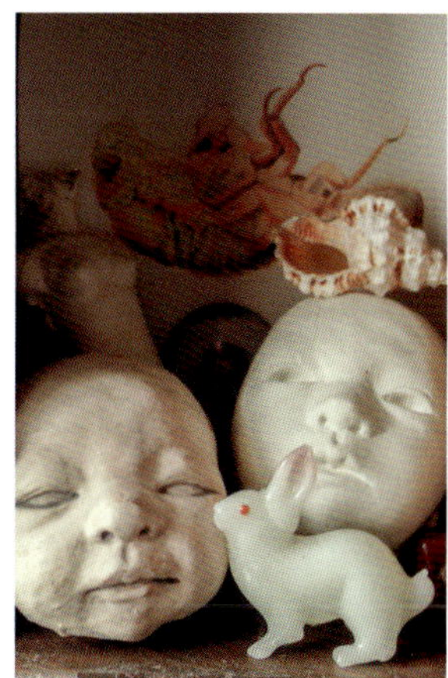

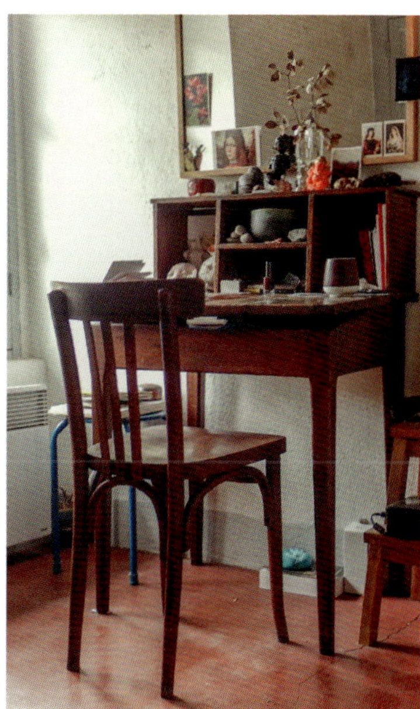

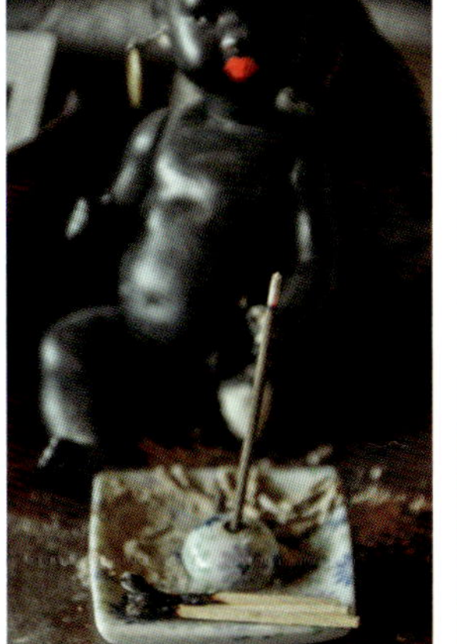

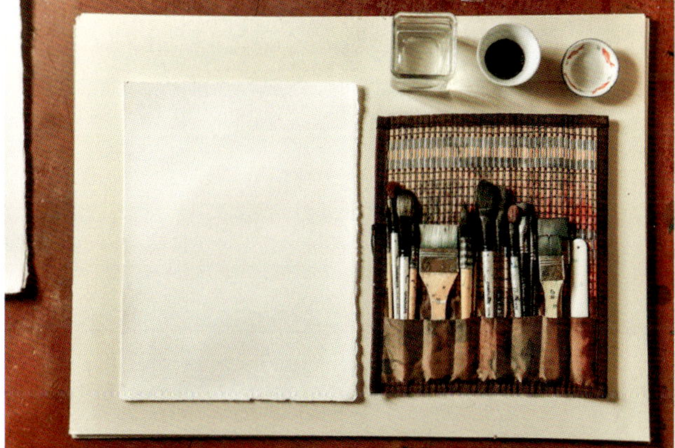

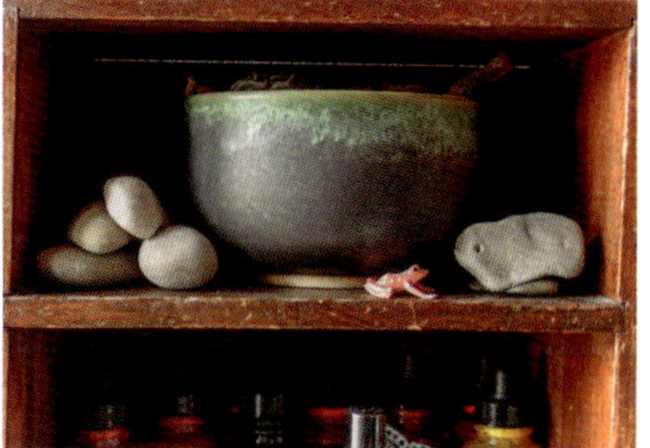

Magali Cazo's workshop

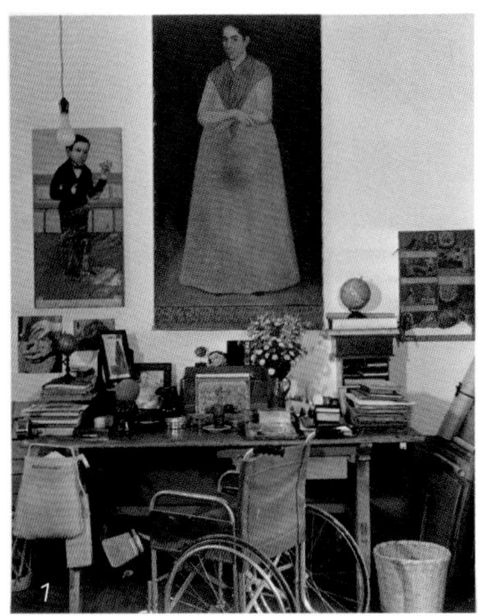

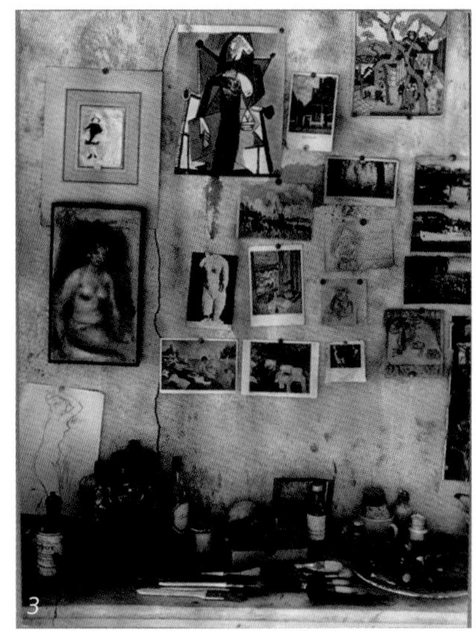

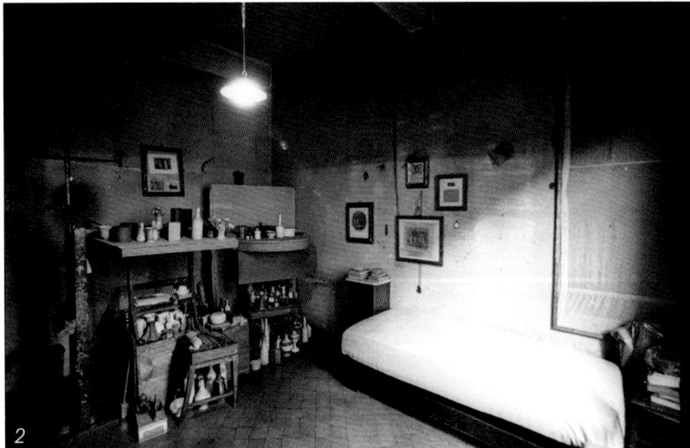

Views of different workshops:

1. Frida Kahlo

2. Giorgio Morandi

3. Pierre Bonnard

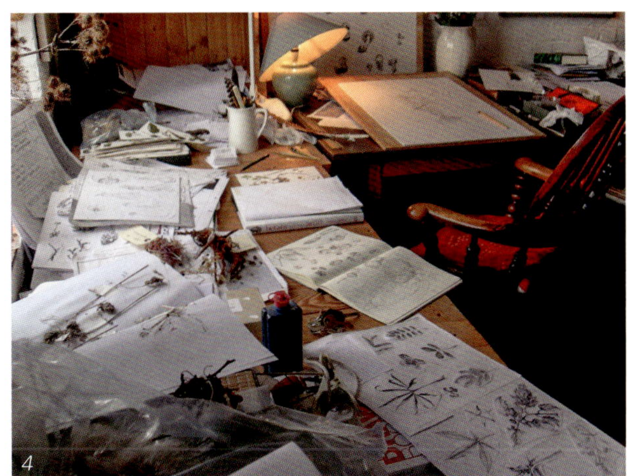

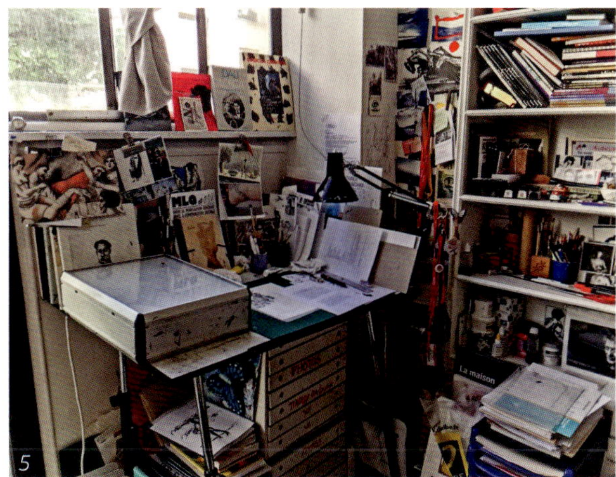

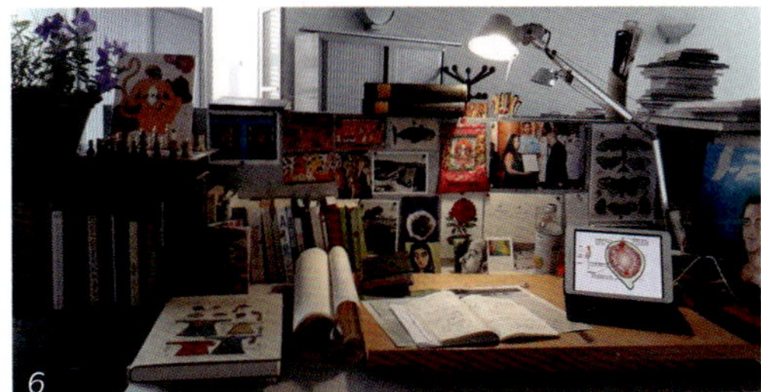

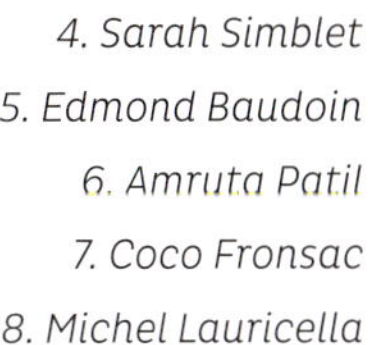

4. Sarah Simblet

5. Edmond Baudoin

6. Amruta Patil

7. Coco Fronsac

8. Michel Lauricella

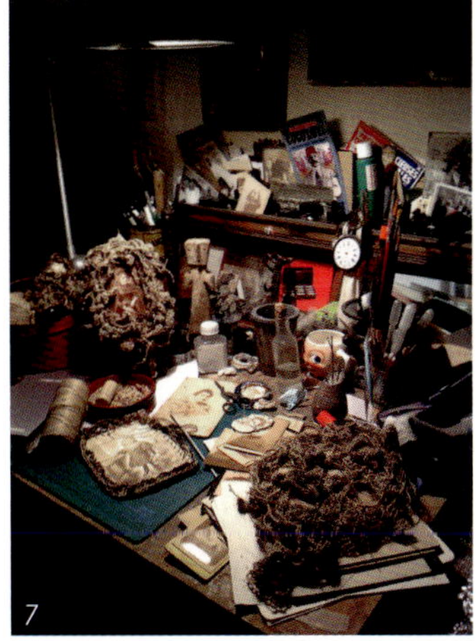

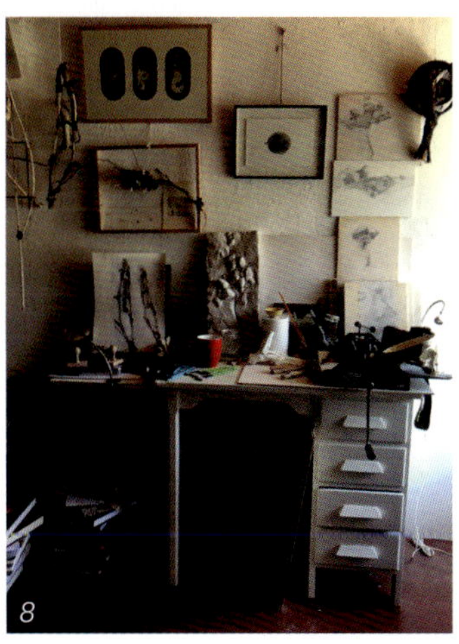

Turned upside down

Art is always more abstract than we fancy. Form and colour tell us of form and colour—that is all.
—Oscar Wilde, *Portrait of Dorian Gray*

Perhaps the greatest difficulty in observational drawing is simply seeing what is before our eyes. We often look more at what we know about an object than what we can observe. Representing reality sometimes involves doing "strange" things: drawing a tiny leg on a character if it is seen in perspective, gluing two objects together when you know they are separate items, etc. For this, it is necessary to retain a certain abstraction, without judgment. This week's exercise will help you do that.

YOUR TURN

Take a blank sheet of paper and a rather dark and thin tool (fine marker, ballpoint pen, sharpened grease pencil).

You're going to reproduce backward.

Choose a drawing with many lines. Turn it upside down and try to forget what it says. Focus your attention on a line somewhere at the top. Follow her. Move forward on the sheet without knowing what you are drawing. If you can't help but name things in your head, stay in abstract notions: curve, angle, right, hollow, relief, shading . . . You can hide the drawing with a blank sheet of paper and discover it as you copy it.

After a while, you will experience a particular, deeper concentration. It's like unplugging your brain and being a pair of eyes! If you are a beginner, chances are you will be surprised of the result.

IF YOU HAVE THE TIME

- Repeat the exercise with a black-and-white photo.
- Try to copy a drawing right side up while preserving the same state of concentration.

Go and see

Edgar Degas (1834–1917), drawings
Vincent van Gogh (1853–1890)
Lucian Freud (1922–2011)

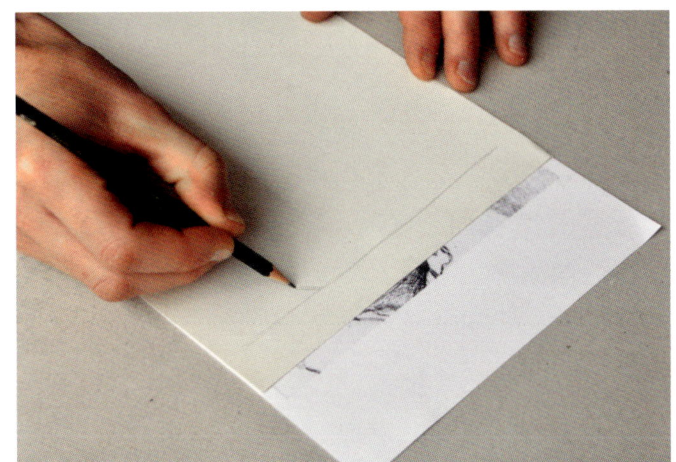

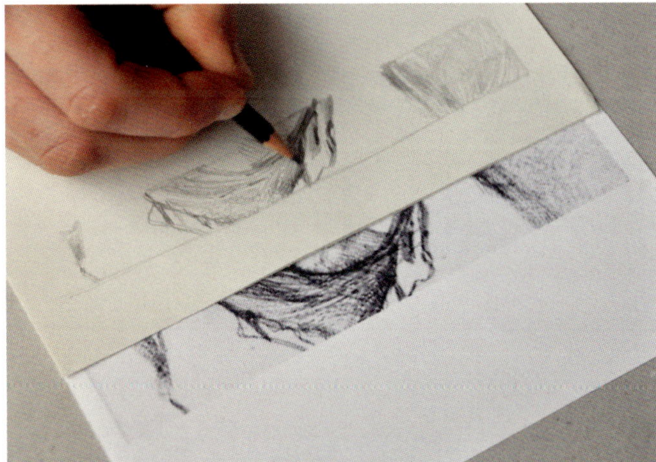

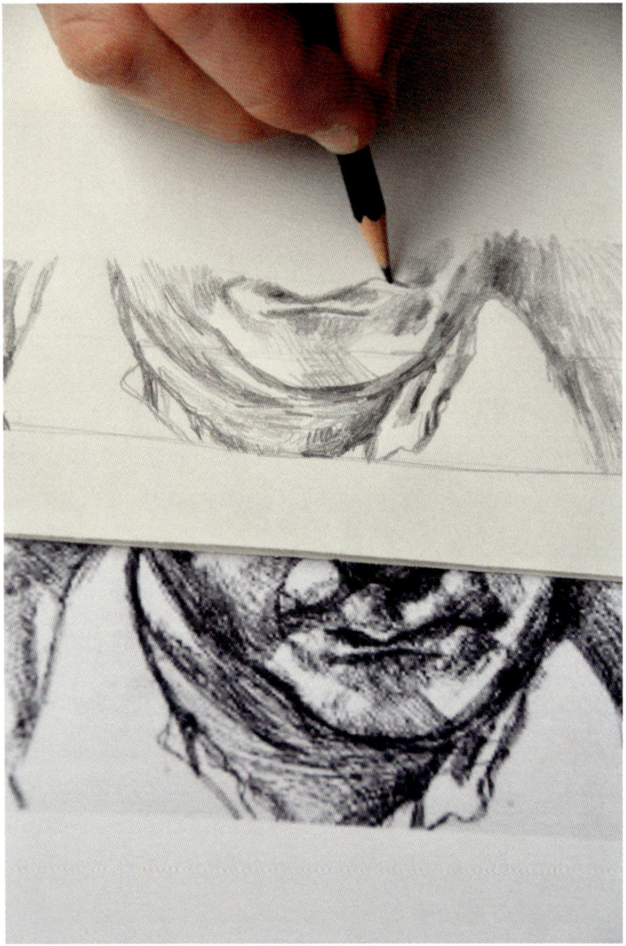

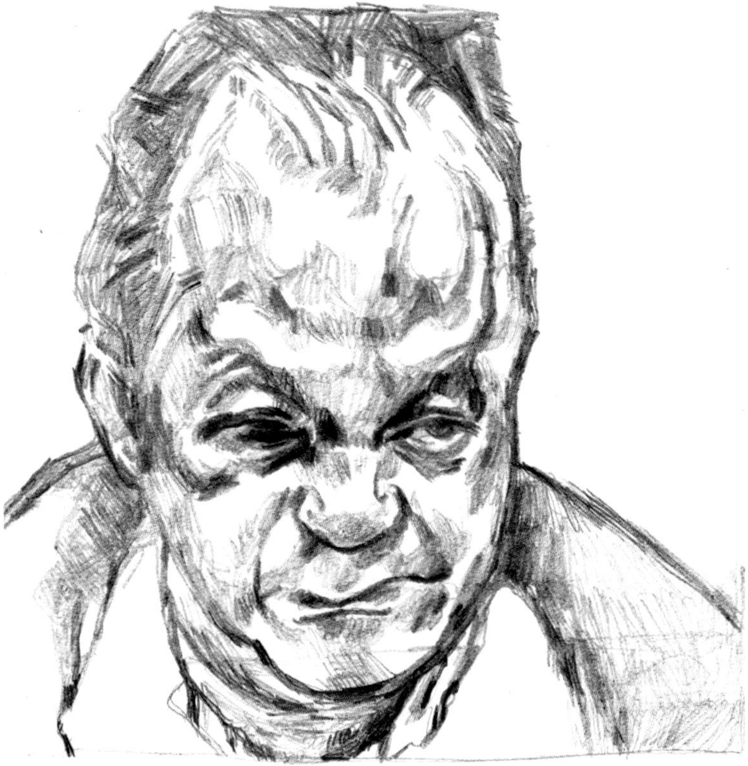

Based on Lucian Freud's Head of Bruce Berna

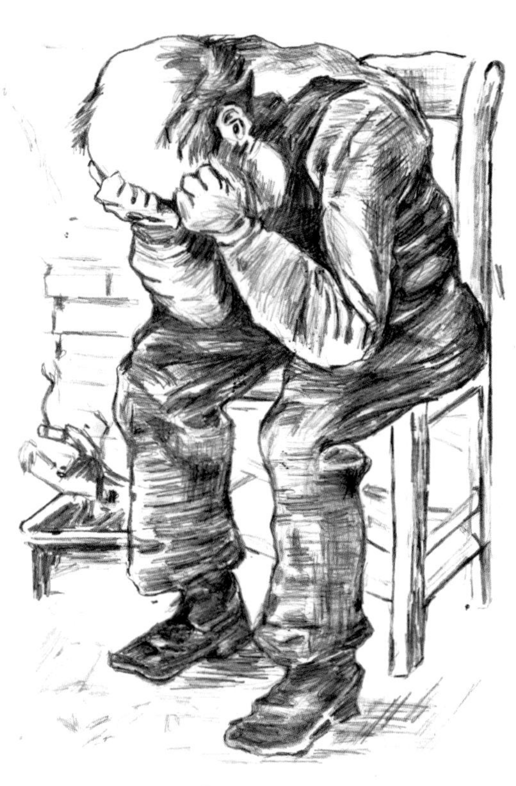

Based on Vincent van Gogh's Sorrowing Old Man (At Eternity's Gate)

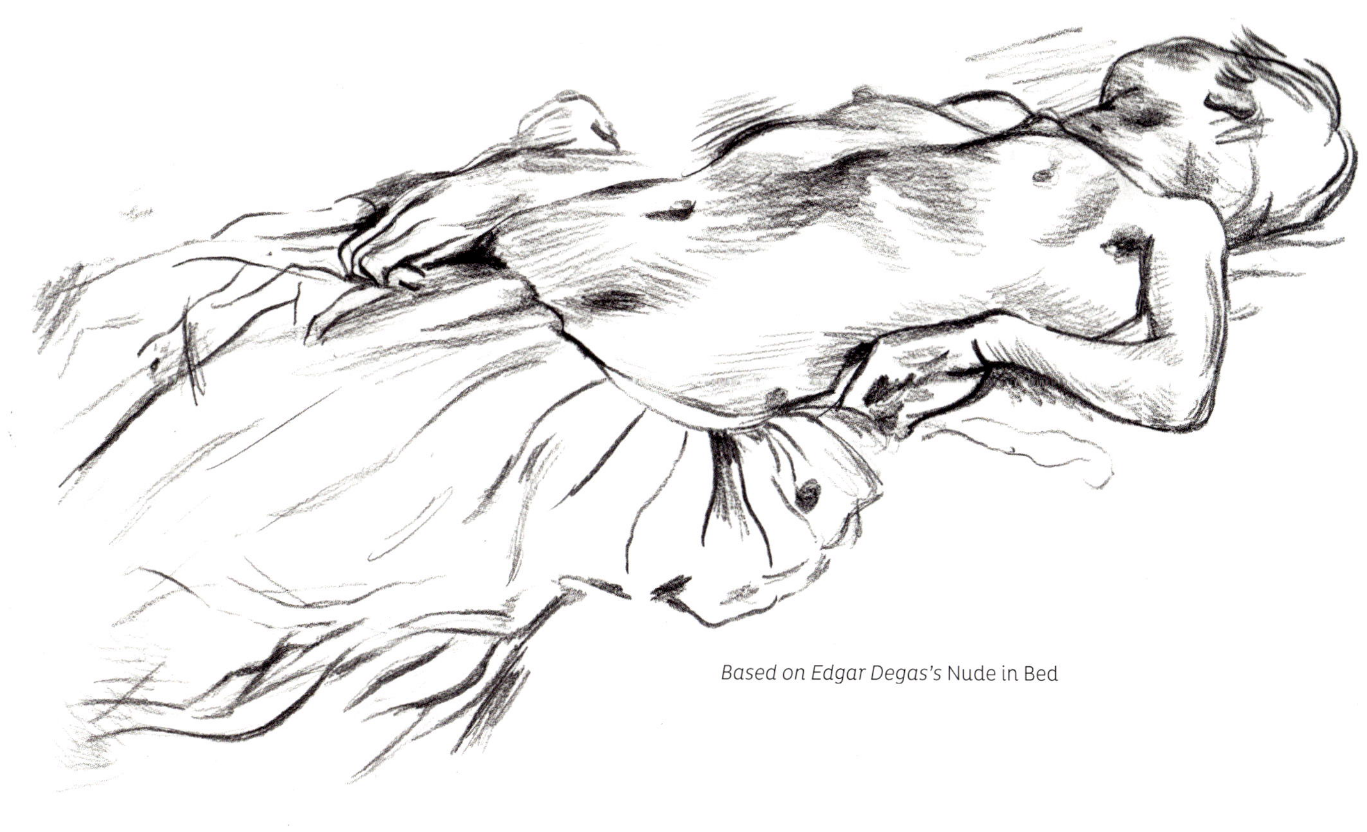

Based on Edgar Degas's Nude in Bed

Drawing a walk

You have to lose yourself, if you're to draw that. The drawing has to be the locus of an incredible self-renunciation, if you're to be a vector of such a world.
—Fred Deux, *Paroles d'artiste*

Most adults stopped drawing a long time ago, as we would stop singing, dancing, or writing under the pretext that we are not virtuoso. What a pity! The only interest of drawing may be to accompany our thinking, meditate, or look more acutely.

The following exercise has only one objective: the simple pleasure of drawing and seeing. The line will be like a memory in your mind's eye. You will see that a drawing can exist outside the expectation of a specific result.

YOUR TURN

Take a blank sheet of paper and a fairly dark and thin tool (fine marker, ballpoint pen, or sharpened grease pencil).

Your hand will serve as a model for you. Position it so that it creates hollows and reliefs in the palm. Look deep into it and choose a starting point for your walk. Place your pencil on the blank sheet of paper and, without looking at your drawing, move forward at the same pace as your eyes on the lines of your hand. Record the slightest crease, the slightest bump. Walk through this tiny landscape as if you were an ant; your line is there only to testify to this walk.

This experience will certainly allow you to achieve good concentration. Repeat as many times as you like by changing the position of your hand. Now, keeping the same level of concentration, start drawing your entire hand, this time looking at its contours. You are allowed to look at your drawing from time to time to check where your line is and eventually return inside the shape to draw a fold or nail.

IF YOU HAVE THE TIME

- Draw other models in the same way: feet, objects, fruit, etc.

Go and see

Soluto (born in 1961), drawings
Moises Mahiques (born in 1976)
Olivier Théuin (contemporary)

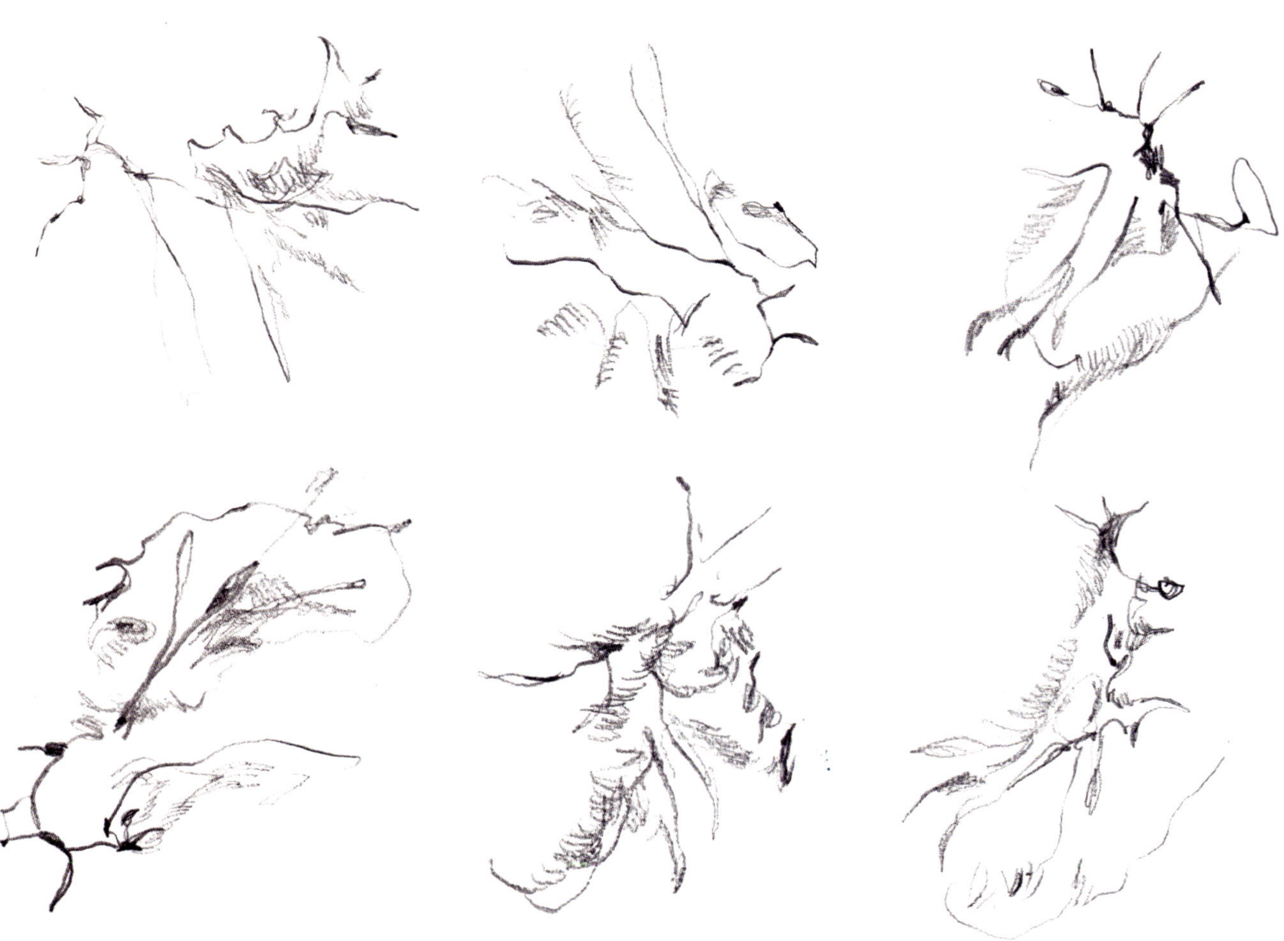

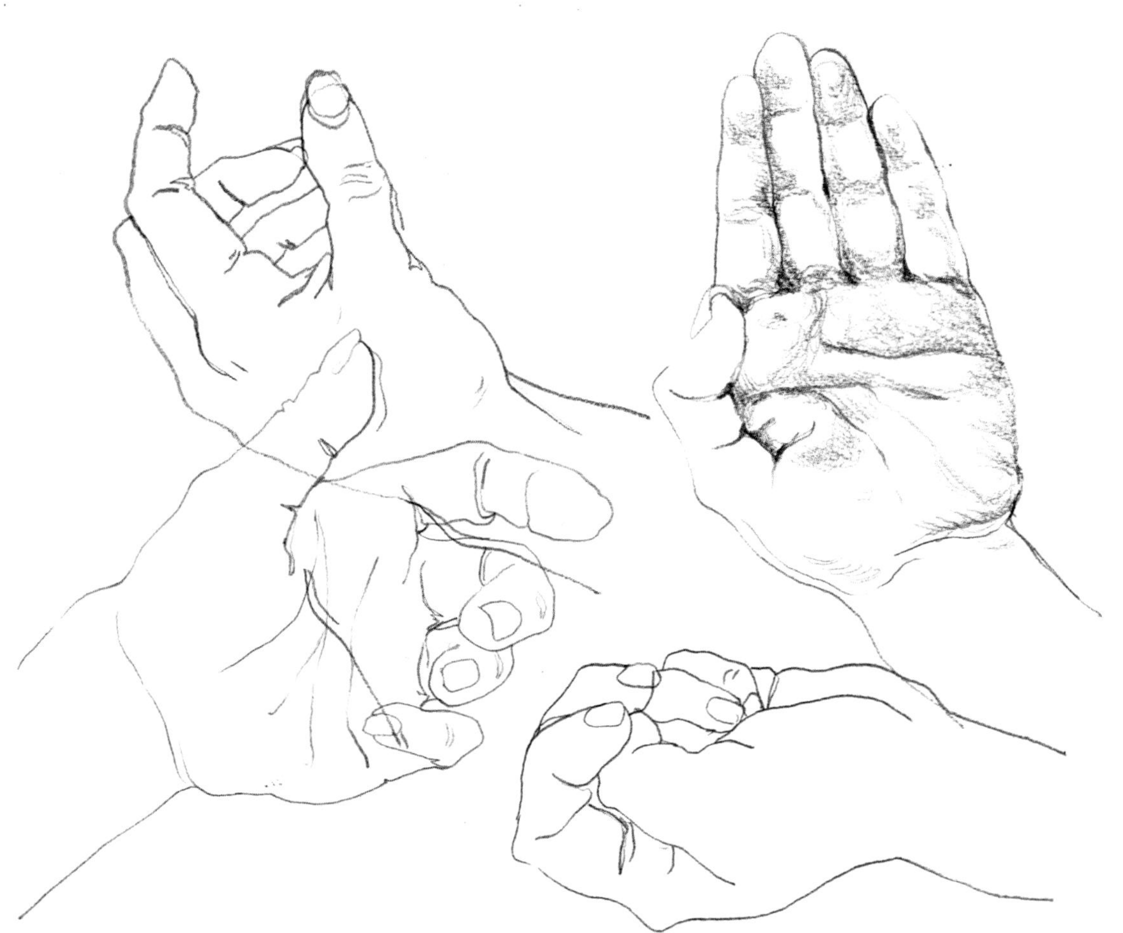

Blink your eyes, close one eye.

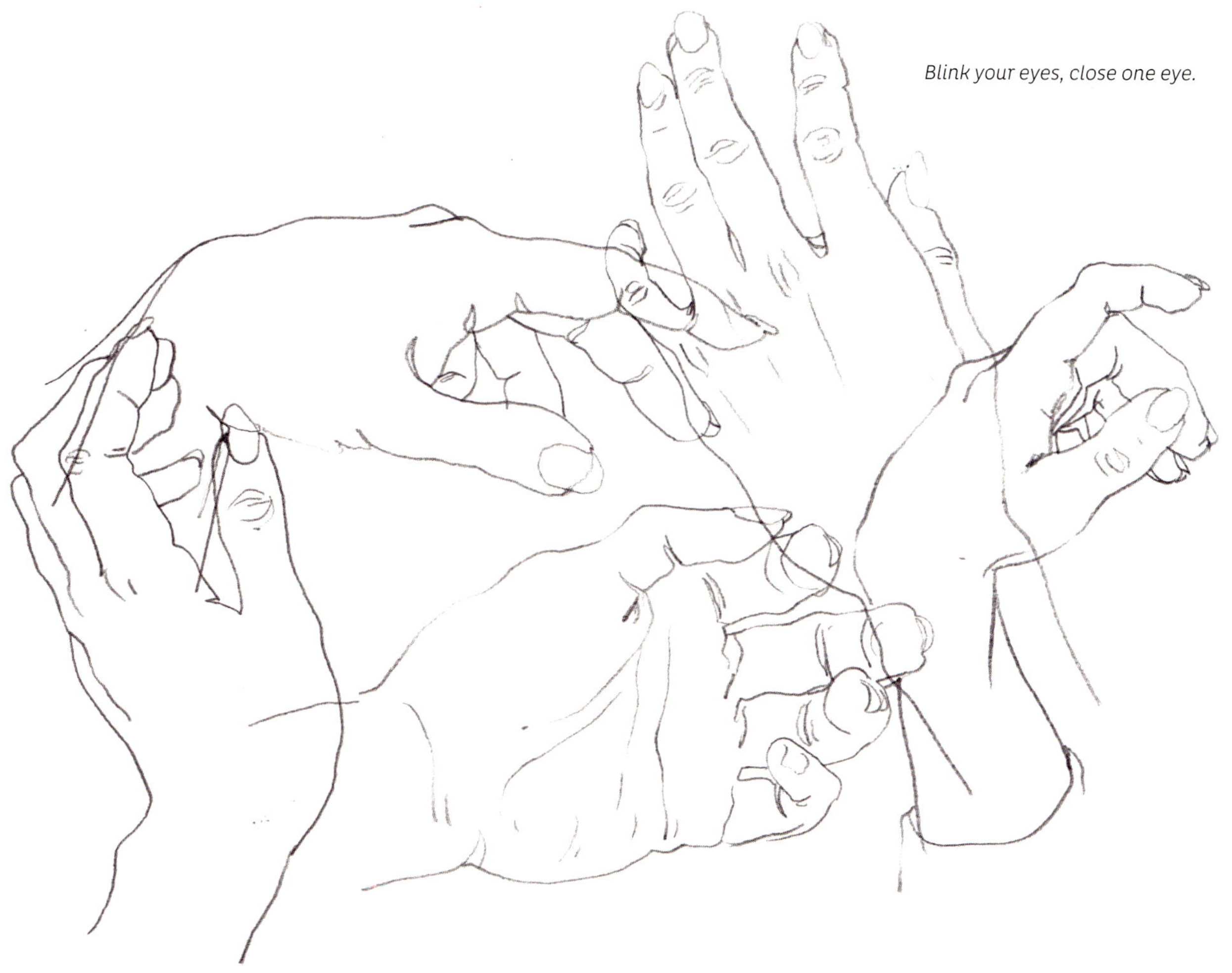

Continuous line

A line is a living entity in itself; it has a skeleton, flesh, a vital energy; it is a creature of nature like the rest.
—Fabienne Verdier, *Passagère du Silence*

Too much caution can harm a drawing. You have to learn to let go, not to be afraid to draw, not to look for the right line from the beginning. One can very well gradually approach a shape by tracing around it, inside it, through it. Search by tracing, without restraint. Quite often, the right line will be between two lines, but the feeling of accuracy will be omnipresent.

YOUR TURN

On the support of your choice, work with an ordinary pencil or—this is the ideal opportunity—a ballpoint pen or felt.

You're going to draw in one go! Without repeating your gesture, in the most fluid way possible.

Rotate your tool in all directions; learn to point your hand in all directions. First, look for the general shapes before going into detail. Do not put your hand on the support; lift your wrist and draw lightly during the first few minutes. When you feel the possibility of specifying, retrace your lines, increasing the pressure on the tool.

Try to fight against the tendency to press hard to correct mistakes: press hard at the end of the drawing to clarify it. The construction lines and the whole process remain visible, which can provide an additional vibration to your image.

IF YOU HAVE THE TIME

- Draw in space with flexible (galvanized) wire, like Nina Ivanovic.

Go and see

Alberto Giacometti (1901–1966)
Rémy Jacquier (born in 1972)
Nina Ivanovic (born in 1986)

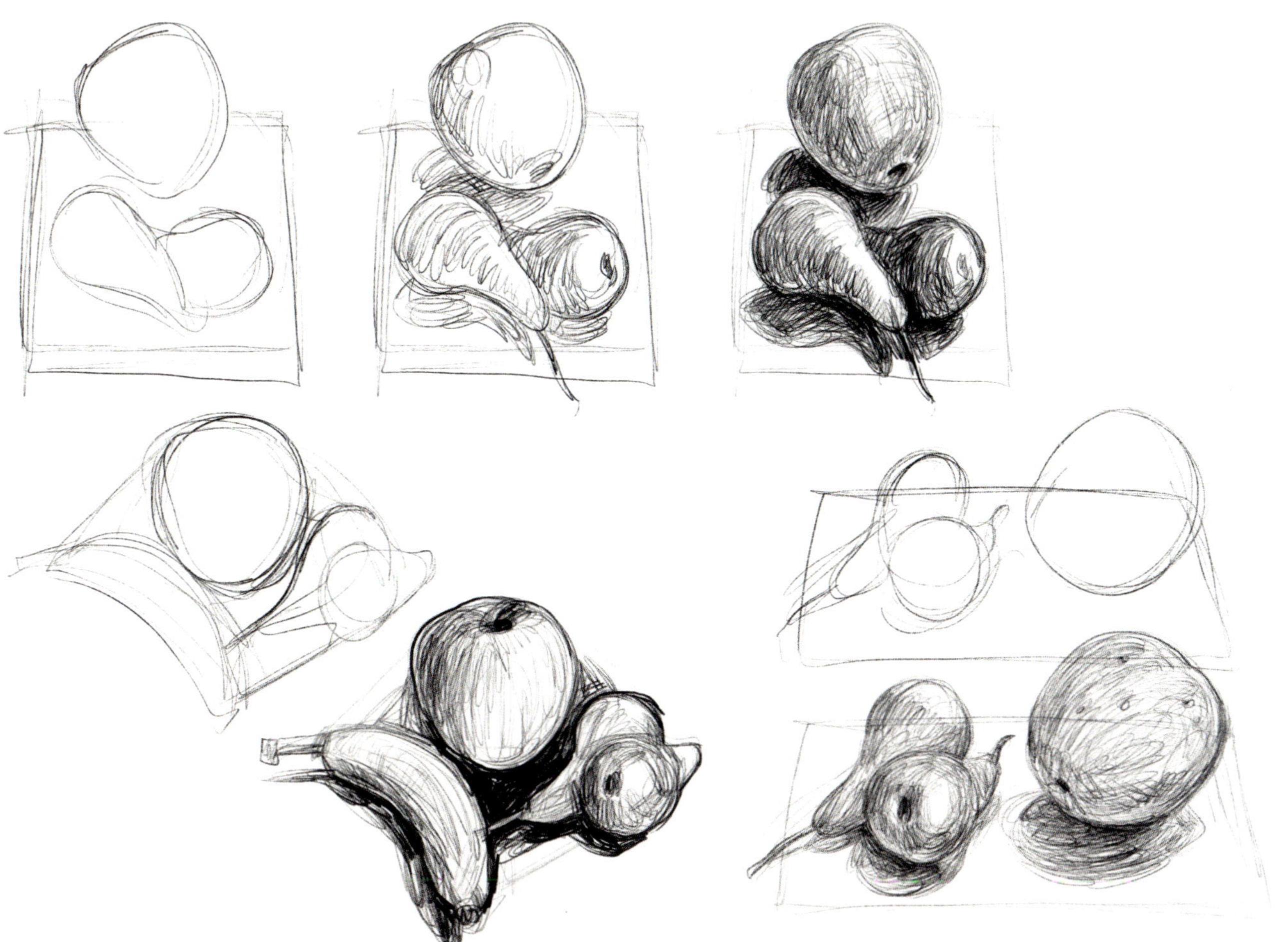

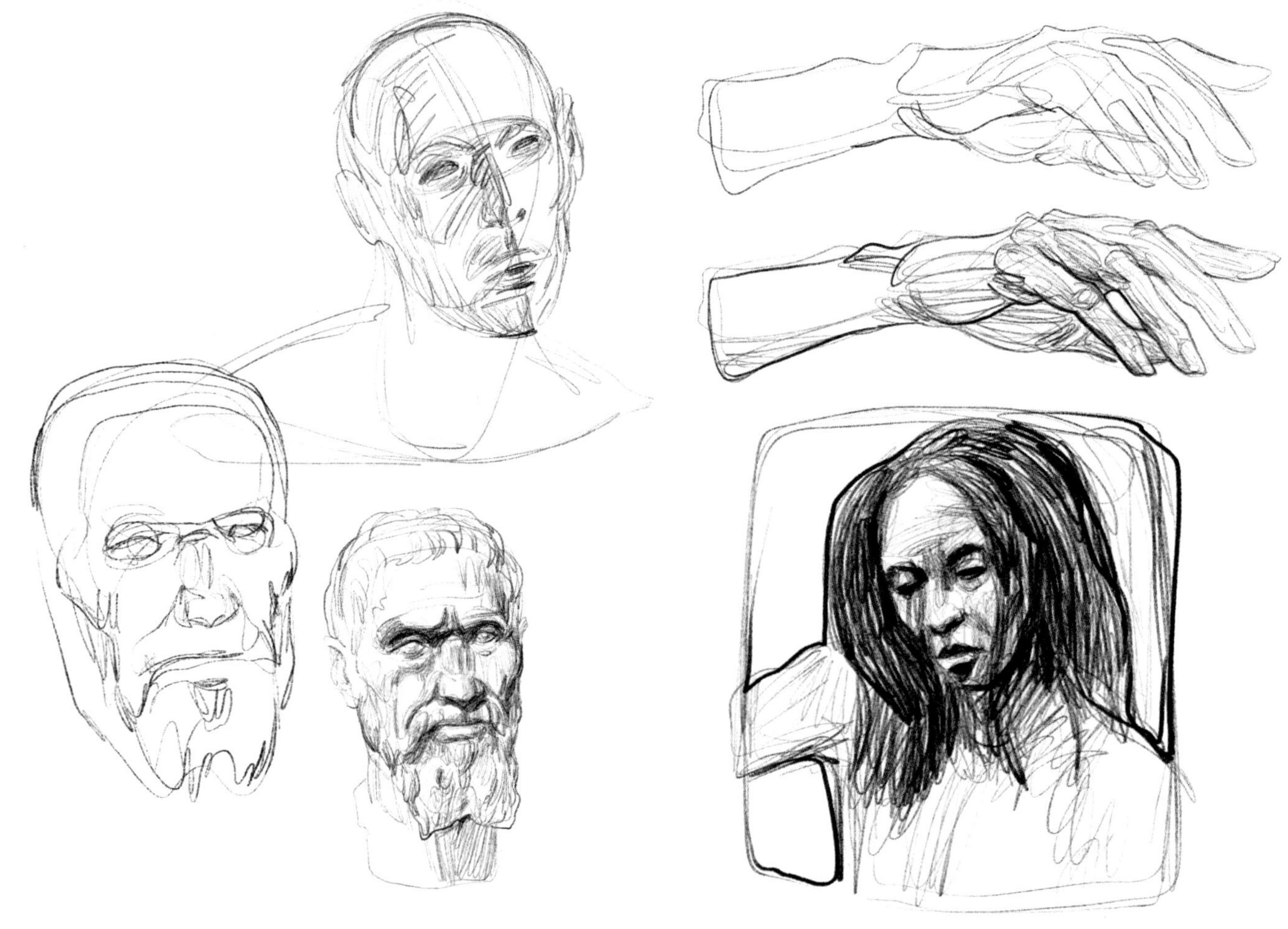

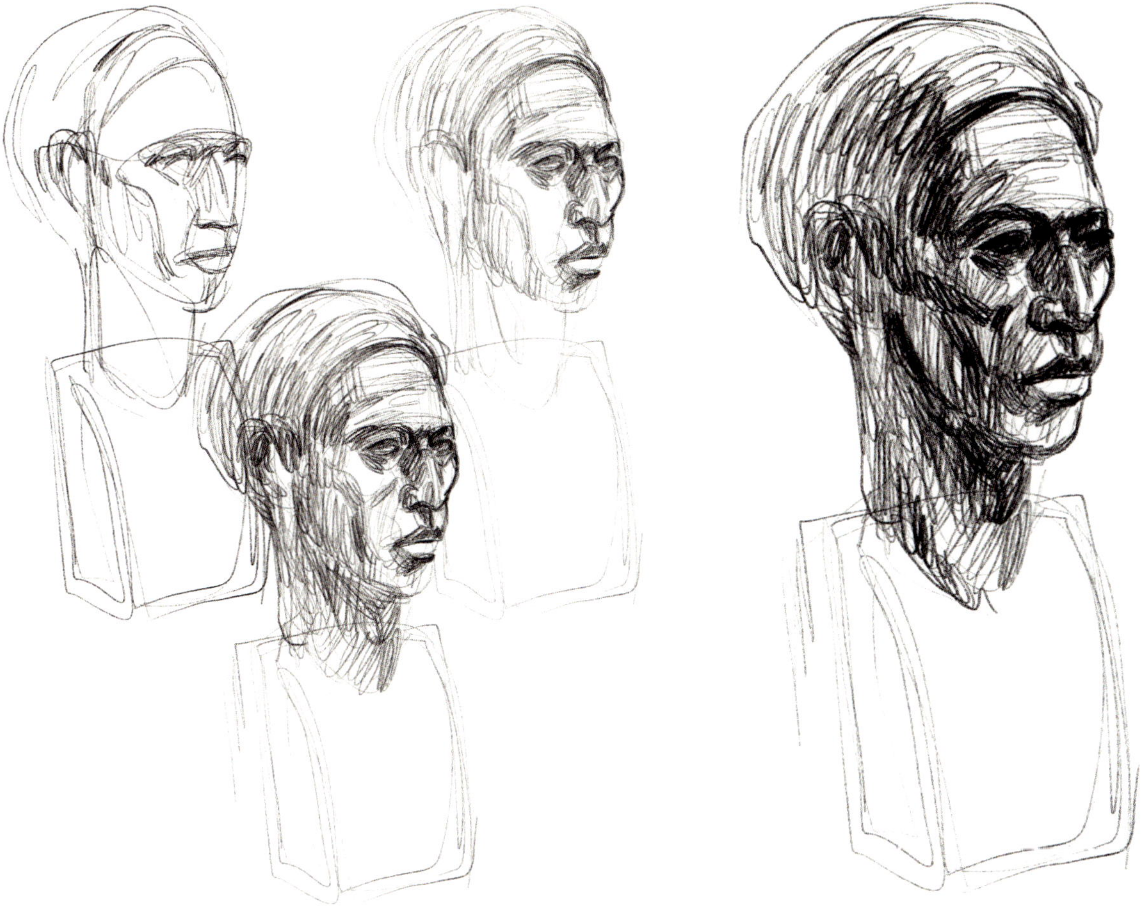

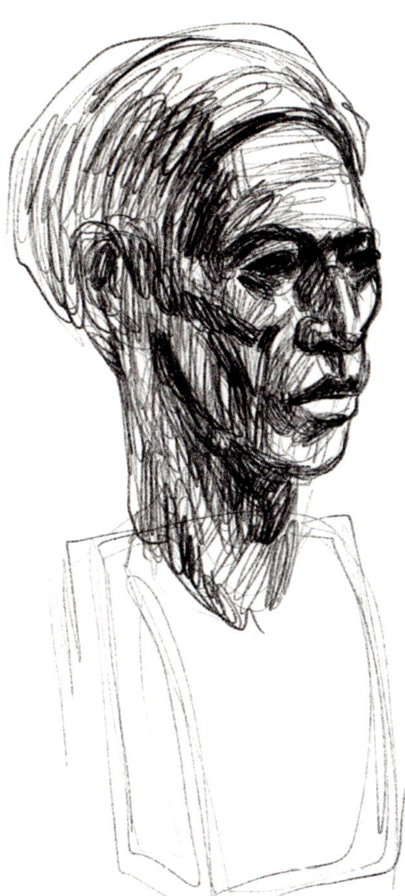

Line segments

A line is a dot that went for a walk.
—Paul Klee

When you have a pencil in your hand, your eyes tend to break up the shapes and to focus on details. We are tempted to draw little by little, and we lose sight of the whole, the proportions, and the composition. This week's exercise will allow you to draw without going into detail. It is a real gymnastic, which consists of drawing while keeping a global vision.

YOUR TURN

Take A4 sheets of paper, plus an ordinary pencil (HB or 2B) or a ballpoint pen.

Choose a simple object: a piece of fruit, for example. Put it on a table in front of you. To represent it, you will use only line segments! The lines can follow the contours or cross your pattern.

First, assess its overall proportions, the height/width ratio. Then, gradually, refine your drawing by reducing the length of your line segments until it follows the curves, at the very end of the process.

IF YOU HAVE THE TIME

• Multiply the patterns, choosing more and more complex ones. Match two or three objects.
• Combine two techniques: for example, an ordinary pencil (lead) and a ballpoint pen.

Go and see

Piet Mondrian (1872–1944), *The Silver Tree*, 1911
Maria Helena Vieira da Silva (1908–1992)
Antonio López García (born in 1936), *Membrillero*, 2007

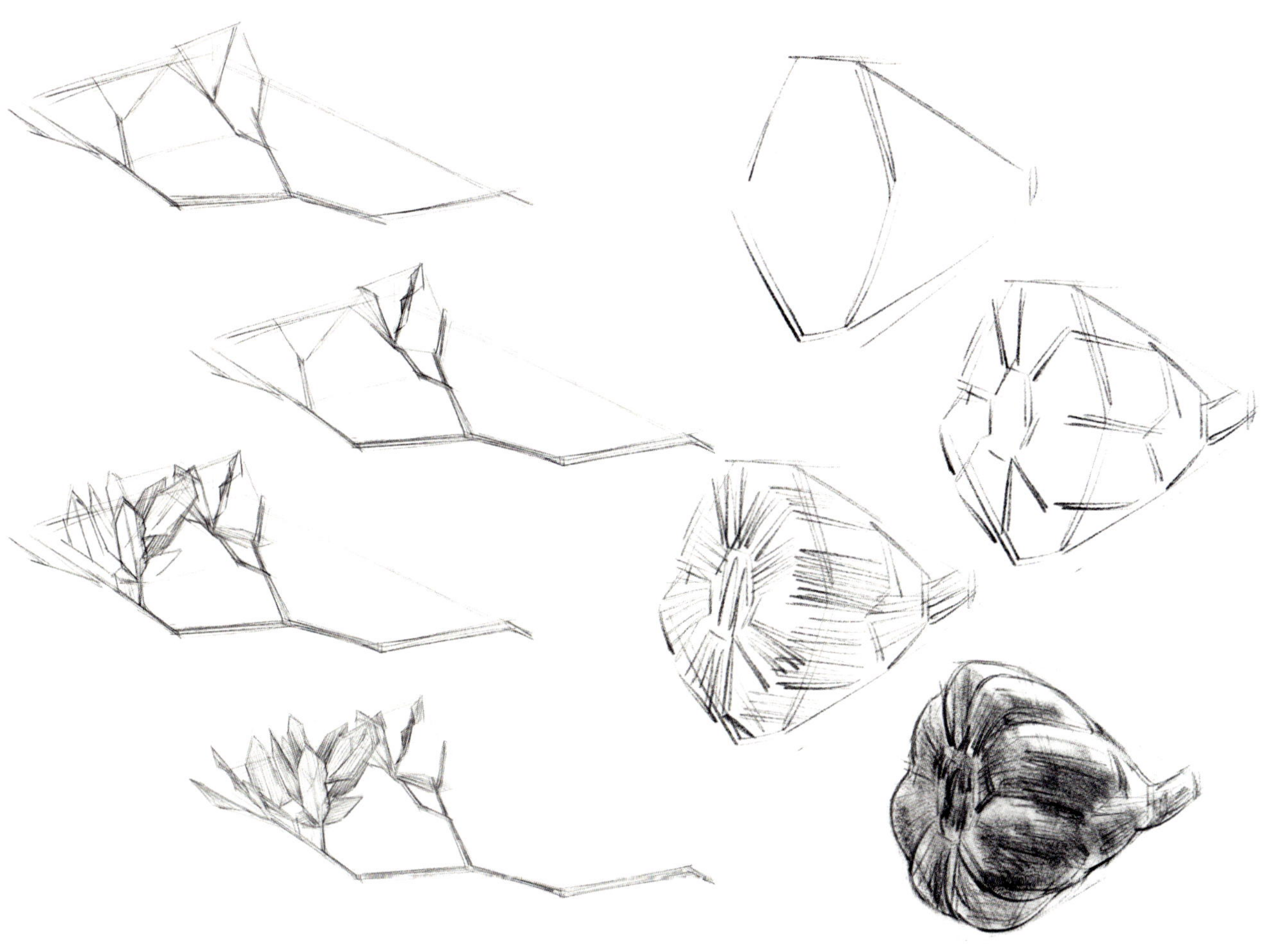

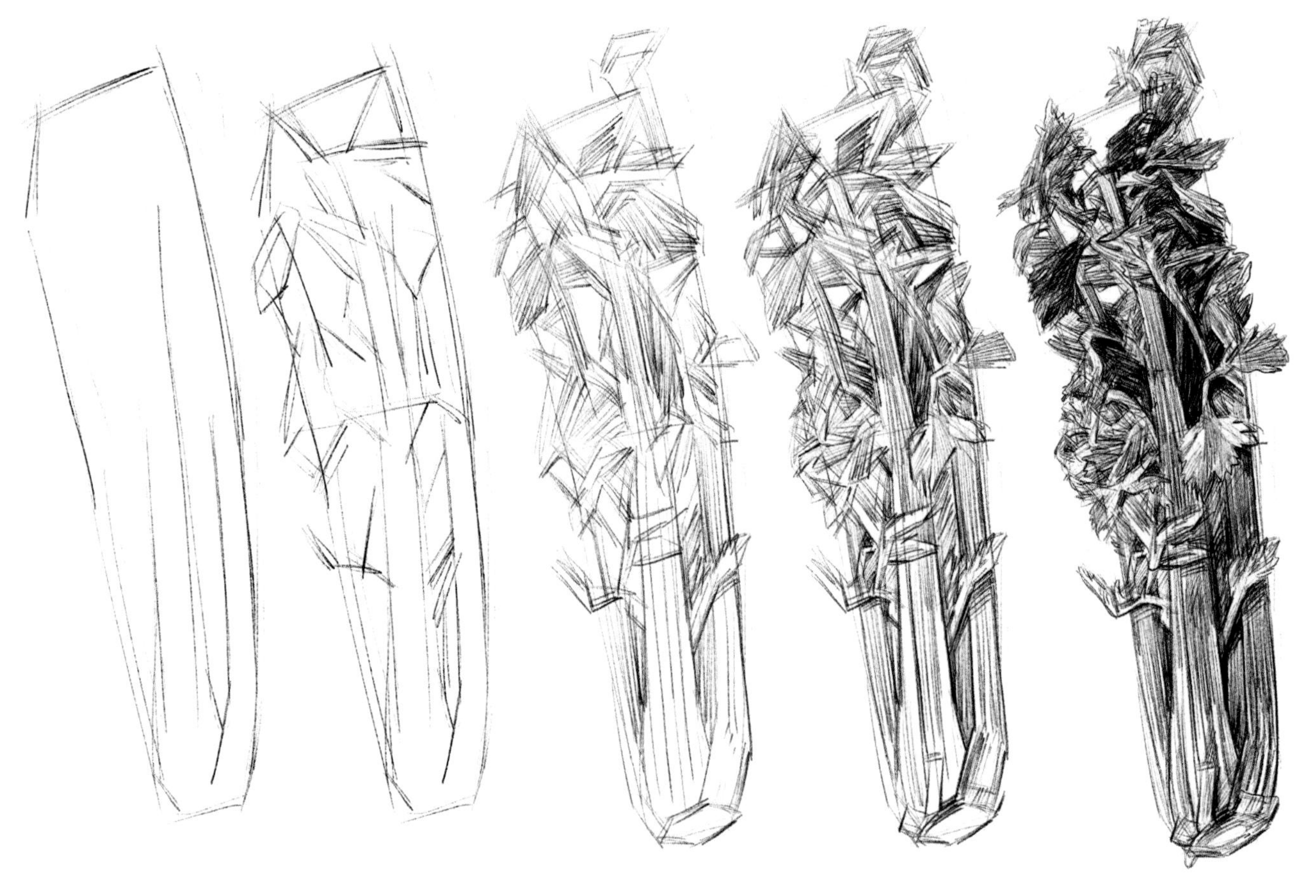

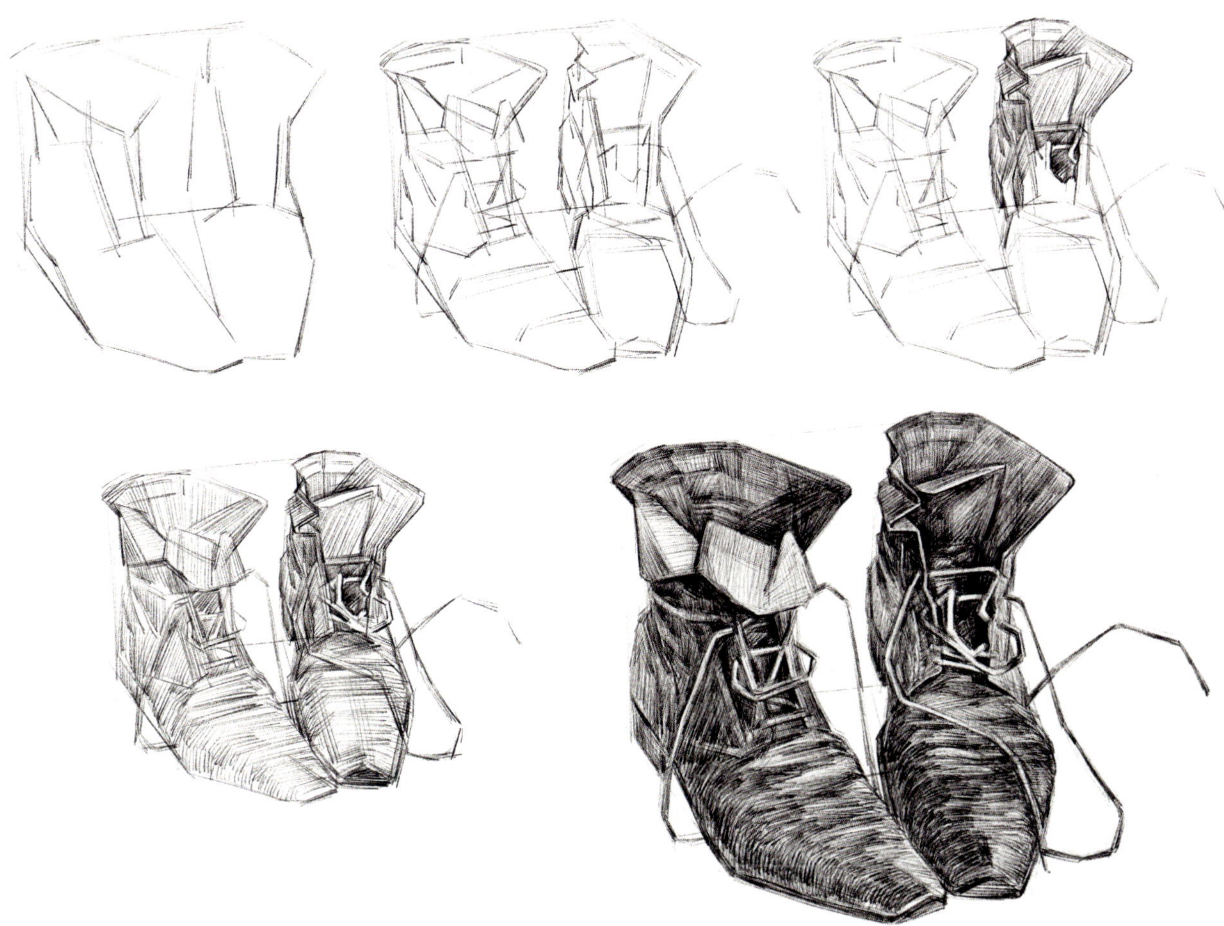

Chinese shadows

At first, have eyes only for the whole.
—Jean-Auguste-Dominique Ingres

This week, like the previous one, is devoted to the global vision. These exercises should also allow you to feel the weight of things, their mass. A little like a sculptor, you will have to evaluate from the outset the amount of material needed to represent your design.

YOUR TURN

Take A4 sheets of paper and bring tools with very wide lines: marker, wide felt pen, blunt-tip graphite, or even a simple pencil held at a steep angle to draw with the flat of the lead.

Put an object on your table. You must represent its silhouette, its mass. Be careful: you will be tempted to draw the contours and color the inside of the delimited shape. It's not about that, but about approaching your drawing directly by its mass. Try to orient your gesture in the direction of form, not just to trace in the natural direction of your dominant hand. Learn to draw by drawing in all directions.

IF YOU HAVE THE TIME

- Put several objects together and consider them as a single form.
- Try to imagine the hidden areas of objects placed in the background.

Go and see

Henri Matisse (1869–1954), *Les découpages de papier*
Michel Ocelot (born in 1943), the animated film *Princes and Princesses*
Pomona Zipser (born in 1958)

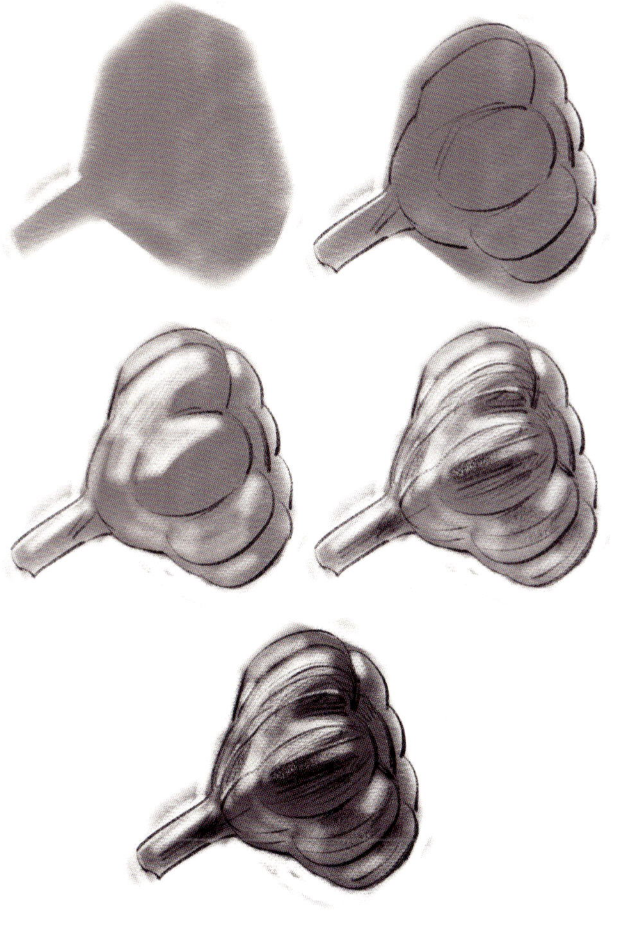

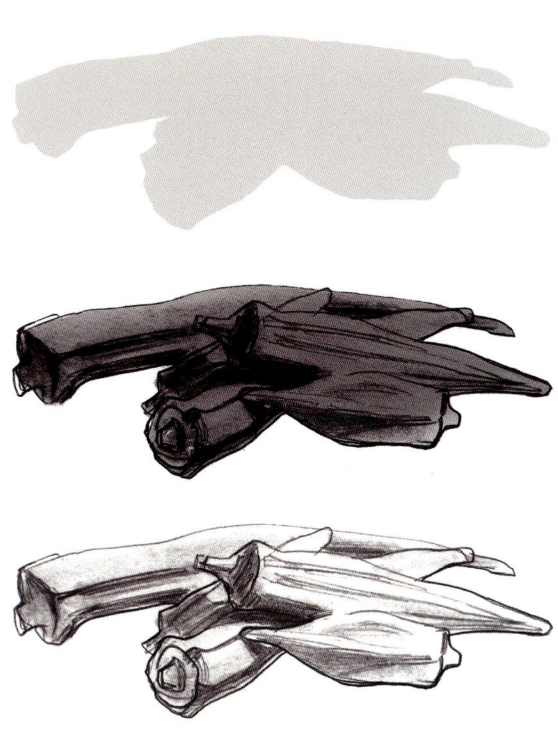

Several adjoining elements form a new entity that can be melted into a single mass.

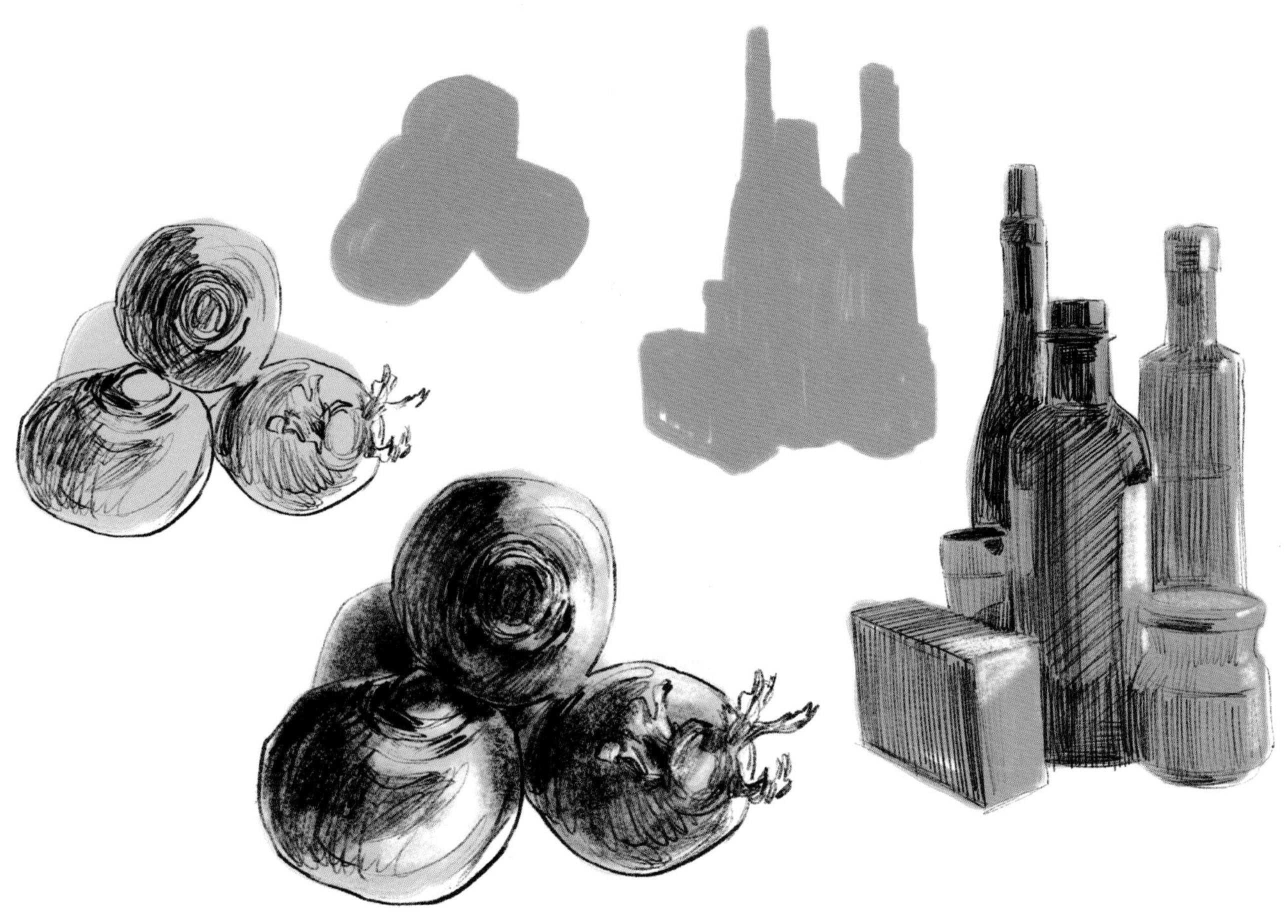

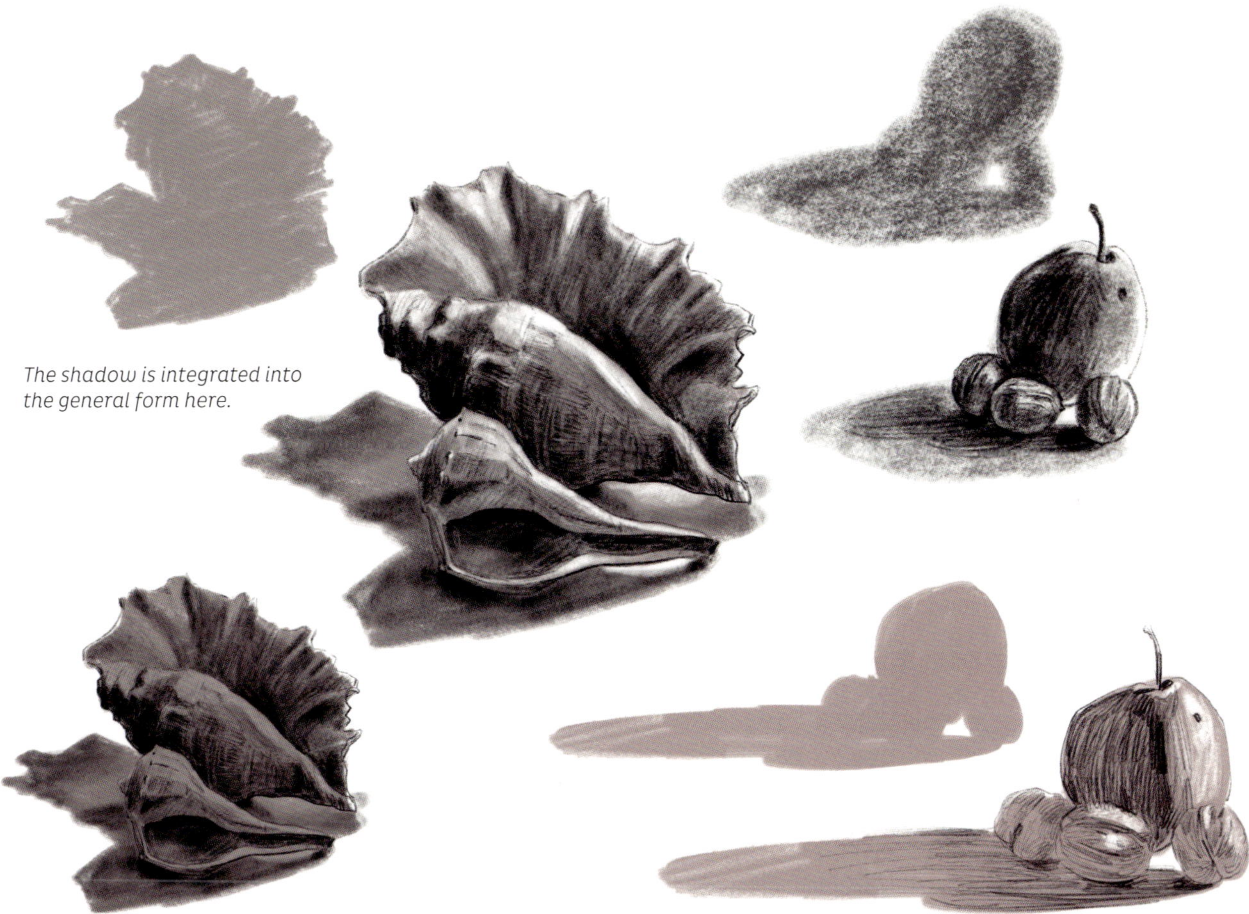

The shadow is integrated into the general form here.

Ink stains

Black is the refuge of color.
—Gaston Bachelard

This week, you will work on abstraction, in black and white, in order to focus on drawing qualities related to matter and contrast rather than form.

YOUR TURN

Use india ink and various tools: feathers, brushes, plants, hair, fabric, salt (coarse and fine), dishwashing liquid, cotton swabs, spray, plastic bag, repositionable tape, etc. Look around you to see what could be useful for your exploration.

Spread your ink in several pots, from the purest to the most diluted, in order to have black, gray, and clear water.

The ideal solution is to use a wash brush (or one per pot, if you have several) and heavyweight A5 or A4 paper (from 250 g), which will not warp when moistened. If your budget is modest, your basic equipment may be simpler, but that doesn't have to stop you: you can get great results and enjoy yourself with the cheapest tools.

Sit back and let yourself be carried away by the material. Start, for example, by moistening your paper with clean water, drip a drop of black ink on it, and admire! With this technique, we often have the impression that the image is created by itself. India ink allows you to experience countless possibilities: dilutions, diffusions, imprints, superimpositions, drips. Don't avoid accidents—provoke them, because that is the best way to discover new possibilities.

IF YOU HAVE THE TIME

- Work with larger formats and larger brushes.
- Try different colors with colored inks or watercolors.

Go and see

Zao Wou-ki (1920–2013), *Les encres*
Anish Kapoor (born in 1954), *Les dessins*
Fabienne Verdier (born in 1962)

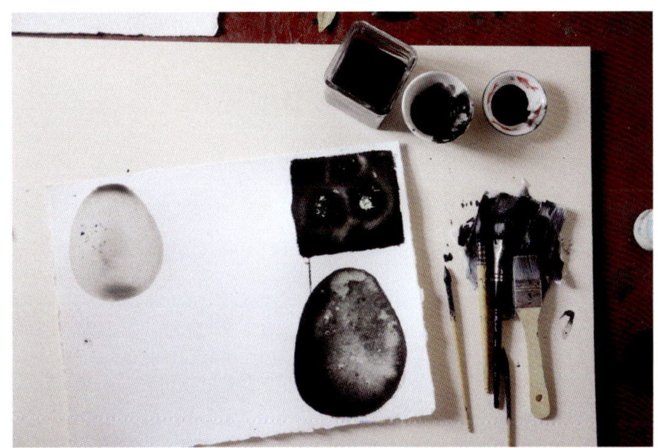

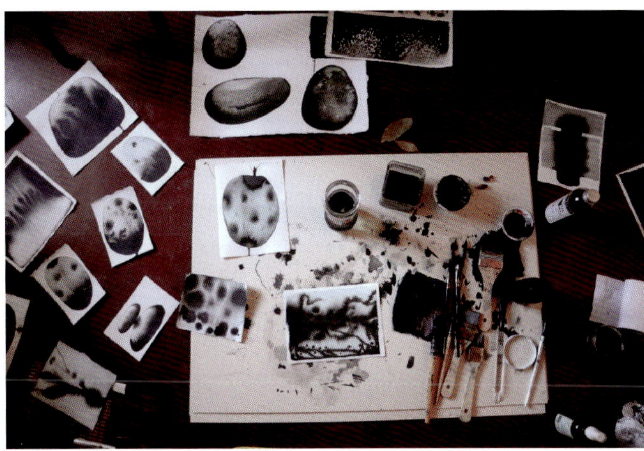

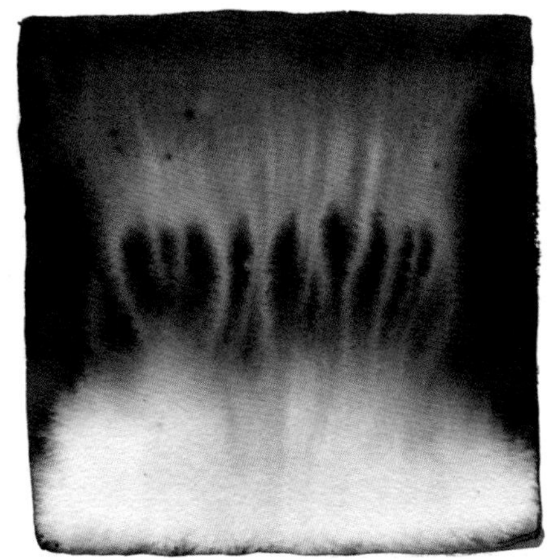

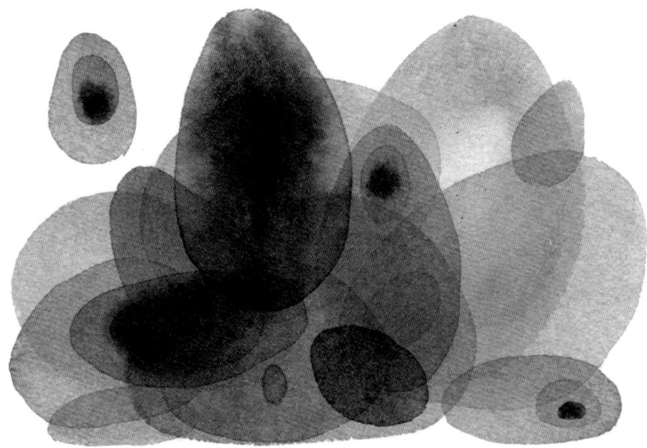

Let each shape dry before adding a new stain so that the overlaps are clear.

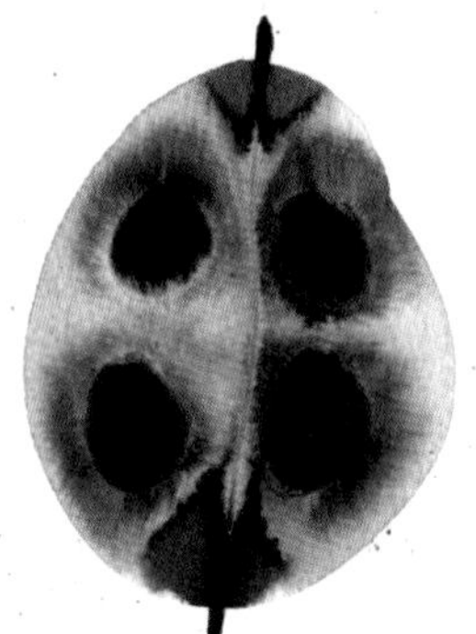

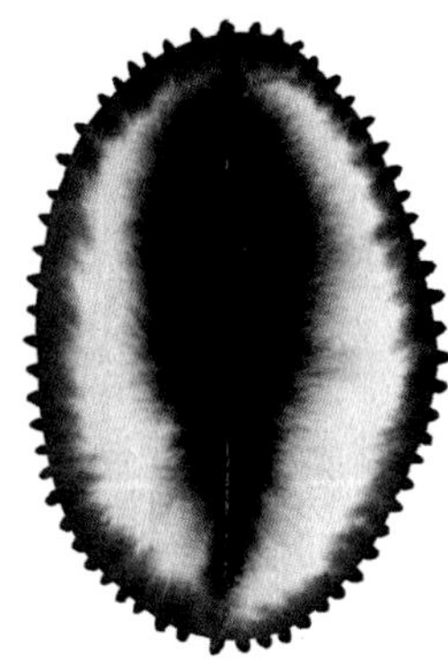

A hair deposited on the still-wet ink draws the central line.

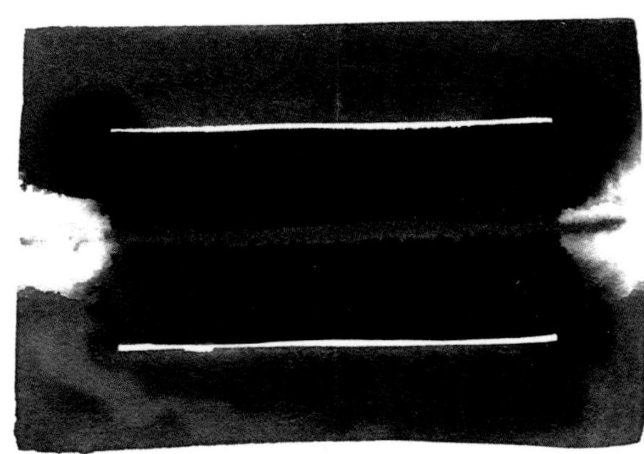

The white lines are left in reserve.

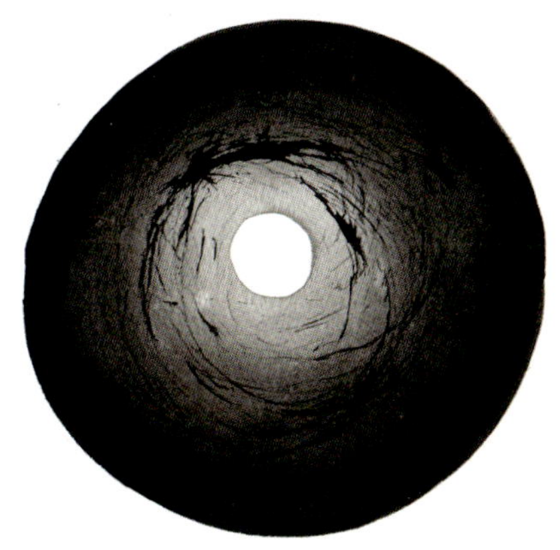

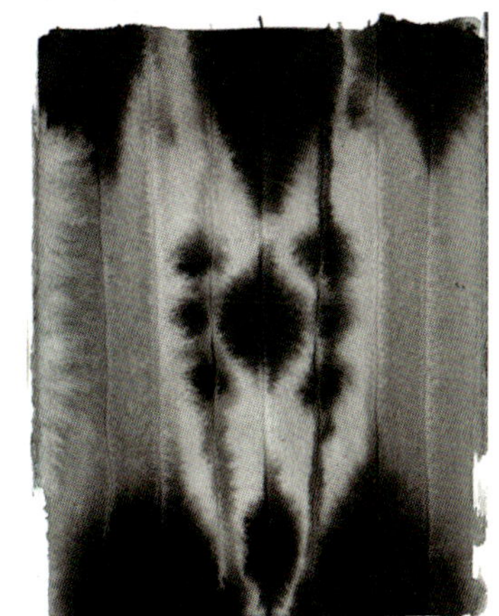

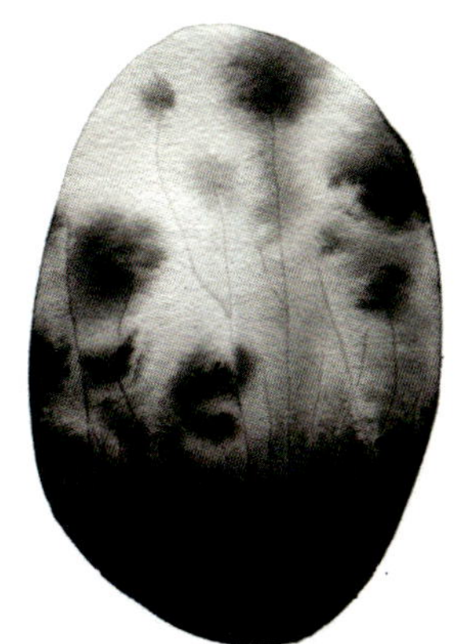

The lines are due to scratches.

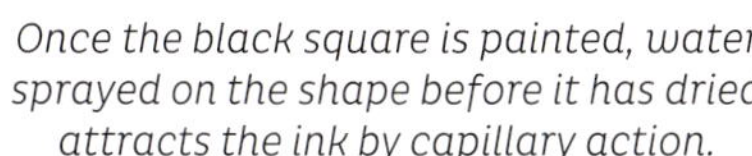

Once the black square is painted, water sprayed on the shape before it has dried attracts the ink by capillary action.

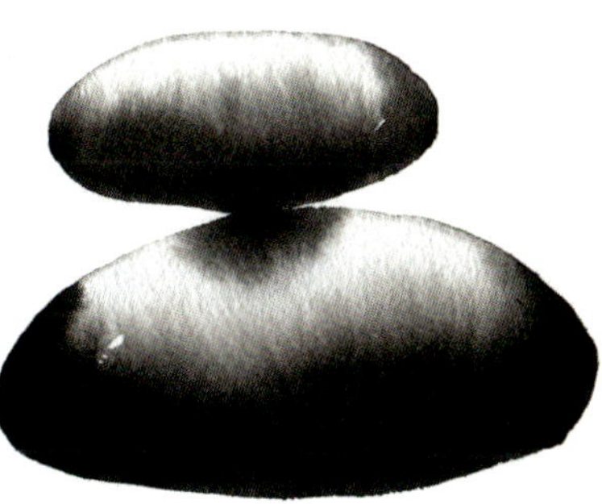

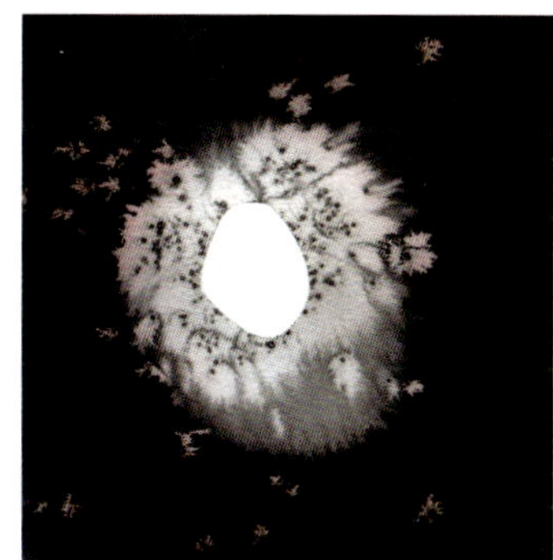

Salt grains repel ink.

Silhouettes

One does not become enlightened by imagining figures of light, but by making the darkness conscious.
—Carl Gustav Jung

You have carried a lot experiments that have helped you understand how ink reacts. Now, use these discoveries to represent "something."

YOUR TURN

Look for models to reproduce (photos or objects) and visualize them in as Chinese shadows (see week 6).

Use the same equipment as last week; make yourself comfortable with all your tools at hand.

Use water to draw the silhouette of your model (i.e., its mass and not its contours).

Place your brush inside the shape and look for the edges (we often tend to draw the outline first and then fill in, which leaves a small margin for error). Put black on the wet form: it will diffuse evenly and fill the silhouette, making the form appear as if by magic.

Keep in mind that it is a matter of accepting that the ink has a say in things: play with it without restricting it, and tolerate any distortions.

If, after several attempts, the exercise seems too difficult, start with a light pencil before moistening the surface.

IF YOU HAVE THE TIME

- Work on the values: wet the paper only where the shadows are, letting the black fill them, leaving the lighter part of the paper to represent the light.

Go and see

Antony Gormley (born in 1950), *Les encres*
Kara Walker (born in 1969)
Yann Bagot (born in 1983), Chaos series

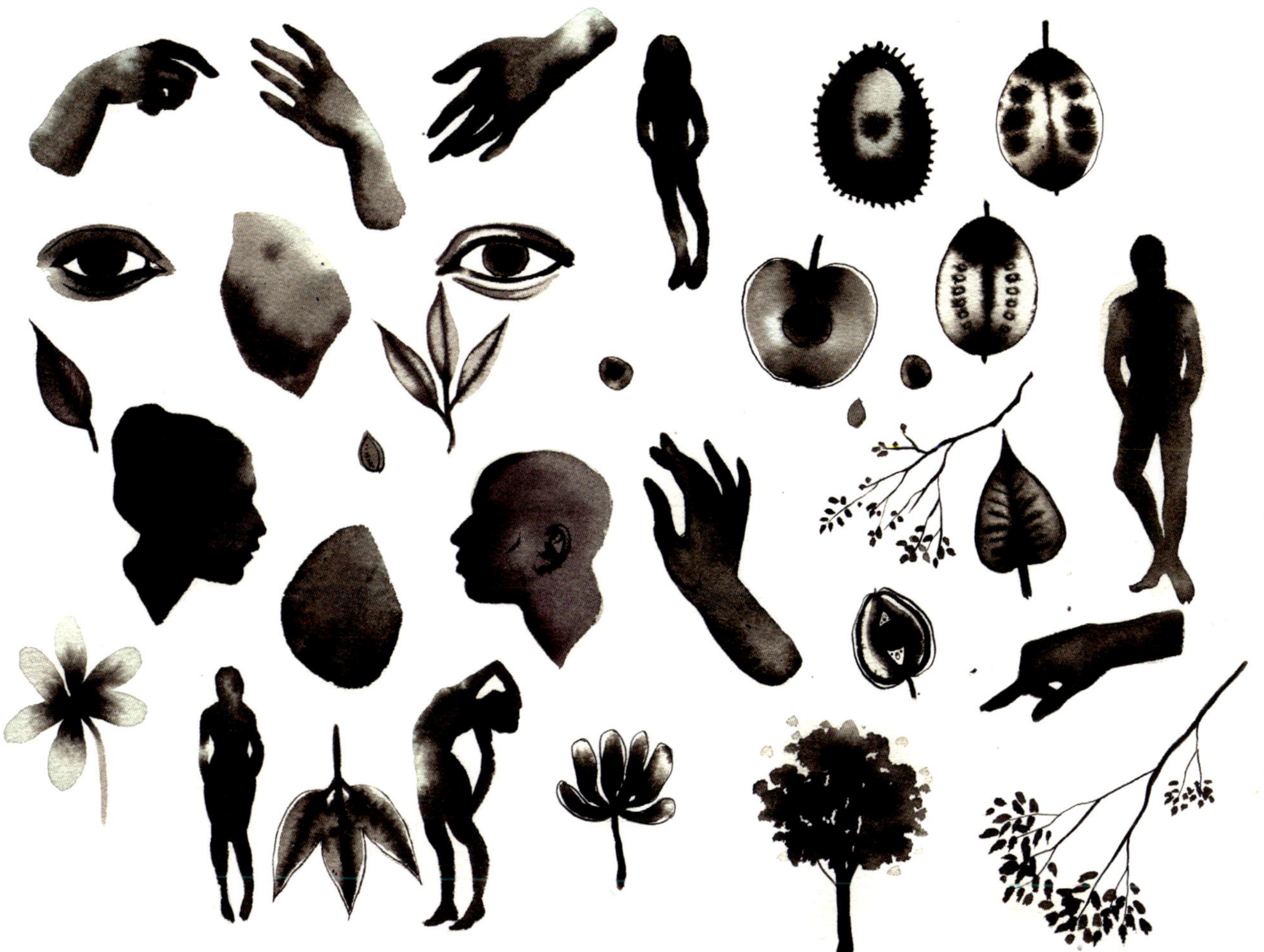

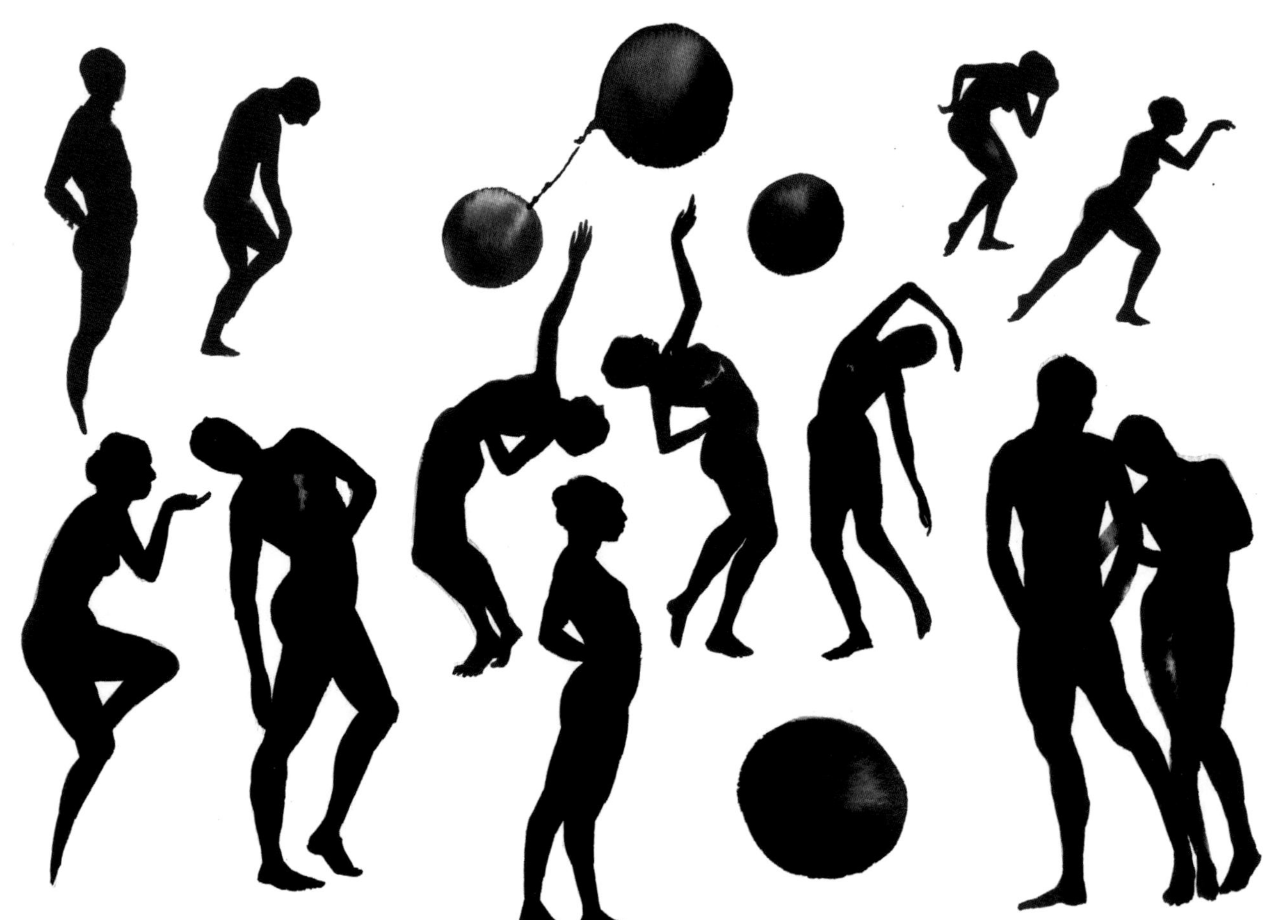

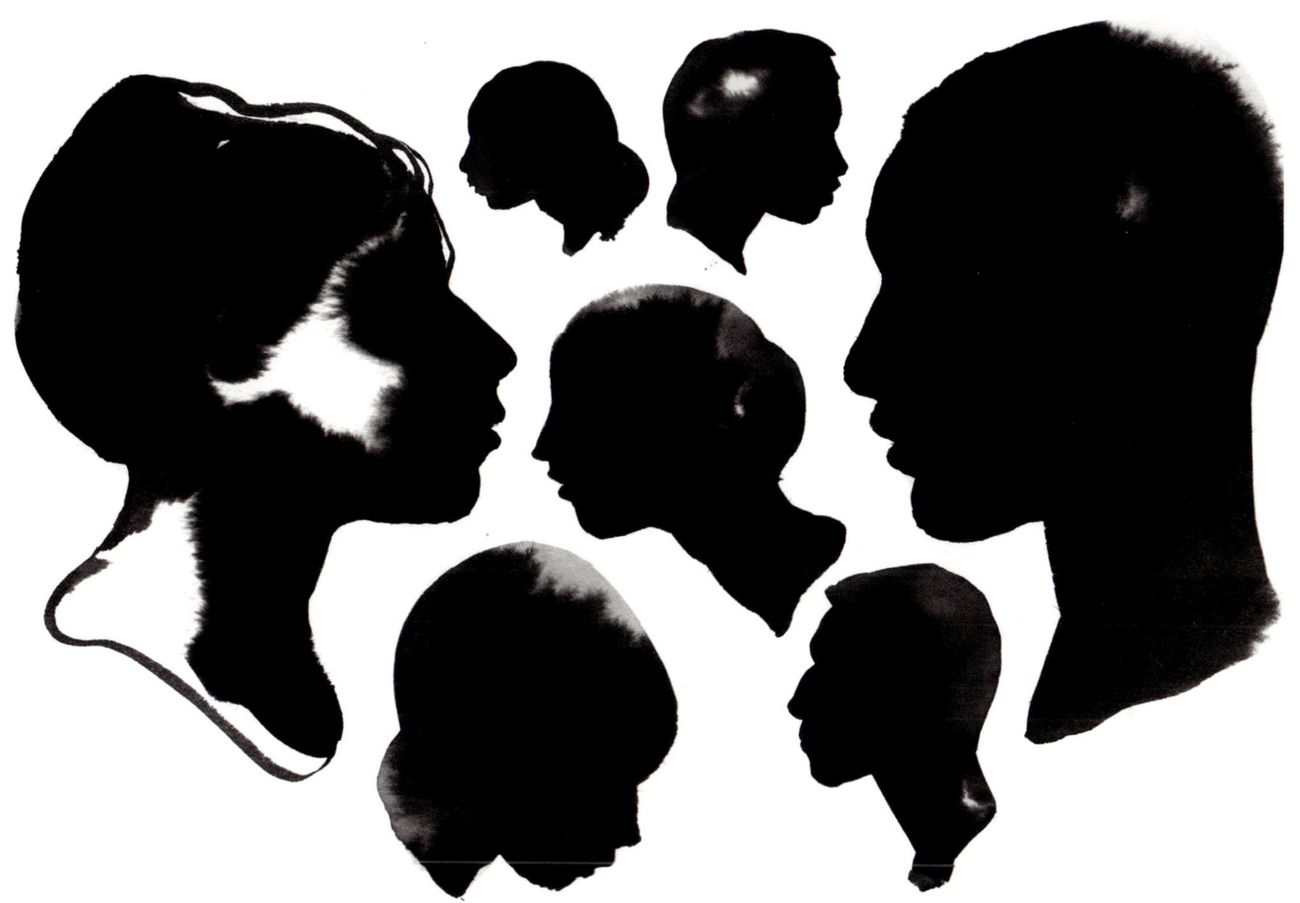

Full and empty

What is between the apple and the plate is also painted. And to me, it seems as difficult to paint the in-between as it is to paint the thing.
—Georges Braque

When we look at an object, we easily forget what surrounds it. However, the background of our sheet of paper is a surface in the same way as the representation of the motif will be. This way of conceiving and feeling space makes it possible to increase the density of the composition. All the shapes thus delimited, whether full or empty, will be arranged like pieces of a puzzle. The void can become the very subject of your drawing; it can deliberately occupy the main place, allowing you to unbalance your composition on purpose.

YOUR TURN

Take an A4 sheet of paper and a pencil (HB or 2B) or ballpoint pen.

Choose two or three objects. Put them on your table and space them out a little. Try to see them as a new entity. The first indications delimit the general shape that surrounds them.

From a puzzle with ten pieces, you will gradually move, in successive layers, to a more complex puzzle, with a hundred or a thousand pieces!

IF YOU HAVE THE TIME

• Keep the same objects and vary the compositions. Enjoy arranging your composition by premeditating the relationships between full and empty spaces.

Go and see

Chu Ta (1626–1705)
Henry Moore (1898–1986), sculptures and drawings
Sarah Simblet (born in 1972), tree studies

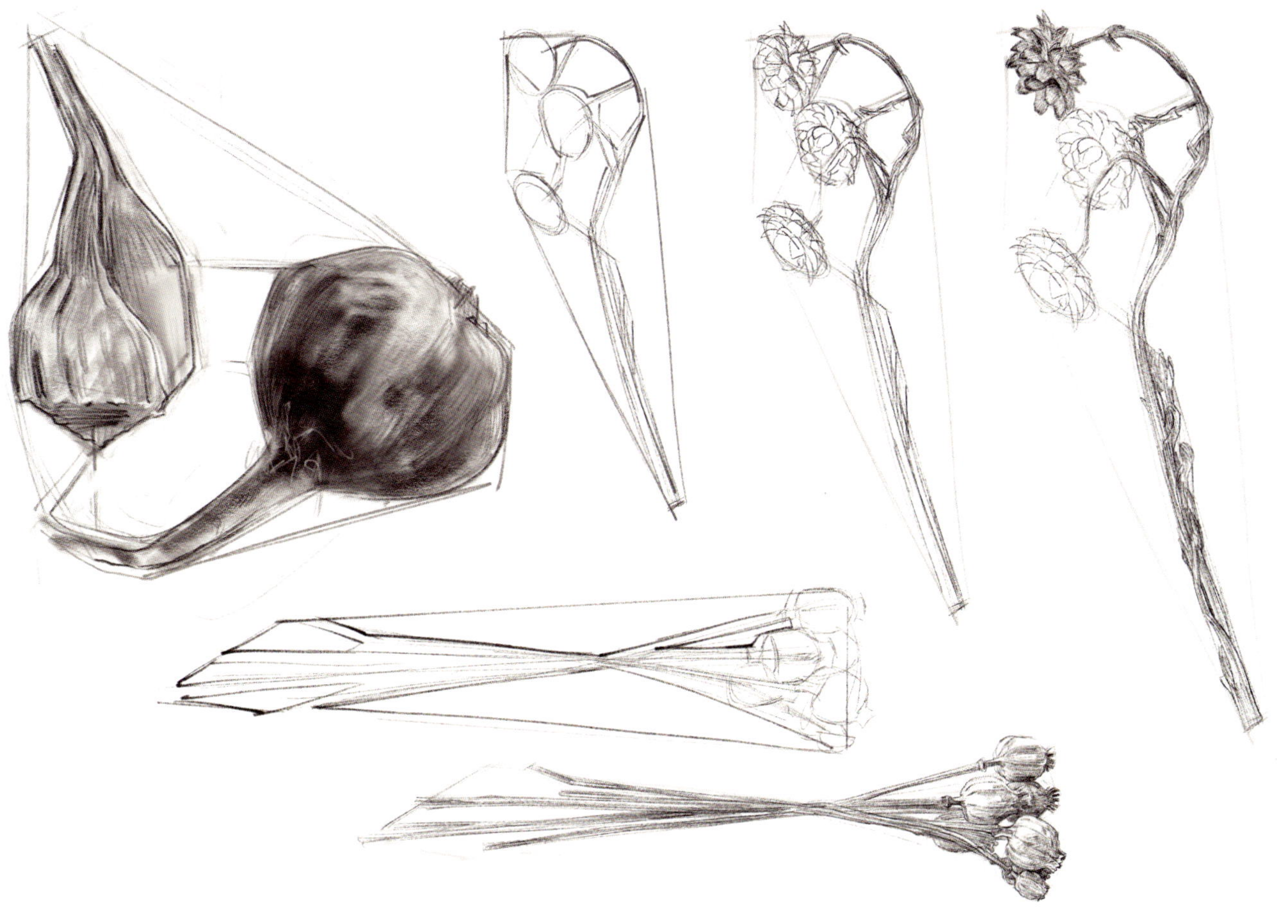

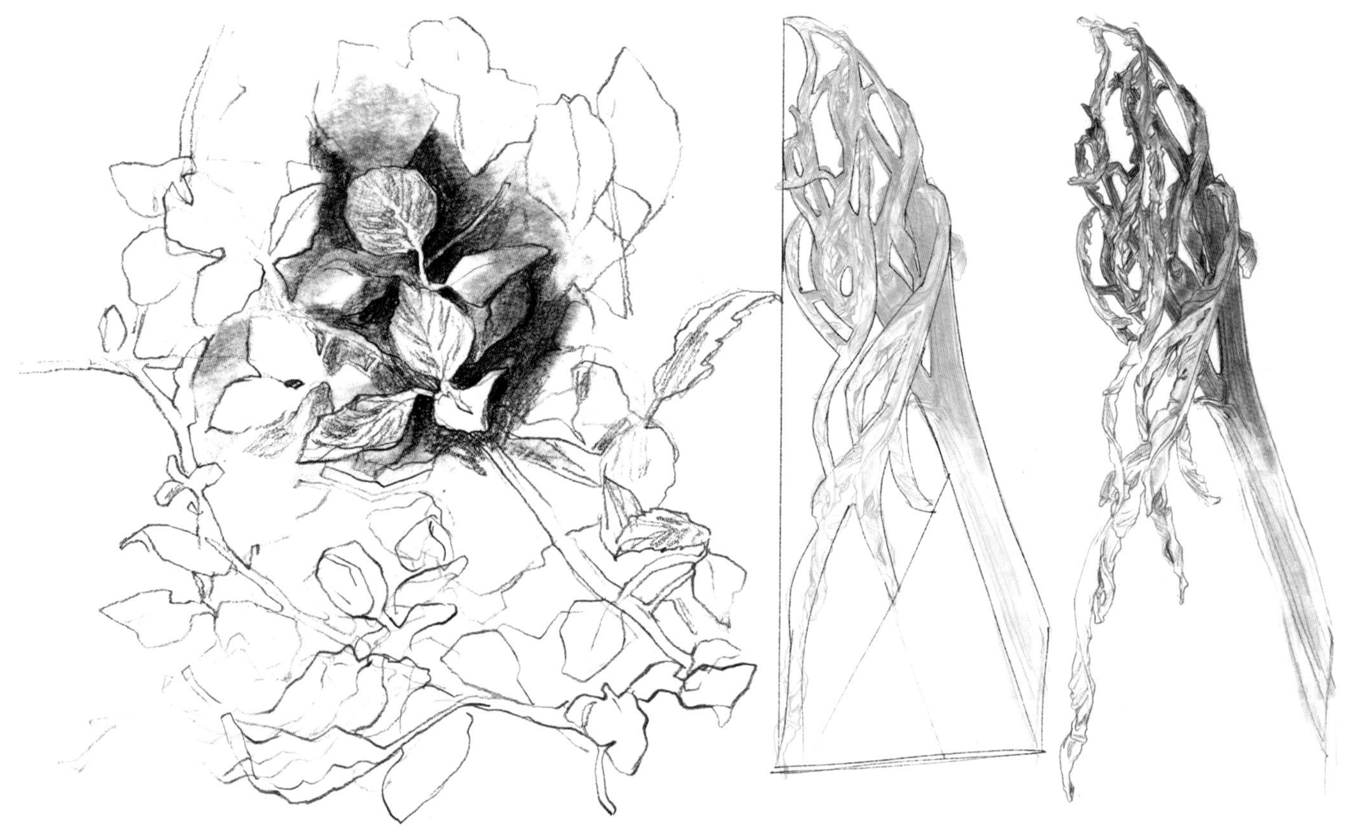

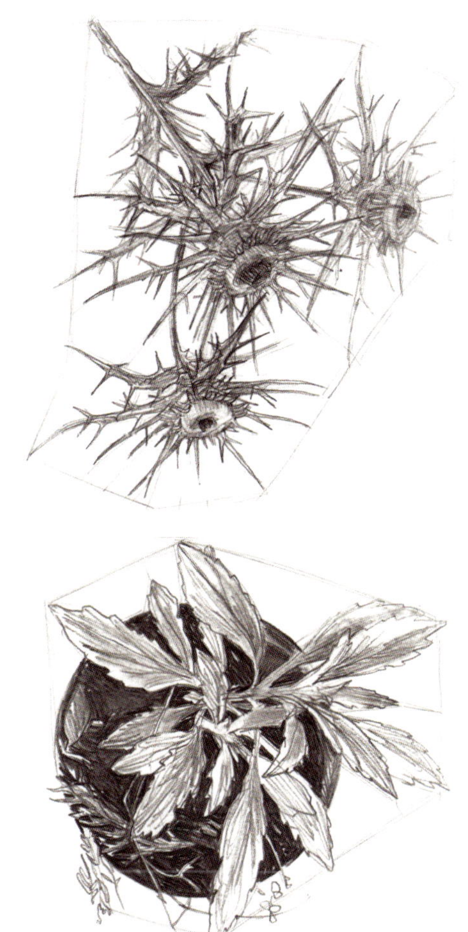

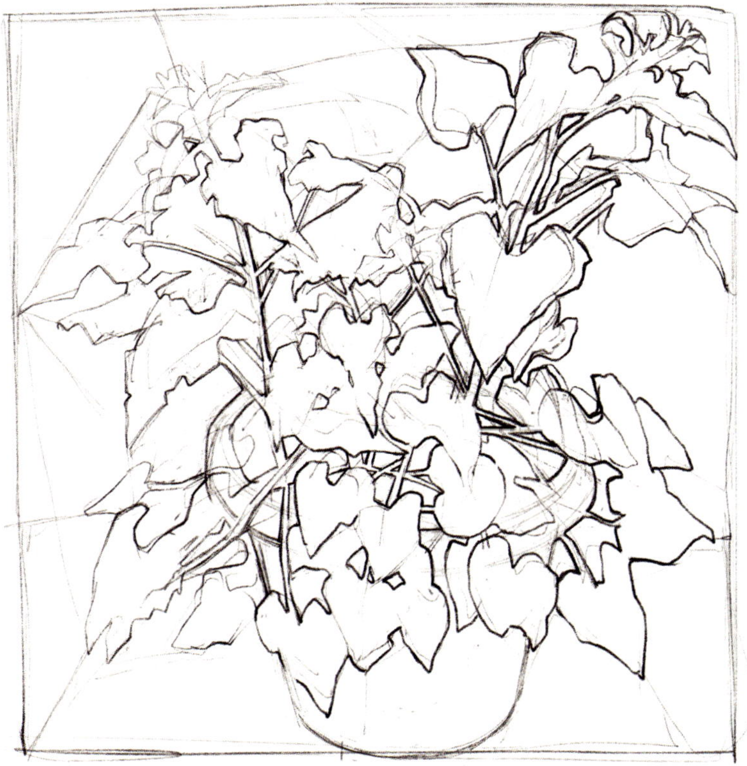

Squaring

What we do with time, time respects.
—Auguste Rodin

This technique of reproduction and enlargement has been used since the Renaissance to make copies as accurate as possible. It facilitates the work by splitting the image into several small boxes.

YOUR TURN

Choose a photo that you would like to reproduce identically, or make one and print it in a large enough size (A5 or A4). Draw a grid of identical squares on it. Transfer this grid to a sheet of the same size. Number the boxes on both grids with numbers and letters on the horizontal and vertical sides to make it easier to find your way around. It is then a question of working square by square in gray or color values. See each of the fragments as an abstraction; together they will recompose, at the end, the most figurative of the drawings. Fill in the boxes by looking at the changes in value or color (or both). Stay "blurred" without contour lines.

IF YOU HAVE THE TIME

- Repeat the experience by enlarging the drawing. Multiply the size of the boxes of your model by 2, 3, 4, 5 . . .
- Get inspiration from D'Arcy Thompson's work: use the grid to deform the model (anamorphosis).

Go and see

Chuck Close (born in 1940)
Ulrike Bolenz (born in 1958)
Borondo (born in 1989), *Les Trois Âges*

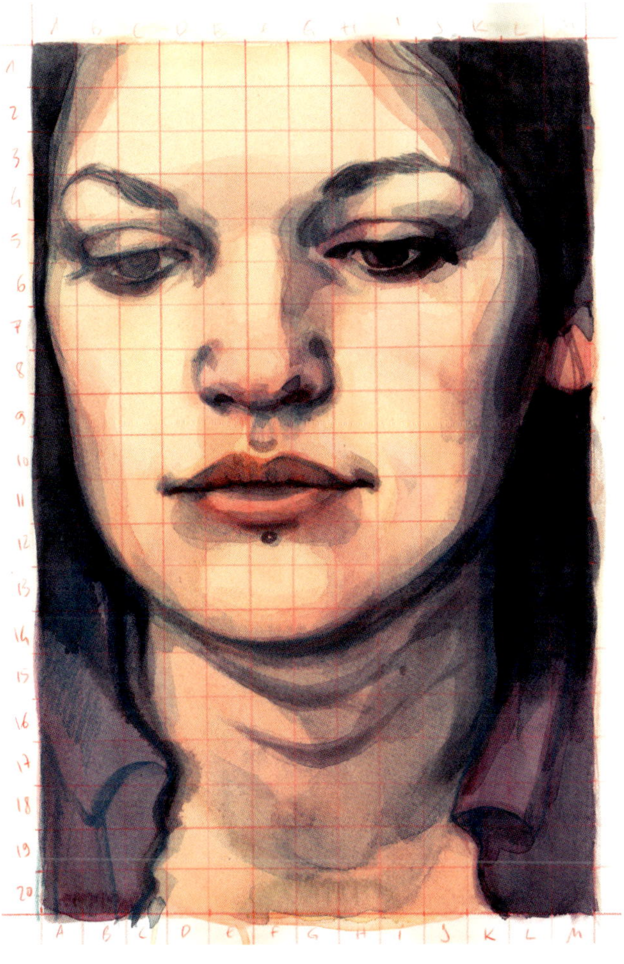

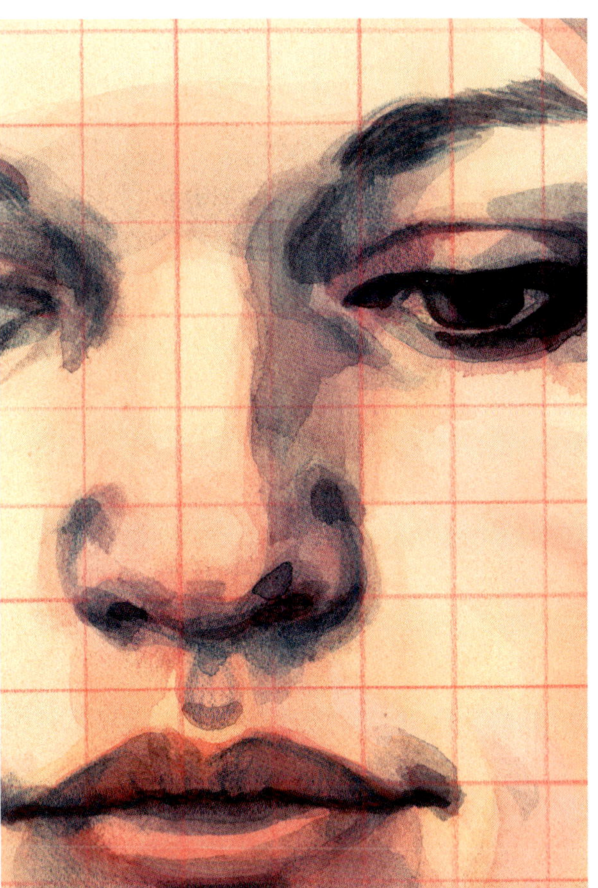

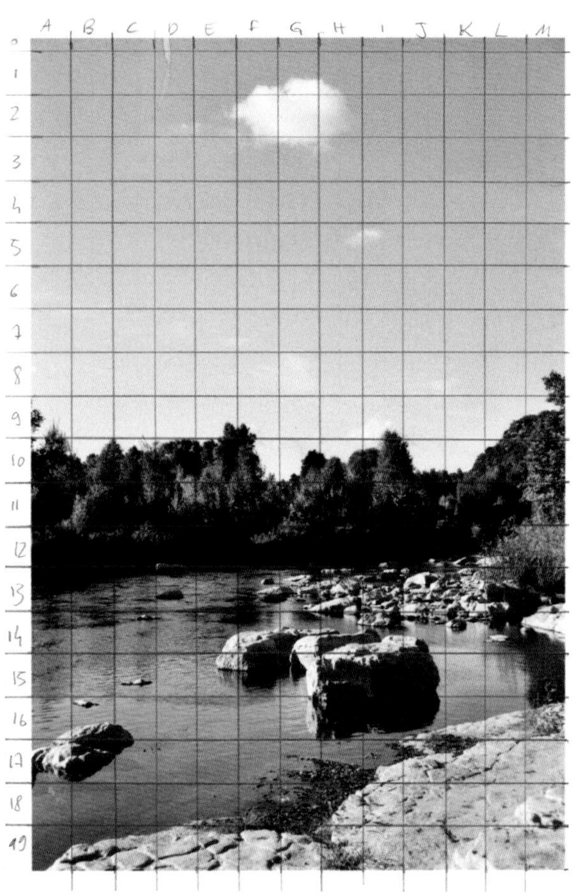

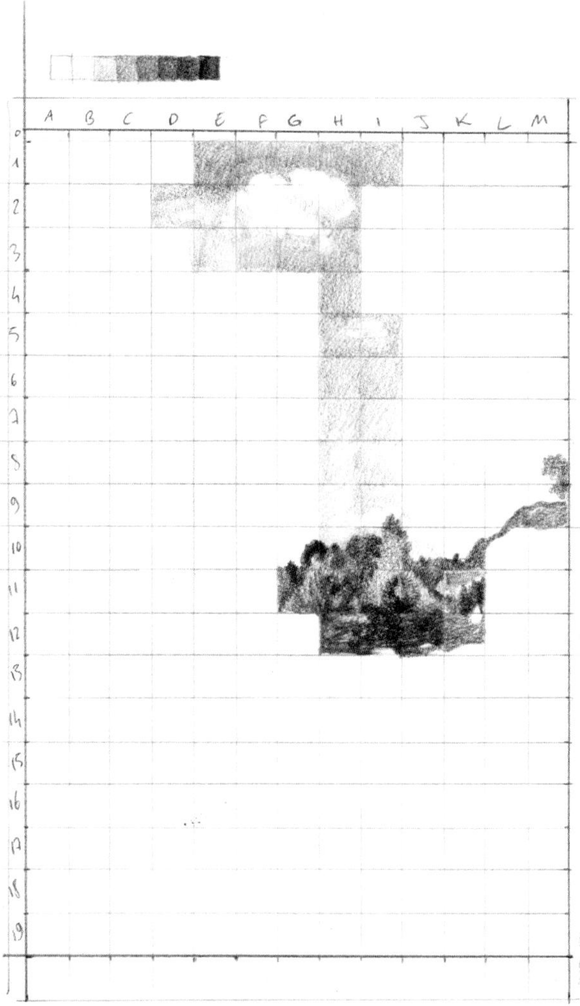

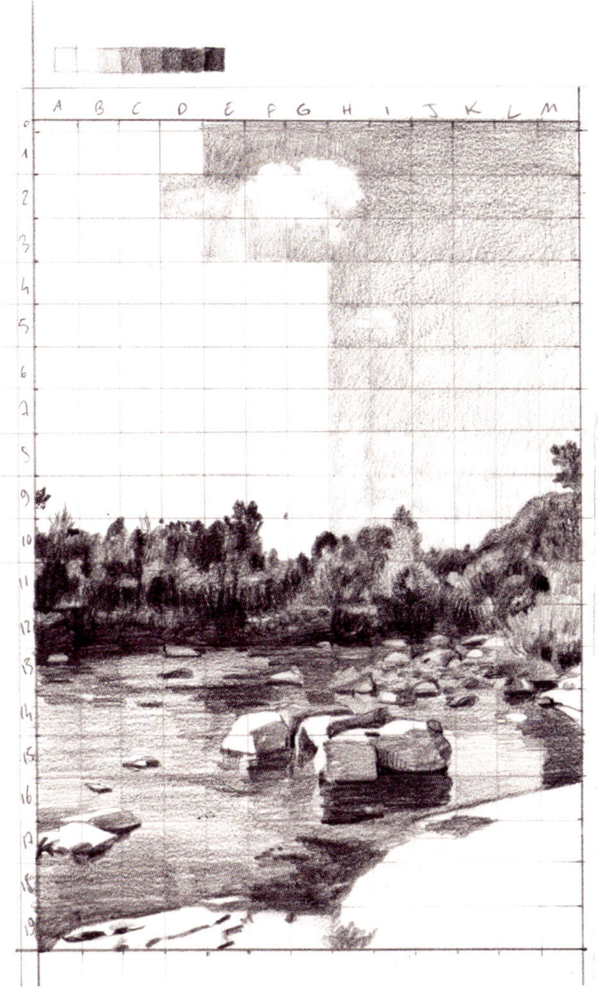

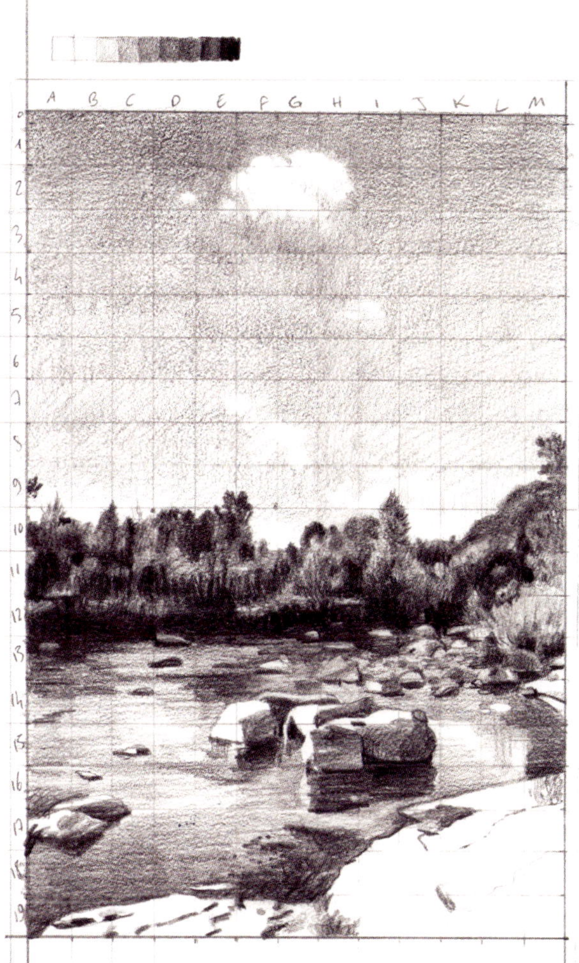
A B C D E F G H I J K L M

Noses and mouths

Only reality is capable of awakening the eye, of tearing it away from its solitary dream, from its vision, to force it to the conscious act of seeing, looking.
—Alberto Giacometti, *Writings*

The most frequent recommendation given in drawing is to start from a global vision before going into details, to avoid errors of proportion. It is excellent advice. However, in the next few days, you will not follow it! You will start with the smallest details, without any prior construction. You will use the same concentration as in weeks 2 and 3 and retain an abstract perception, to draw eyes, noses, mouths, and ears.

YOUR TURN

Observe these facial fragments very closely, on yourself and on relatives. It is important to change your point of view to enrich your vision. This experience of observing details will lead to drawing fragments of well-known faces as if you had never seen them before.

Choose a pencil or ballpoint pen and basic paper. Look at a fold or hollow and follow it until it meets another one, which will lead you in another direction, without any prior idea of your destination. Let yourself be captivated by this new world to explore.

IF YOU HAVE THE TIME

- Make a full-page fragment (A4) to work in even more detail.
- Draw a whole face in the same state of mind, without construction or landmarks.

Go and see

Maurits Cornelis Escher (1898–1972), *Eye*
Alina Szapocznikow (1926–1973)
Iris Legendre (born in 1988)

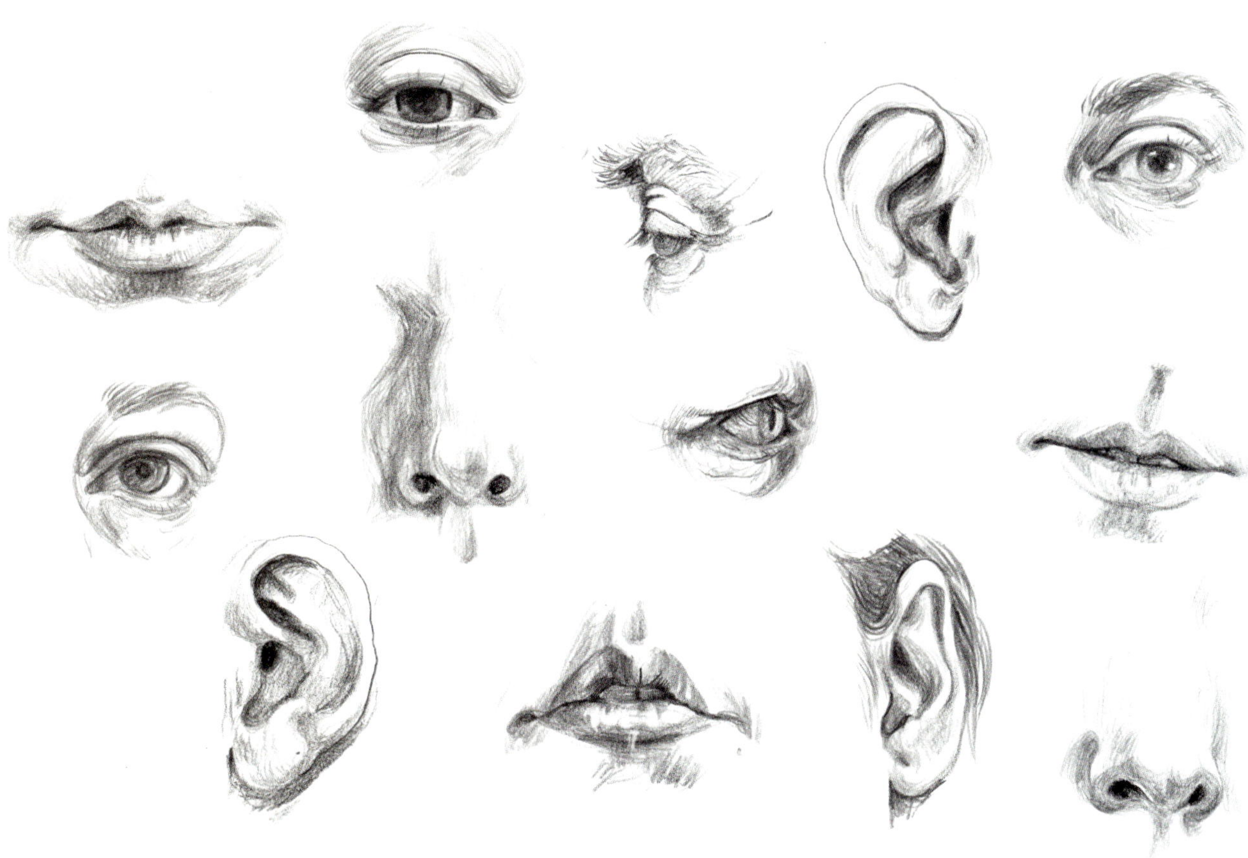

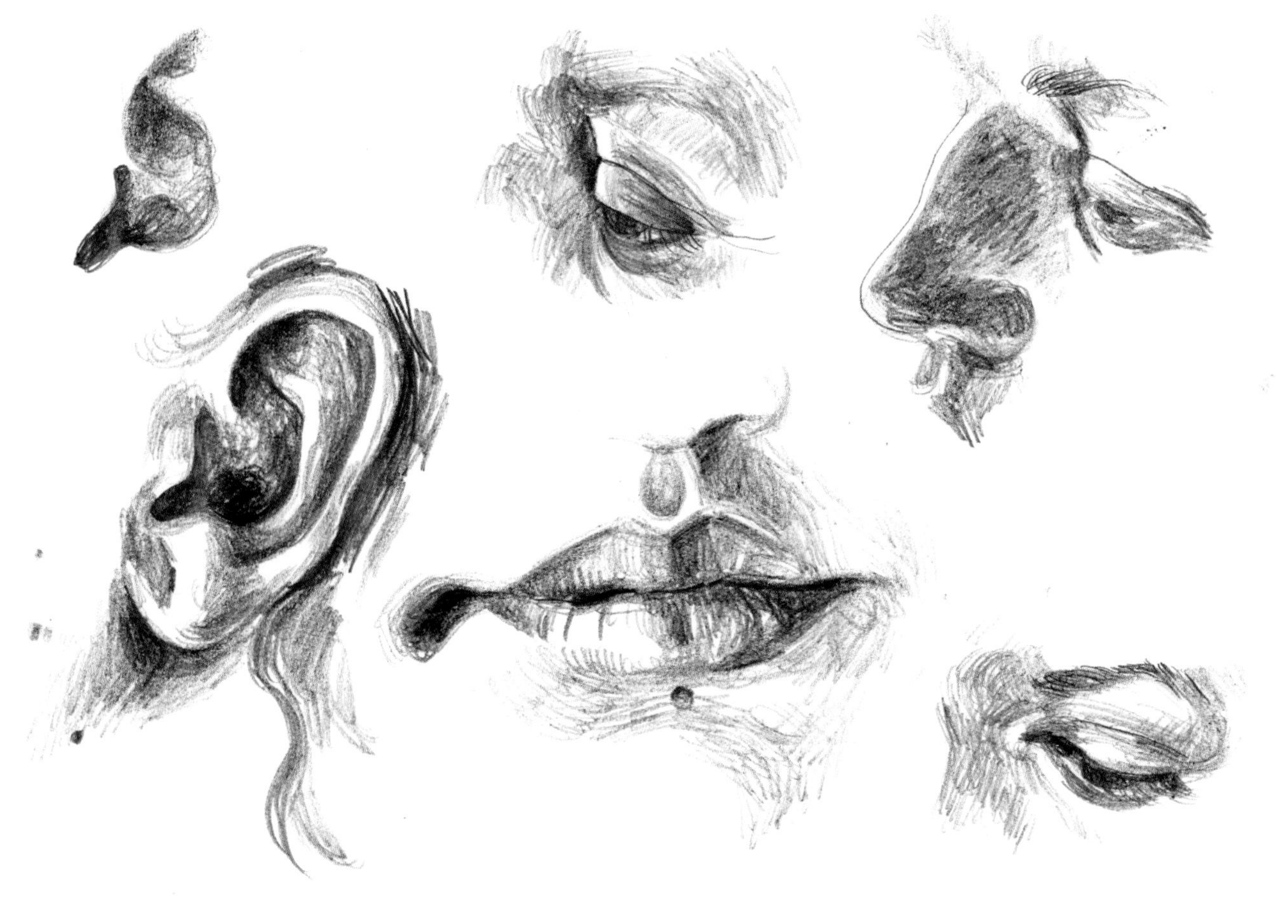

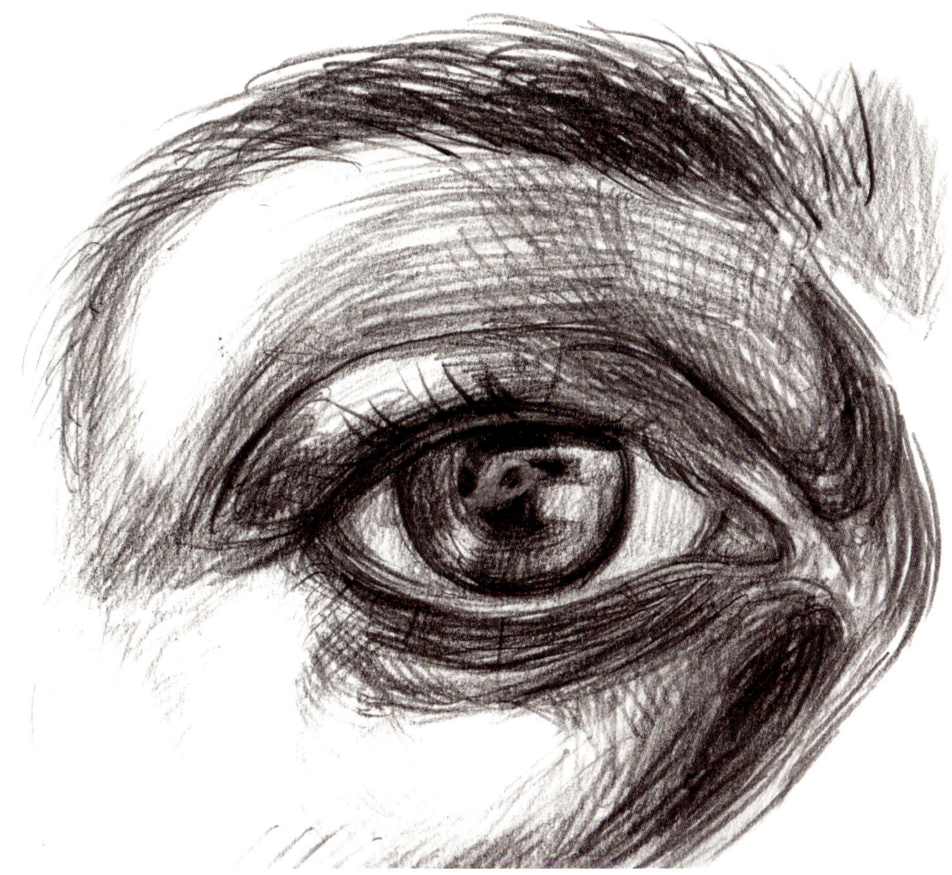

The bigger the drawing, the more you will have to treat the details with precision.

Portraits

He did not paint his models from the outside, but identified with them and proceeded as if he was painting his own portrait.
—Jean Renoir about his father, the painter Auguste Renoir

The aesthetic canon does not coincide with all faces, but it will help you identify the specific characters of each.

YOUR TURN

Free format and technique.

Have someone close to you pose, use photographs, or stand in front of a mirror.

If your model is in profile, imagine the volume of her skull under the hair or skin: her ovoid shape, wider at the back, narrower at the forehead. Draw the limits of the face and lower jaw and then move up under the skull, midway along the width of the head. It is behind this point that we will affix the ear. Be careful: we often tend to place it much farther forward. Then draw the eyes at midheight. The height of the nose can be adjusted to determine the distance between the underside of the nose and the chin. Place the cheekbones; make them reach the attachment point of the jaw behind the ear. The ear is at nose level.

Then draw a front view; the space between the eyes is the length of an eye and the width of the nose, at the nostrils. The corners of the lips align with the center of the eyes.

After a few sketches of proportions, multiply the drawings.

IF YOU HAVE TIME

• Have fun distorting and accentuating characters from reproductions of paintings.

Go and see

Helene Schjerfbeck (1862–1946)
Alice Neel (1900–1984)
Benjamin Björklund (born in 1986)

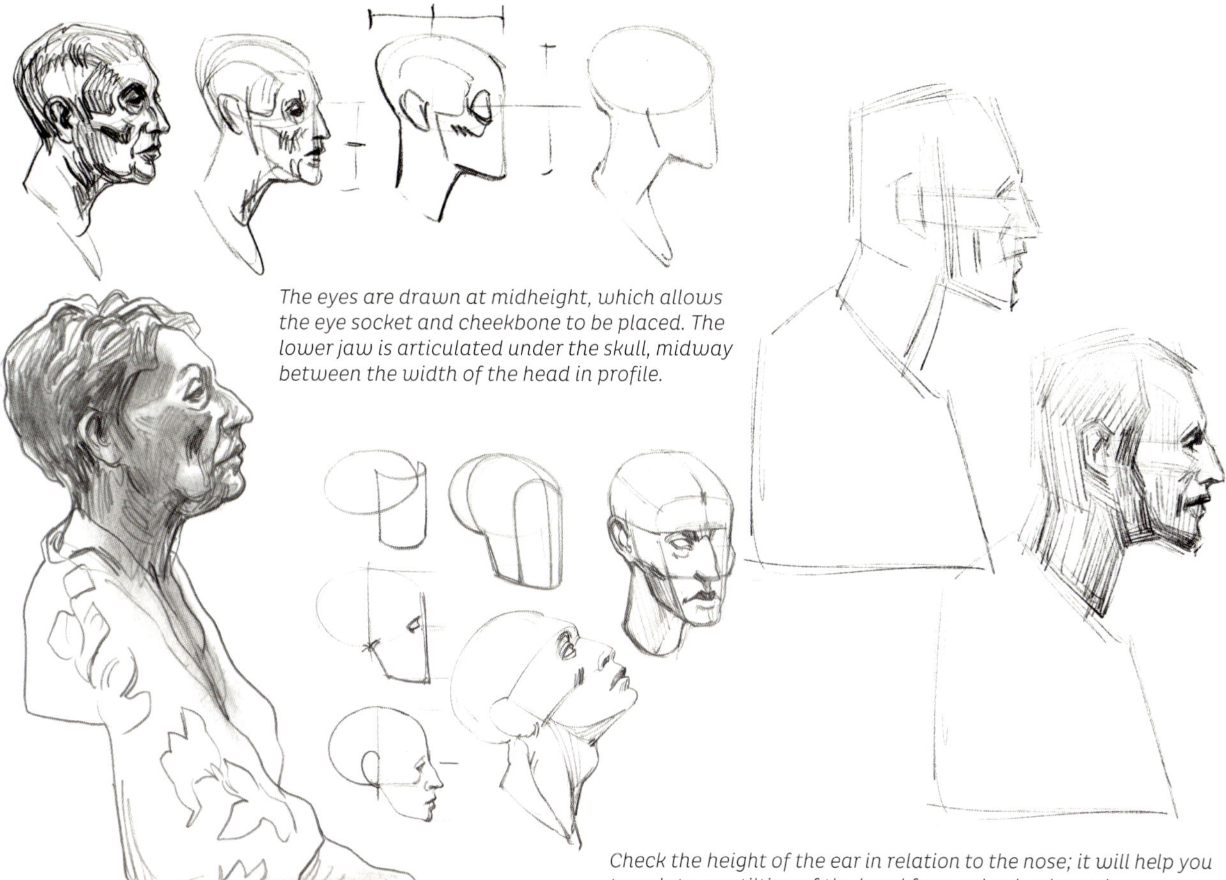

The eyes are drawn at midheight, which allows the eye socket and cheekbone to be placed. The lower jaw is articulated under the skull, midway between the width of the head in profile.

Check the height of the ear in relation to the nose; it will help you translate any tilting of the head forward or backward.

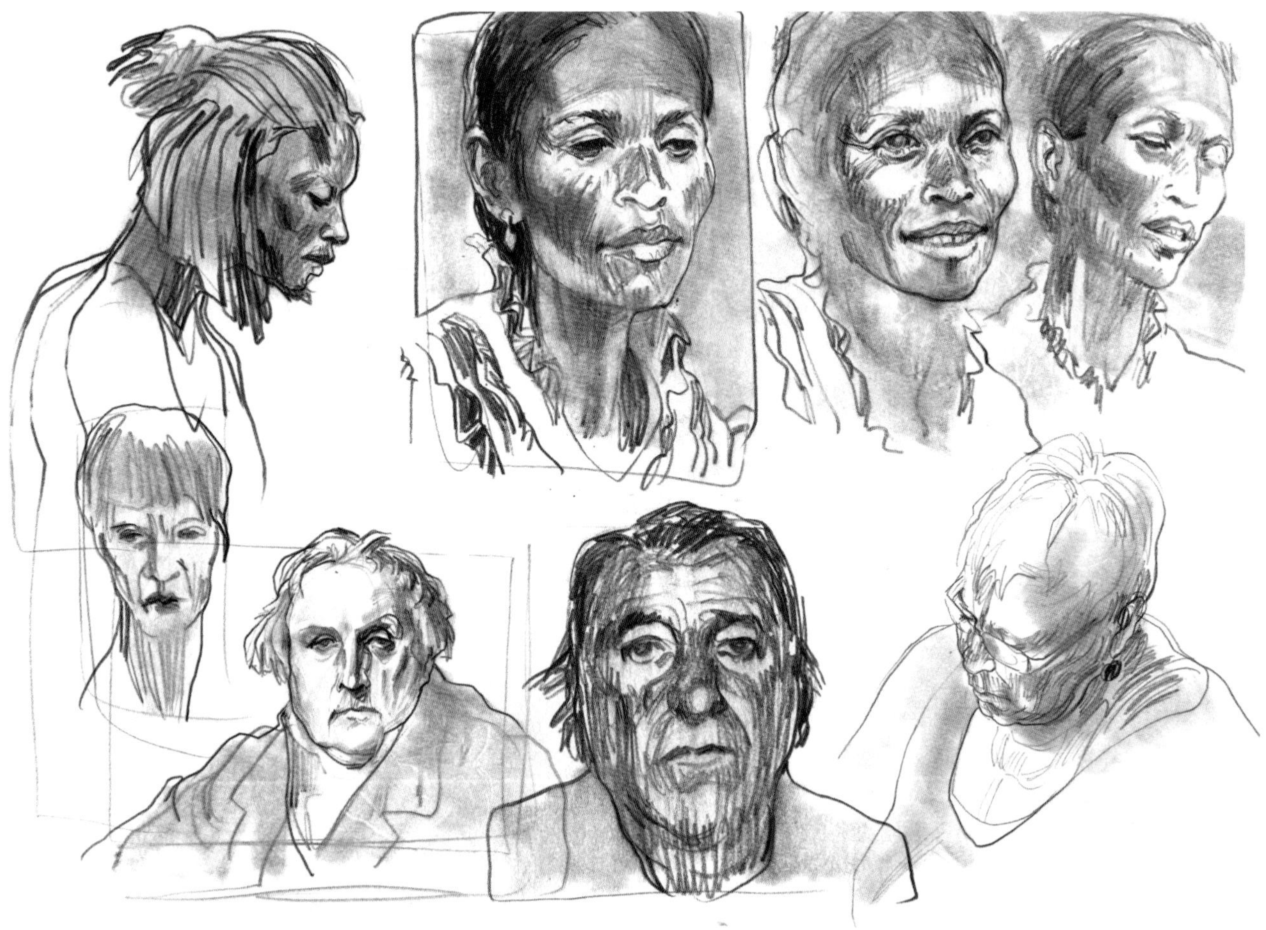

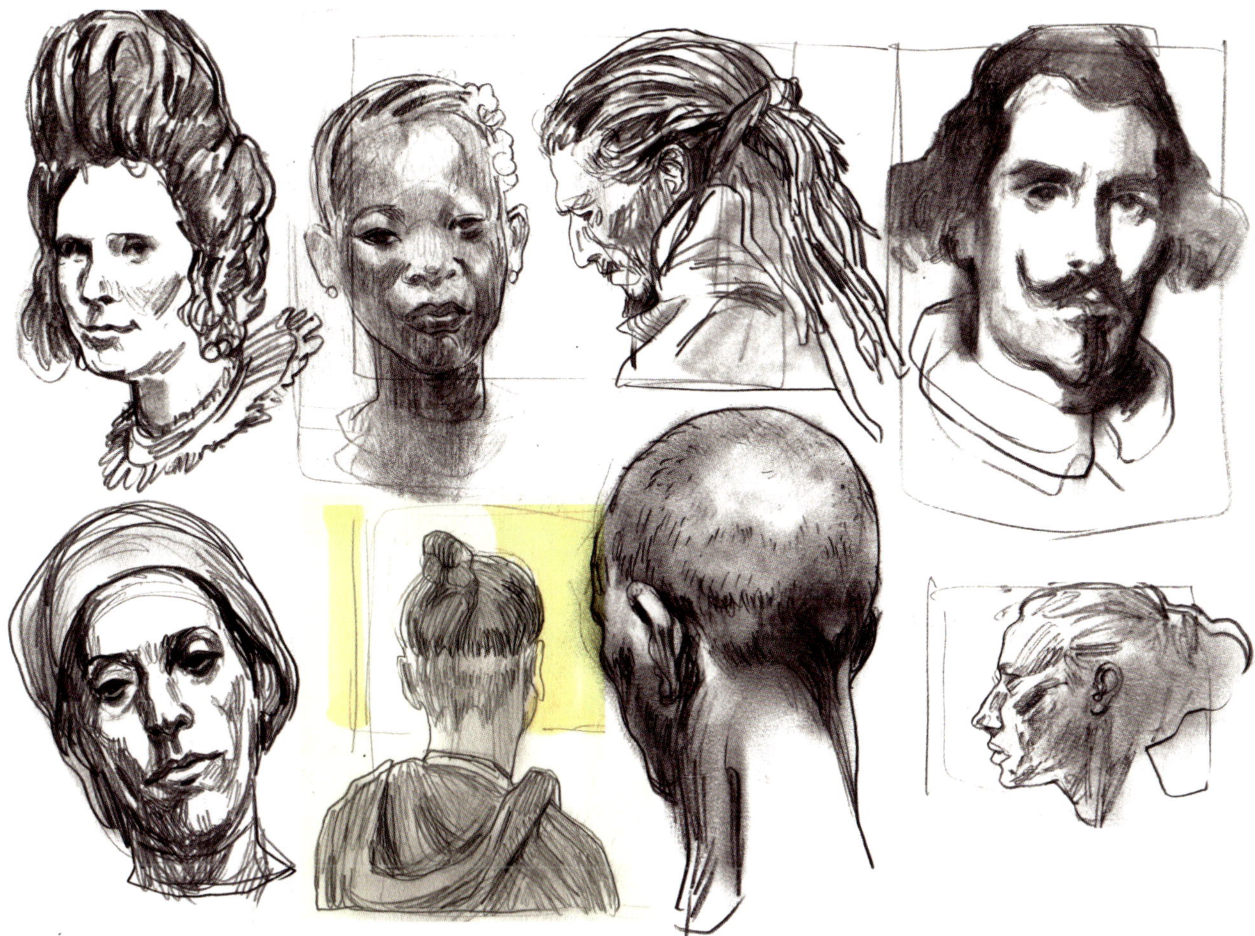

Perspective

Oh, what a sweet thing this perspective is!
—Giorgio Vasari, *Life of Paolo Uccello*

We are going to reduce the rules of perspective to a few notions: the horizon line is at eye level, and all the parallel lines converge toward the same point placed on this line.

You won't be able to place all the points—a certain number will be out of scope, but that's okay: just know that the parallels converge toward the same point somewhere on this line. They move up or down depending on whether they are below (e.g., on a level with your table) or above (e.g., the ceiling) your eye level.

YOUR TURN

Take a large sheet, preferably at least A3, a dry pencil (H or 2H) for construction, and a greasier pencil (2B or more) to detach your volumes from the construction.

Place simple-shaped objects on your table: stacks of books, boxes, etc. Draw your perspective grid: the horizon line and the vanishing lines. Feel free to move the objects around to make this exercise easier, by having at least one escape point in your frame. Bring back all the shapes to parallelepipeds; you will find the middle of each by drawing their diagonals.

Place a desk lamp nearby and observe the drawing of the drop shadows (you will find in the following pages how to build them in perspective).

IF YOU HAVE THE TIME

- Take the risk outdoors to check these notions. Draw what surrounds you by reducing all complex shapes to simple shapes: boxes and cylinders.

Go and see

Erich Kettelhut (1893–1979)
François Schuiten (born in 1956)
Marion Tivital (born in 1960)

All parallels converge toward infinity.

1 is the vanishing point of the table.

2 the vanishing point of the box.

The horizon line is at your eye level, projected infinitely, or on your wall or any obstacle.

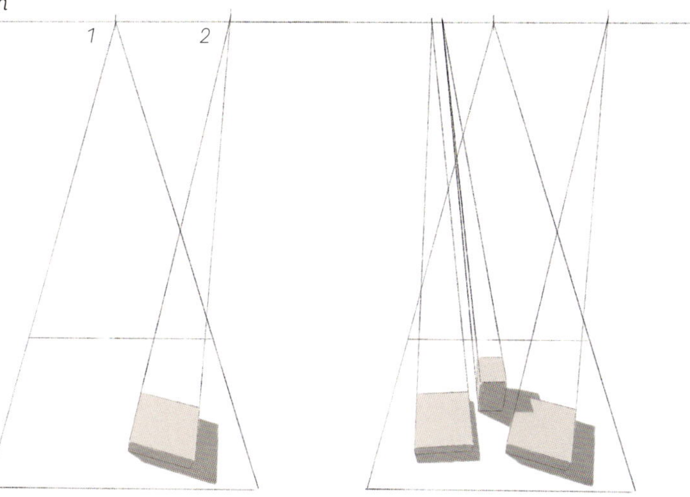

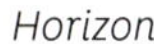

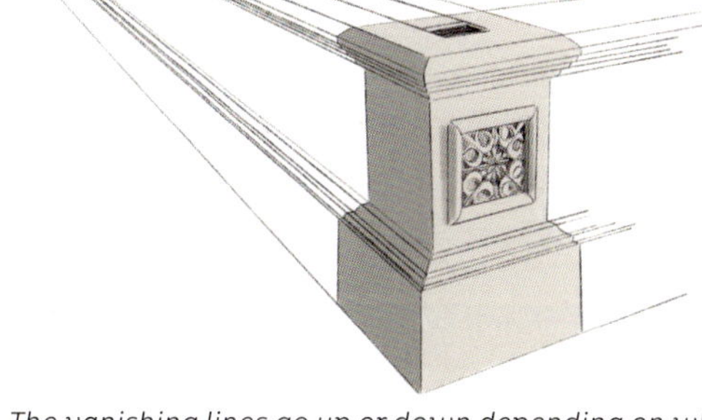

The vanishing lines go up or down depending on whether they are below or above the height of your eyes.

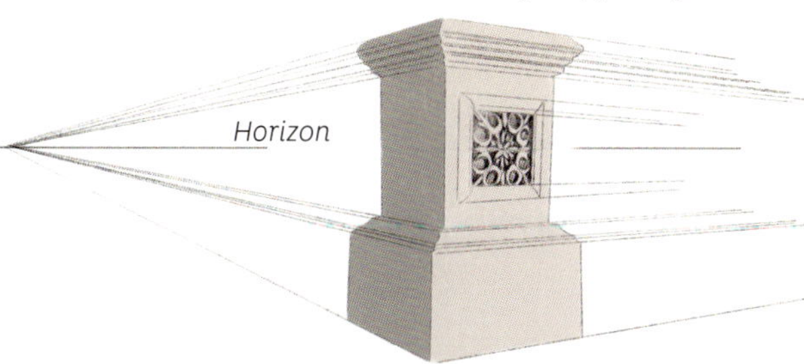

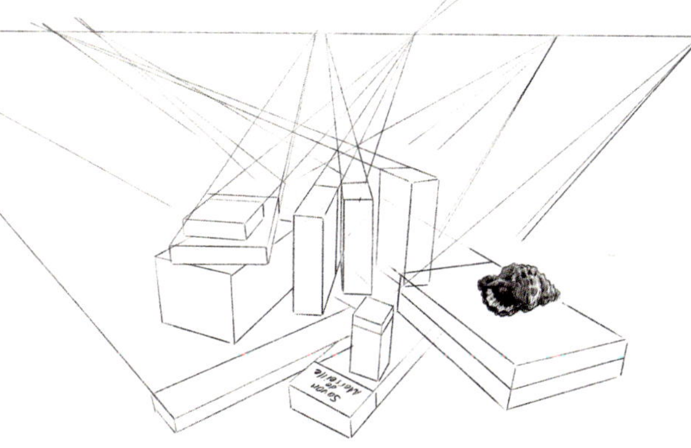

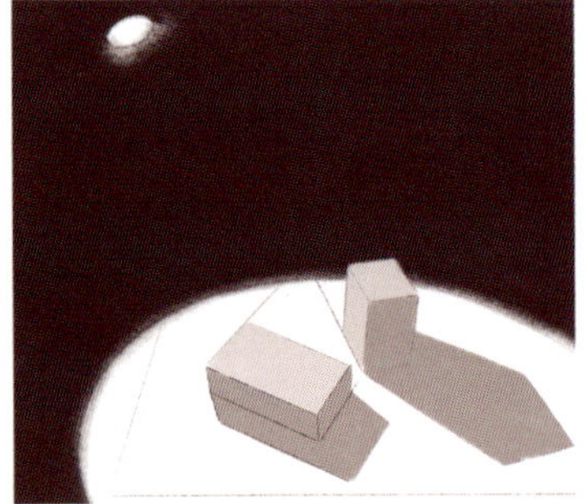

A desk lamp will serve as a light source.

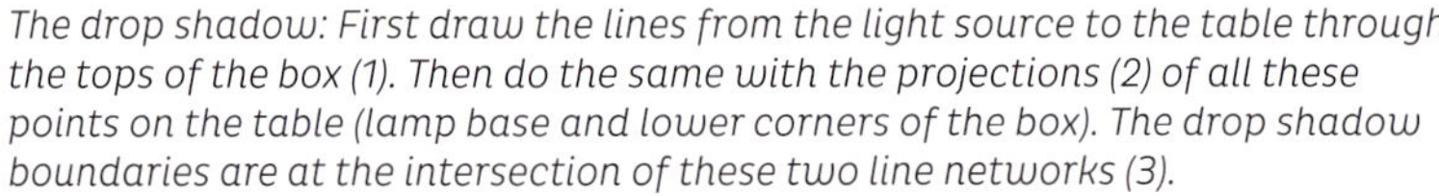

The drop shadow: First draw the lines from the light source to the table through the tops of the box (1). Then do the same with the projections (2) of all these points on the table (lamp base and lower corners of the box). The drop shadow boundaries are at the intersection of these two line networks (3).

Here, the construction requires that the height of the first box be transferred to the plumb of the light source (4), the lamp base, to find the angle deviated from the drop shadow of the second box (5).

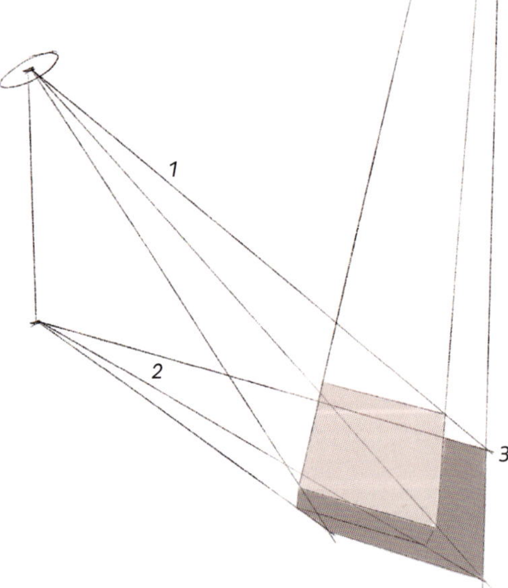

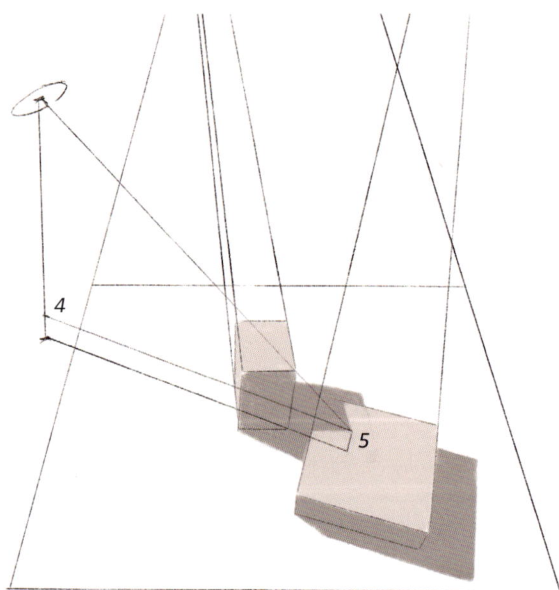

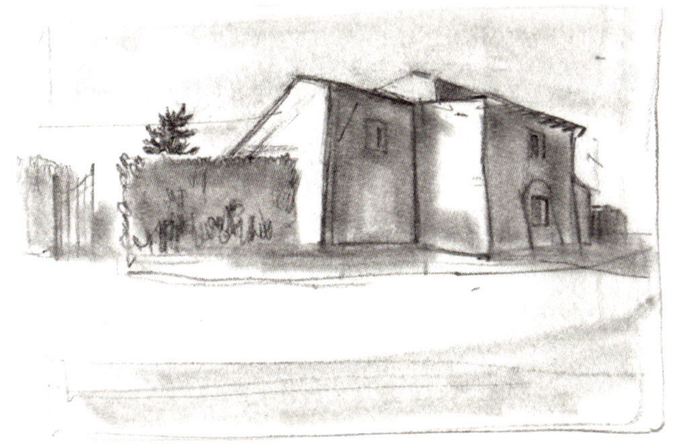

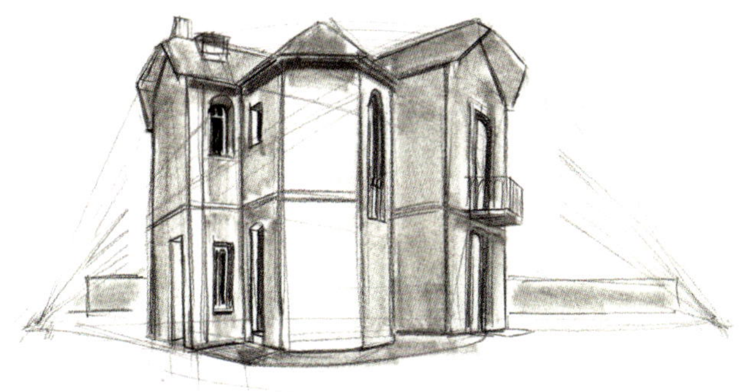

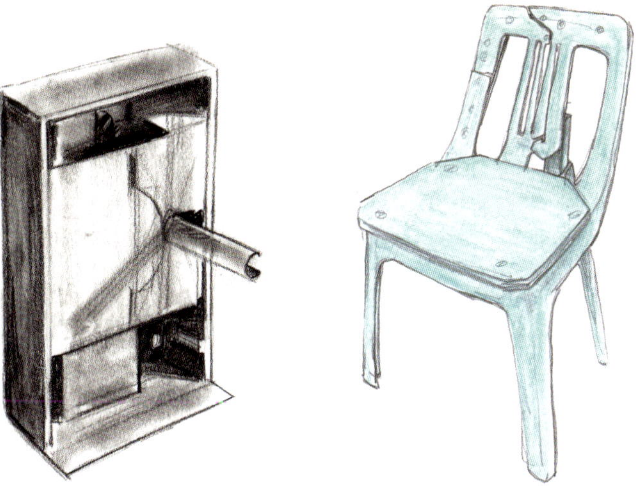

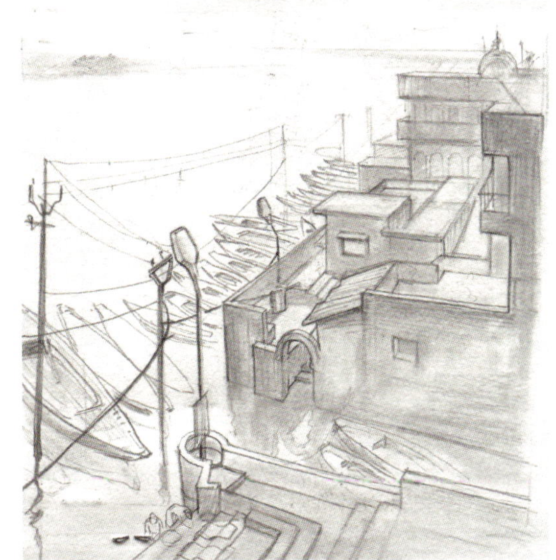

In the box

Any object in the world is capable of constituting a basis of fascination and enlightenment for anyone.
—Jean Dubuffet, *Anti-cultural Positions*

Following on from the previous exercise, you will draw parallelepiped shapes (which therefore have at least one vanishing point on the horizon). These forms will delimit spaces to be structured, to be invested—really small enclosed universes that condense games of full and empty spaces, spots of light and shadow.

YOUR TURN

You can use last week's tools: a large format, preferably at least A3, a dry pencil (H or 2H) for the construction, and a greasier pencil (2B or more) to detach the volumes of the construction and add the shadow areas.

Place a drawer or sewing box, or a tool box, shoebox, toy box, etc., but with its contents on your table. Start by delimiting the volume of the box in perspective, taking care to respect its proportions. The diagonals allow you to find the middle of a surface in perspective.

Then draw the contents of the box. Organize the whole thing by relying on the rhythms of light and shadow. This is not about making a very realistic drawing: this work by light and shadows helps you put the spaces into simpler shapes.

IF YOU HAVE THE TIME

• Multiply the drawings; make the exercise more complex by choosing compartmentalized boxes, with lids, etc.

Go and see

Betye Saar (born in 1926)
Claes Oldenburg (born in 1929), *False Food Selection*
Daniel Spoerri (born in 1930)

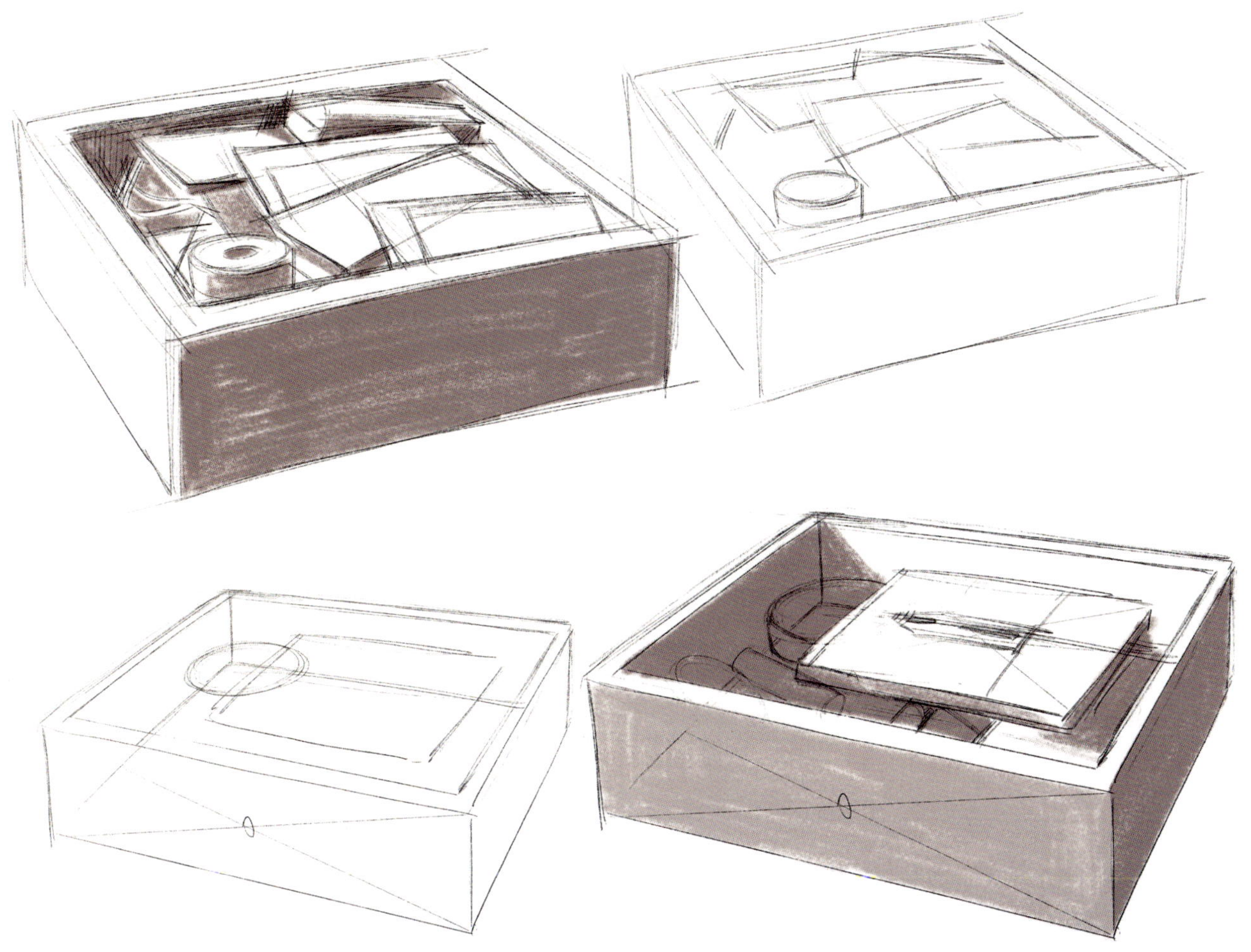

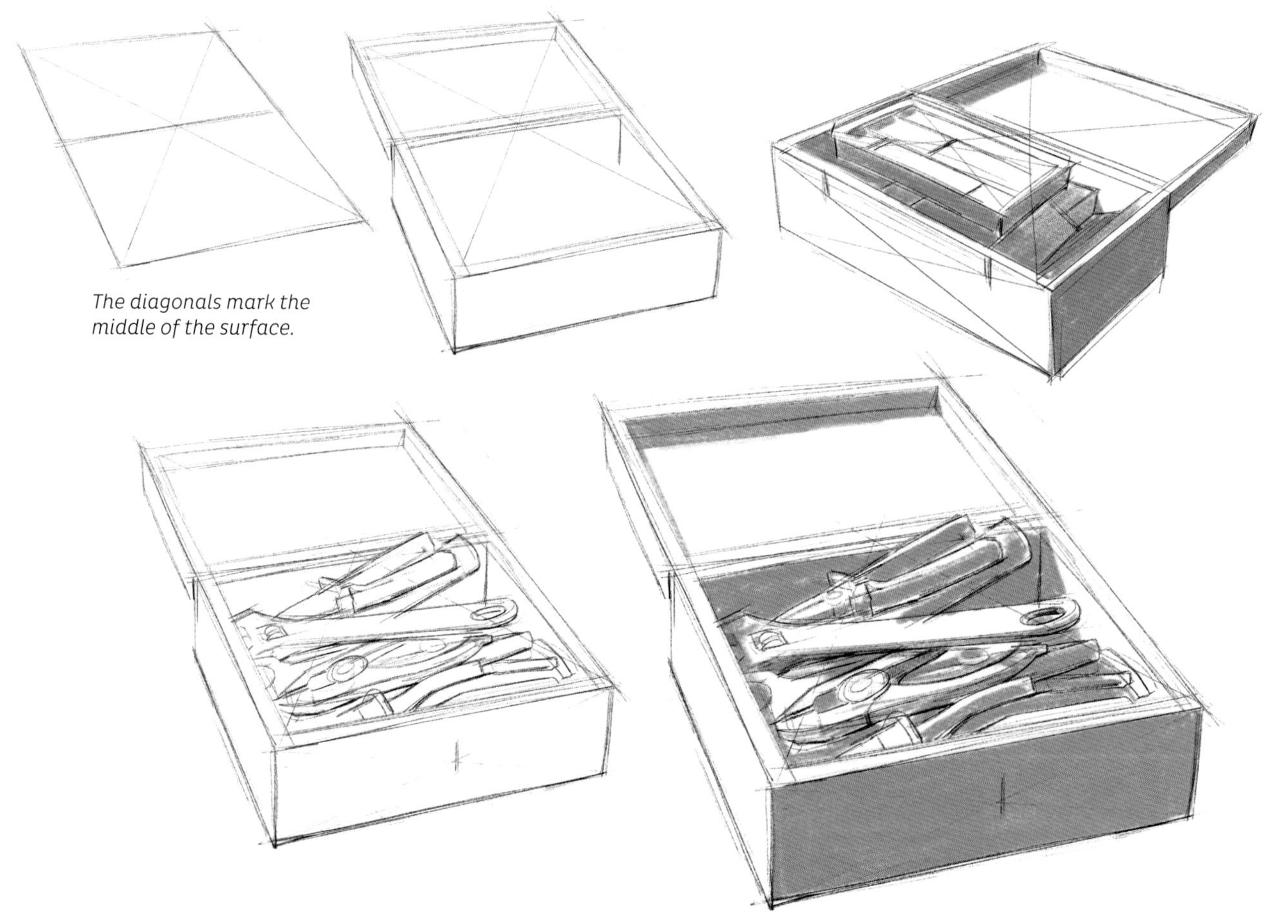

The diagonals mark the middle of the surface.

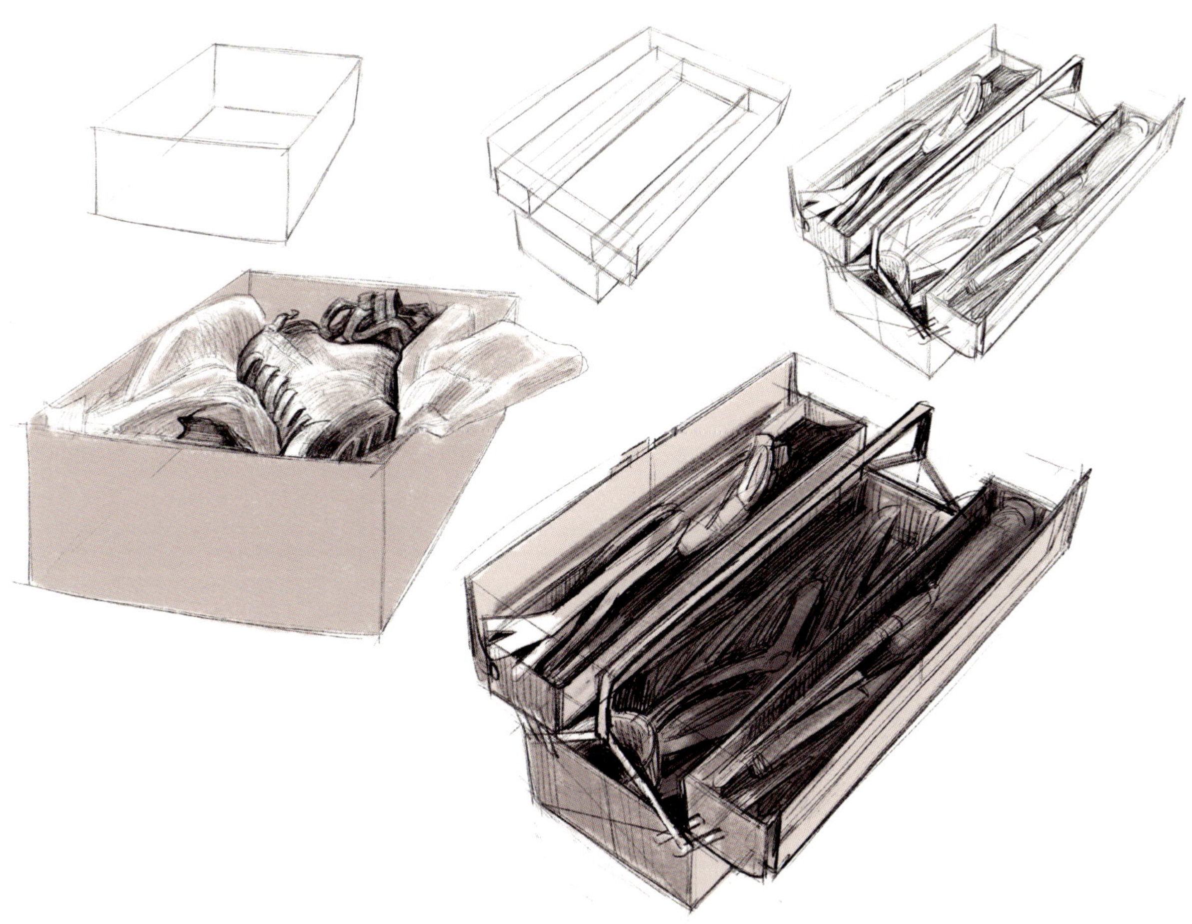

Automatic drawing

I feel more like an experience than a painting.
—Cy Twombly, *Paroles d'artiste*

This week will be devoted to the pleasure of drawing, in a purely intuitive approach to drawing. We have all experienced this practice since childhood: we scribble before we even learn to speak! It will be easy for you to reconnect with this pleasure.

YOUR TURN

Take a blank sheet of paper (A4 or smaller) and a fine tipped tool. Start by drawing an abstract shape somewhere in the blank of the page. Add other shapes to it; soon, from trace to trace, you will be carried away by your own writing.

Do not try to represent anything: it is not a question here of "succeeding" in doing a drawing but of experiencing a motif that builds itself. Let yourself be surprised. As long as you enjoy it, blacken your format and observe what wants to appear. The image can continue over the days, little by little bit. It's an endless story!

IF YOU HAVE THE TIME

- Try a more ambitious format. If you feel that your drawing needs to continue beyond the edges of the sheet, there is nothing to stop you from sticking "extensions" to it.
- Add color to one of your compositions.

Go and see

André Masson (1896–1987) and automatic drawing among surrealists
Fred Deux (1924–2015)
Min Jung-Yeon (born in 1979)

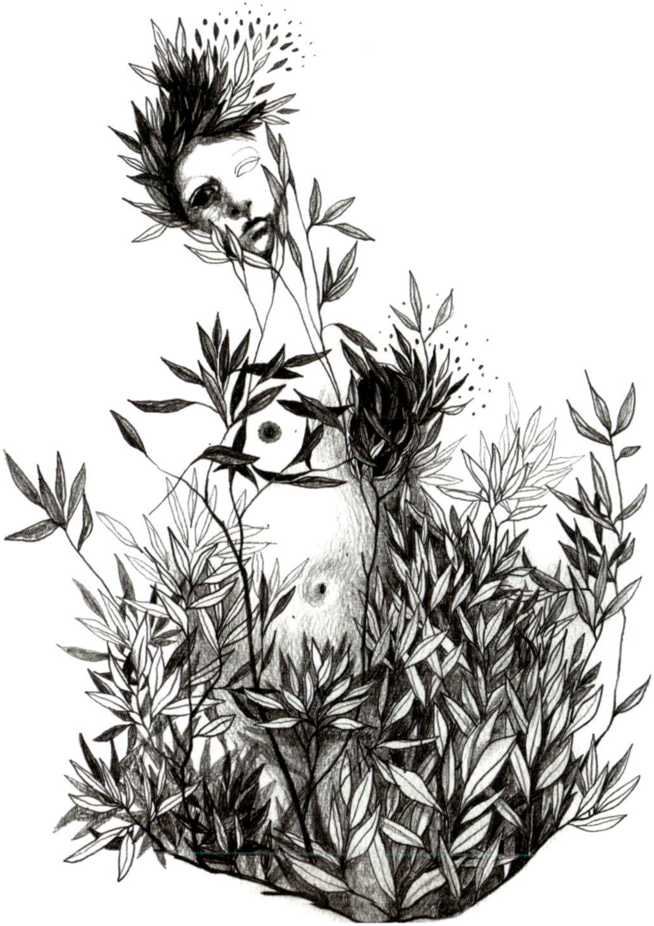

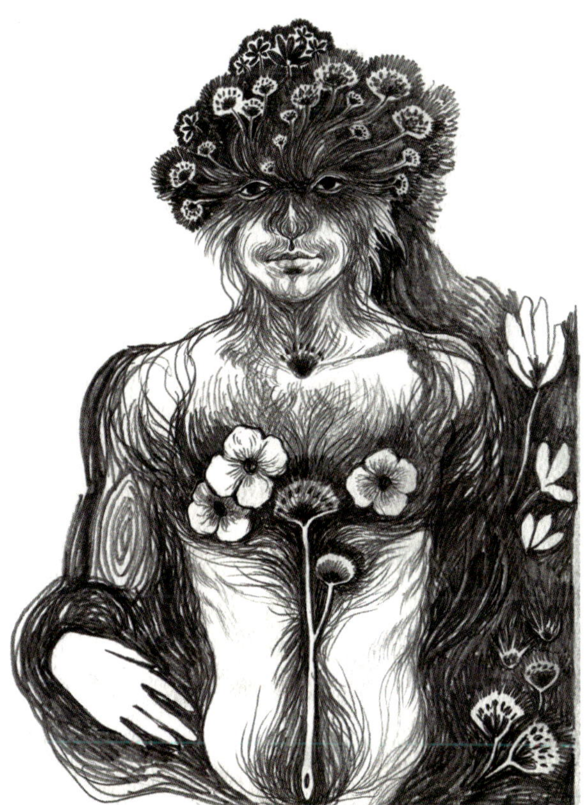

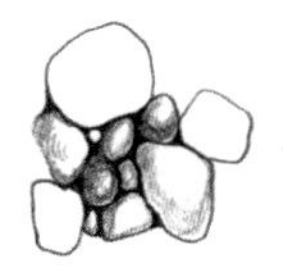

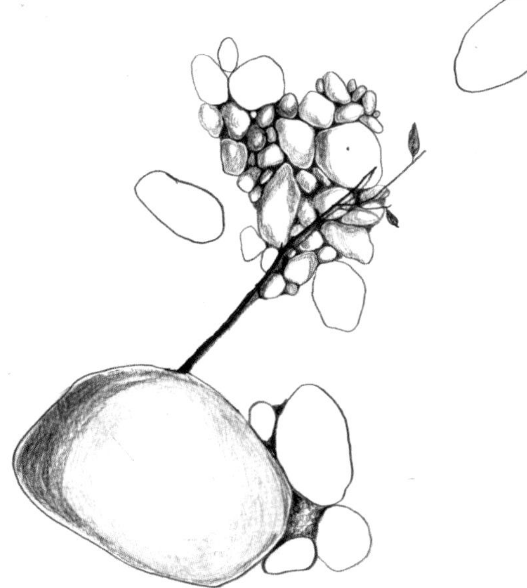

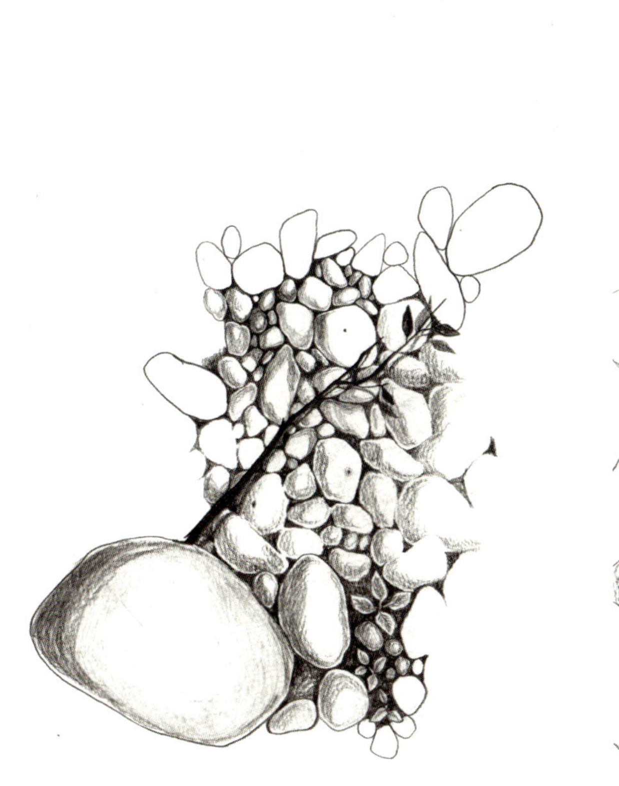

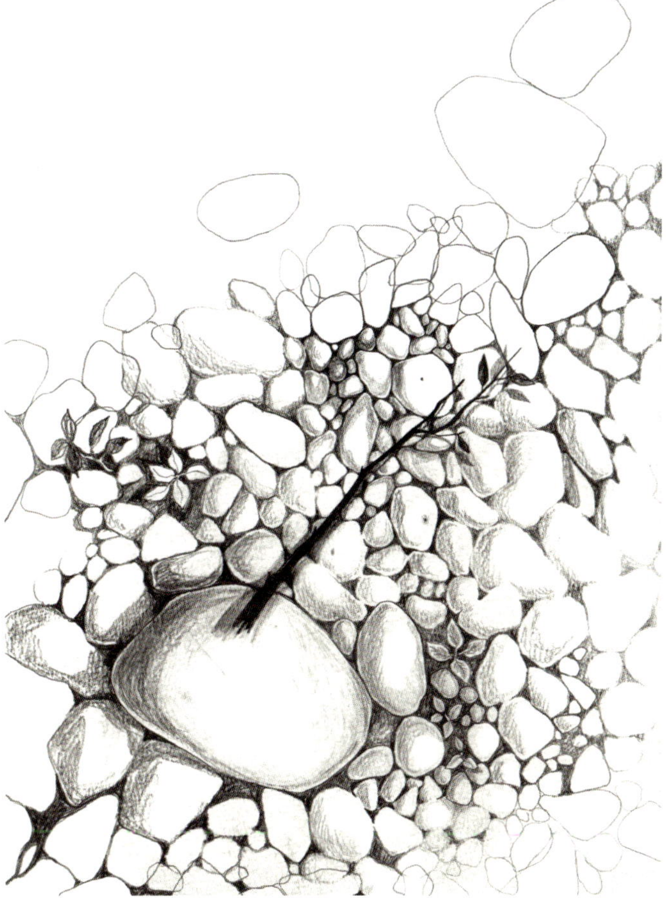

Order out of chaos

Drawing is the art of elimination.
—Max Liebermann, quoted by Paul Klee in *Theory of Modern Art*

Drawing can help us clarify our vision and thus become the source of great satisfaction. The exercise proposed for this week may seem like a real headache, but it reflects one of the components of drawing: simplification.

Faced with the complexity of the world, the abundance of information, we strive to simplify, synthesize, and select. Drawing bears witness to this necessary process and draws its aesthetic potential from it in the eyes of some. For the moment, it is only a question of unraveling networks of complex shapes through drawing, to understand their spatial arrangement.

YOUR TURN

Take a sheet of heavy-duty paper (A4 or A3 size) and tools that can easily correct mistakes (HB pencil and eraser), or digital tools.

Choose a pattern with chaotic, disordered shapes. For example, put a pile of ropes, a pile of branches, or dead leaves on your table. Try to untangle the pattern by following each shape, representing the hidden areas if they help you reconnect the different parts of the same element. Play at untangling this "bag of knots."

IF YOU HAVE THE TIME

• To vary the pleasure, increase the complexity by using more and more disordered subjects. You can also work outdoors and tackle a tree and its network of branches, and more!

Go and see

Sam Szafran (1934–2019)
Monika Grzymala (born in 1970)
Sarah Navasse Miller (born in 1985)

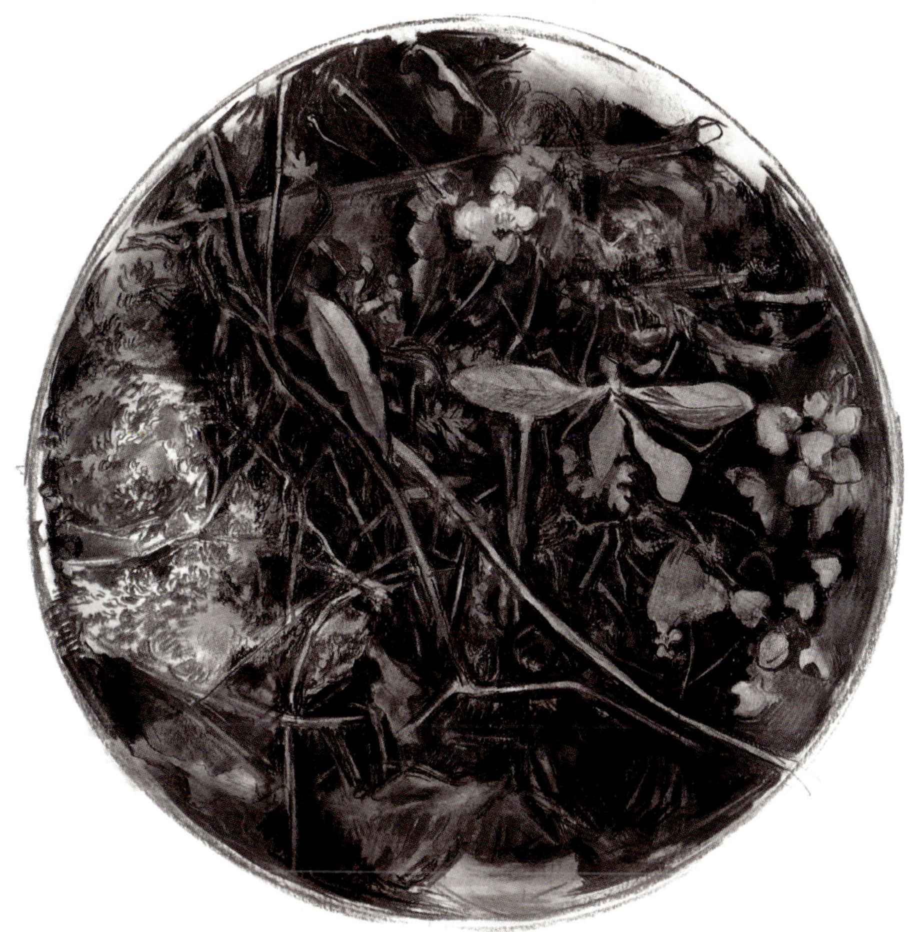

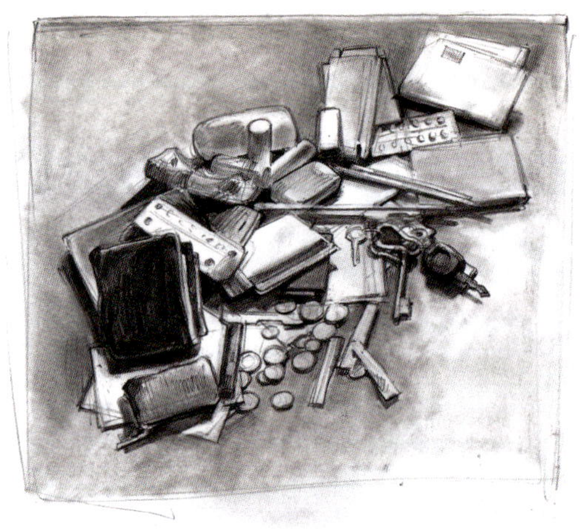

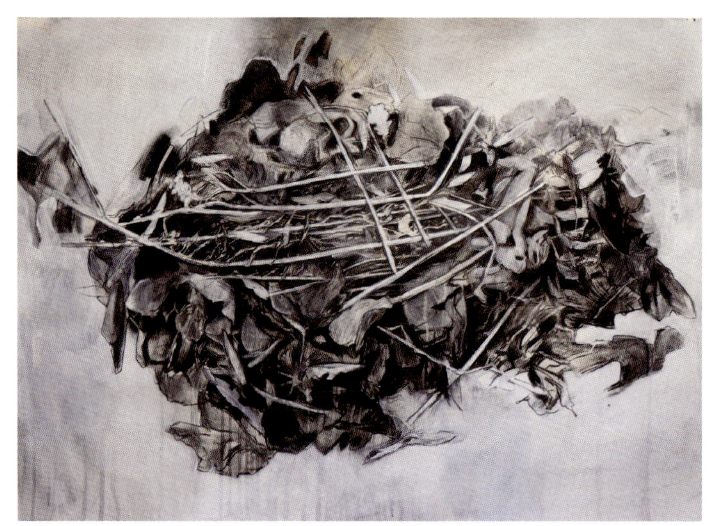

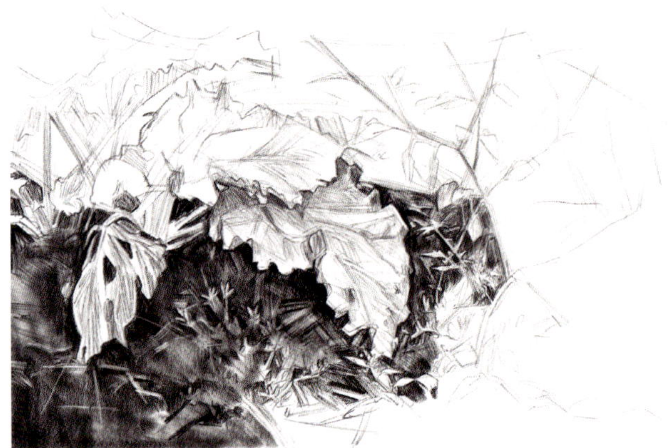

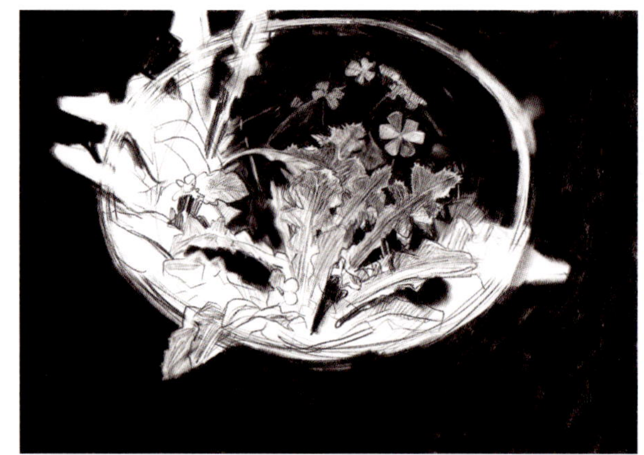

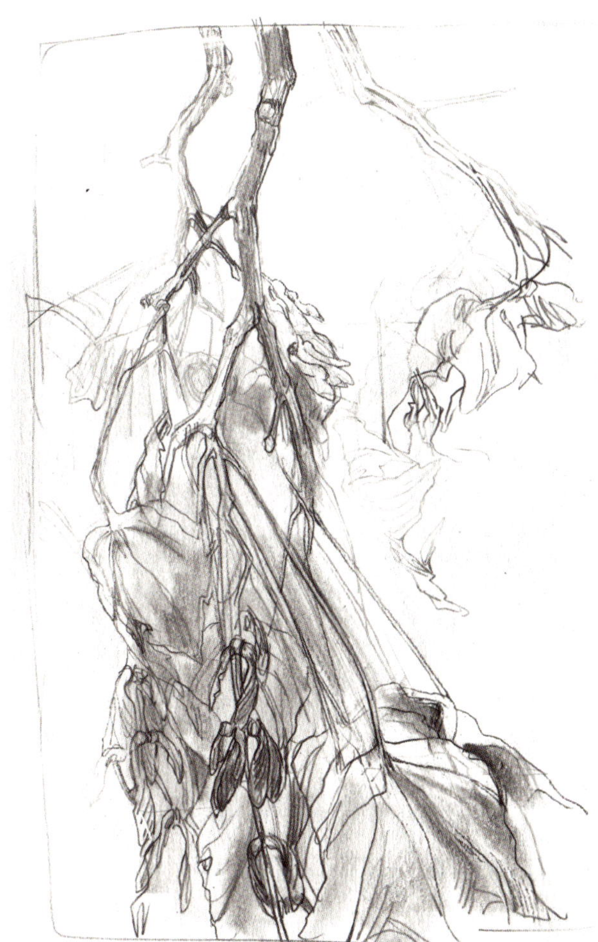

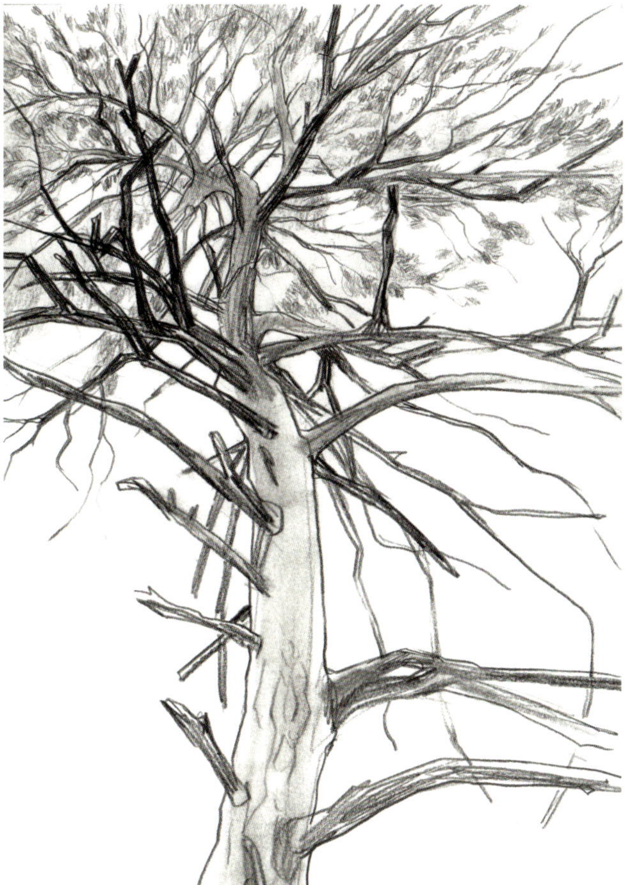

Morph approach

Imagination is the most scientific of all faculties, because only it understands the universal analogy.
—Charles Baudelaire, quoted by Élie Faure in *L'Esprit des formesa*

According to the etymology of the word, morphology is the "study of form." Some natural forms lend themselves more easily than others to an analytical, geometric, Cartesian approach: it is sometimes possible to detect the simple rhythms of their construction and growth. If necessary, this knowledge can be used to start a drawing by placing this reading grid.

YOUR TURN

Take the tools of your choice. Layer and digital tools are well suited to this exercise.

Select natural objects: fruit, vegetables, flowers, shells . . .

Observe them at first without drawing them. Try to discover logical construction, a rhythm. Then make sketches and diagrams to explain these shapes through drawing.

Repeat one of these schemes on a larger scale and take your drawing as far as possible.

IF YOU HAVE THE TIME

• Multiply the experience by trying to compose your research and reflections in the form of a real naturalist board. Feel free to add inscriptions, signs, arrows. Any addition is drawing, composition, graphics: it is therefore necessary to balance, to harmonize texts, signs, diagrams, and drawings.

Go and see

Leonardo da Vinci (1452–1519)
Stella Ross-Craig (1906–2006)
Terryl Whitlatch (born in 1961)

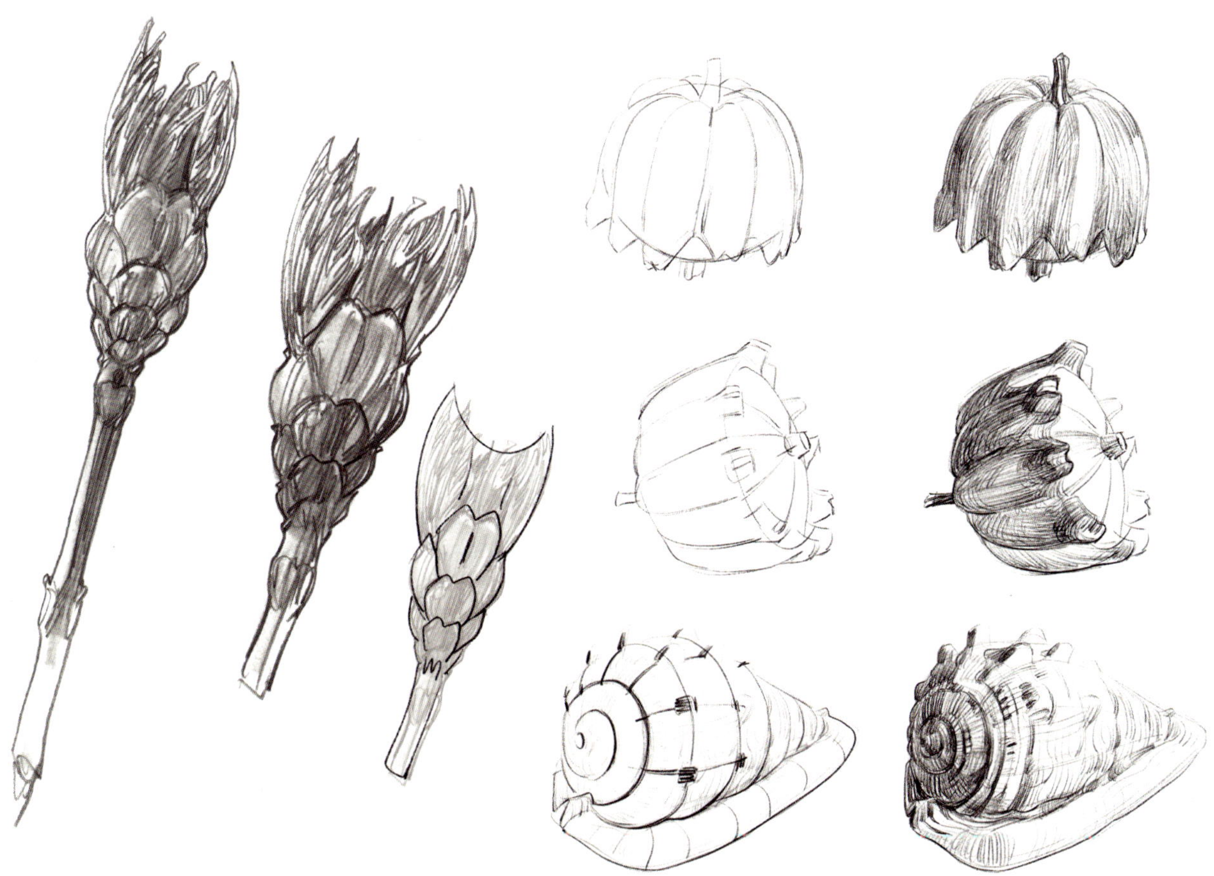

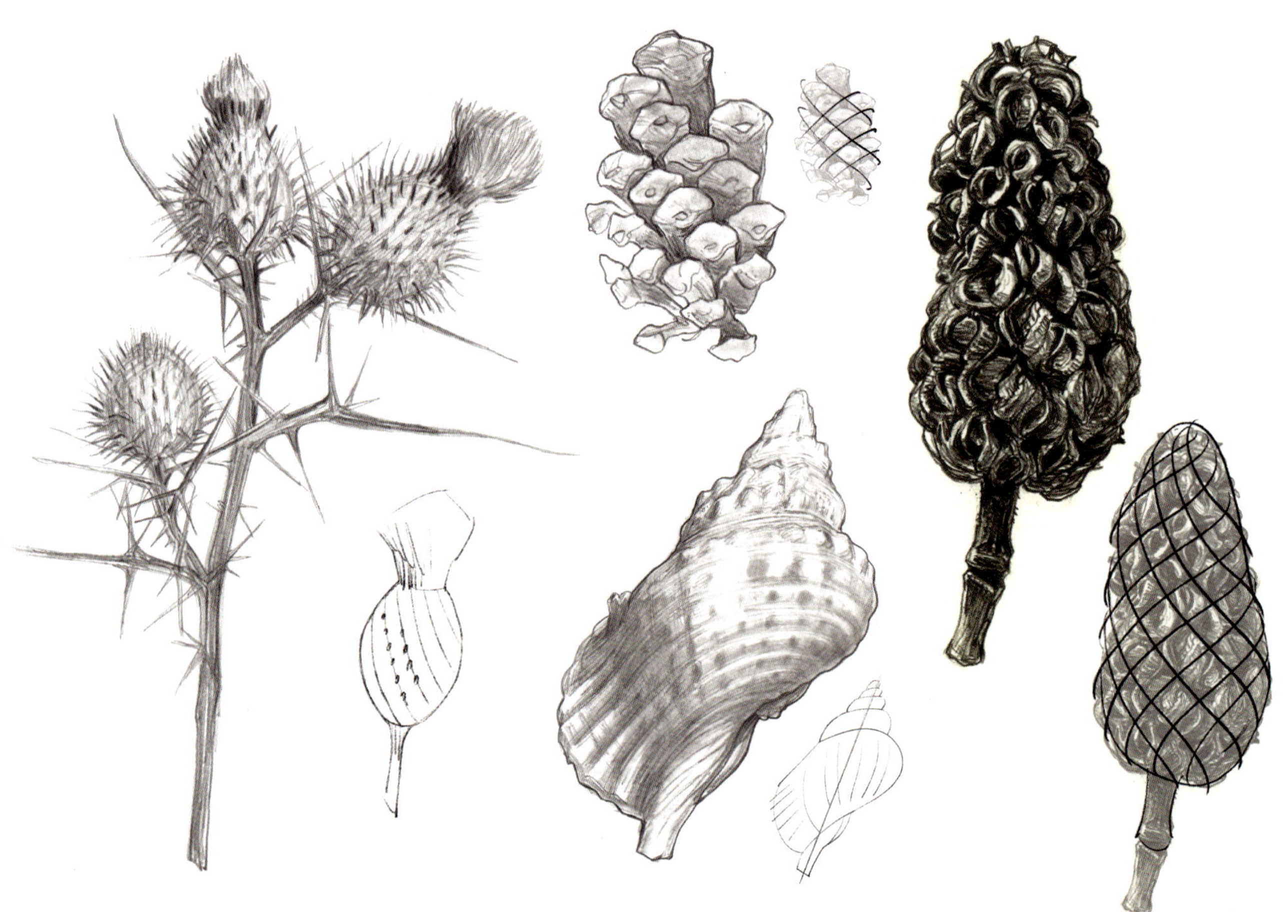

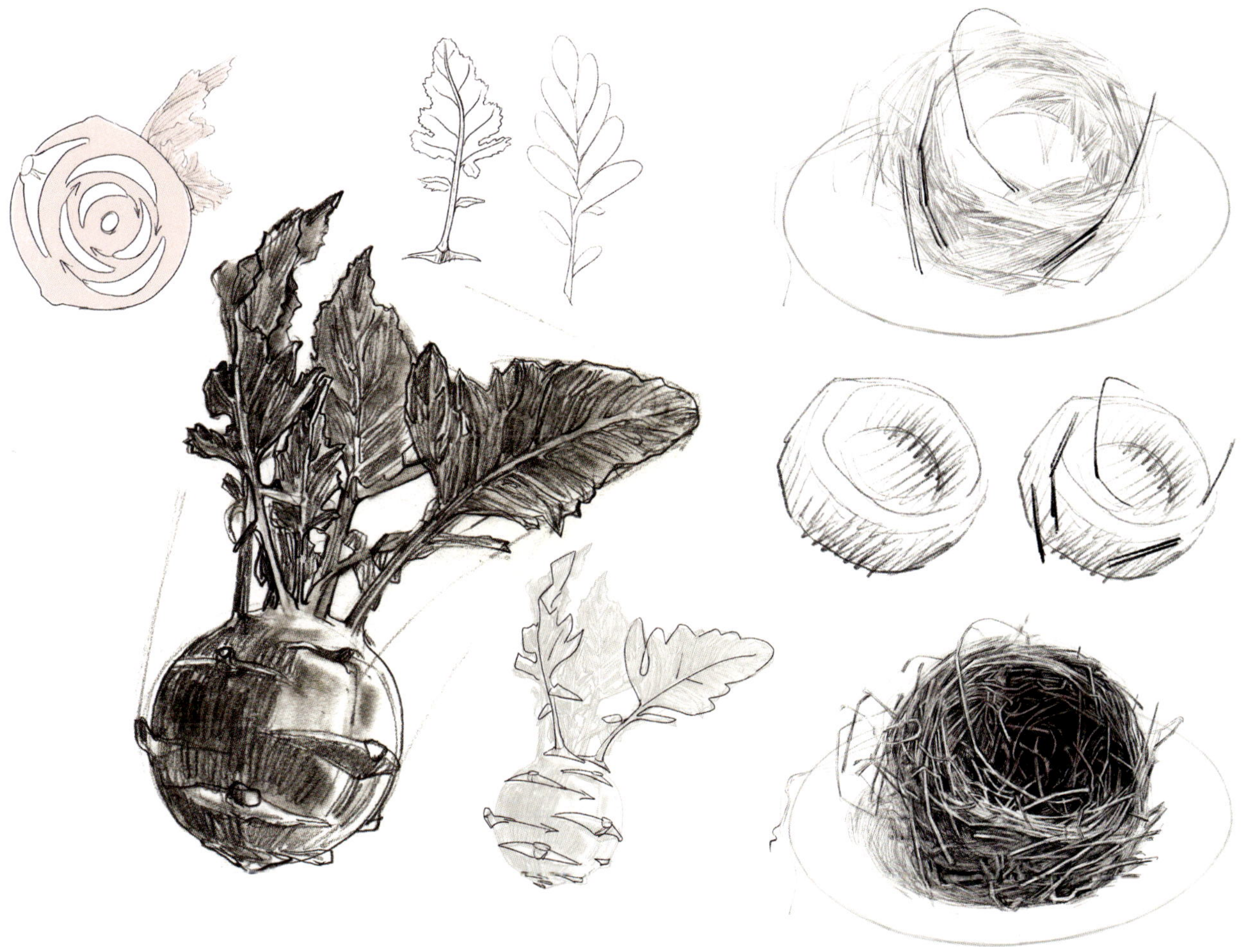

Deforming mirrors

There is no exquisite beauty... without some strangeness in the proportion.
—Edgar Allan Poe, *Ligeia*

In previous proposals, you have learned how to build characters accurately: now have fun deforming bodies. By distancing yourself a little from the rigor of proportion, this type of exercise provides relaxation that encourages the development of freer and more-personal expression. Cartooning also develops the qualities of observation: one must have understood the forms to exaggerate them.

YOUR TURN

Use the tools of your choice (pencil, crayon, ballpoint pen, fine felt pen, felt-tip brush, ink pen). Look for pictures of human beings, preferably naked (see "Resources," p. 222). Draw a frame on a sheet of paper that has different proportions to the subject, and make sure that the body touches all four sides of the shape you have drawn. For this exercise, anything goes: the body can be stretched, folded, inflated. . . . The only imperative: the sides are real barriers, they cannot be exceeded, and the body must fit inside.

IF YOU HAVE THE TIME

- Repeat the experience without the frame. Deform as you wish.
- Choose models with a unique morphology and accentuate their characters in order to move toward caricature.

Go and see

André Kertész (1894–1985), *Les Distorsions*
Carlos Nine (1944–2016)
Nicolas Presl (born in 1976)

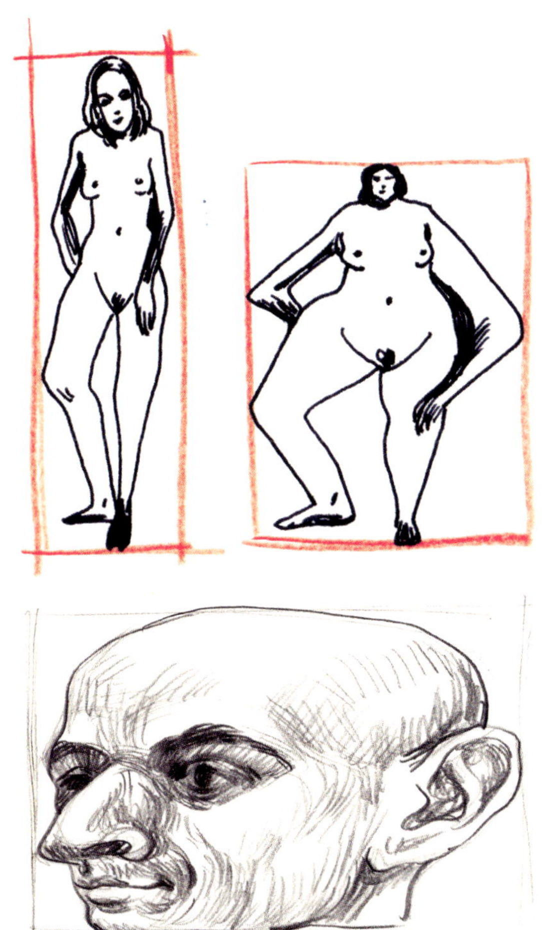

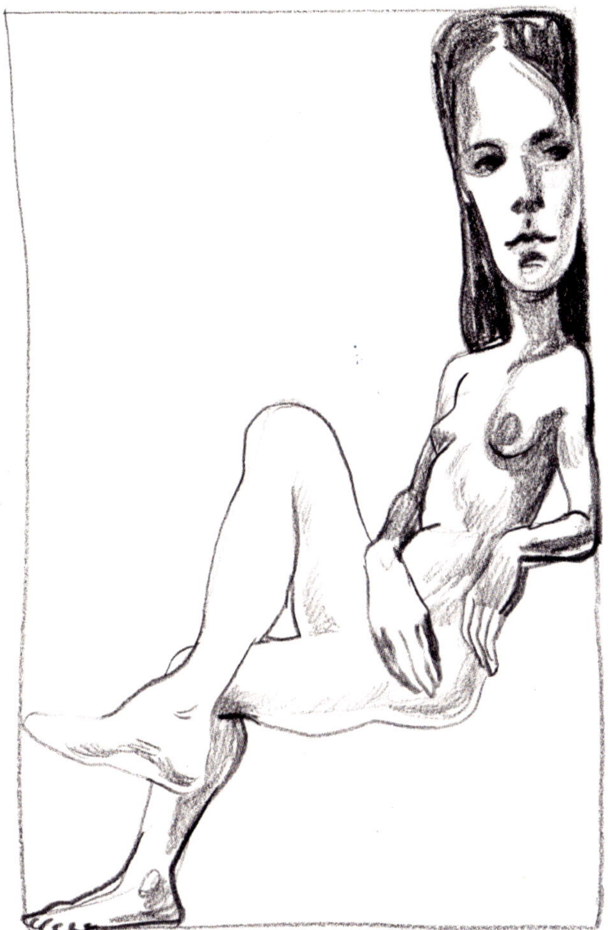

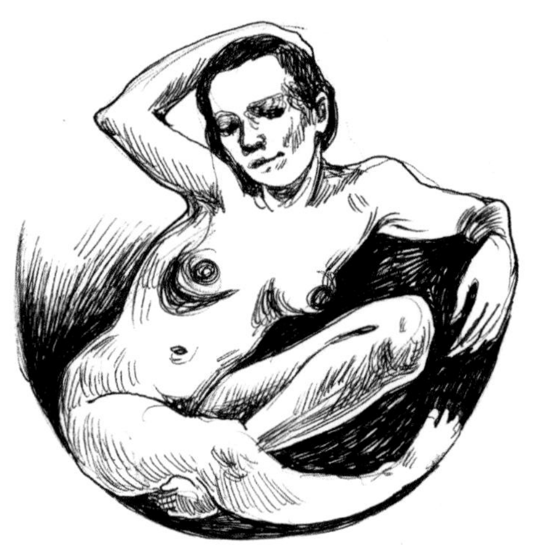

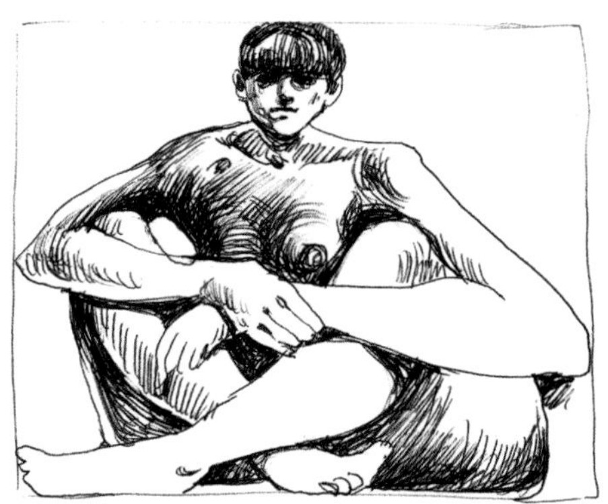

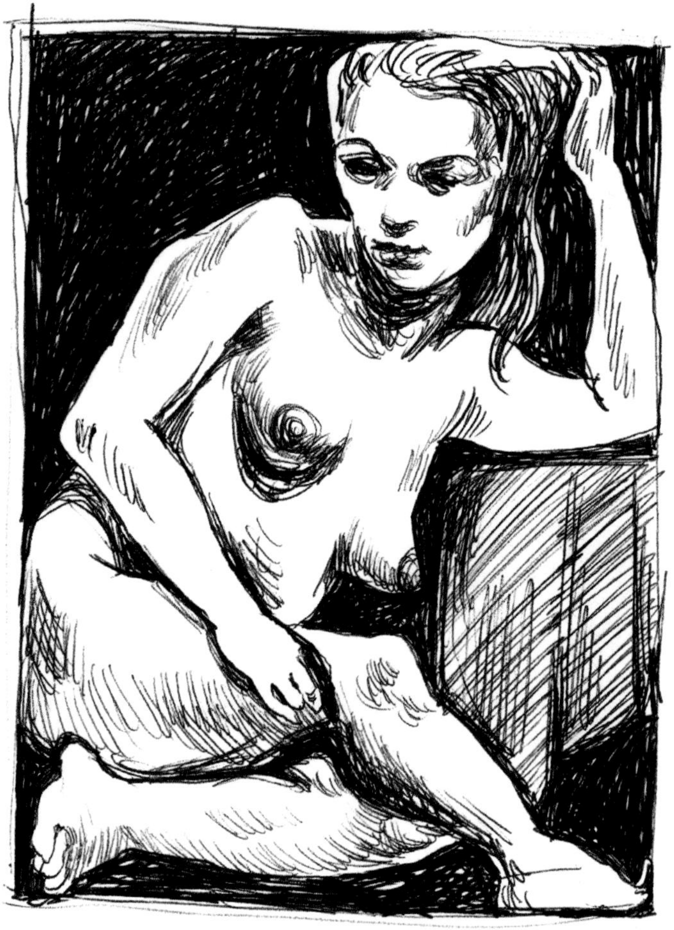

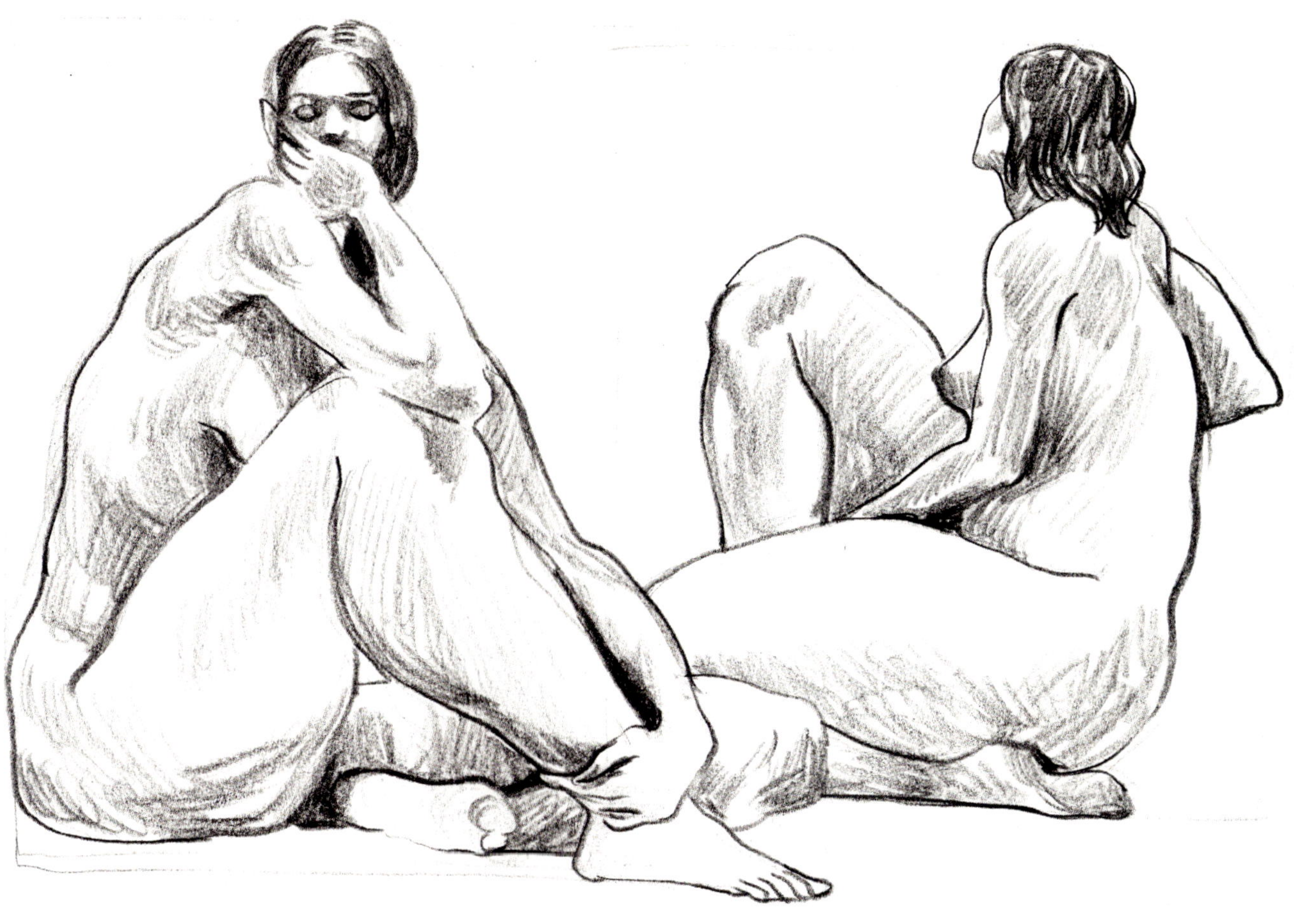

A window on the world

Art is nature seen through a temperament.
—Maurice Denis

Drawing on a pattern means confronting space, depth. You may feel the need to reframe by placing a paper window, a reduced size of our support, in front of your eyes. This practice, widespread among landscape painters, is useful in channeling the gaze and refocusing the composition. Translating the depth, in front of us and out of the field, is a delicate task. The atmospheric perspective (which consists of creating the illusion of depth through a gradient of colors and the progressive attenuation of contours), the depth of field, and its photographic blur effects complete the use of the linear perspective described in week 13.

YOUR TURN

Free format and technique. If you work outdoors, think about your comfort: a place to sit down can quickly become necessary!

Choose drawing outdoors rather than from a photo, in order to learn how to manage the depth between the different shots. Quickly take into account the framing, composition, and what you want to highlight. Stay true to the strongest impression. You will have to fight against the desire to say everything, to show everything.

IF YOU HAVE THE TIME

• Draw the same pattern at different times of the day; observe the changes in light.

Go and see

Rembrandt (1606–1669), the engravings
Jean-Baptiste Sécheret (born in 1957)
Sue Bryan (contemporary), *Landscapes*, 2017

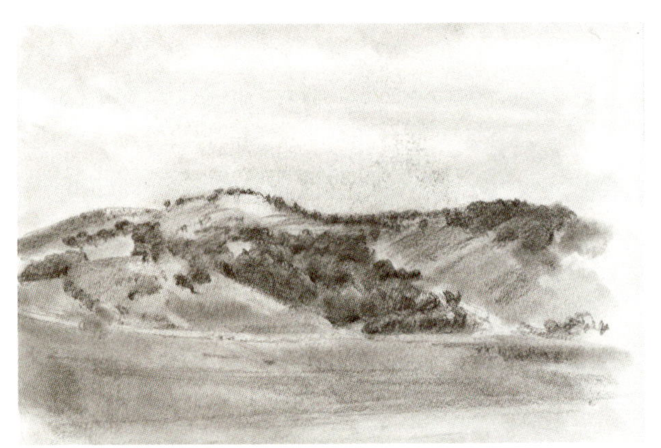

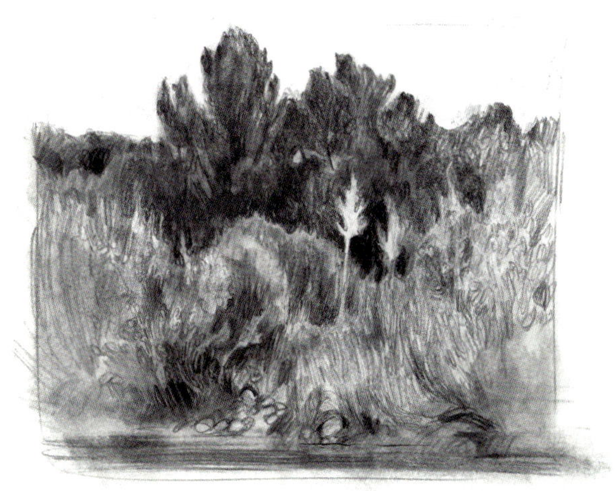

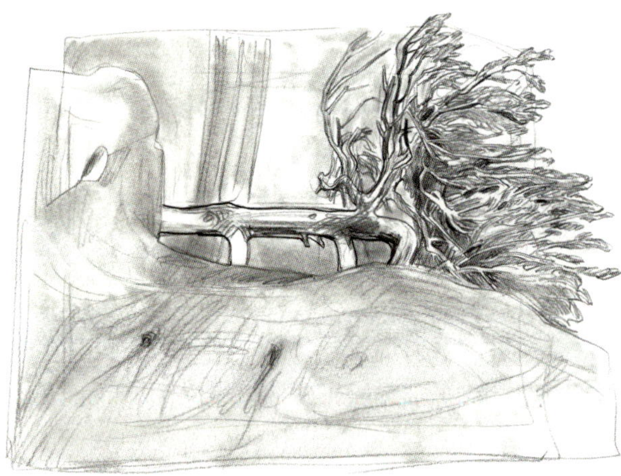

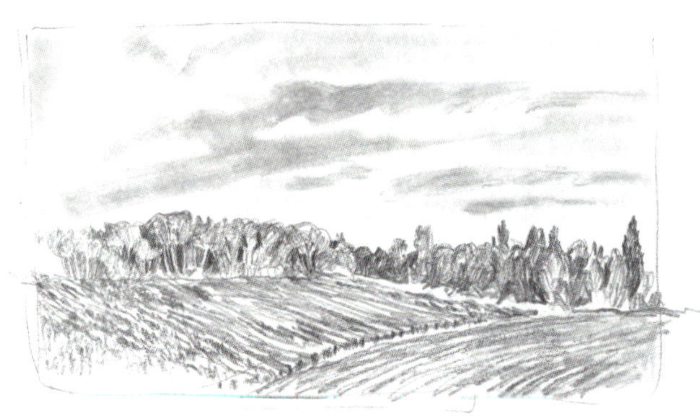

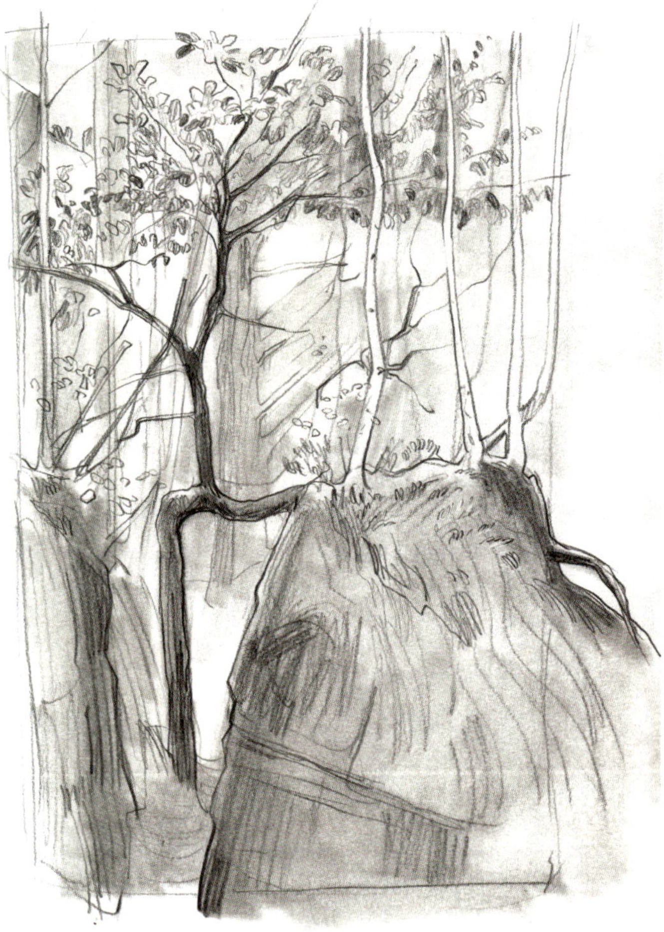

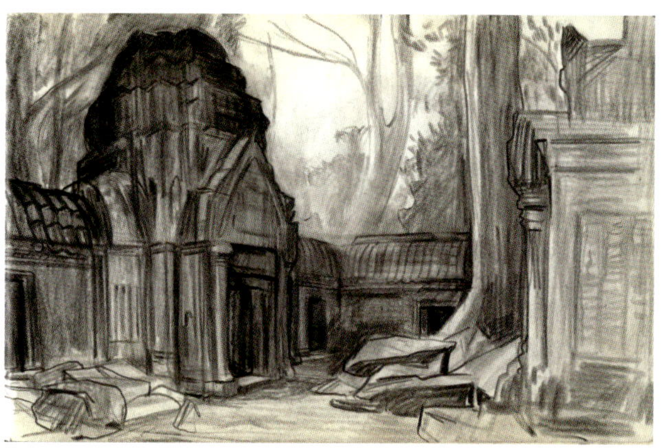

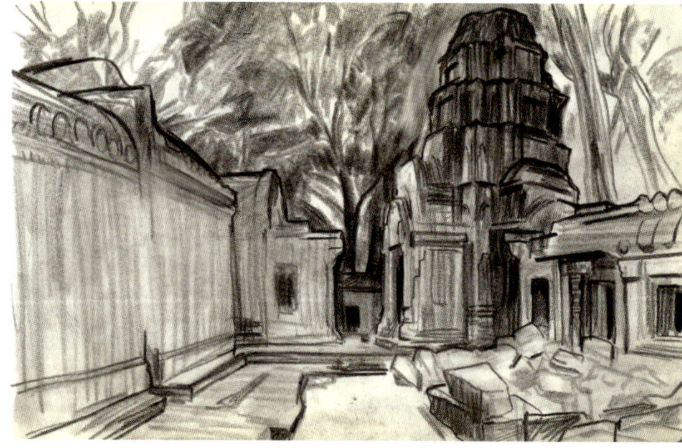

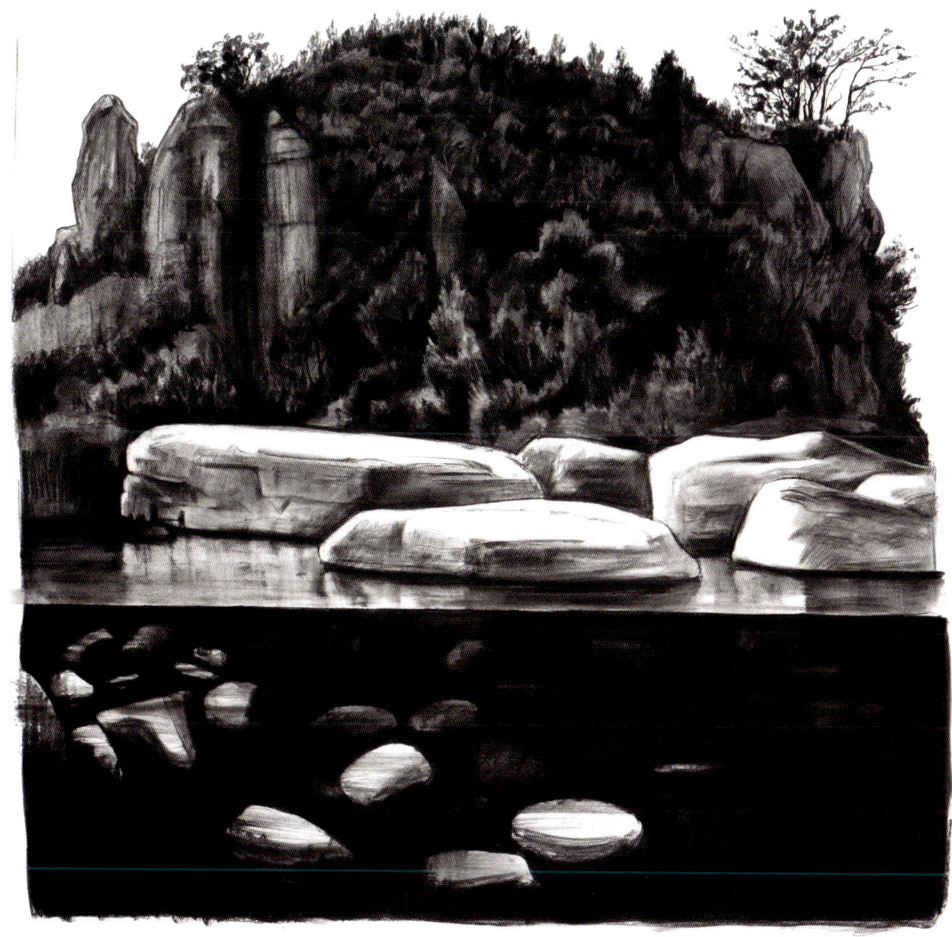

Landscaped body

The human figure is what interests me most deeply, but I have found principles of form and rhythm from the study of natural objects such as pebbles, rocks, bones, trees, plants etc.
—Henry Moore

The change of scale makes us lose ground. Microcosm and macrocosm merge and interpenetrate each other. Drawing can easily give us access to this poetic, illusionist game. Imagine that you are the size of an insect, and walk around your body, move around on your skin, walk around bushes of hair, climb a bony peak.

YOUR TURN

Use the tools and support of your choice.

You can choose a knee or an ankle as a model. Your left hand can become a world. You can also draw a relative, about 20 centimeters from his skin. A contrasting light will help you translate hollows and bumps, valleys and hills.

It is better to draw from nature than from a photo, in order to make this exercise a real experience. The slightest body fragment can then be viewed from several angles of view, subjected to multiple lighting. It will always appear different to you. The goal here is to expand the space. It will not be necessary to "cheat" by accentuating distances by depth effects (by attenuating the "distance," for example), but especially by carefully framing so that the evocation of the landscape is well conveyed.

IF YOU HAVE THE TIME

• Reverse the process! From a landscape, on a pattern, or from a photo, show a body or a fragment of a body: draw, for example, a hill like a belly or a shoulder.

Go and see

Matthäus Merian the Elder (1593–1650)
Edgar Degas (1834–1917), *Côte escarpée*, pastel
Karin Rosenthal (born in 1945)

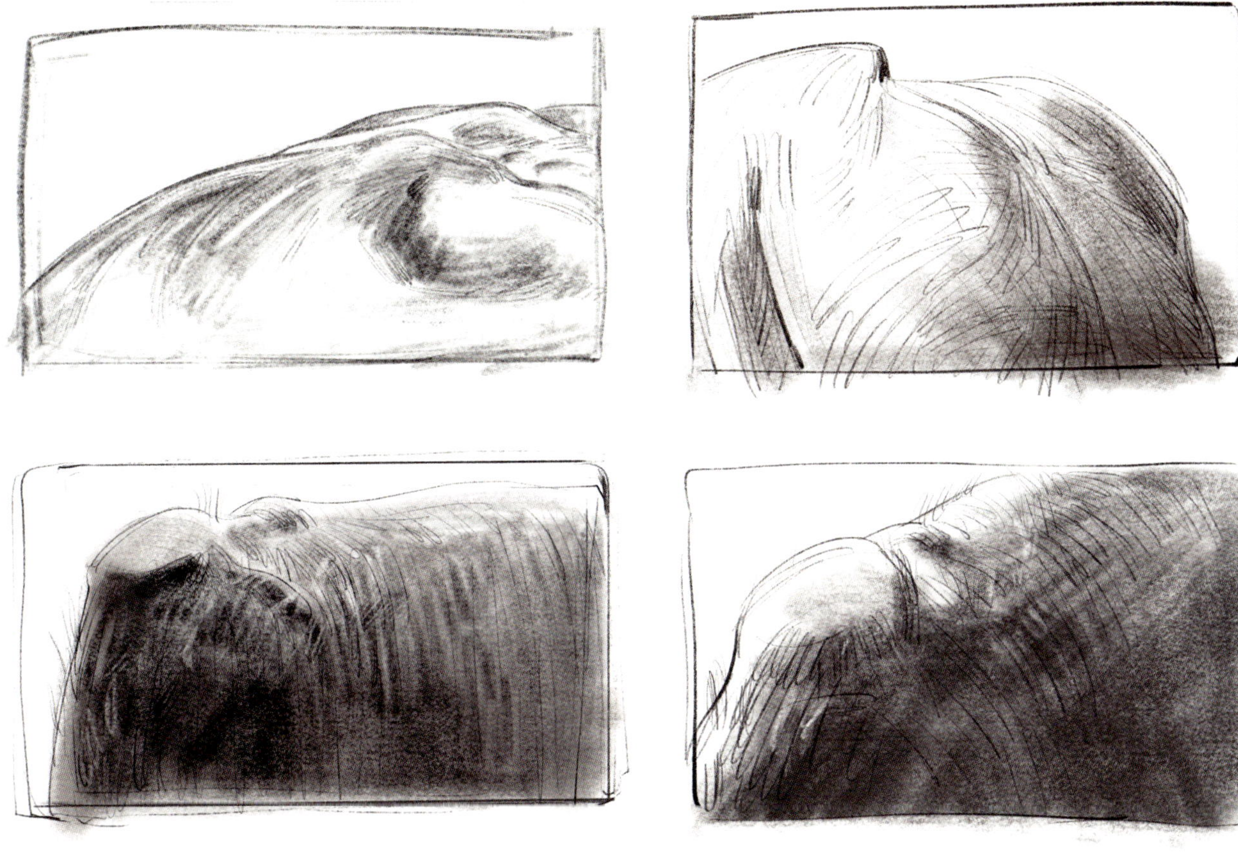

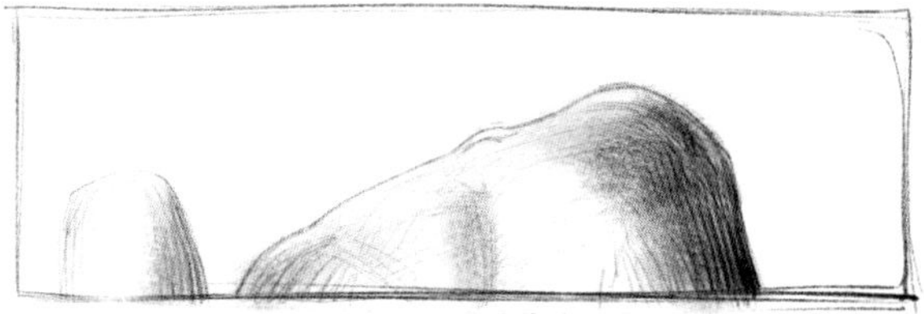

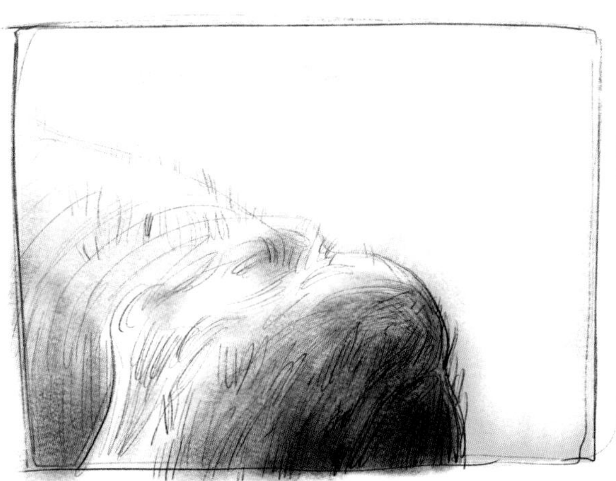

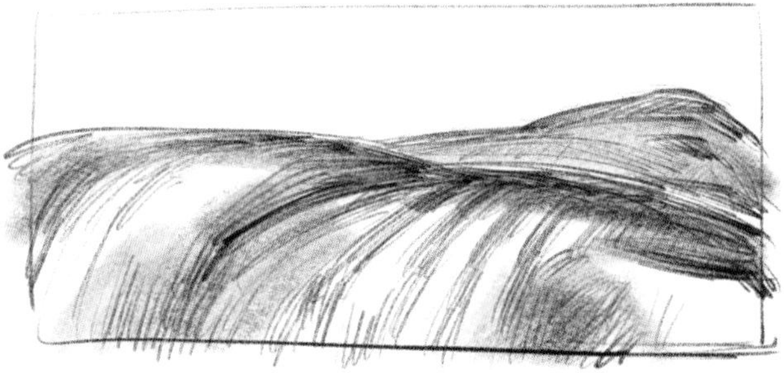

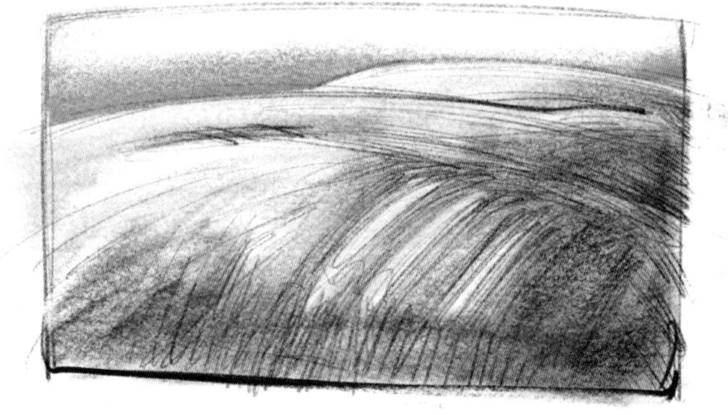

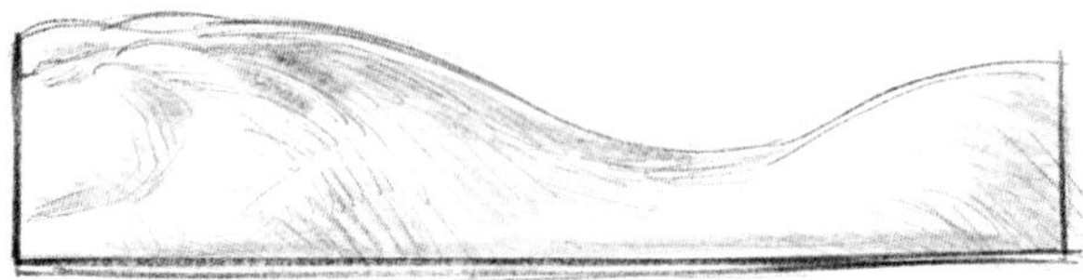

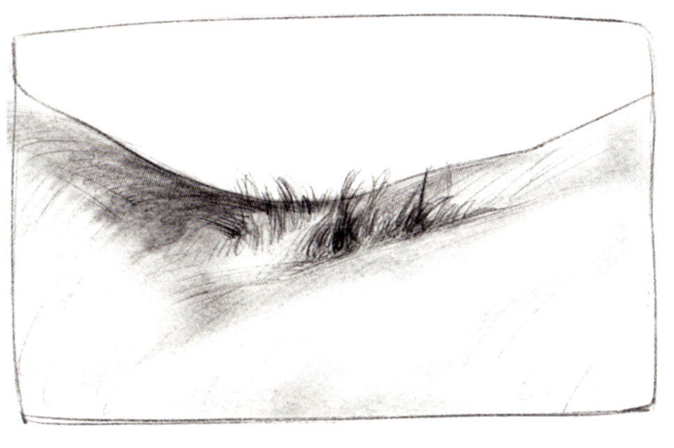

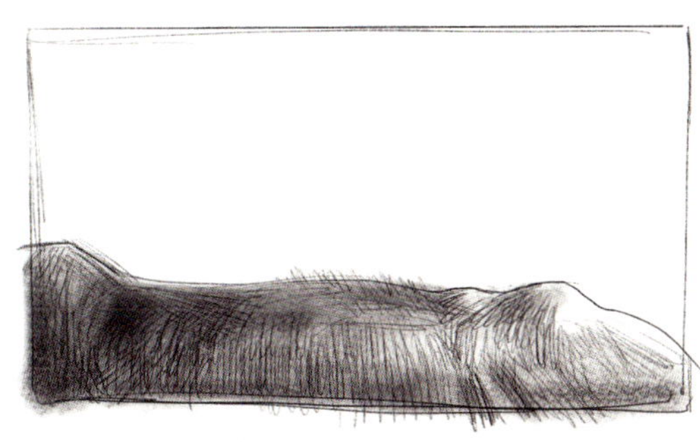

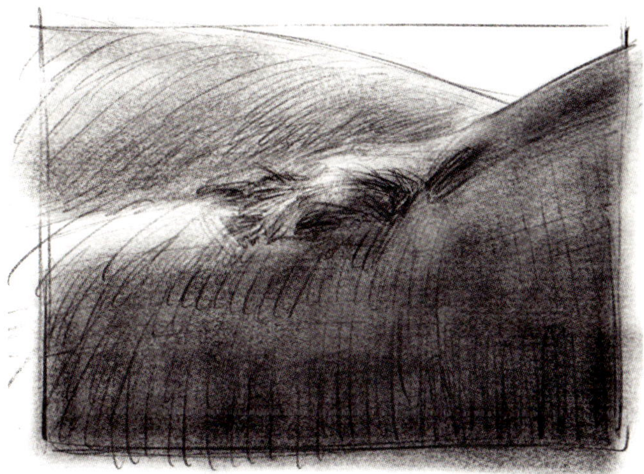

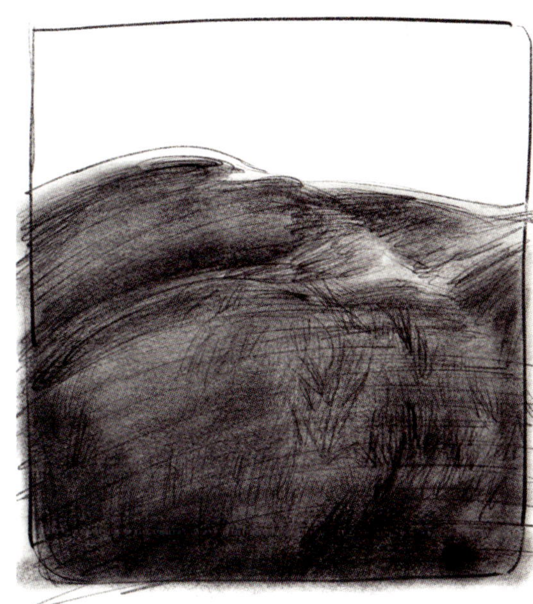

Drawing texts

I cross out words so you will see them more; the fact that they are obscured makes you want to read them.
—Jean-Michel Basquiat

Many artists have associated text with images, using collage techniques or the expressive properties of handwritten writing. Any text element (e.g., letters, typography, words, sentences, paragraphs) can also be designed, without taking into account its meaning, such as an abstract form with graphic components (proportions, intensity, contrast, etc.).

YOUR TURN

Use a sheet of paper (A4 minimum) and the tools of your choice, possibly extracts from newspapers and magazines: in this case, a pair of scissors and a tube of glue are a must.

You can make an observational drawing, or entirely imaginary. Let the words come to you (which usually never fail to assault the mind when you draw!) and make them an engine of inspiration, of creative play. Draw, write, draw in the same way, always considering writing as a drawing line.

To thwart our tendency to decipher texts, look at your image upside down or in a mirror and ask yourself if it "holds up" visually.

IF YOU HAVE THE TIME

Use newspapers or magazines. Choose the techniques according to the paper qualities. Paint a coat of white gouache or gesso on these supports and draw over them, playing with the printed patterns, meaning, and shapes of the visible words.

Go and see

Cy Twombly (1928–2011)
Massimo Nota (born in 1959)
Tracey Emin (born in 1963)

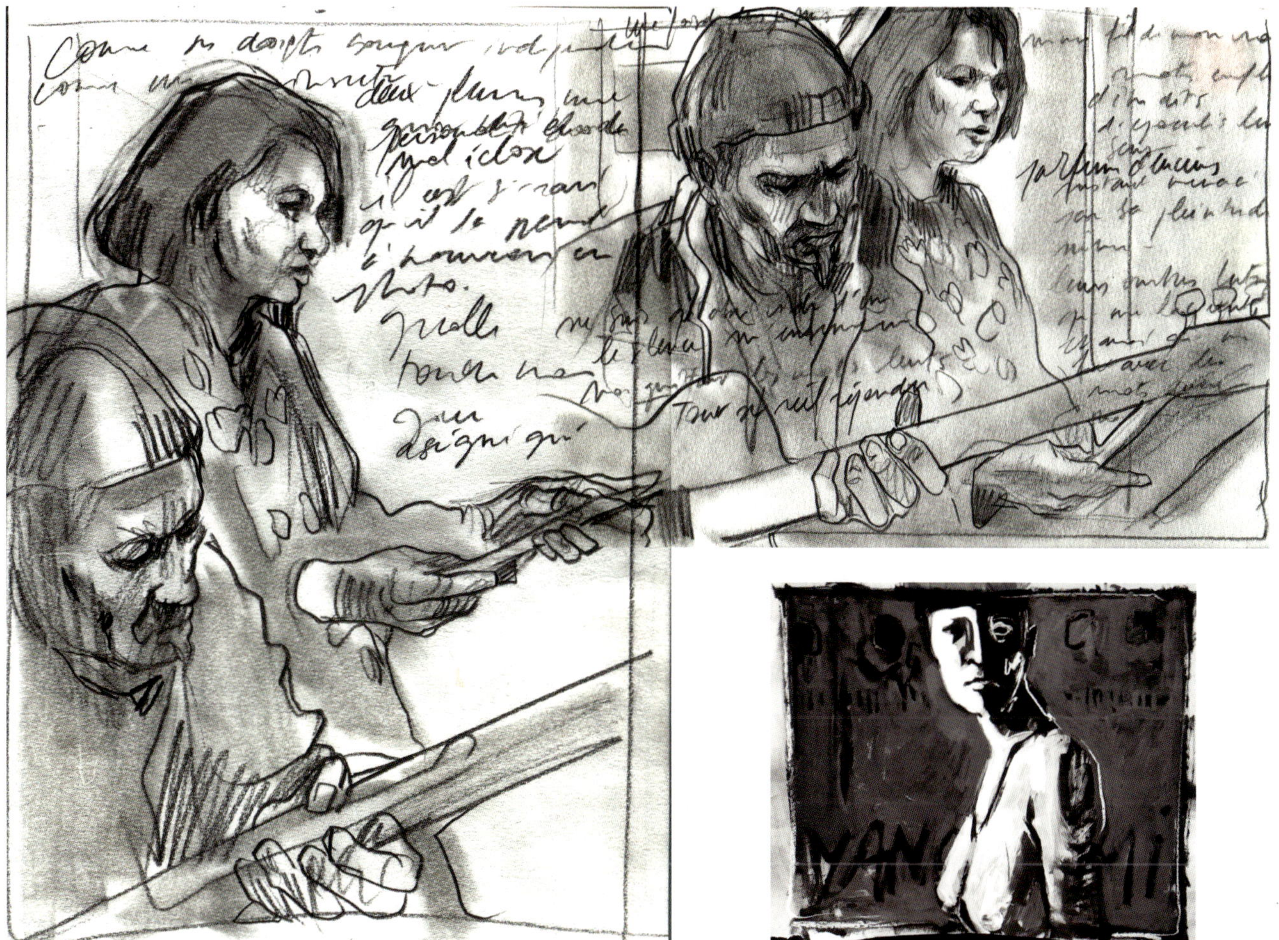

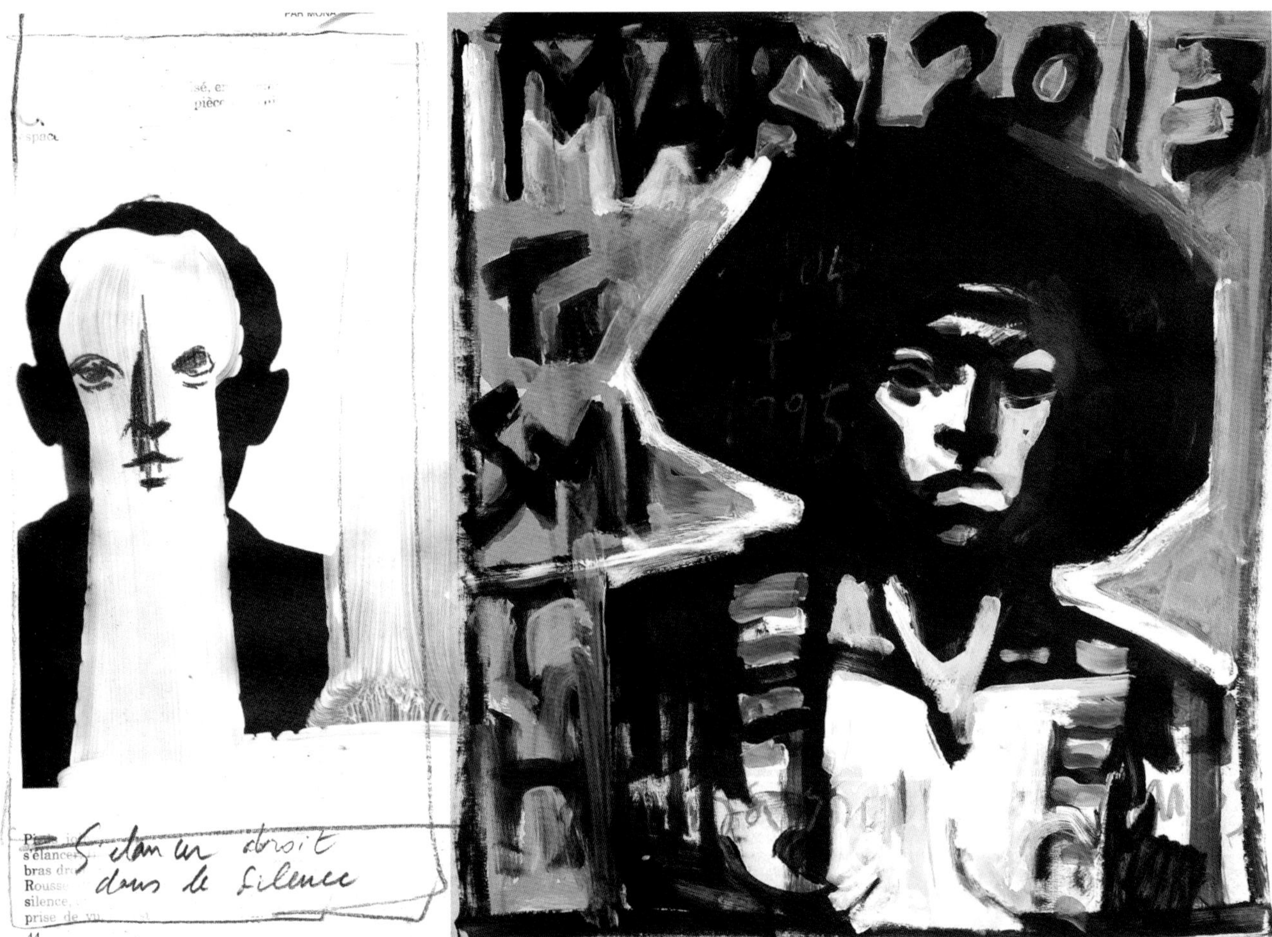
S'élancer droit
dans le silence

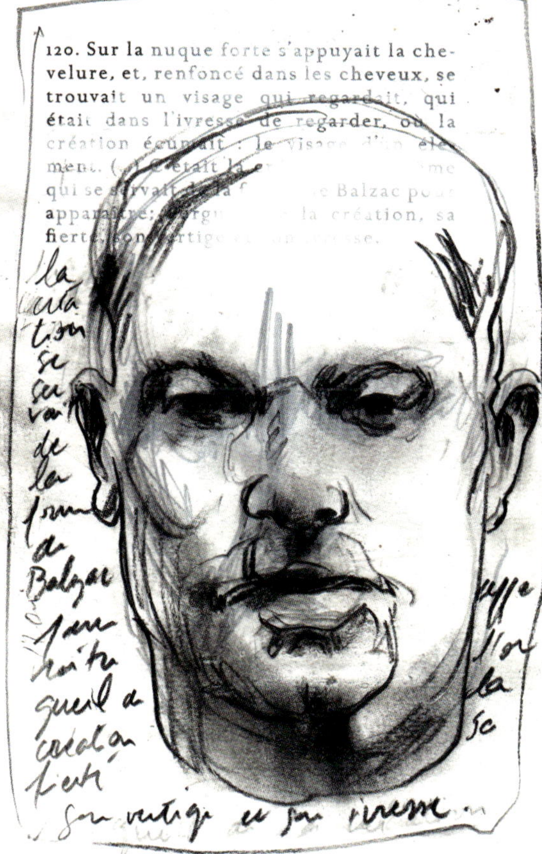
120. Sur la nuque forte s'appuyait la che-
velure, et, renfoncé dans les cheveux, se
trouvait un visage qui regardait, qui
était dans l'ivresse de regarder, où la
son vertige et son ivresse

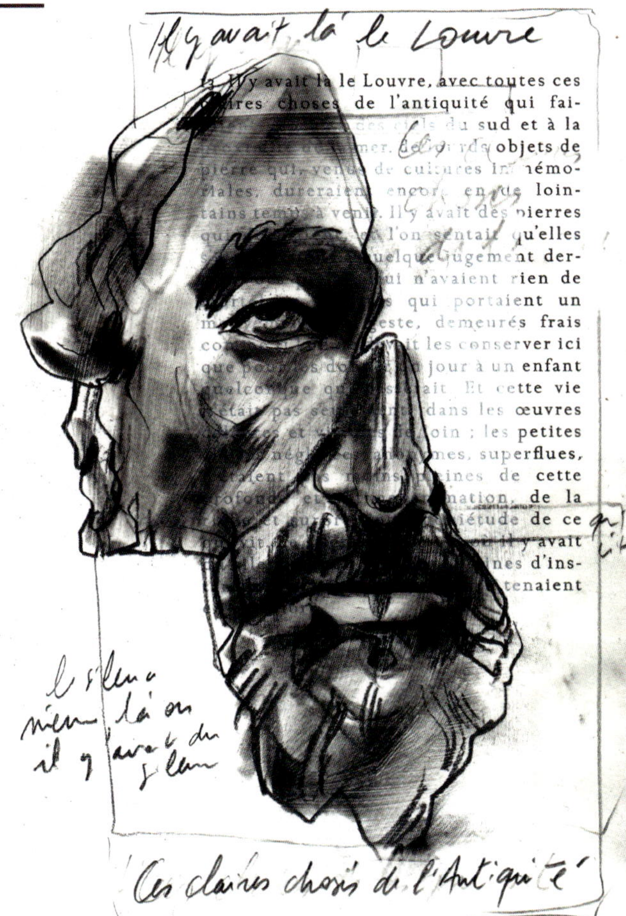
Il y avait là le Louvre
Il y avait là le Louvre, avec toutes ces
Ces claires choses de l'Antiquité

Collages

If you know exactly what you're going to do, what's the point of doing it?
—Pablo Picasso, conversations with Christian Zervos in *Cahiers d'art*

Why don't you trade in your pencils for a pair of scissors? The collage exercise is a good way to create new and surprising images. You will work by assembly and invent another reality.

YOUR TURN

Collect magazines, leaflets, packaging papers, etc. Choose by intuition, without a prior project, the photos that attract you, then cut them out. (Observe how the cuttings are already a form of drawing: one becomes aware of the form by distorting it.)

Bring together a wide variety of topics—characters, animals, landscapes, plants, objects—then try to make connections between these images, without sticking them together. Test different compositions before you decide on the one that "speaks" to you. You can photograph some of the versions to keep them in memory.

An effective collage is of the order of poetry; it speaks to emotions without anyone explicitly understanding what it's saying. . . . It's about finding a balance and accepting a little strangeness. Remember that the simplest is often the strongest: sometimes it is enough to combine two or three elements to compose a striking image.

IF YOU HAVE THE TIME

• Redraw on your collages.
• If you are equipped, reproduce the experience with digital tools (photo-editing software): mimic objects, characters, and animals to create an image bank. Assemble the elements; vary formats, colors, and contrasts until the composite image speaks to you.

Go and see

Hannah Höch (1889–1978)
Julien Pacaud (born in 1972)
Victoria Siemer (contemporary)

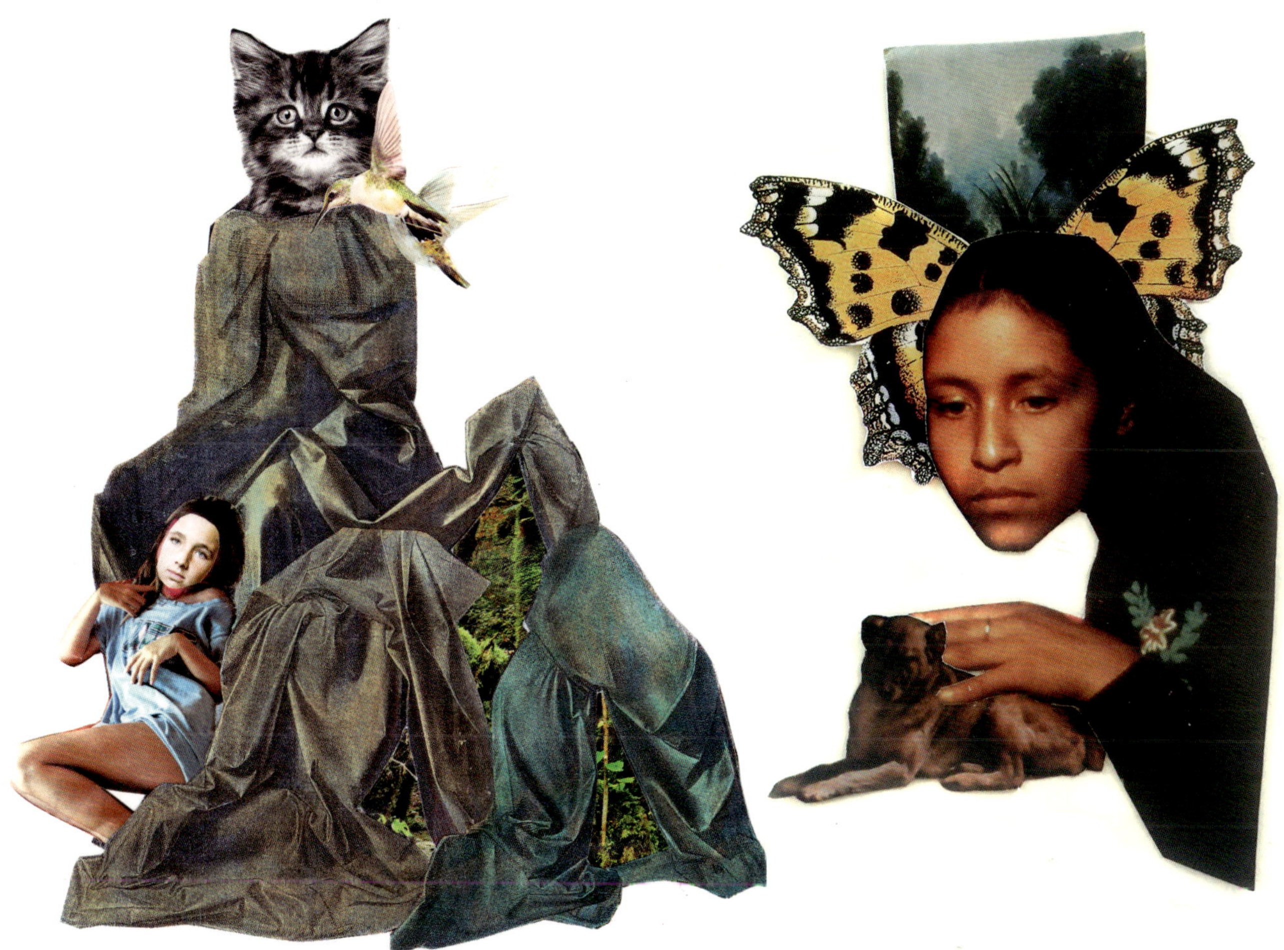

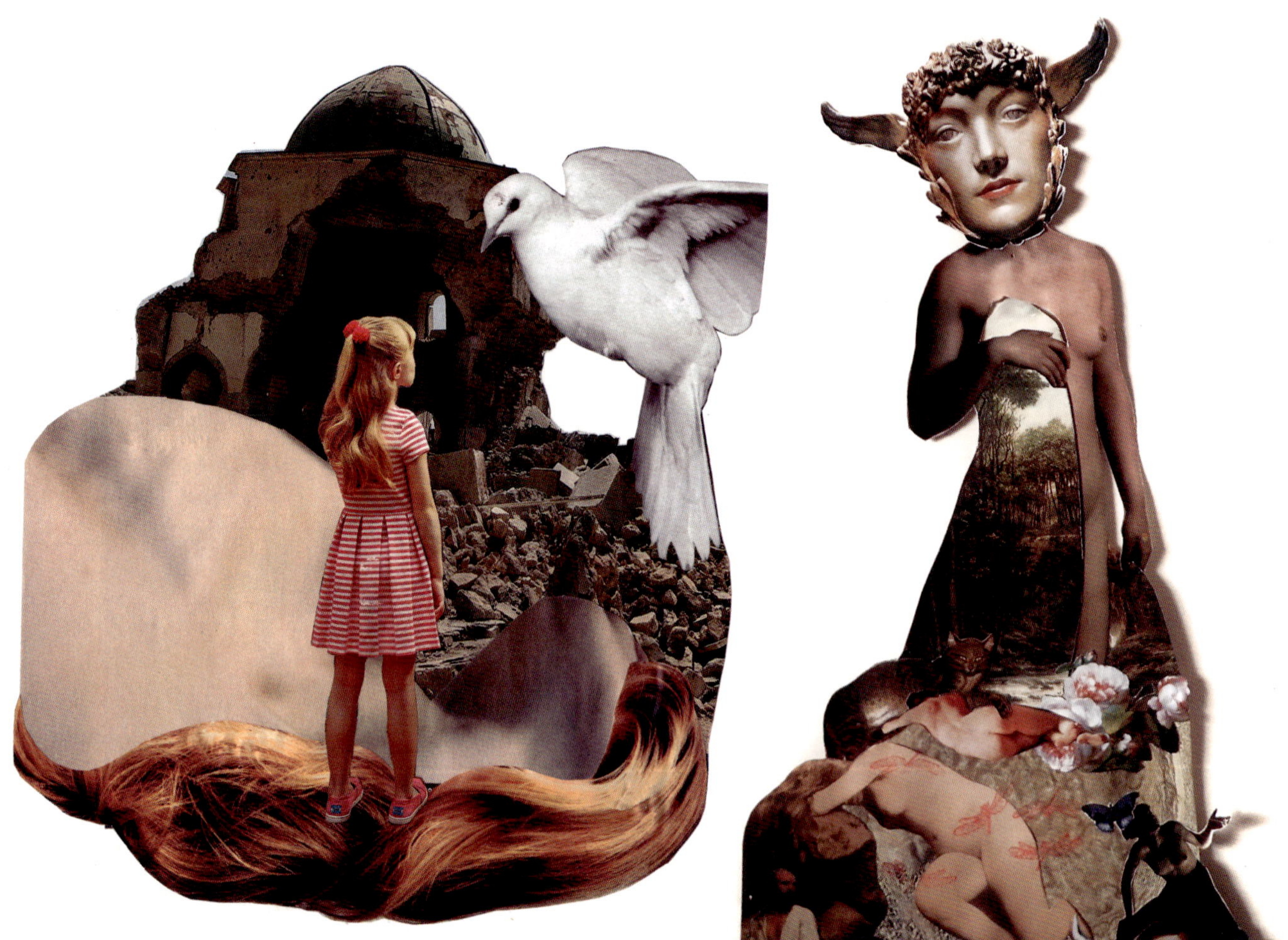

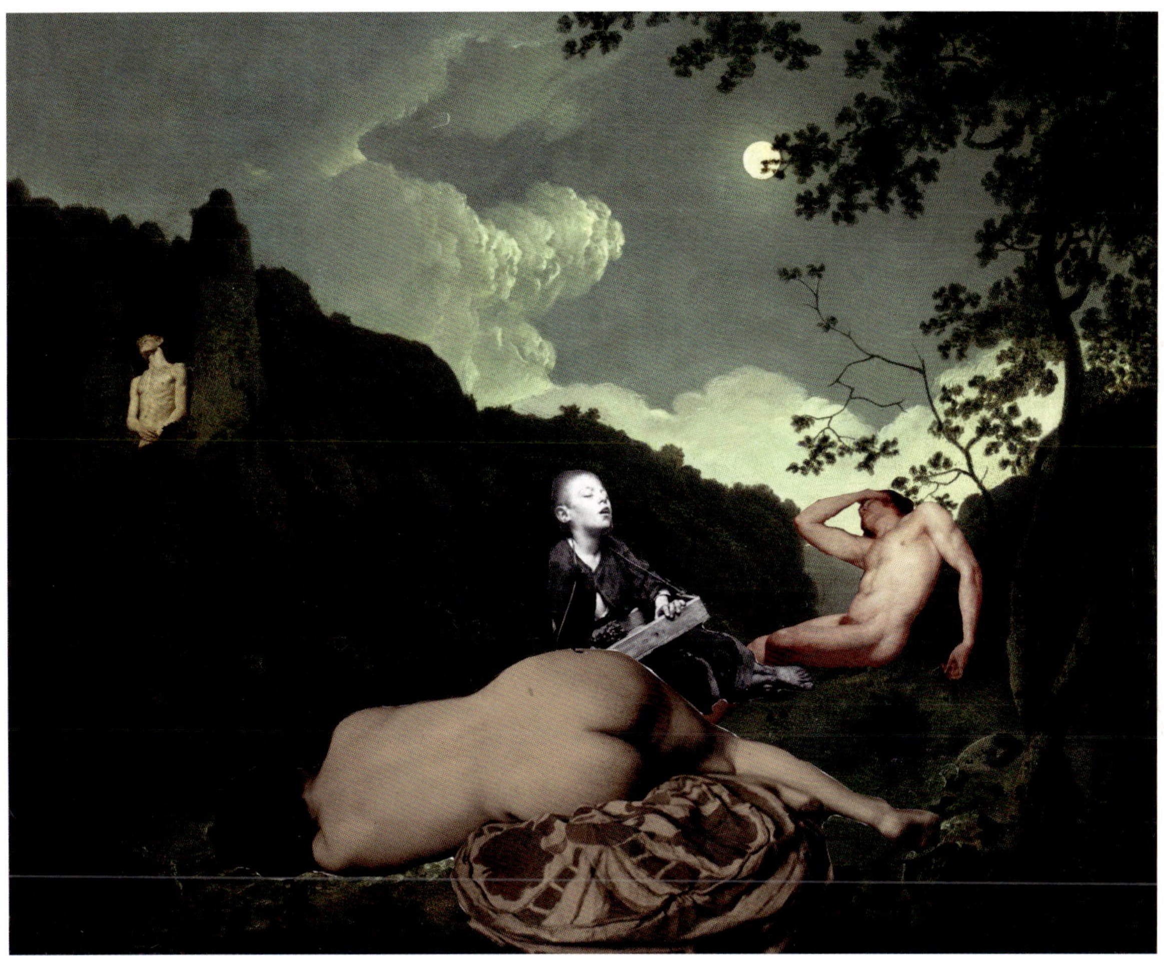

Three primaries

I found I could say things with color and shapes that I couldn't say any other way—things I had no words for.
—Georgia O'Keeffe

Limiting the number of shades used is always a good idea to create a coherent palette image. With the three primary colors, you will avoid too much neutrality and discover the pleasure of pure color.

YOUR TURN

With a felt pen, crayon, or pastel, explore the extent of a colorful range composed only of red, blue, and yellow.

Make a free and colorful interpretation of last week's collage(s): recompose the image, add or remove elements, modify the contrasts . . . it's up to you to redesign the whole so that the image tells what you project in it as well as possible.

Proceed by superimposing colored layers. In the following example, the three primary colors (red, yellow, blue) were duplicated in order to obtain a fairly wide range. If theory wants us to be able to make all the colors of the chromatic circle with red, yellow, and blue, practice proves that it is preferable to use coprimaries for this purpose, such as vermilion red and magenta, lemon yellow and orange, or cyan blue and ultramarine.

IF YOU HAVE THE TIME

• Appropriate this chromatic range and take liberties with it to deal with other subjects. The three primaries remain the basis of your color chart; you can add one or two colors, depending on your desires or needs.

Go and see

Aline Zalko (born in 1977)
Icinori (Mayumi Otero, born in 1985, and Raphael Urwiller, born in 1984)
Brecht Evens (born in 1986)

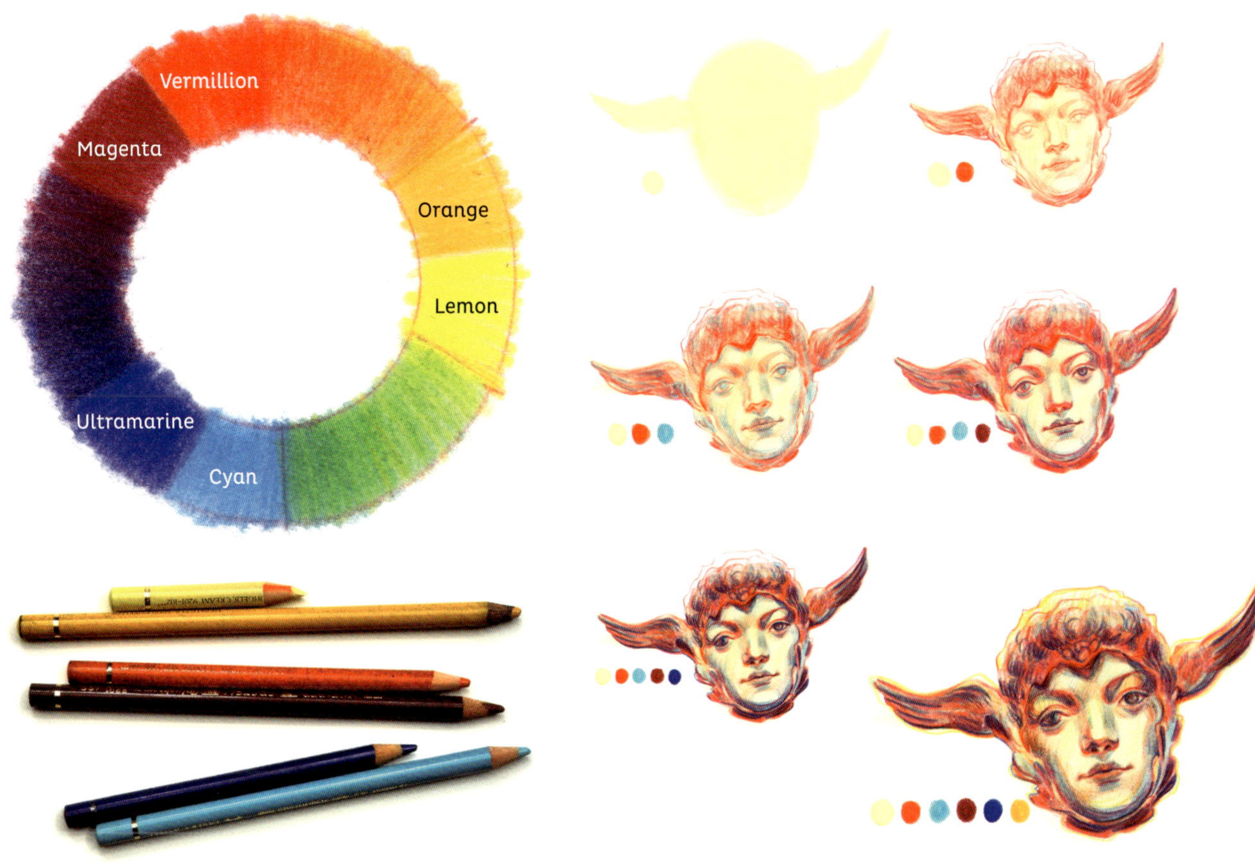
Vermillion
Magenta
Orange
Lemon
Ultramarine
Cyan

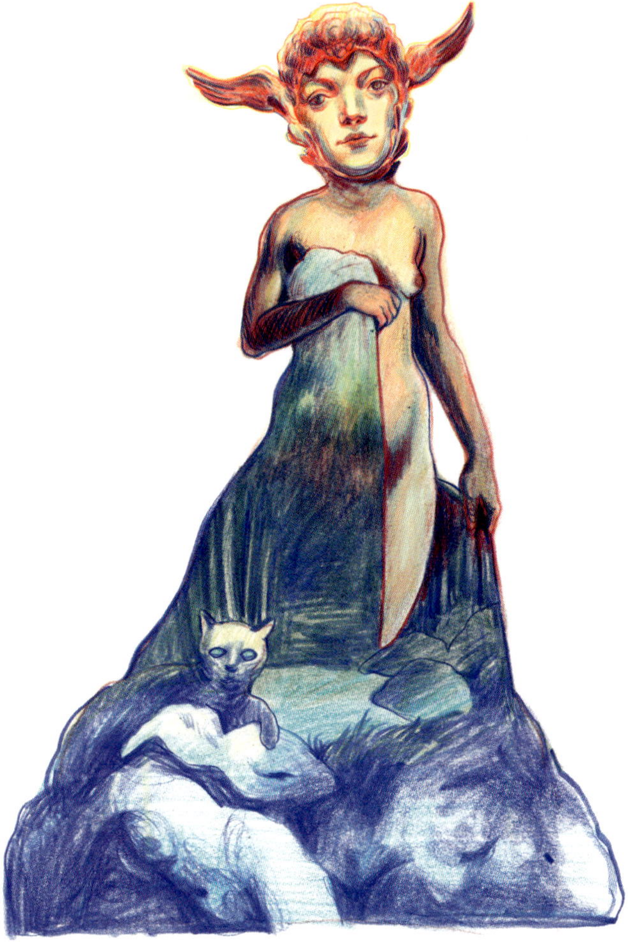

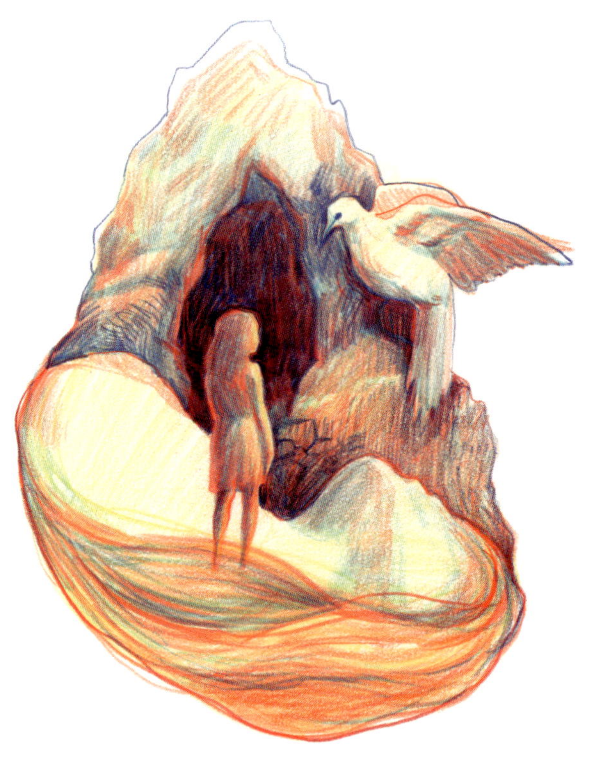

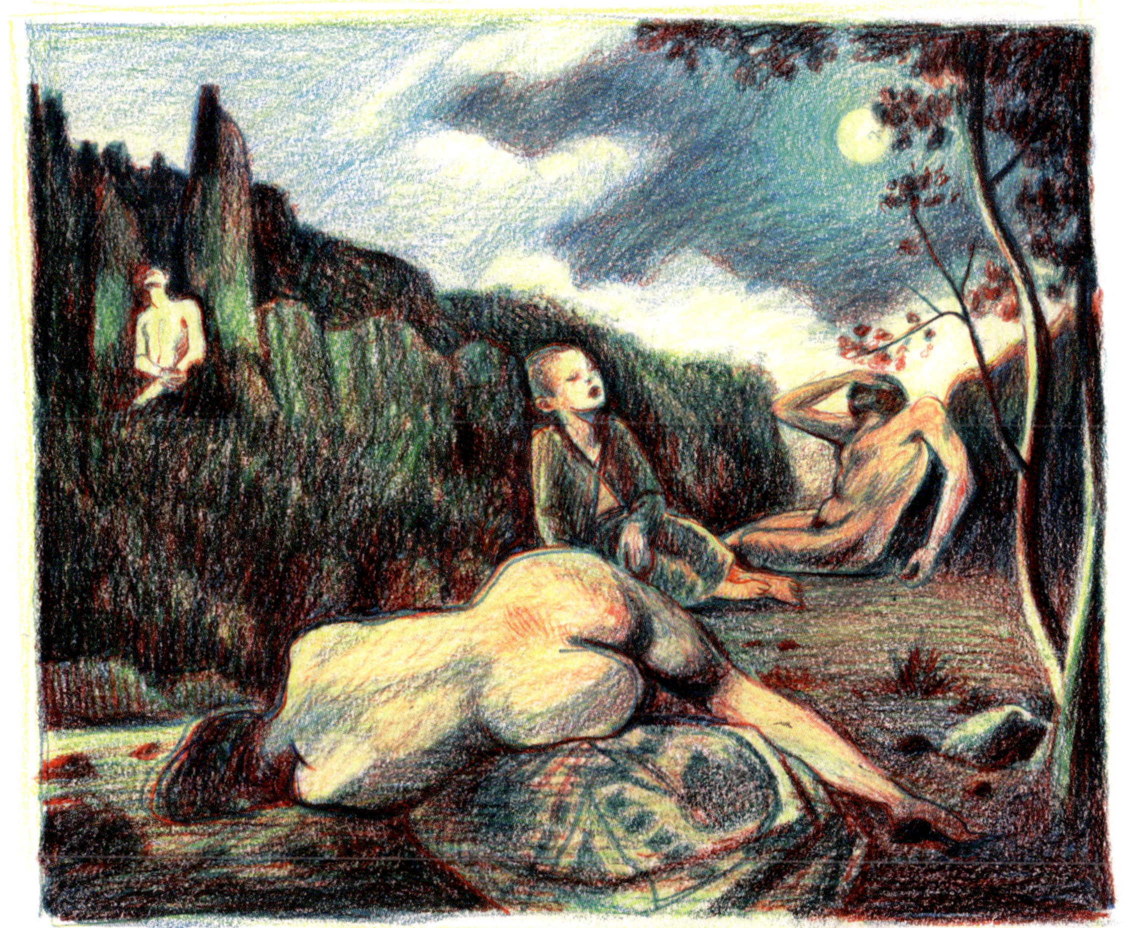

Drawings in three values

It is necessary to draw the shapes of the shadow with a light hand.
—Pierre Bonnard

Spontaneously, lines, contours, tempt us. Yet, we know that reality is quite different. Black-and-white photography restores this to us in solid, nuanced, and more or less contrasted values. This exercise brings us closer to this result. In order to facilitate the approach, we suggest that you reduce the range of values to three shades: white (the one of your support, which you can treat "in reserve" or erase), medium gray, and black.

YOUR TURN

Use a minimum A3 format and a greasy graphite lead 2B to 9B (blunt-tip pencil or graphite lead), charcoal, black Conté chalk (2B), black chalk, or black dry pastel, as you wish.

Choose an object from your daily life. Make a color chart of three values (white, medium gray, and black) in three small aligned frames. Depending on your sensitivity and the possibilities of your tool, you will get a more or less contrasted range, but try in any case to distinguish clearly between the differences in values.

Start with the medium gray. Draw with the least amount of distance possible of this value. You will be tempted to add nuances, but the purpose of the exercise is to draw using only the three values of your "palette." It is up to you to select the closest of the three on your color chart.

IF YOU HAVE THE TIME

• Gradually enrich your range with new values (4 or 5), but always take the time to make a color chart beforehand.

Go and see

Ernest Pignon-Ernest (born in 1942)
Richard Laillier (born in 1961)
Peter Morrens (born in 1965)

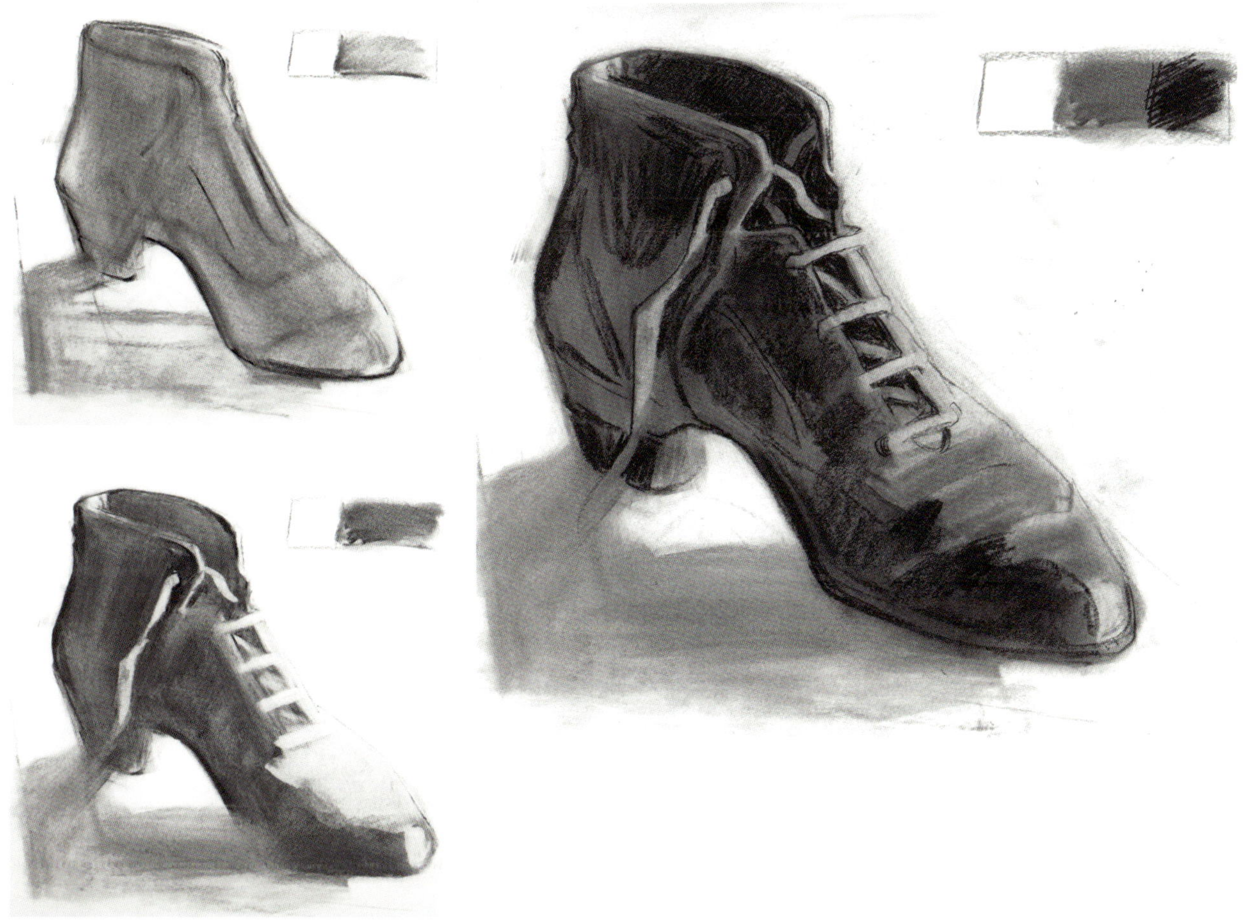

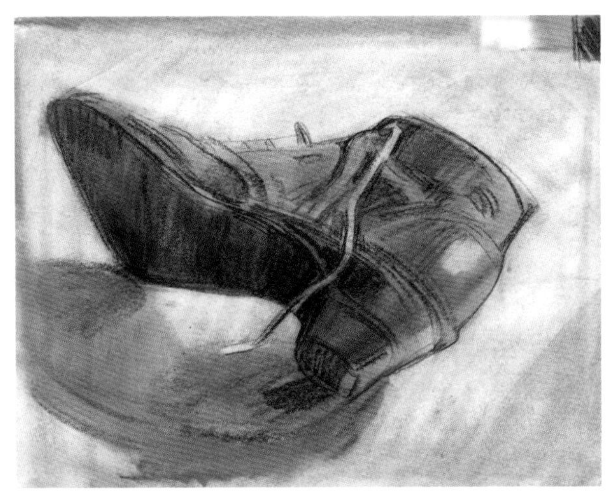

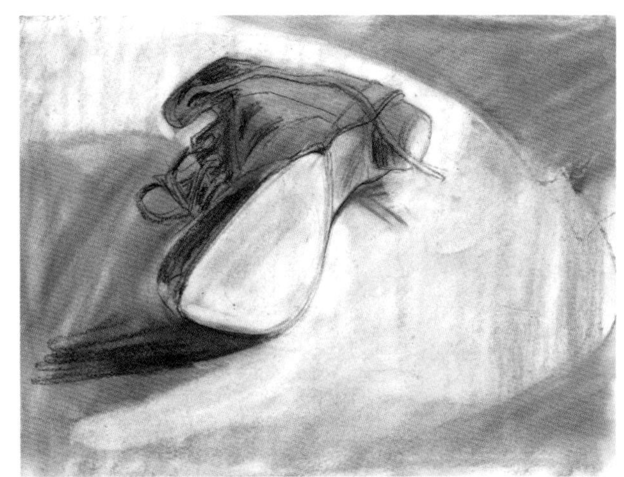

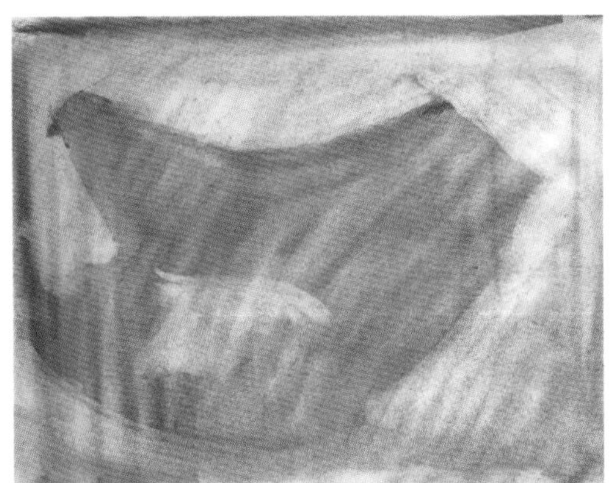

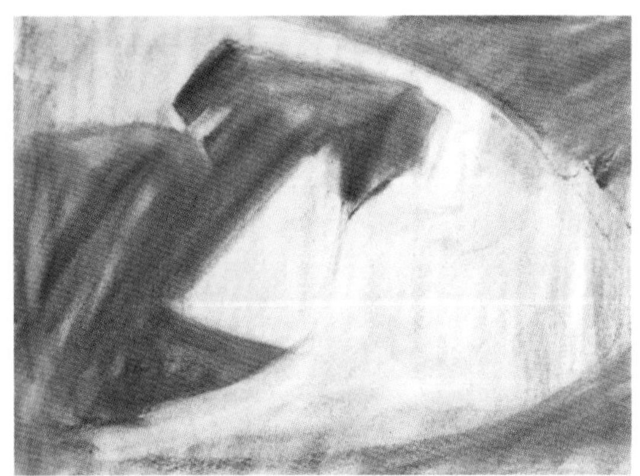

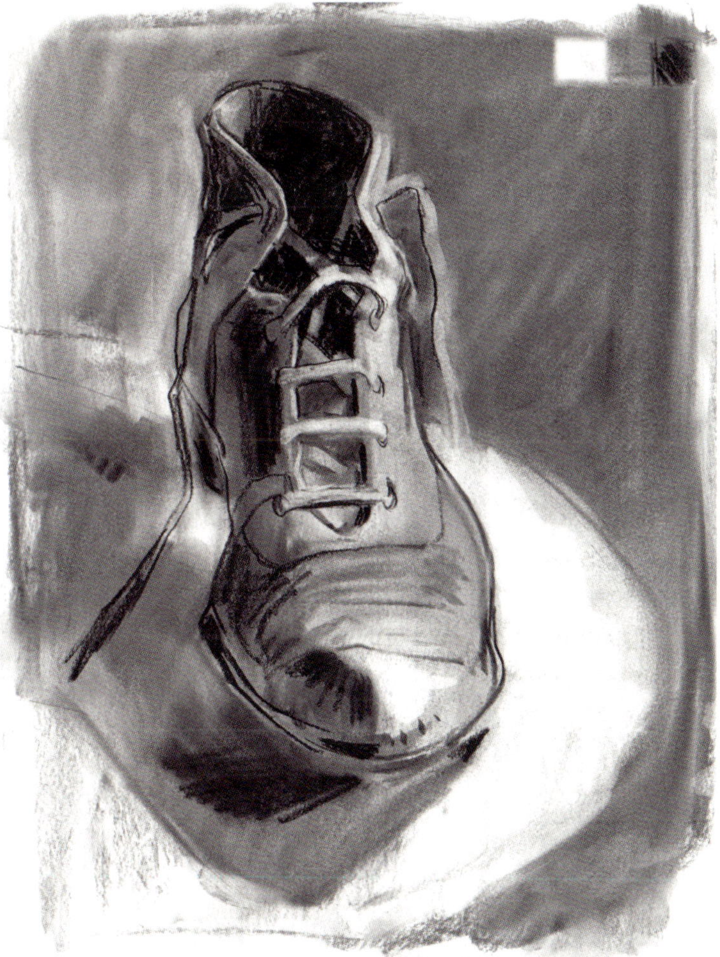

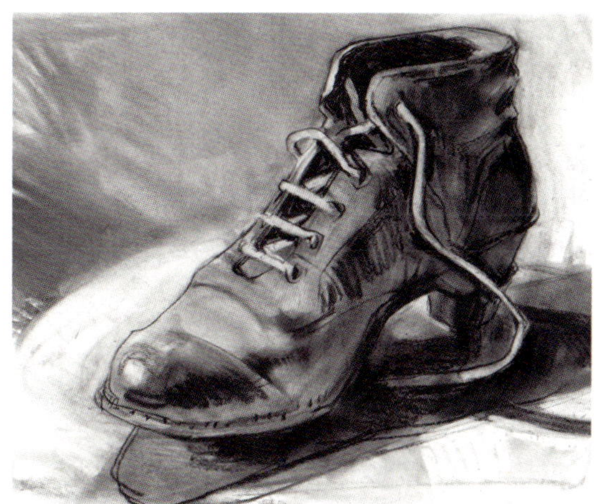

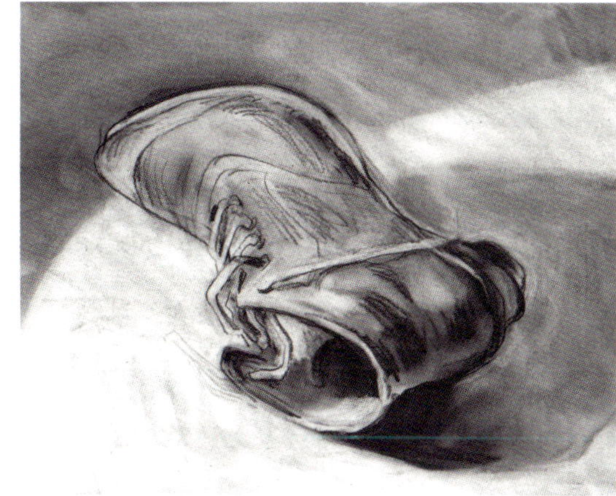

Monotypes

Inspiration forms nothing without matter.
—Alain, *Système des Beaux-Arts*

SA monotype is a single print (hence its name): a drawing made on a sheet of paper affixed to a surface coated with typographic ink (or oil paint). You draw by exerting pressure with your fingers or any tool.

The goal this time is to play more with the materials, to give them a share in the expression and an expressive charge even if—and perhaps because—you won't control everything. The uncertainties of the outcome create more or less happy but mostly evocative surprises.

YOUR TURN

Use a smooth support (metal, glass, or Plexiglas) in the format of your choice. The use of an ink roller is not necessary. Coat this plate with a thin layer of typographic ink.

Cover it with a sheet of paper that isn't too thick. Draw on this sheet by pressing. First, conduct some experiments to evaluate the effects and transformations associated with the transfer. Works by famous painters freely inspire the examples presented: Le Caravaggio, Rubens, Velasquez.

Note: Monotype usually refers to a drawing made entirely in typographic ink on a support and then transferred to paper by using a printing press.

IF YOU HAVE THE TIME

- Use your failed results: they can be excellent bases for drawings. Feel free to use them again with the technique of your choice. Degas repainted his in pastels.
- If you have carbon paper sheets, you can achieve similar effects by drawing on them with a ballpoint pen. Try it!

Go and see

Thierry Van Hasselt (born in 1969), *Brutalis comic strip*
Sophie Lécuyer (born in 1987)
Tekla McInerney (contemporary)

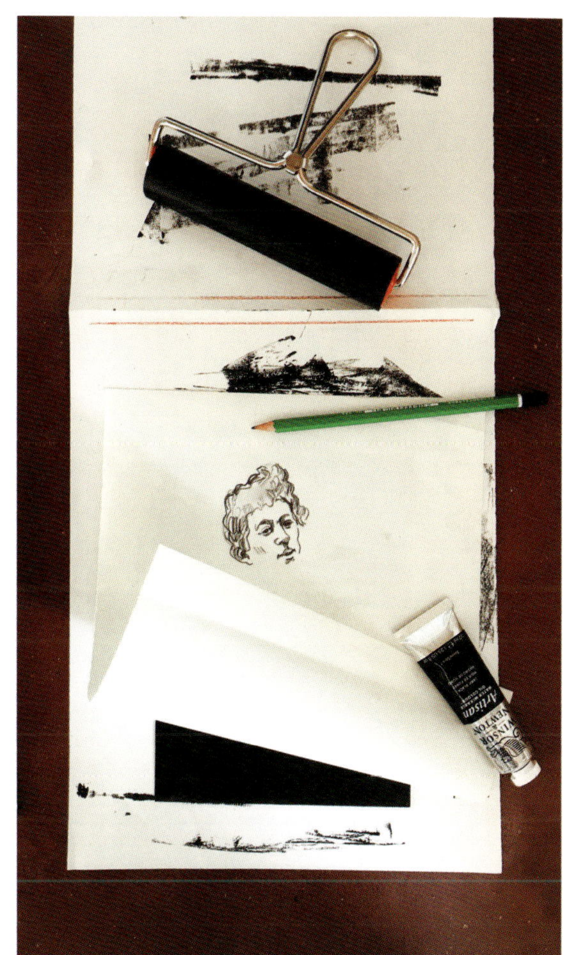
Artisan

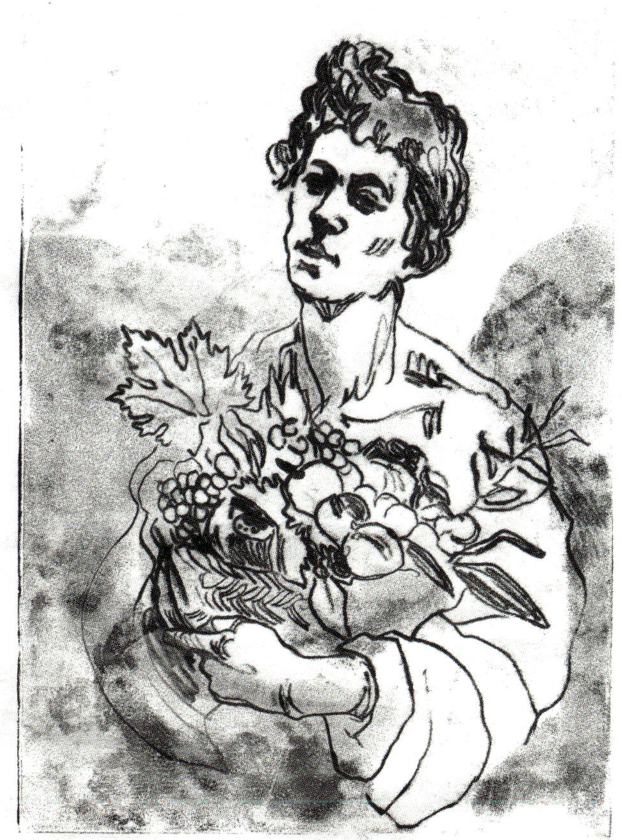

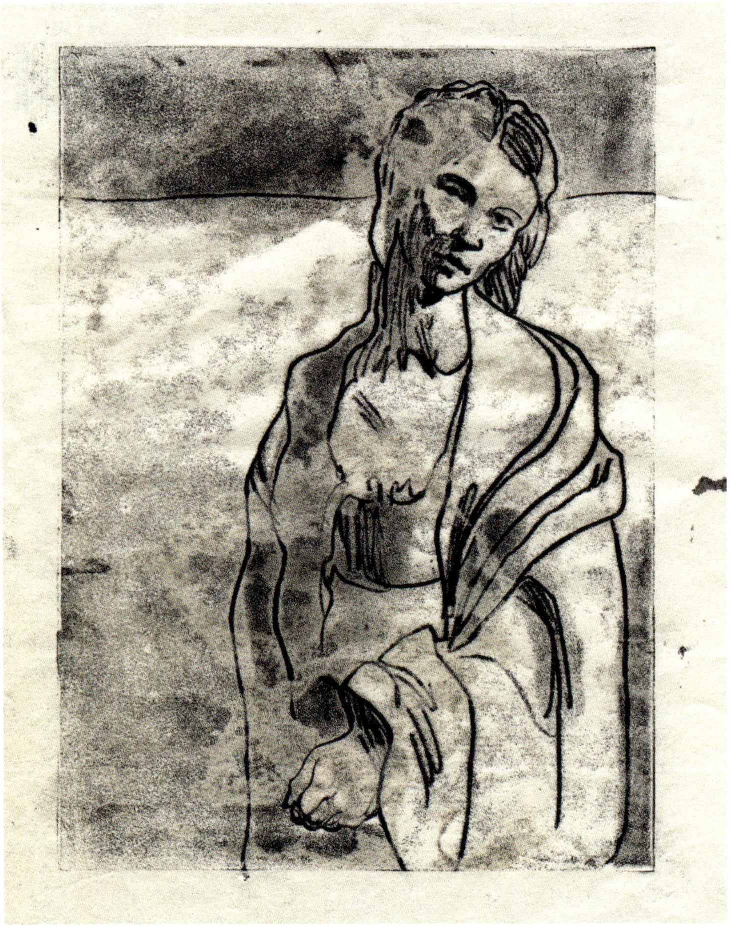

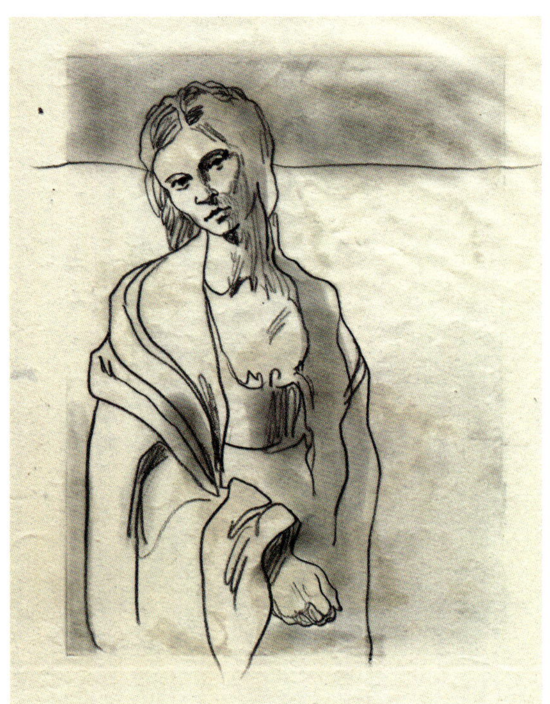

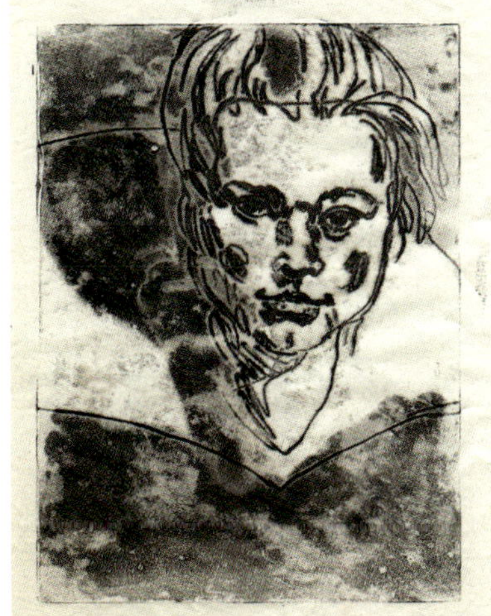

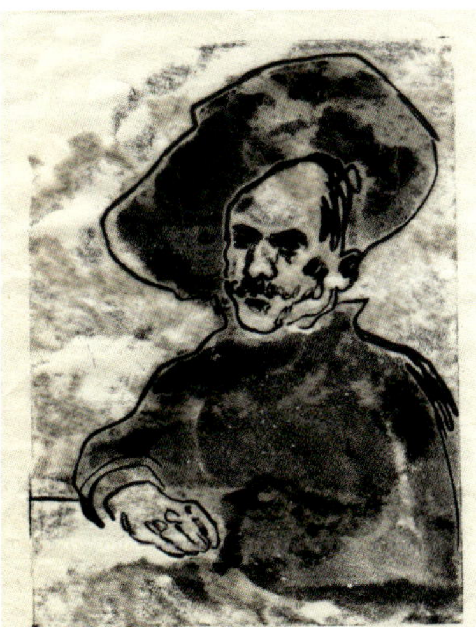

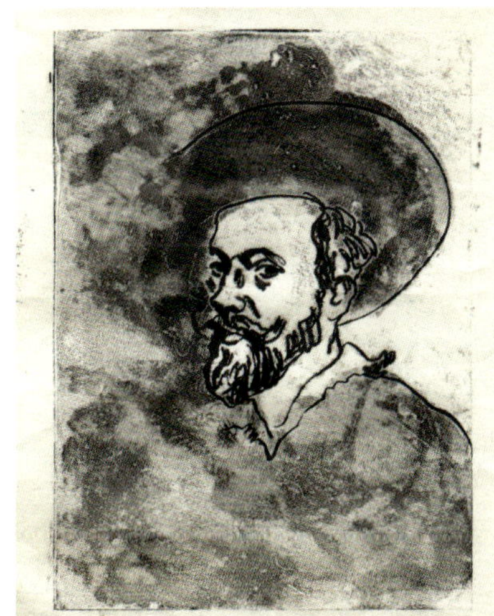

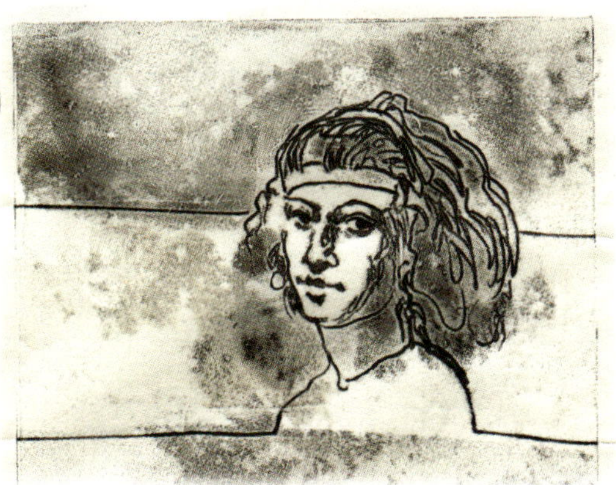

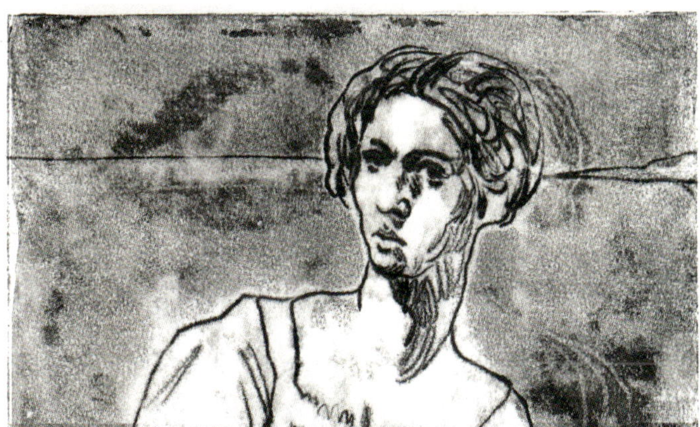

Midterm review

It's what I do that teaches me what I'm looking for.
—Pierre Soulages

If you have followed the rhythm proposed by this book, you have been drawing for six months now! You may have found the right pace according to the constraints of your daily life. Whether you spend one hour or one day a week or five minutes or several hours a day in this practice, the important thing is to maintain a certain regularity so that this new habit settles into your life and finds its place in it.

It is now a question of taking a short break and looking at your work to see how closely it represents your vision and your center of interest.

YOUR TURN

Spread out all your drawings. Go over them slowly, one by one, and answer a few questions in writing. Which are your favorite drawings? Why? Which drawings did you enjoy doing the most? Are these your favorites? Which ones were the most difficult? Are you rather proud of them or disappointed?

Do you find there are some similarities between certain images? Which ones?

Have you had any preferred techniques? Etc.

Continue this dialogue with yourself. You might find that you enjoy it and decide to repeat the experience from time to time (or even daily). There is no right or wrong answer. It's just a matter of questioning and taking a step back to understand yourself better.

Now, select some drawings to compose a series. Juxtapose the images that you think belong to the same family, or those that, even if they are different, create a story together.

What do you see? What emerges from this series?

IF YOU HAVE THE TIME

• Complete the series you have just made by doing drawings that fit into the same theme and color scheme.

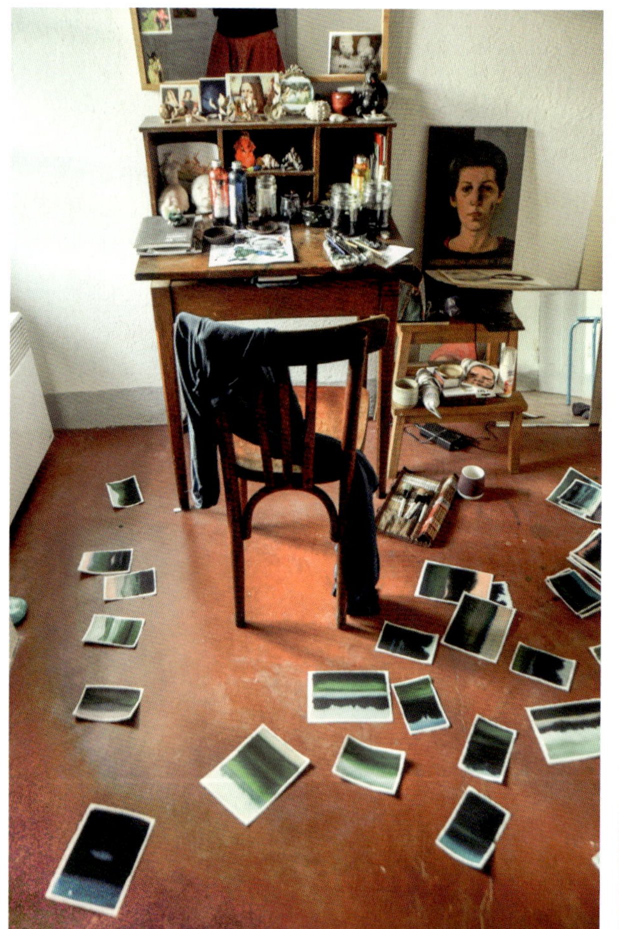
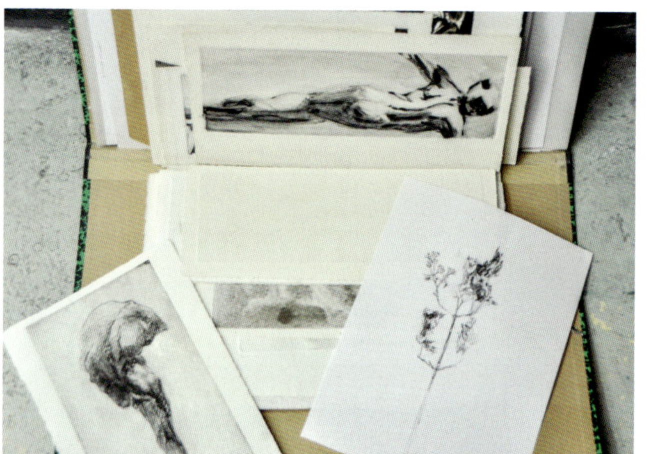
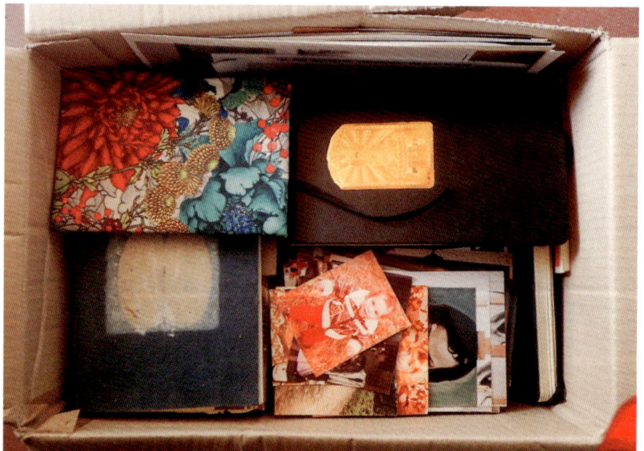

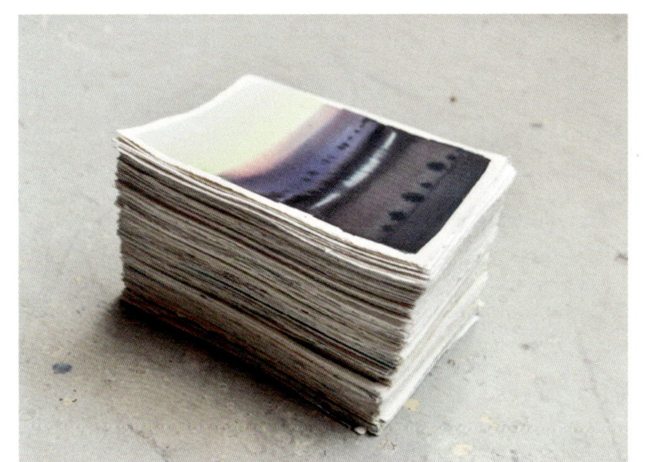

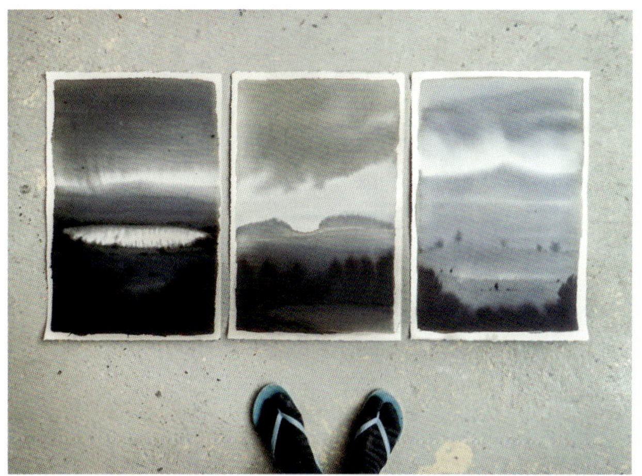

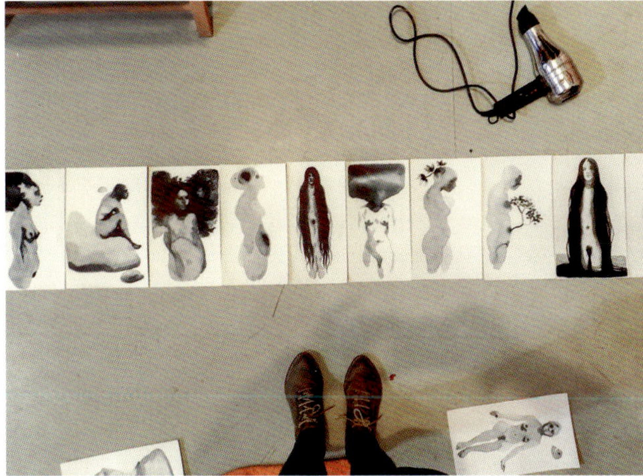

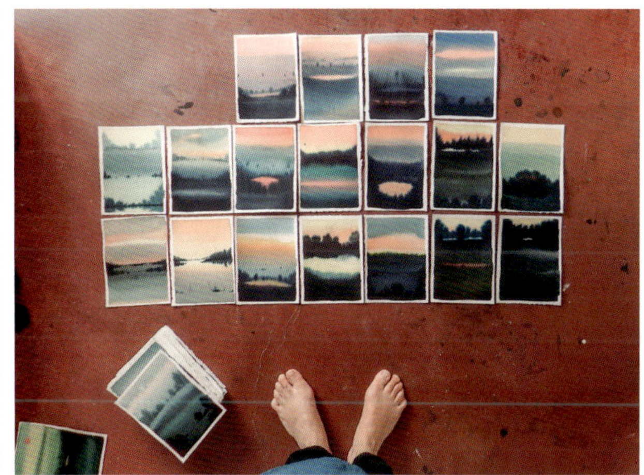

Based on

It's by copying that we invent.
—Paul Valéry

Our journey in creation is also built through contact with other people's work. It is sometimes difficult to ignore the artists we admire. Don't avoid influences that come and go: they are often there to nourish your expression. Once assimilated, they mix with your "dough" and enrich it without taking away its uniqueness.

YOUR TURN

Choose one of the artists whose work you admire, and adopt his manner of working, just for a few drawings.

Analyze what makes its expression so special. What tools did he use? Is the energy it gives off calm or nervous? Do you imagine that the artist used careful, fast, or systematic strokes to create this piece?

It is not a question of making a copy, but of working on one of your personal subjects by putting yourself in the shoes of another artist.

IF YOU HAVE THE TIME

- Imitate artists who seem to you to be the opposite of your language in drawing; this will enrich your writing.
- Do a drawing that pays tribute to or parodies a work known to everyone, such as Leonardo da Vinci's *Mona Lisa*, Velasquez's *Meninas*, or Milo's *Venus*!

Go and see

Roy Lichtenstein (1923–1997)
Coco Fronsac (born in 1962), *Chimères et Merveilles*
Rémi Wyart (born in 1983)

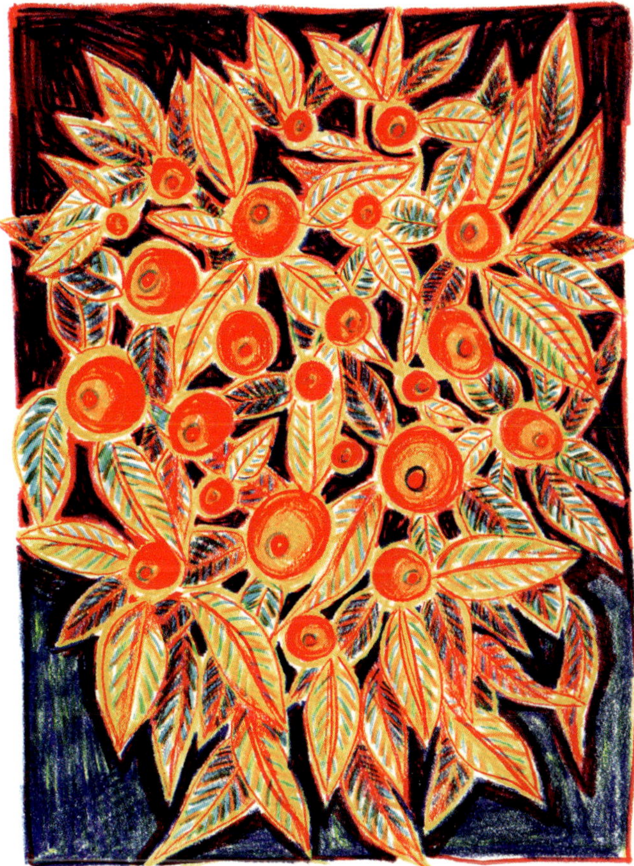

Based on the work of Séraphine de Senlis

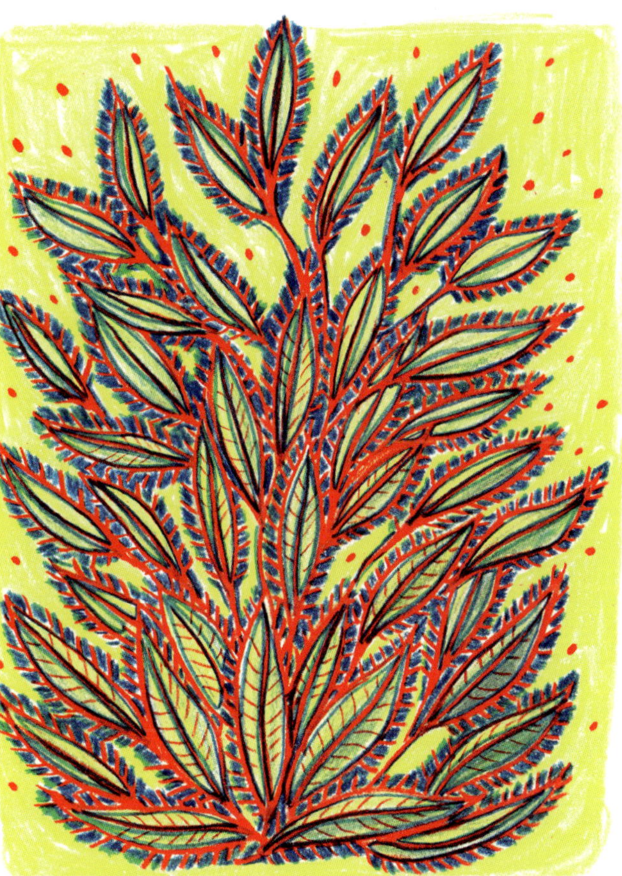

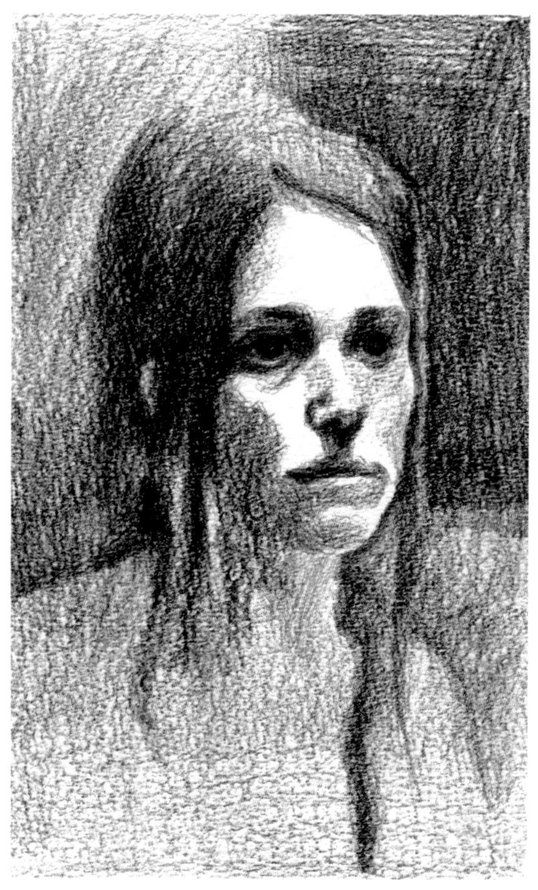

Based on the work of George Seurat

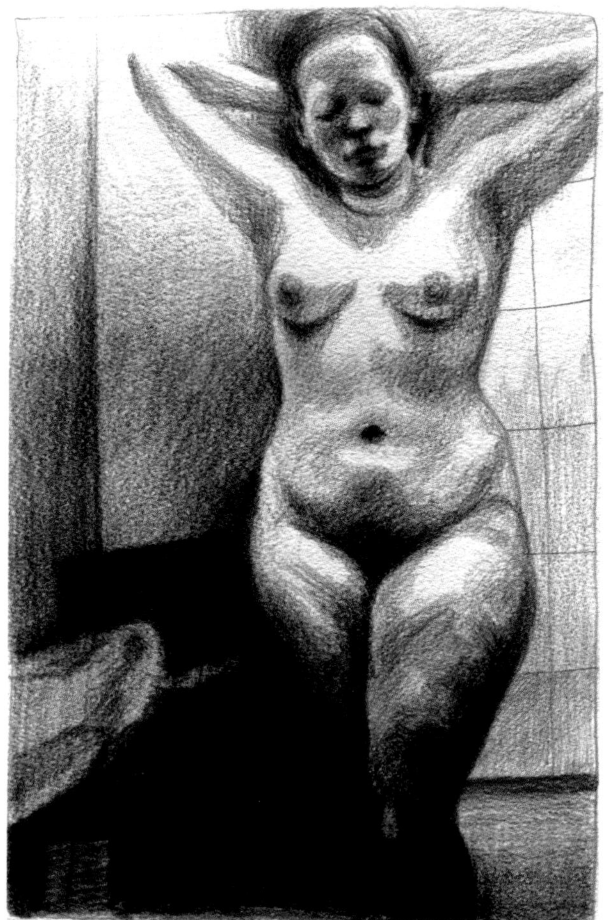

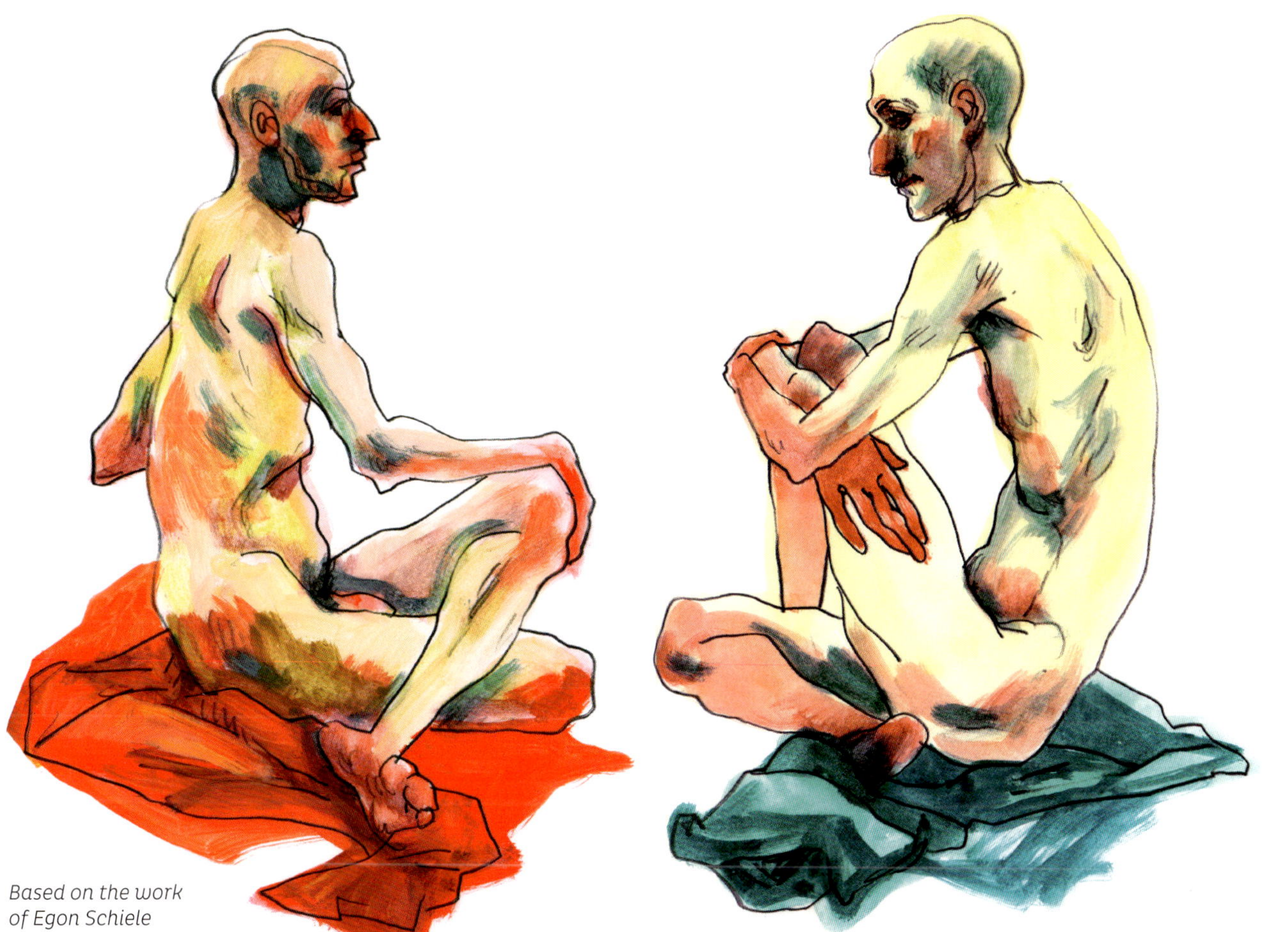

Based on the work of Egon Schiele

Hands and feet

An artist's function is very clear: he must open a studio and repair the world, in fragments, as it comes to him.
—Francis Ponge

The extremities, hands and feet, often worry artists. We recognize their great expressiveness, but they seem complicated to draw. These parts of the body are ultimately no more or less difficult to treat than others and require time and practice. Therefore, we will dedicate this week to them.

YOUR TURN

Your notebook can be the ideal support for this research. Use the tools of your choice and don't hesitate to vary the pleasures.

Draw your left hand, then your right hand. Use a mirror if necessary. Draw the hands of those around you. Do the same with your feet and those of your loved ones! Choose drawing from nature; if not, take pictures.

Try to identify the general proportions before you focus on the details. Consider the hand as a natural clamp, respecting the orientation of the thumb, and the foot as a natural shock absorber if it is curved. Study its impact on the ground as it supports the body's weight.

IF YOU HAVE THE TIME

- Choose hands that are holding an object. Draw the object first, trying to respect its volume. Then draw the hand enclosing it and hiding some parts of it. Play with transparency.

Go and see

Anatomical ex-voto
John Coplans (1920–2003)
Frédérique Lucien (born in 1960)

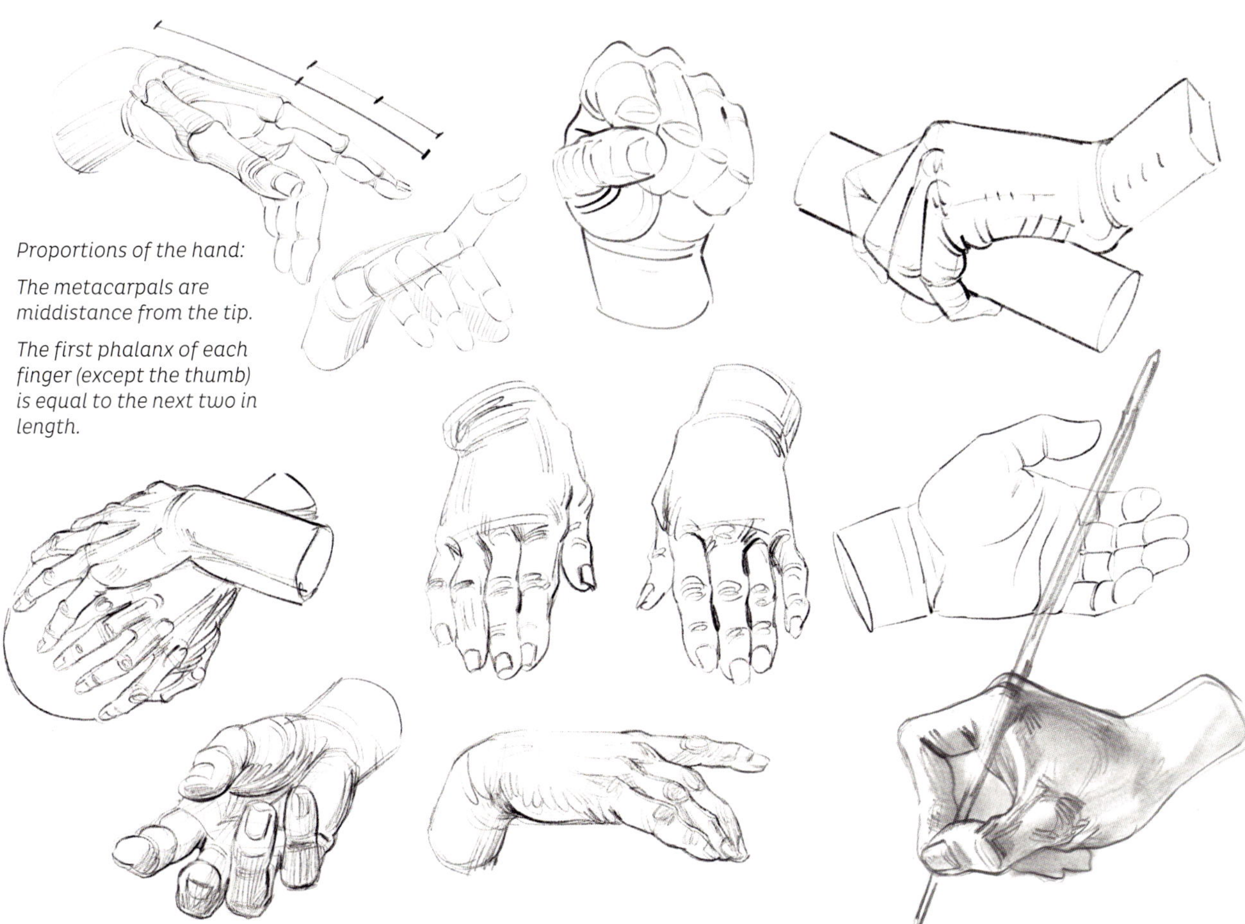

Proportions of the hand:

The metacarpals are middistance from the tip.

The first phalanx of each finger (except the thumb) is equal to the next two in length.

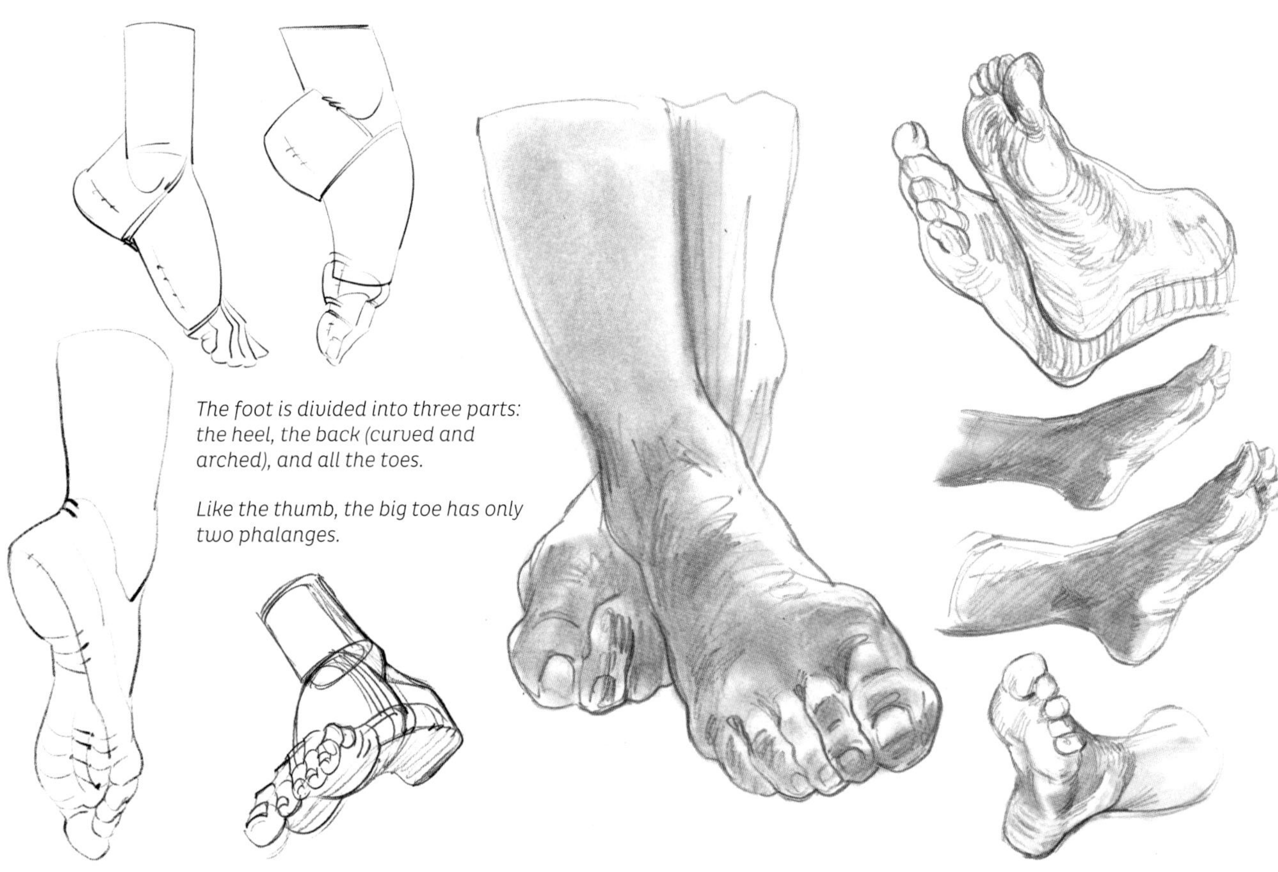

The foot is divided into three parts: the heel, the back (curved and arched), and all the toes.

Like the thumb, the big toe has only two phalanges.

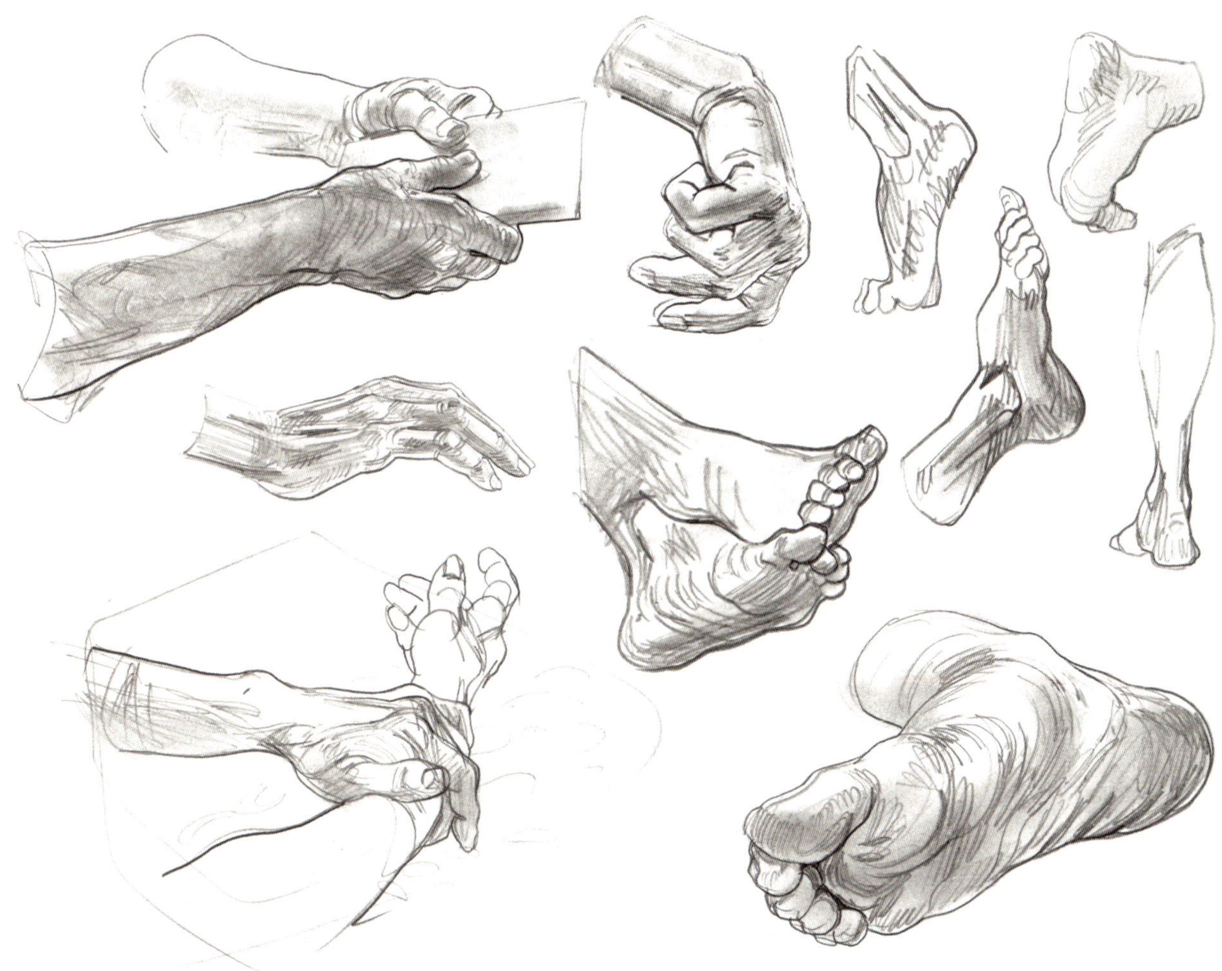

Draperies

Nothing is as beautiful as gravity in the fleeting folds of the sea's undulations or the almost eternal folds of the mountains.
—Simone Weil, *Expectation of God*

The representation of draperies has long been part of classical learning. Even if the allegories dressed in ancient robes are no longer in vogue, drapery remains a subject worthy of interest for its structured (fabric pan, clothing pattern) and organic (flexibility, fluidity, evocation of the body) aspect. In addition, drapery subjected to direct lighting makes it possible to analyze the effects of light, in particular the return of light in shadows, reflections, and reverberations (if the support, or a neighboring shape, is clear, it will tend to reflect light and become a secondary light source).

YOUR TURN

Use a large-sized sheet of paper (A3 minimum, demi-raisin, raisin, or more) and a tool such as charcoal, black or red chalk, or graphite (2B to 9B). (Note: demi-raisin and raisin are French drawing paper sizes, equal to 32.5 x 50 cm and 50 x 65 cm, respectively).

Place a piece of fabric in front of you that is folded in on itself. Draw it, paying attention to the effects of light.

Repeat the exercise with a pile of clothes. Draw it while remaining focused on the idea that it evokes a landscape. Walk around the pattern by mentally expanding the distances.

IF YOU HAVE THE TIME

- Cover an object with a piece of fabric and try to translate its shape through the interplay of folds, tensions, and points of support.
- Repeat the experiment with patterned fabrics and have fun reproducing the pattern interruptions according to the folds.

Go and see

Antoni Tàpies (1923–2012)
Christo (1935–2020) and Jeanne-Claude (1935–2009)
Kaarina Kaikkkonen (born in 1952)

Same lighting

Dark surface

Light surface

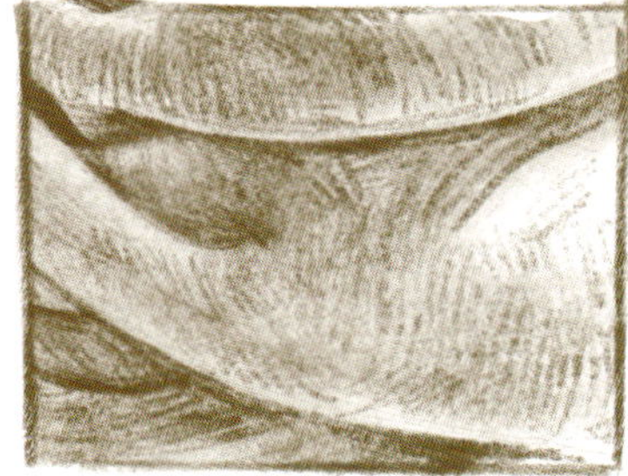

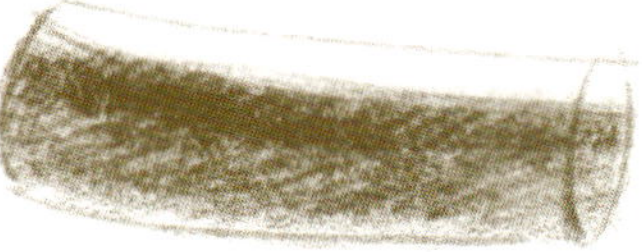

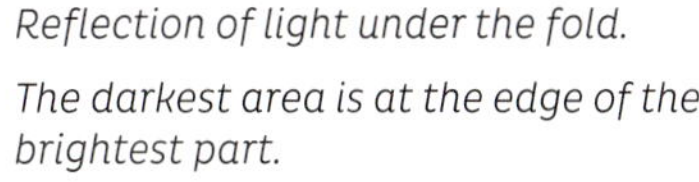

Reflection of light under the fold.

The darkest area is at the edge of the brightest part.

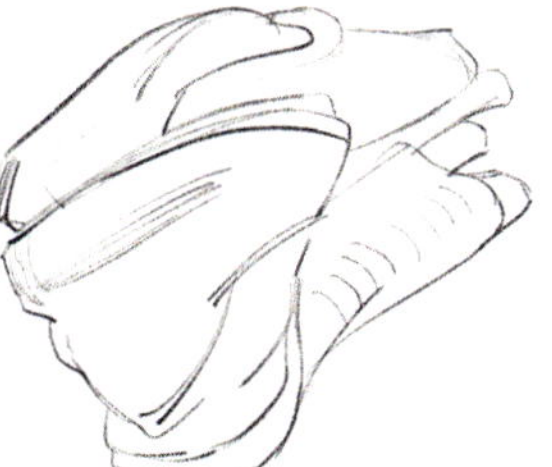

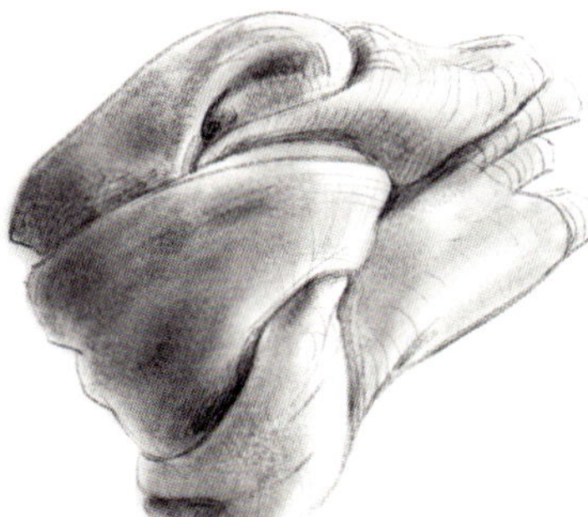

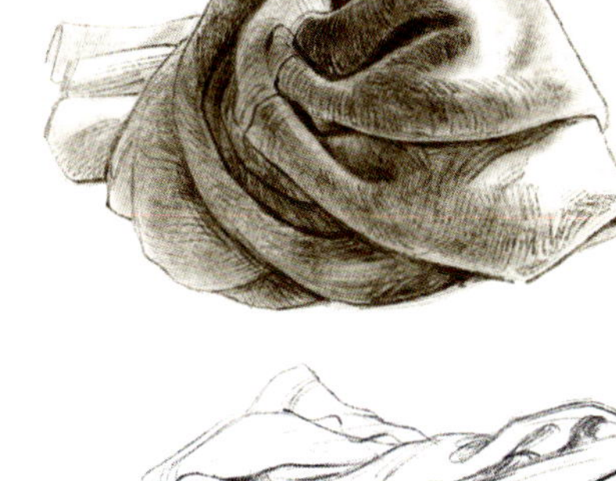

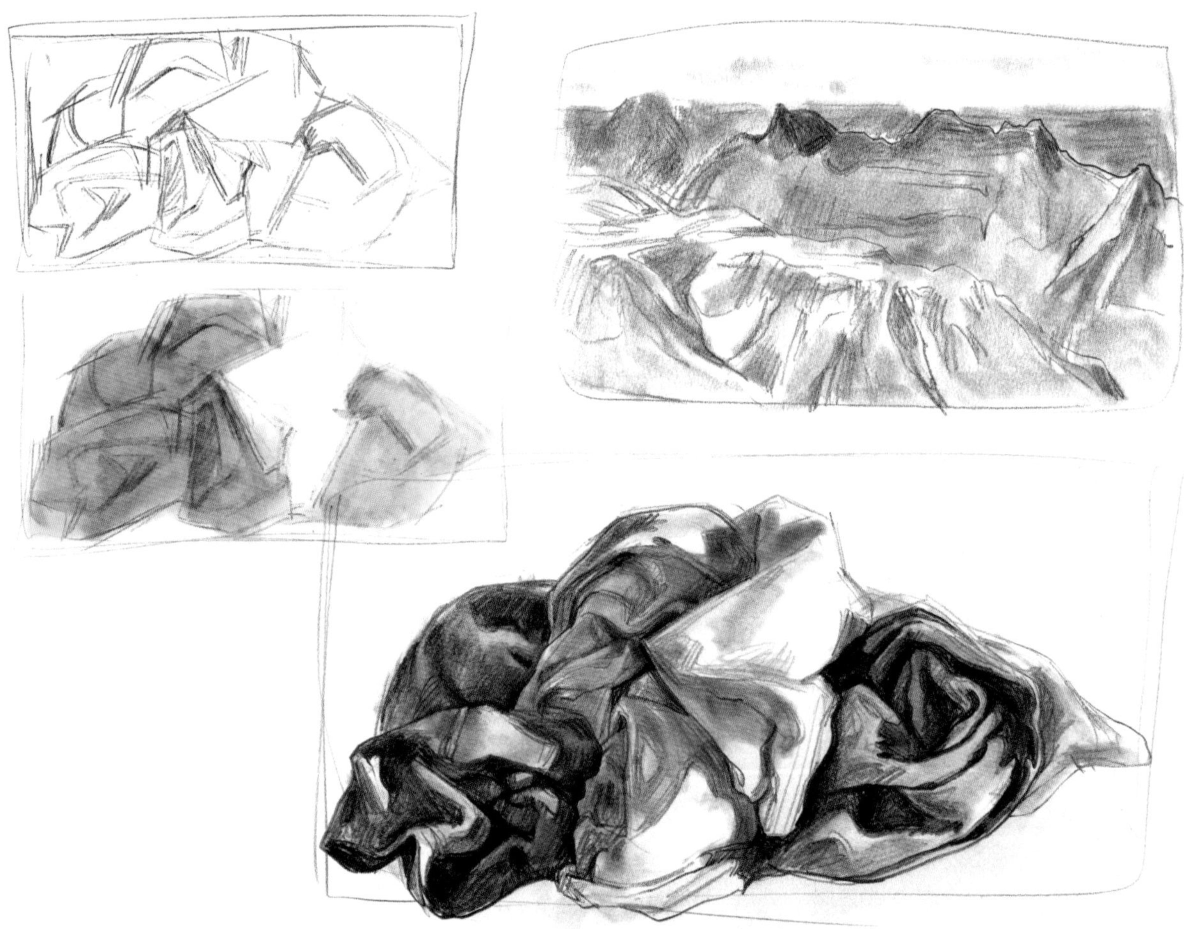

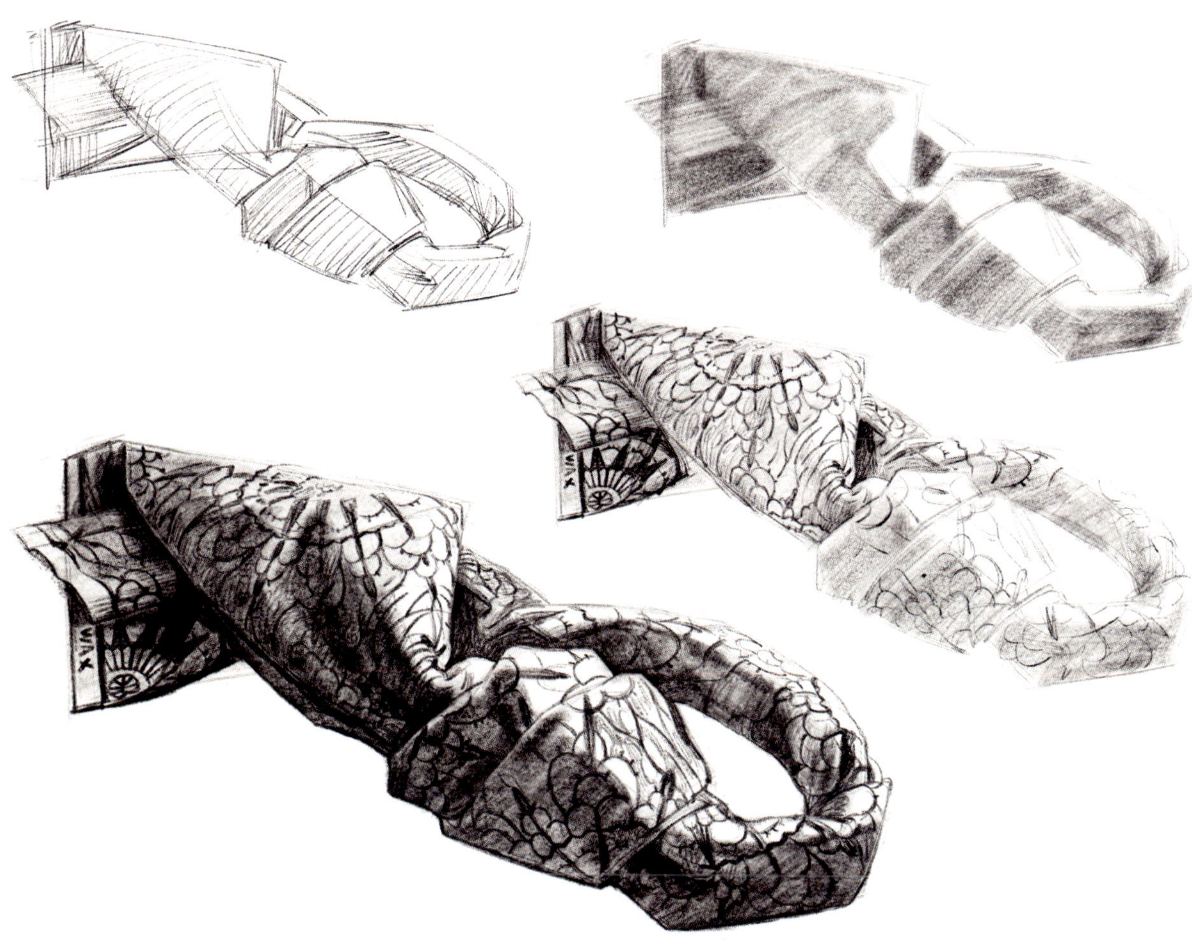

Complementary

One tone is only one color, two tones is a chord; it's life.
—Henri Matisse

Interpret a black-and-white photo in color. The objective is to invent a colored range and to learn how to translate values (e.g., light gray, medium gray, dark gray, black) into colors. The aim is to create an effective chromatic range by limiting the number of shades and basing it on a contrast that has a great impact: the contrast of complementary colors.

YOUR TURN

You can do this exercise with a colored pencil, felt pen, or pastel. Choose only four colors: one light and one dark for each of the two complementary shades.

The complementary ones are diametrically opposed on the chromatic circle. Each of the three primaries has a secondary color as a complement: red is opposite to green, yellow to purple, and blue to orange. By mixing them and playing on their opacity, this apparently very small range can be extended and will allow you to keep a certain coherence.

The complementary color can be an "intruder." Used in a smaller proportion than the main hue, it will have the function of revitalizing the image by punctuating it with small strokes. It is useful also to unsaturate and darken a color (for shadows).

Use the observation drawing methods tested beforehand (weeks 4, 5, 6, and 9) to set up your composition in a global way, directly with the clearest tool as in the following example.

IF YOU HAVE THE TIME

- Try out the other complementary pairs.

Go and see

Lorenzo Mattotti (born in 1954), the Nell'acqua series
Emmanuelle Houdart (born in 1967)
Daria Petrilli (born in 1970)

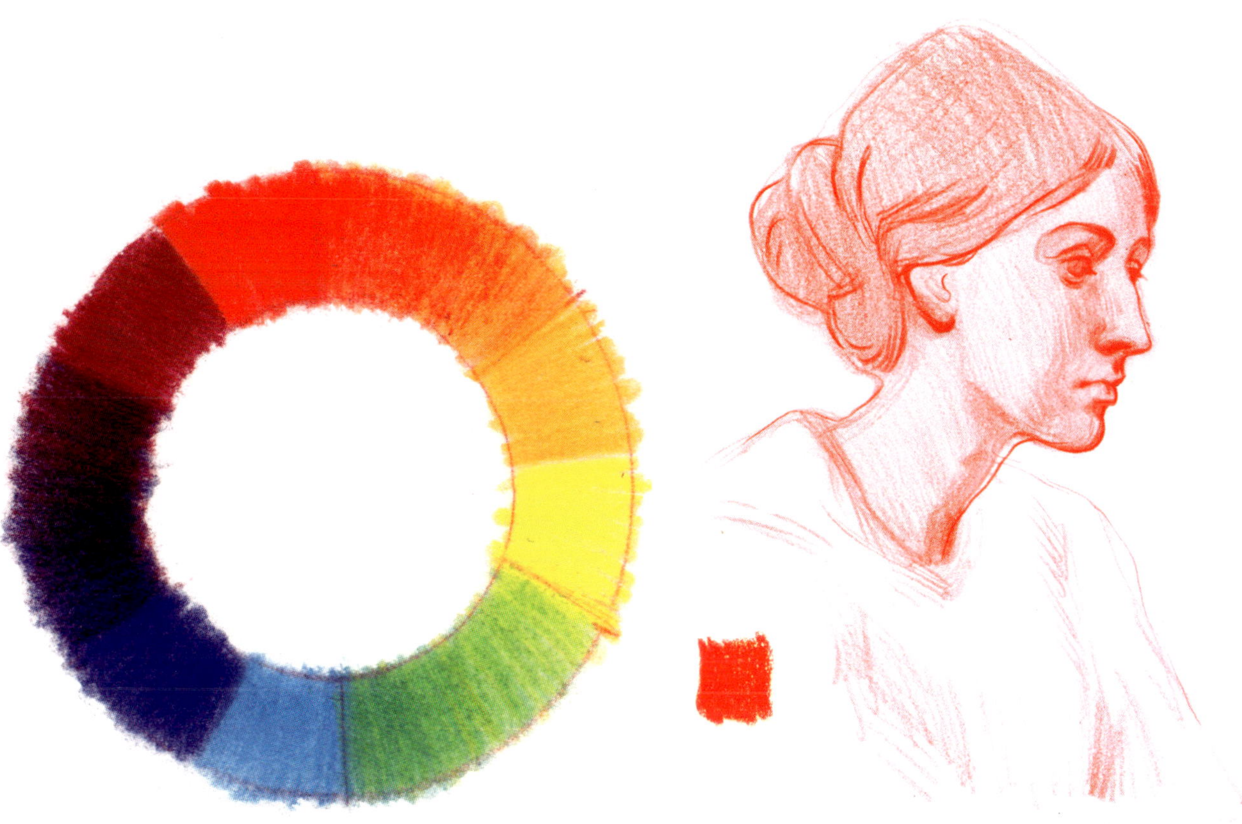

The complementary colors are opposite on the chromatic circle.

Based on a portrait of Virginia Woolf by Julia Margaret Cameron

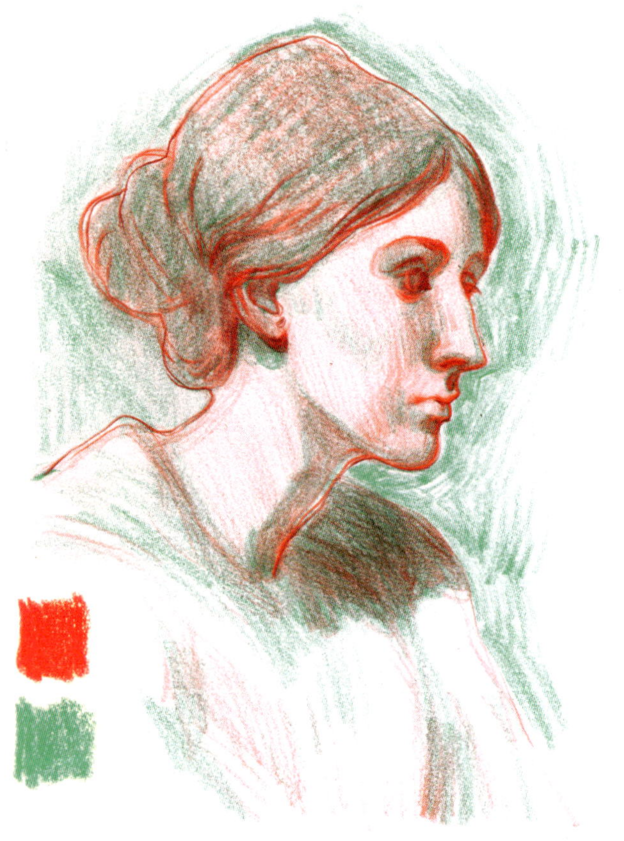

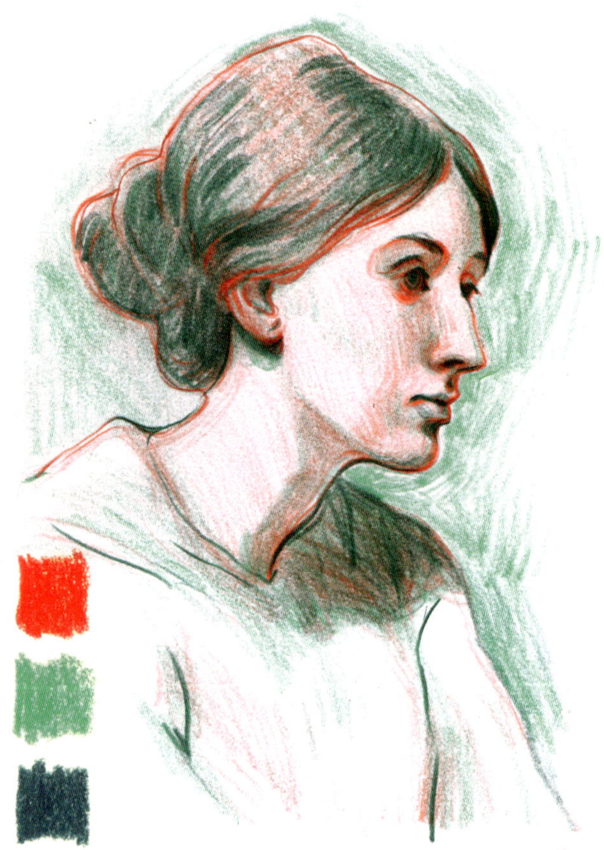

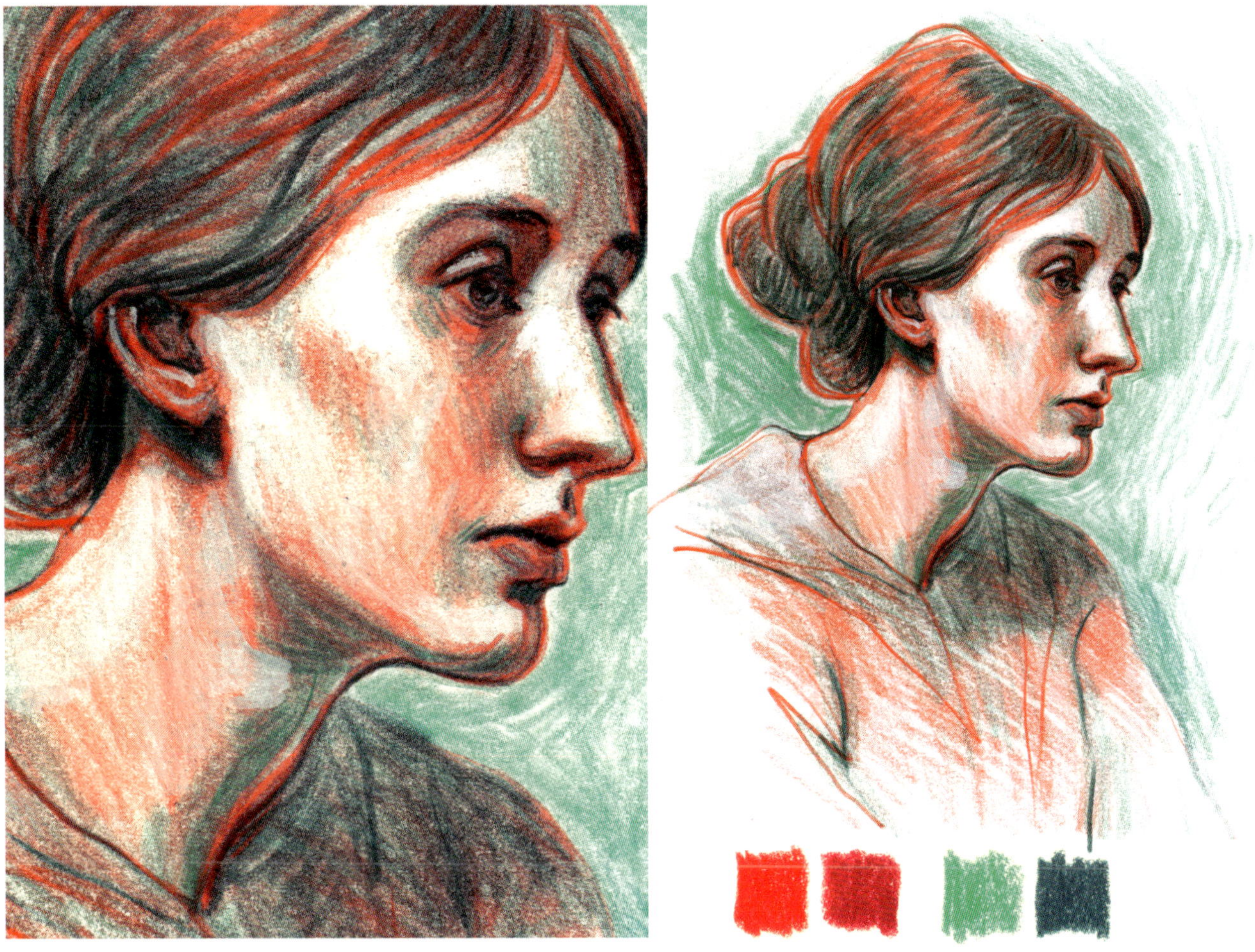

Unlikely objects

The forms of things unknown, the poet's pen
Turns them to shapes and gives to airy nothing
A local habitation and a name.
—William Shakespeare, *A Midsummer Night's Dream*

You are going to make an improbable object using pieces of string and natural (plants, stones) or manufactured (boxes, nuts, keys) elements. Tinker with what you want; try to vary the textures. Choose materials, shapes, and associations that you will enjoy drawing.

The achievement of this objective is an integral part of the exercise. You may even discover a taste for this type of manipulation, and it may become your way of expression! This is an opportunity to assemble elements that you would like to see combined into a single design. This object deserves a certain care to become rich, evocative, and poetic. It must make you want to draw it!

YOUR TURN

Drawing techniques and supports of your choice.

This improbable object is your model, your drawing subject. Place it before you and make it the subject of an analytical study by opting for a "naturalistic," descriptive representation.

However, it can also become a phantasmagorical support, its representation revealing what you like about this object and what it makes you think of.

IF YOU HAVE THE TIME

• Create a family of objects from an imaginary culture: jewelry, utensils, tools, weapons, symbolic objects, etc.

Go and see

Dieter Appelt (born in 1935), Erinnerungsspur—Statische Vibration
Gérard Titus-Carmel (born in 1942), *The Pocket Size Tlingit Coffin*
Judith Scott (1943–2005)

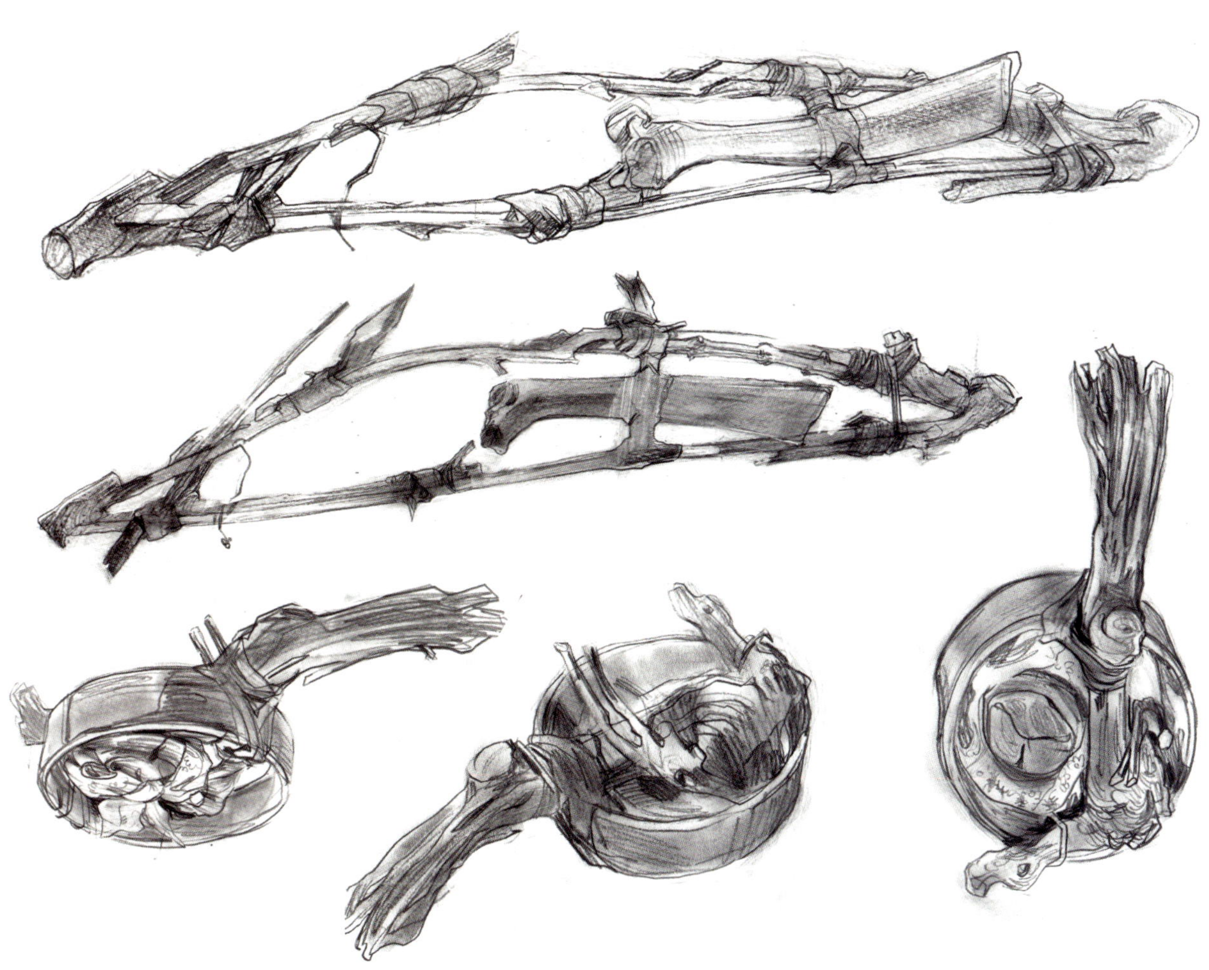

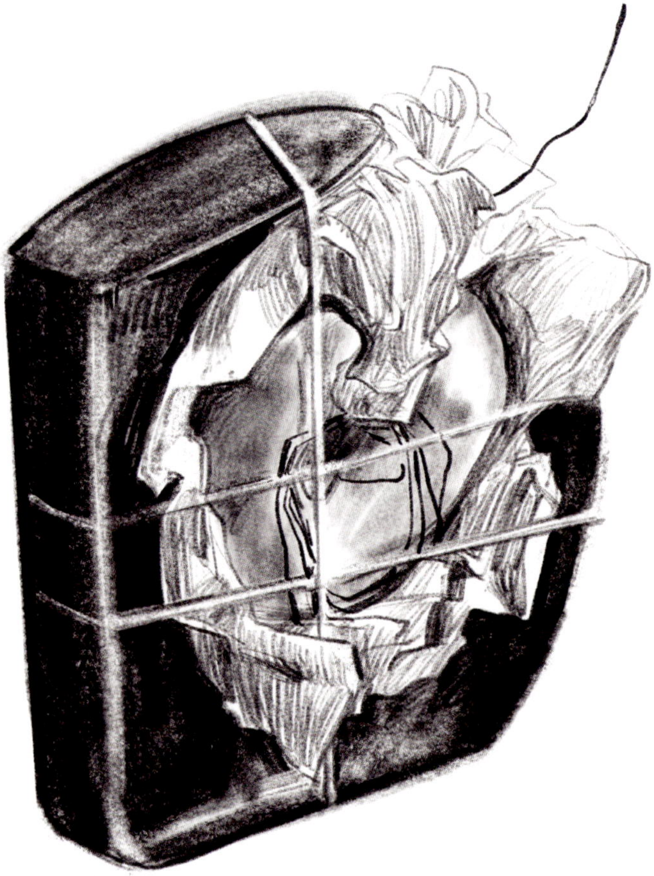

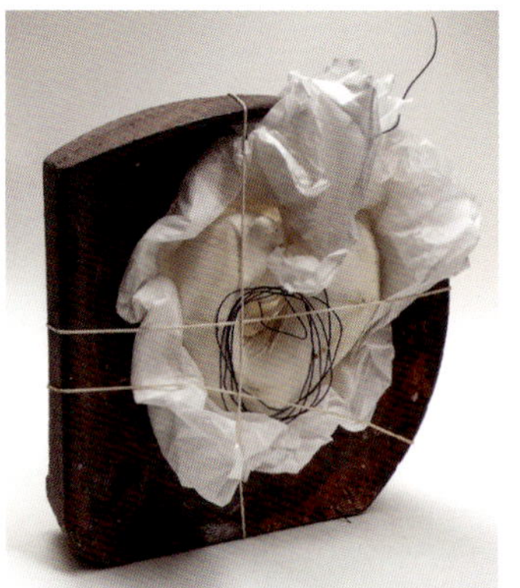

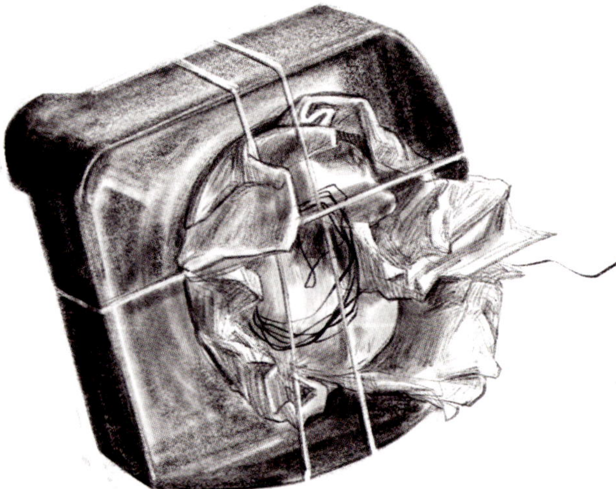

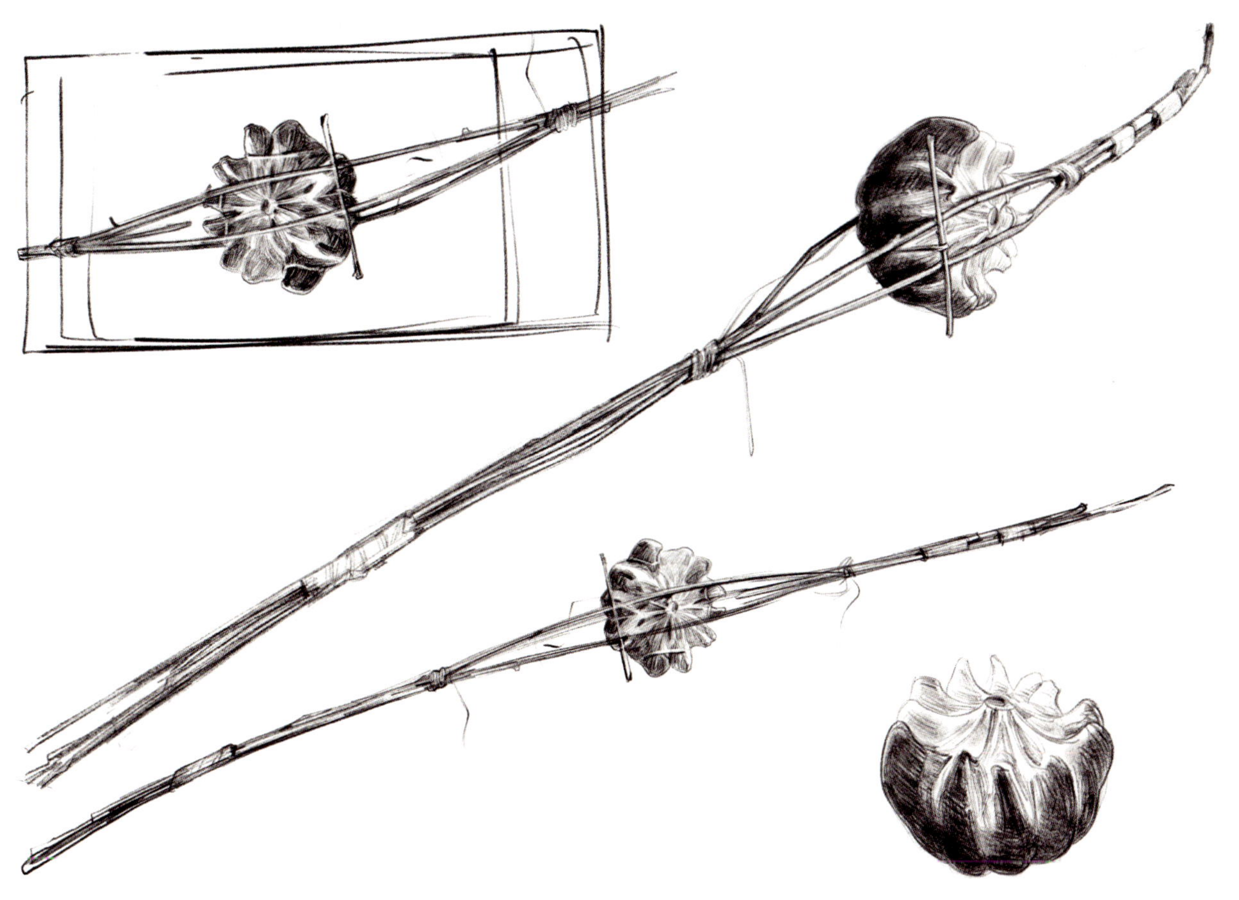

Metamorphoses

Remember that it costs nothing to stop from time to time to look at the stains on the walls, the ashes of the fire, the clouds, the mud, or other similar things in which, if you observe them, you will find wonderful ideas that awaken the painter's imagination.
—Leonardo da Vinci, *Treatise on Painting*

We know our tendency toward anthropomorphism, our ability to give human forms or expressions to the things around us. These metamorphoses and evocations are essential in a creative, poetic approach.

This imaginary game also often makes it possible to find a primer in the representation of a motif: a cloud resembling an animal, for example. In a fun way, we offer you the opportunity to transform the objects of your choice!

YOUR TURN

All techniques and supports are possible. Digital layers and tools are very suitable for this exercise.

Look around for objects that evoke other shapes, and work on their metamorphosis through drawing. You can keep your ideas poetic or make your vision explicit.

IF YOU HAVE THE TIME

- Follow Leonardo da Vinci's advice to the letter; his quotation begun above continues as follows: *"that awaken the painter's imagination to new inventions such as battle scenes, animals, and men, as well as various compositions of landscapes and monstrous things, devils and others, which will be to your credit, for in confused things the genius awakes to new inventions."*

Go and see

Charles Philipon (1800–1862)
Pablo Picasso (1881–1973), *The Bull, 11 lithographs*
Jean-Olivier Héron (1938–2017)

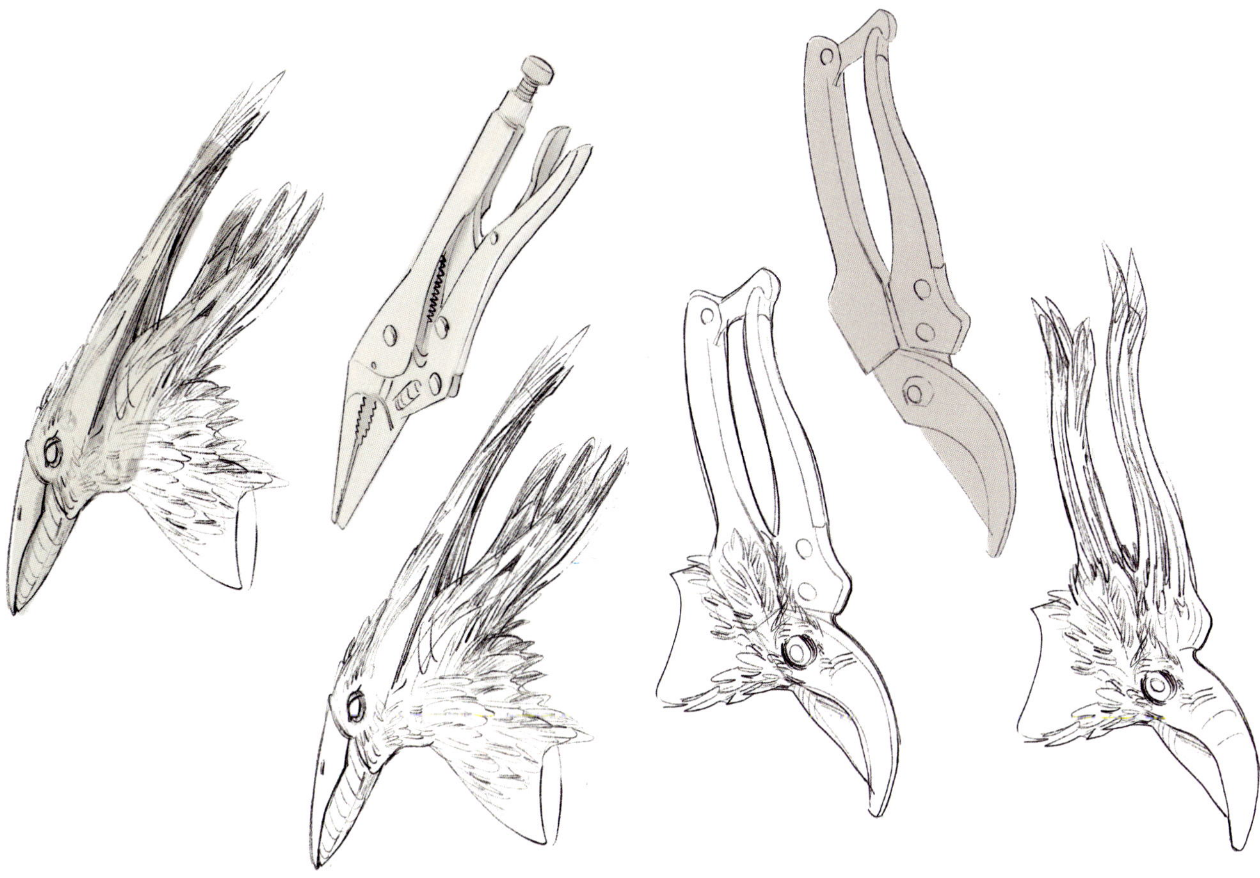

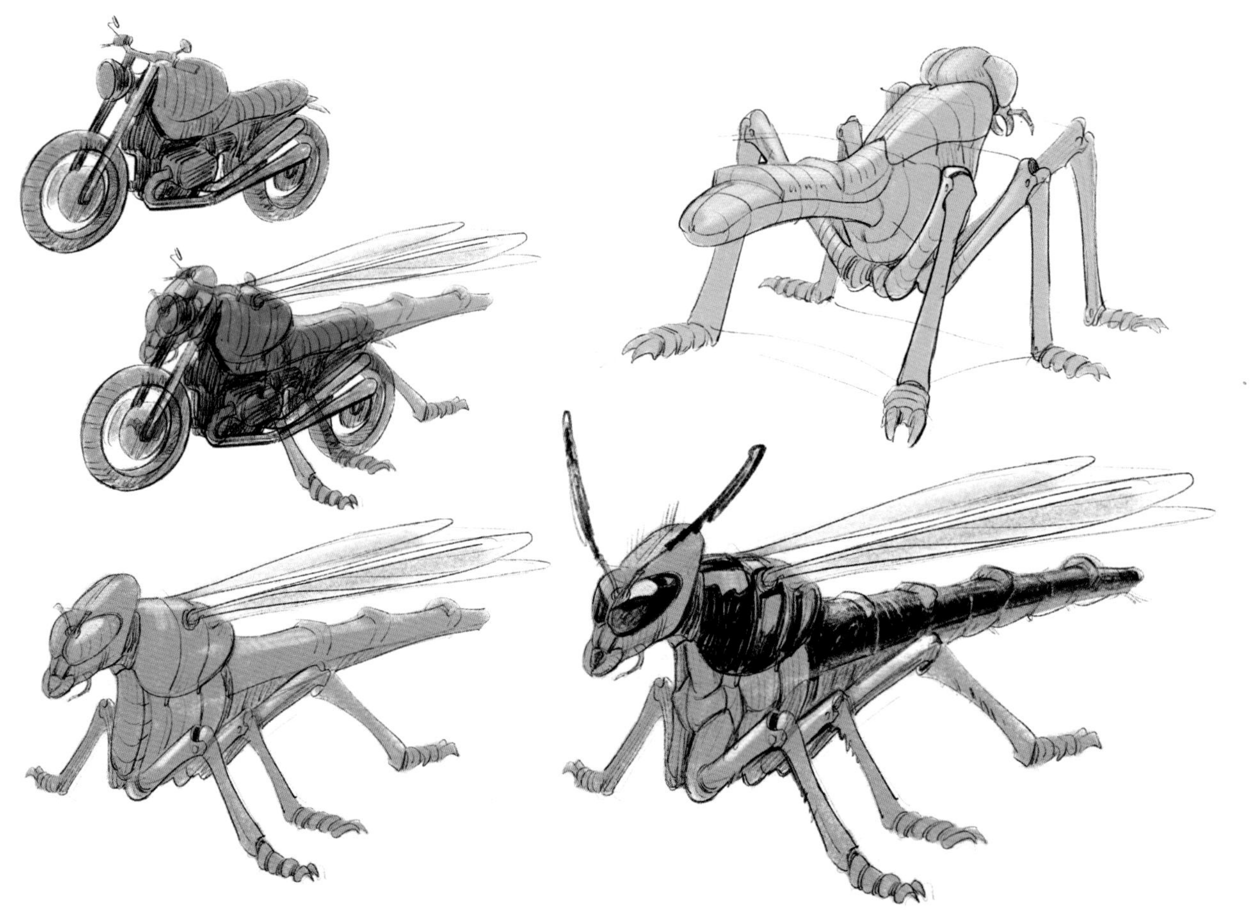

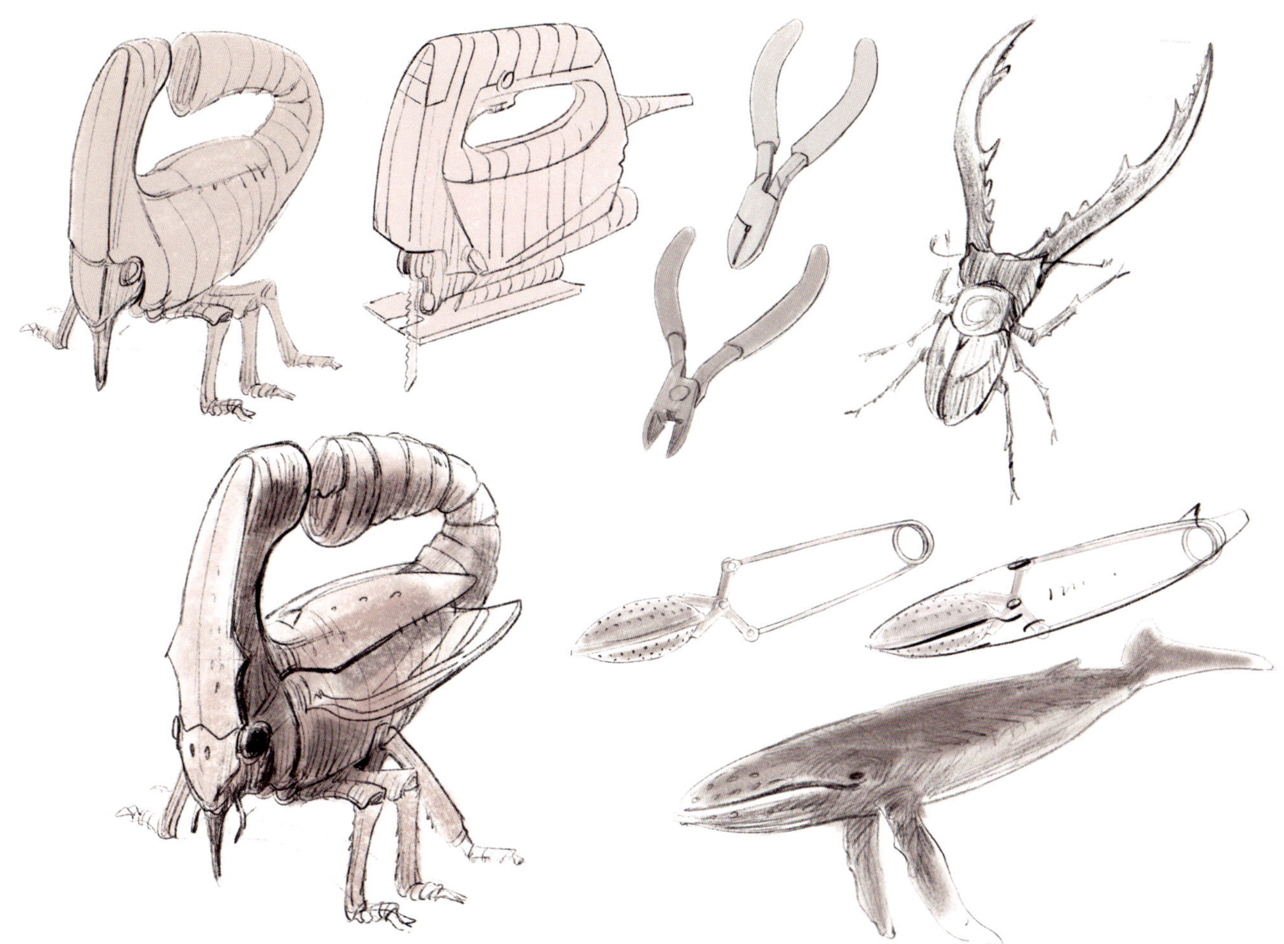

First and second roles

... he noticed for the first time some small figures in blue, that the sand was pink, and finally, the precious substance of the tiny patch of yellow wall ...
—Marcel Proust, *Swann's Way*

When we look at a set of objects, a group of characters, we naturally do not give the same importance to all the elements of this scene. We select information and prioritize it. We distribute leading and supporting roles, so to speak, and we place the extras and the set.

YOUR TURN

Use an A4 sheet of paper (minimum) and a simple HB or 2B pencil, or a ballpoint pen, for placement. Change the tool in order to contrast the presences of the different actors of your image.

Put some objects on your table. You are going to direct the regard of an imaginary observer and indicate to him by purely graphical means a stratagem which of these different elements has the leading role in your image. To do this, you will use composition: central or offset, cantilevered, in a vacuum zone, unbalanced, etc.

You will be able to highlight this or that part of your drawing by using different lettering: more accurate, more contrasting, with another tool, etc.

IF YOU HAVE THE TIME

- Compose in a way that guides the gaze by playing with frames of multiple shapes: square, panoramic, circle, etc.

Go and see

Henri de Toulouse-Lautrec (1864–1901)
Max Beckmann (1884–1950)
Balthus (1908–2001)

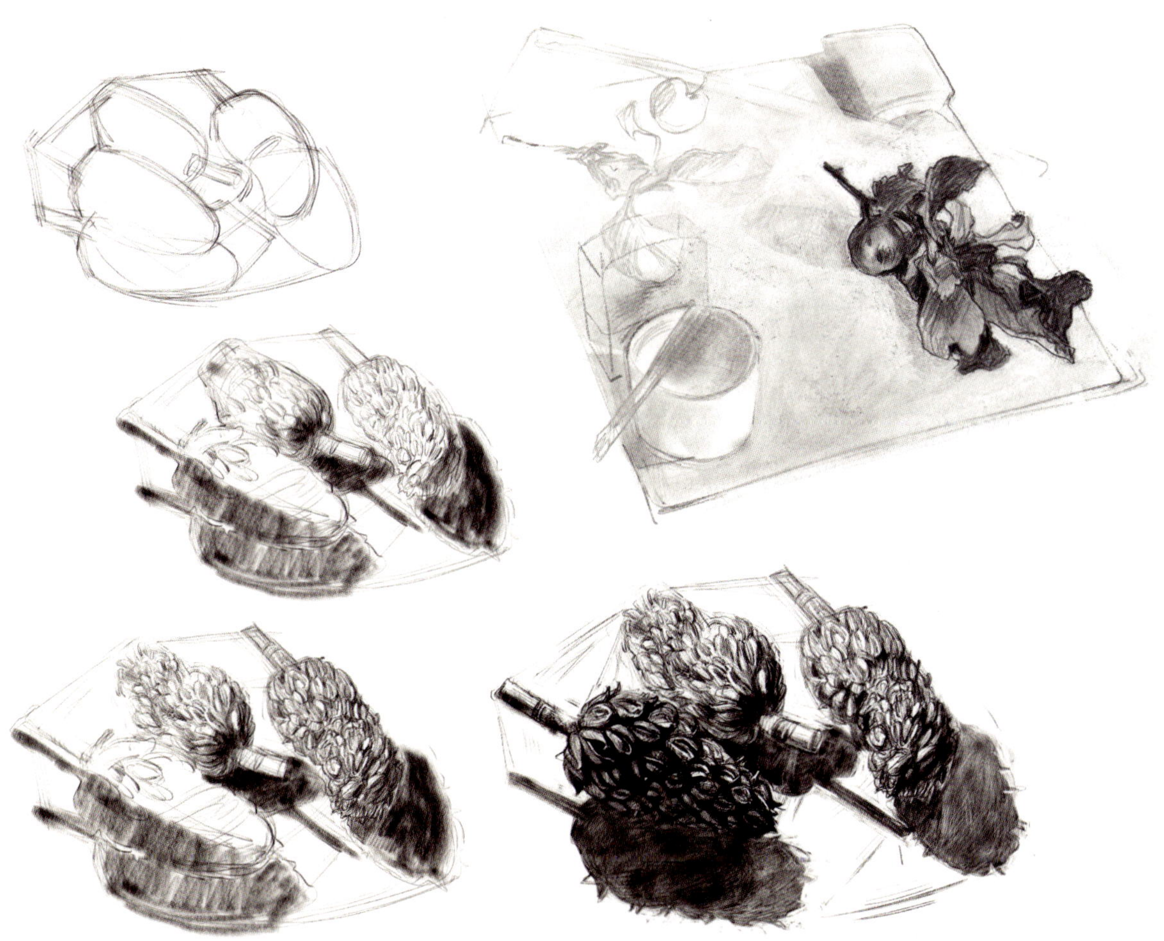

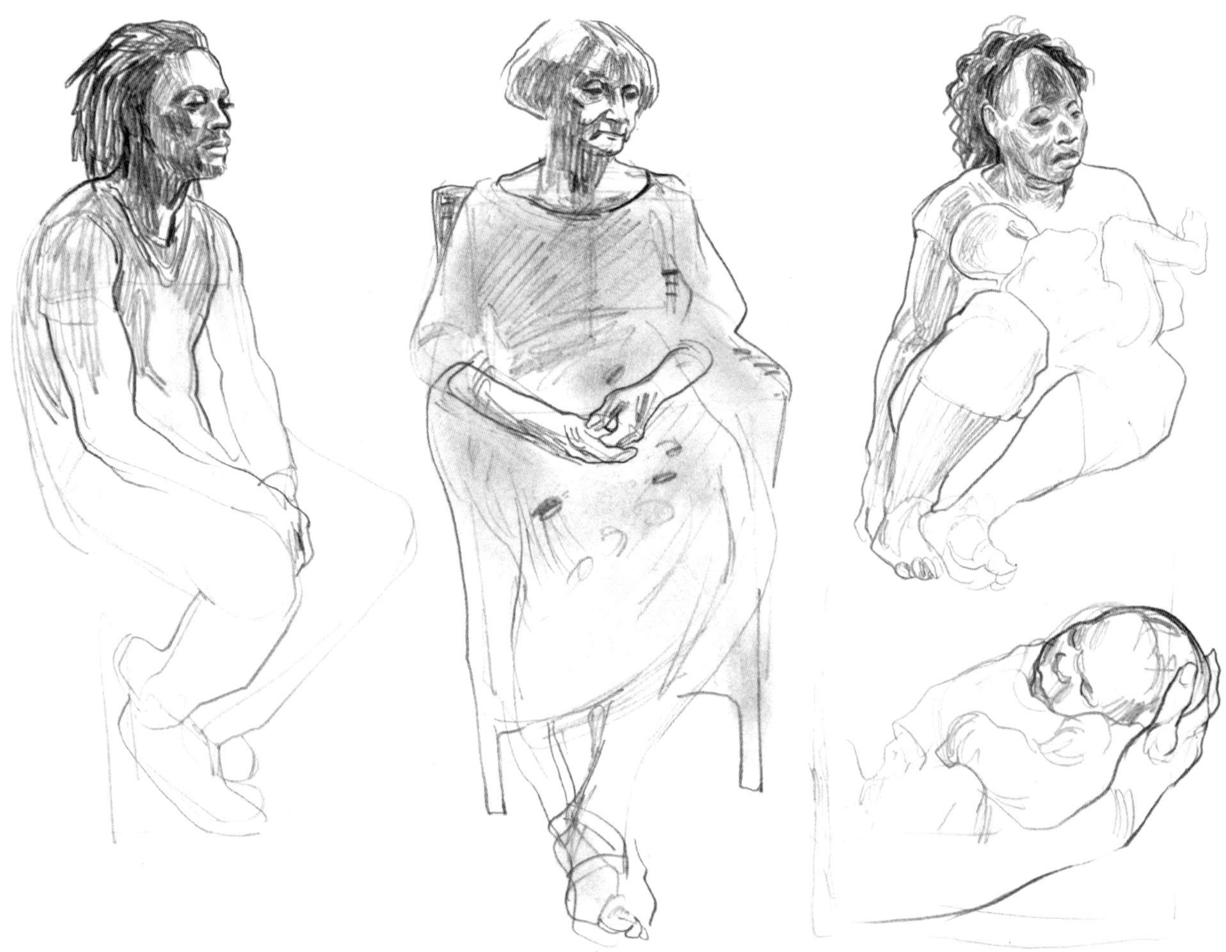

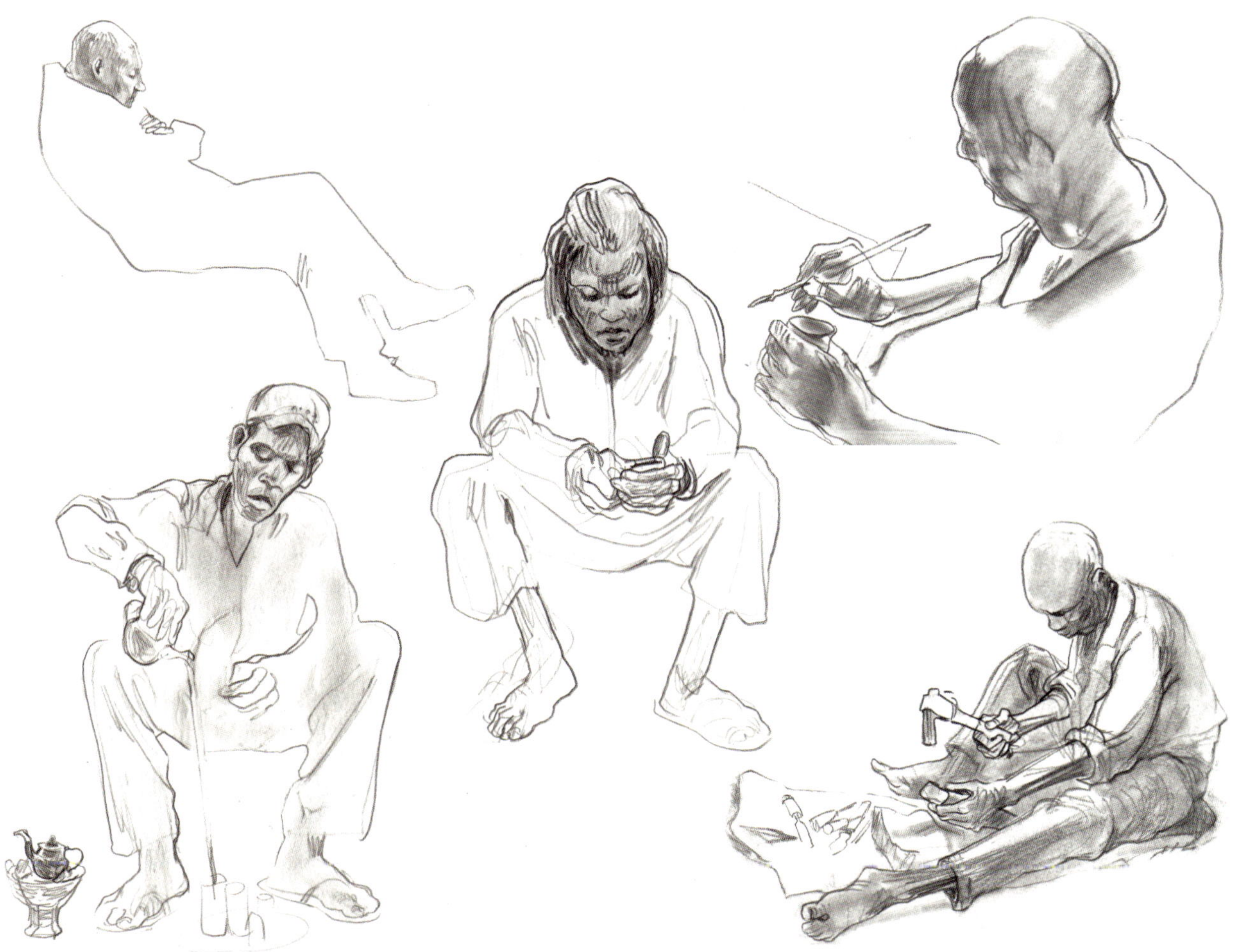

Self-portraits

Human growth does not occur from the bottom upwards but from inside to outside.
—Franz Kafka, in Gustav Janouch's *Conversations with Kafka*

This week you will be doing a "self-portrait in a mirror" exercise. Drawing yourself leaves no one indifferent: some people particularly appreciate the experience, while others hate it! In either case, you will certainly find it instructive.

YOUR TURN

Try to make a new self-portrait every day. Choose the tools that inspire you, with a different point of view, framing, background, and lighting for each one. The idea is to be able to compare different "states" of yourself at the end of the week. It is even more difficult to see yourself as you are than to represent the other as you see it! Focus on what you see more than on the image you would like to give of yourself. Try to consider yourself as if you were an object of study like any other.

If you have only a short time, a quick sketch every day will be enough. The important thing is regularity.

IF YOU HAVE THE TIME

- Set yourself up for a "full-length" self-portrait, in a chosen setting and attitude.

Go and see

Käthe Kollwitz (1867–1945)
Roman Opalka (1931–2011)
Cindy Sherman (born in 1954)

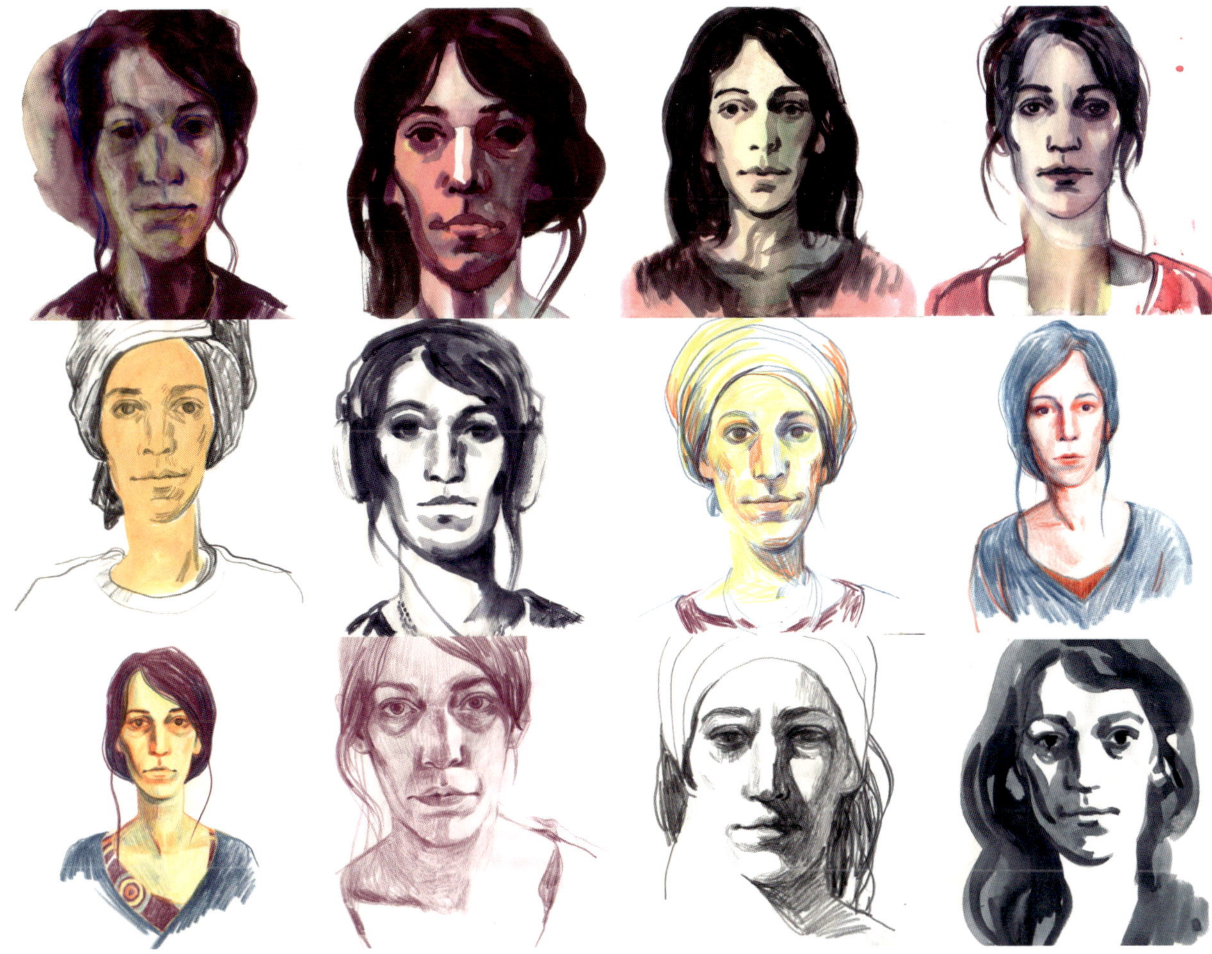

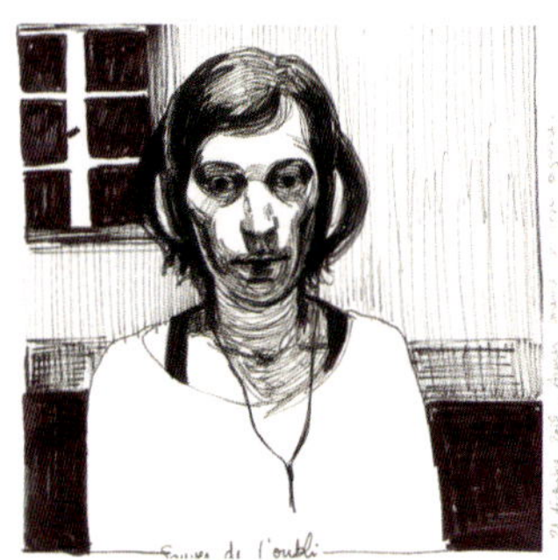

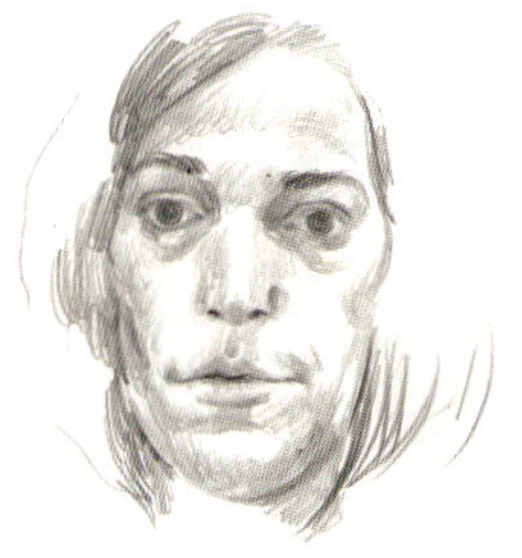

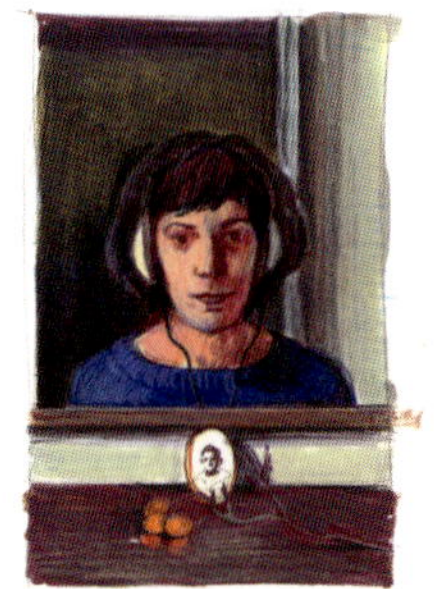

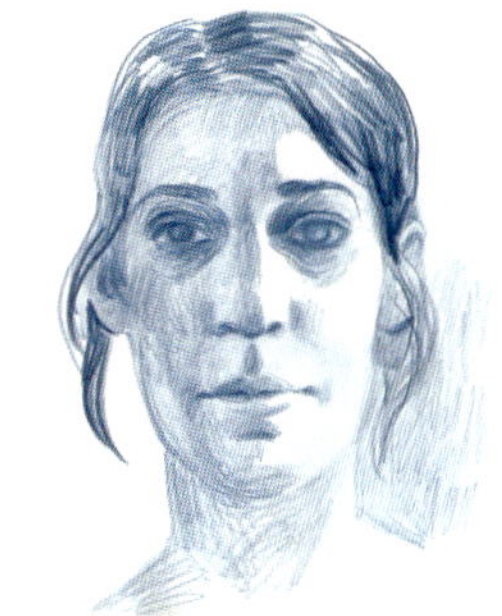

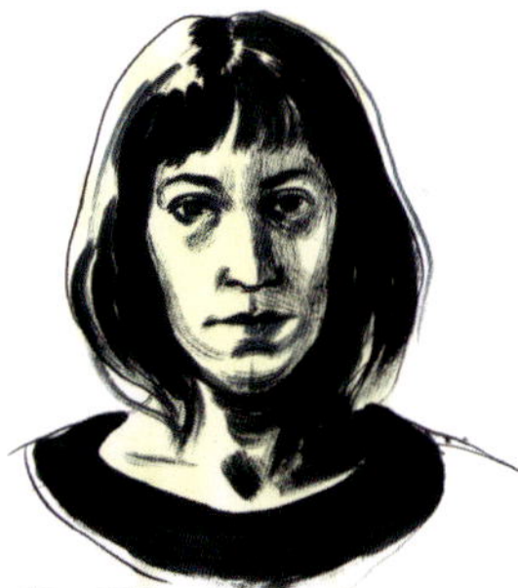
S'il y a des larmes, il y aura des rires…

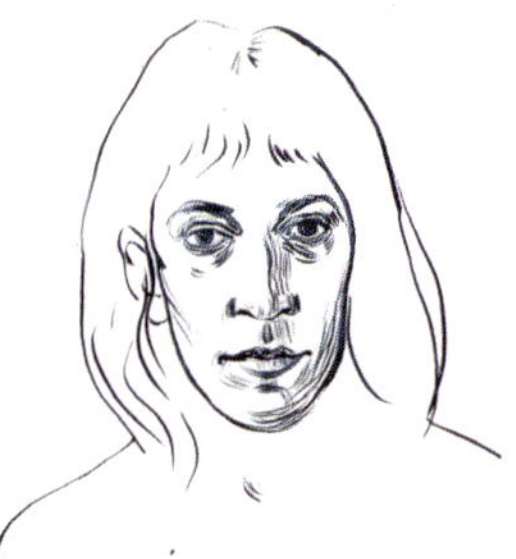

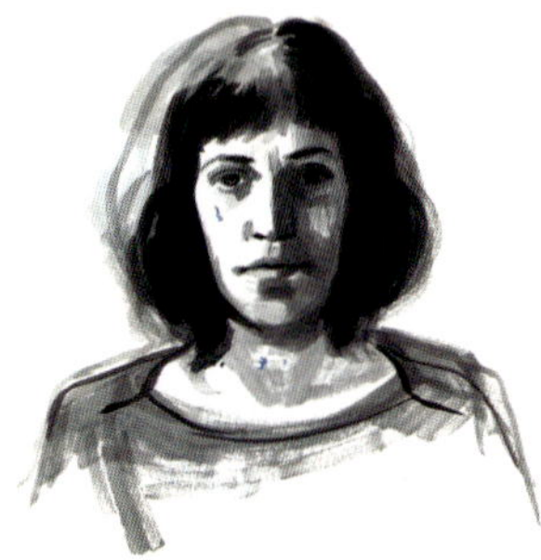

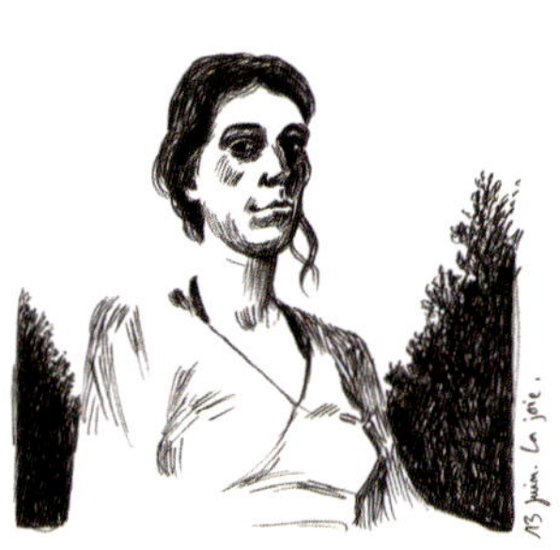
13 juin. La joie.

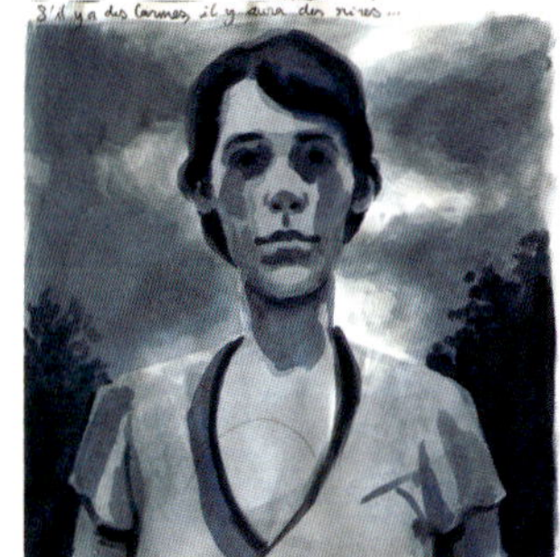

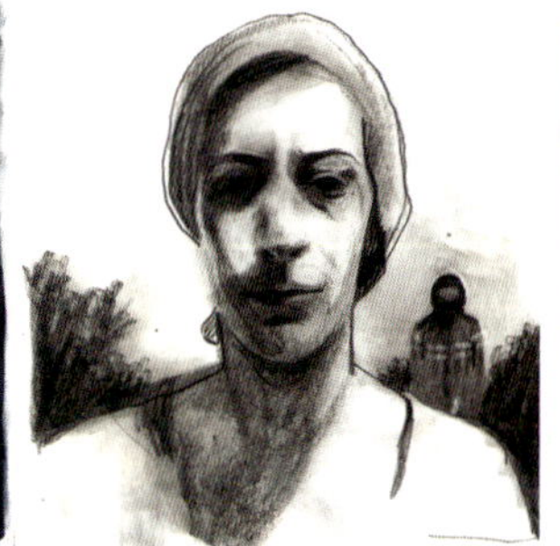

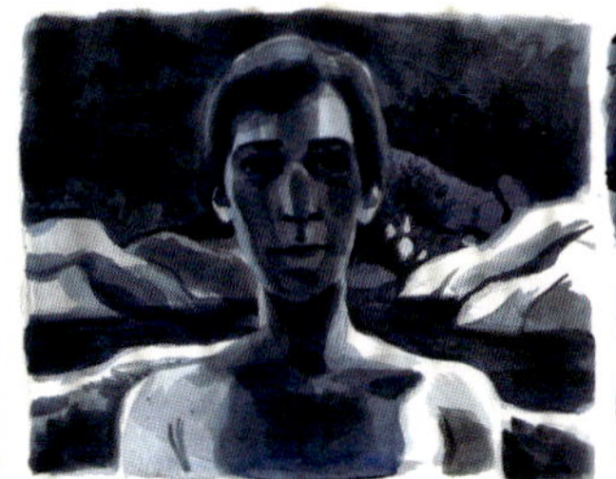

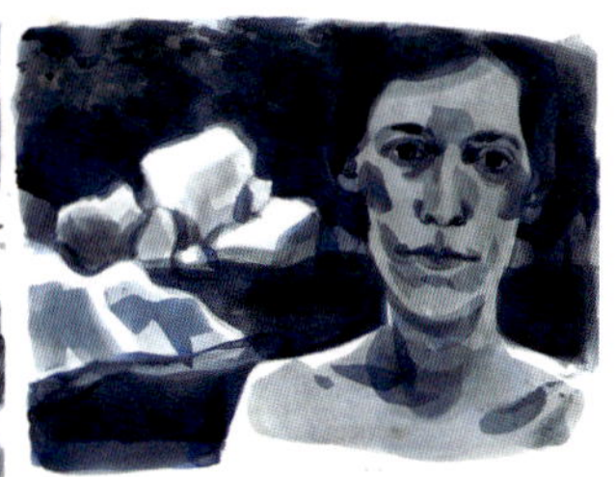

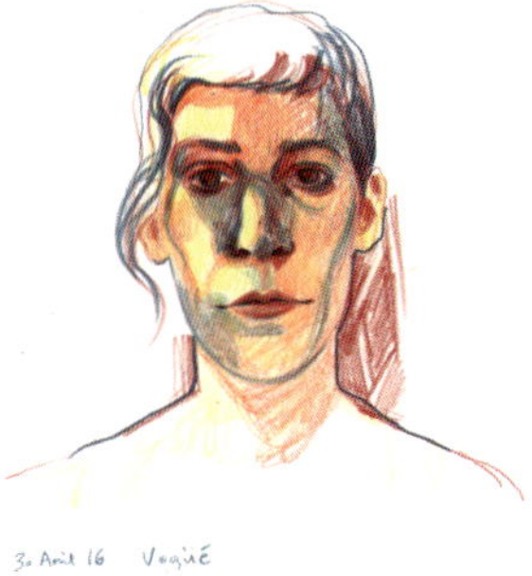

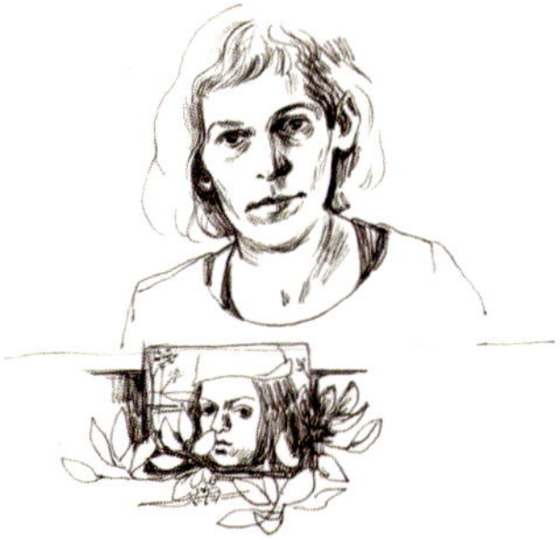

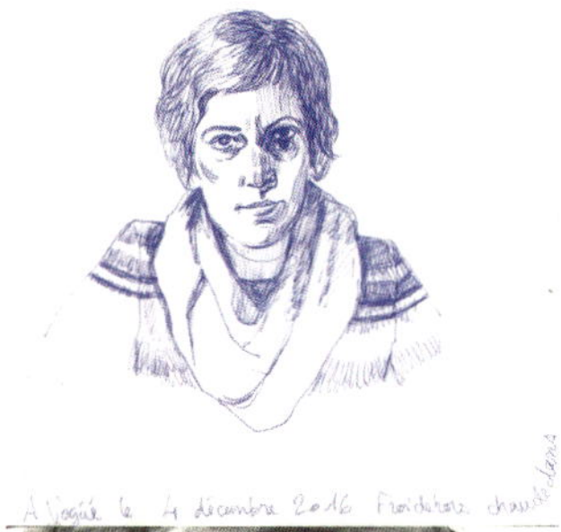

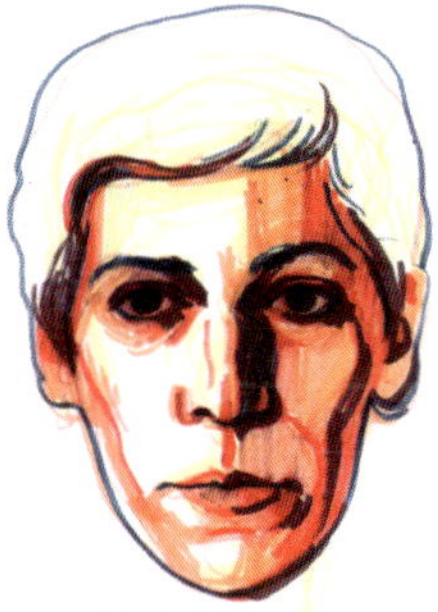

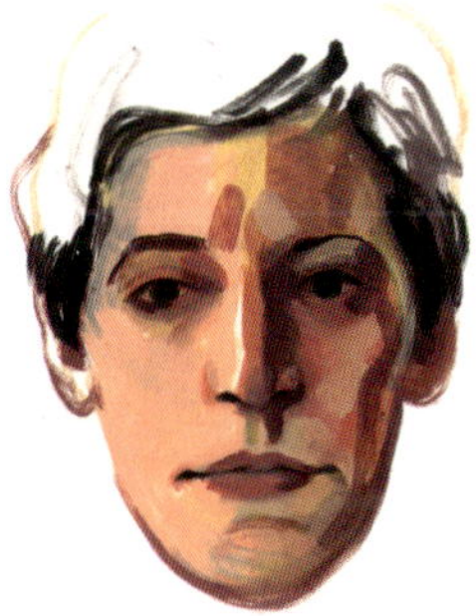

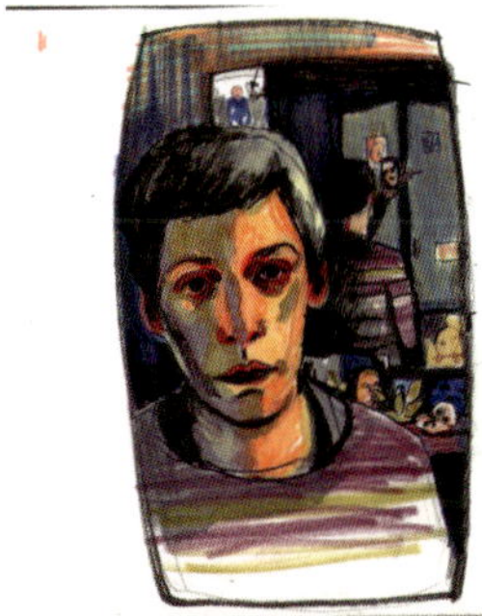

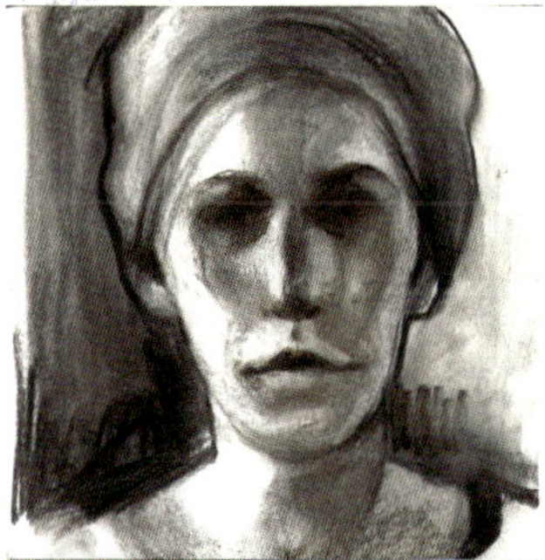

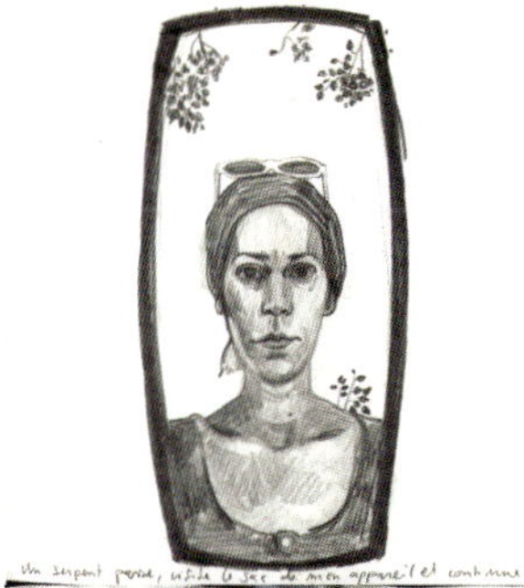

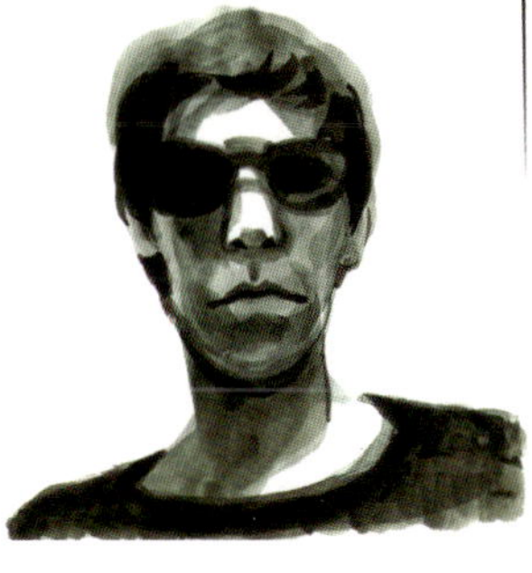

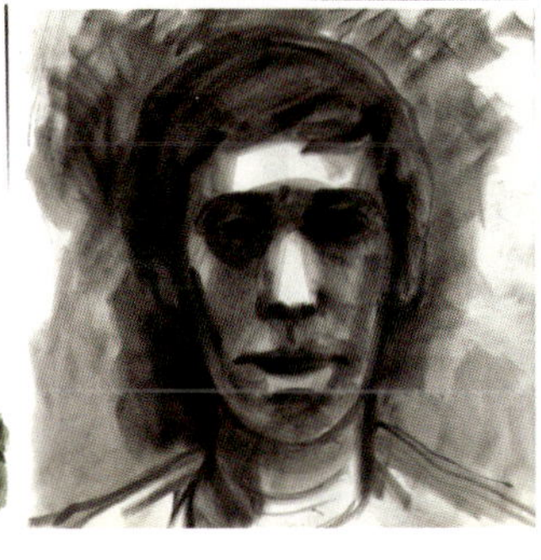

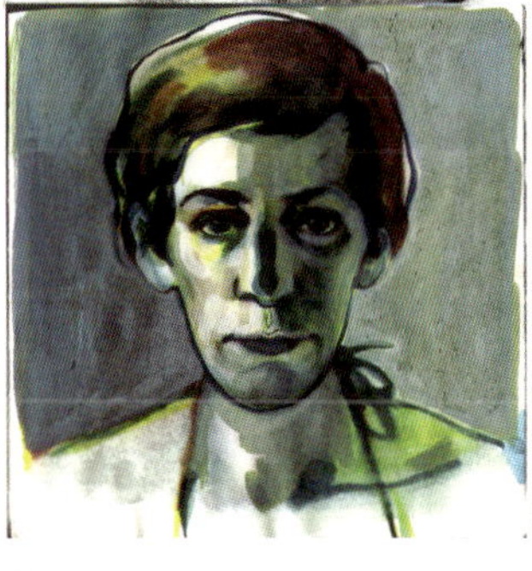

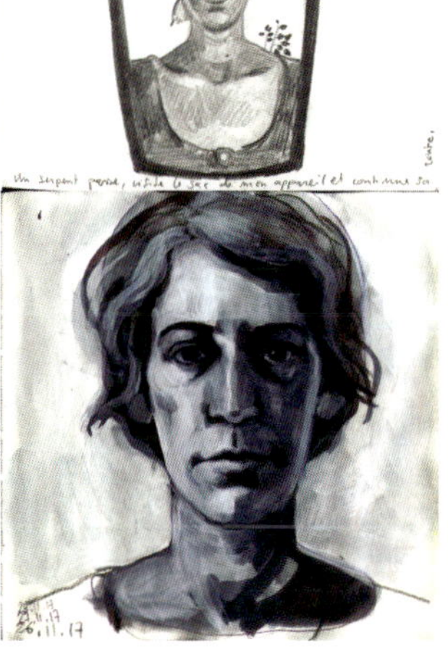

Chrono

So I began to circumscribe the first group in the blink of an eye; if there was not much time, I had at least captured its character.
—Jean-Baptiste Camille Corot

This week, you will impose very short execution times on yourself, which will help you to let go, to stop worrying about the result, and to let yourself be surprised by what happens. Either it works—or it doesn't! Stay the course even if you are not convinced by the results: it will always be an excellent exercise for the eye and the hand. The very short exposure times facilitate the overall vision. Drawing in thirty seconds does not necessarily mean at full speed! Above all, you have to draw differently, finding ratios as a whole, without dwelling on details. It's very good training for drawing on the spot, in the street, in a café, etc.

YOUR TURN

Use sketch sheets and tools of your choice. Choose wide tools (charcoal, marker, etc.). Collect images of subjects that inspire you. A selection of photos of dancers, for example. First, draw your design by using only five line segments. Make the most-appropriate choices. Then make a series of drawings, devoting between ten seconds and three minutes to each.

IF YOU HAVE THE TIME

• Look at your design for about ten seconds without drawing it. Then draw without looking at it.
• This may be the time, if you haven't already done it, to participate in live model-drawing sessions! These short classes are a classic.

Go and see

Auguste Rodin (1840–1917), drawings
Edmond Baudoin (born in 1942)
Cyril Pedrosa (born in 1972), notebooks

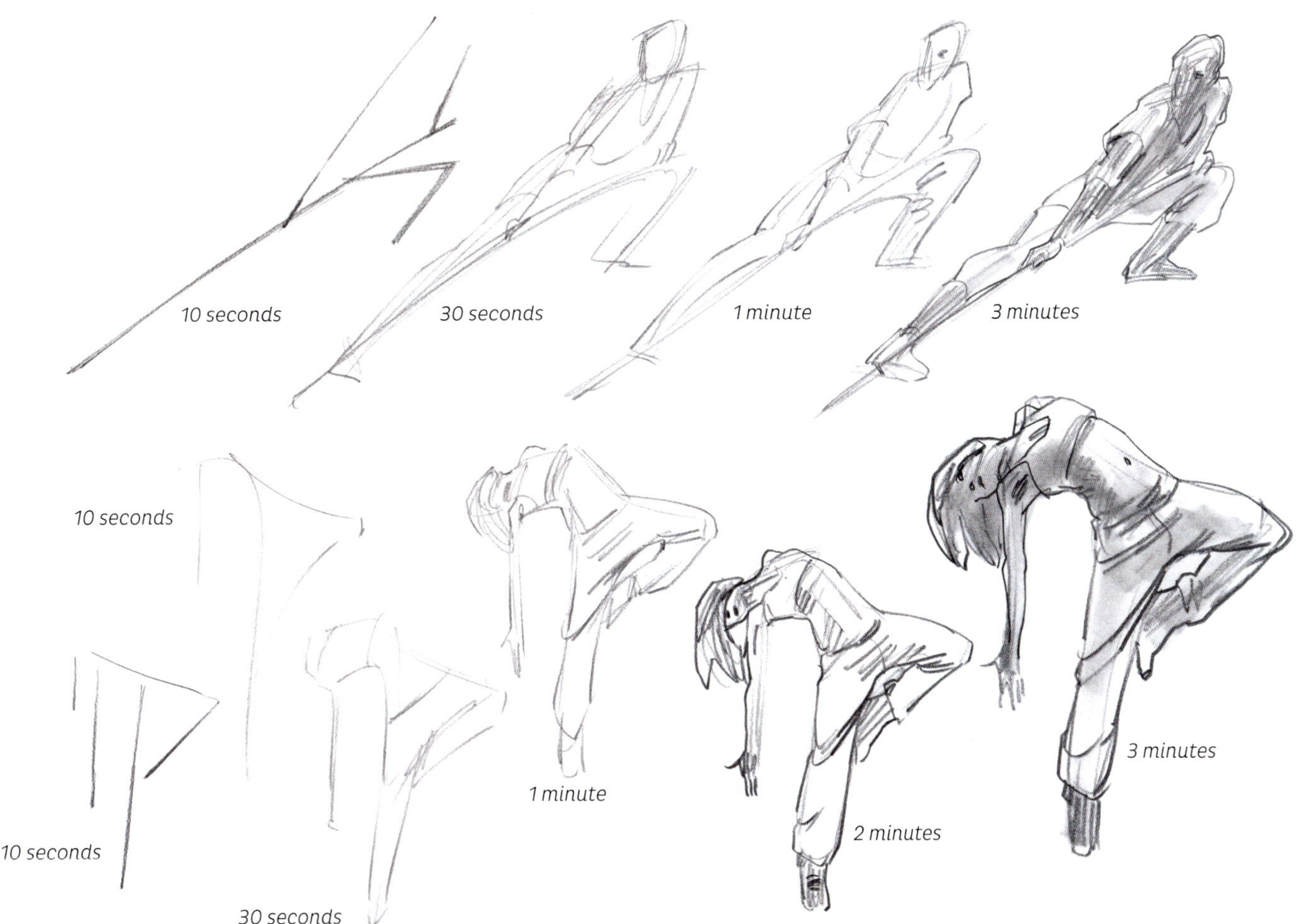
10 seconds
30 seconds
1 minute
3 minutes
10 seconds
10 seconds
30 seconds
1 minute
2 minutes
3 minutes

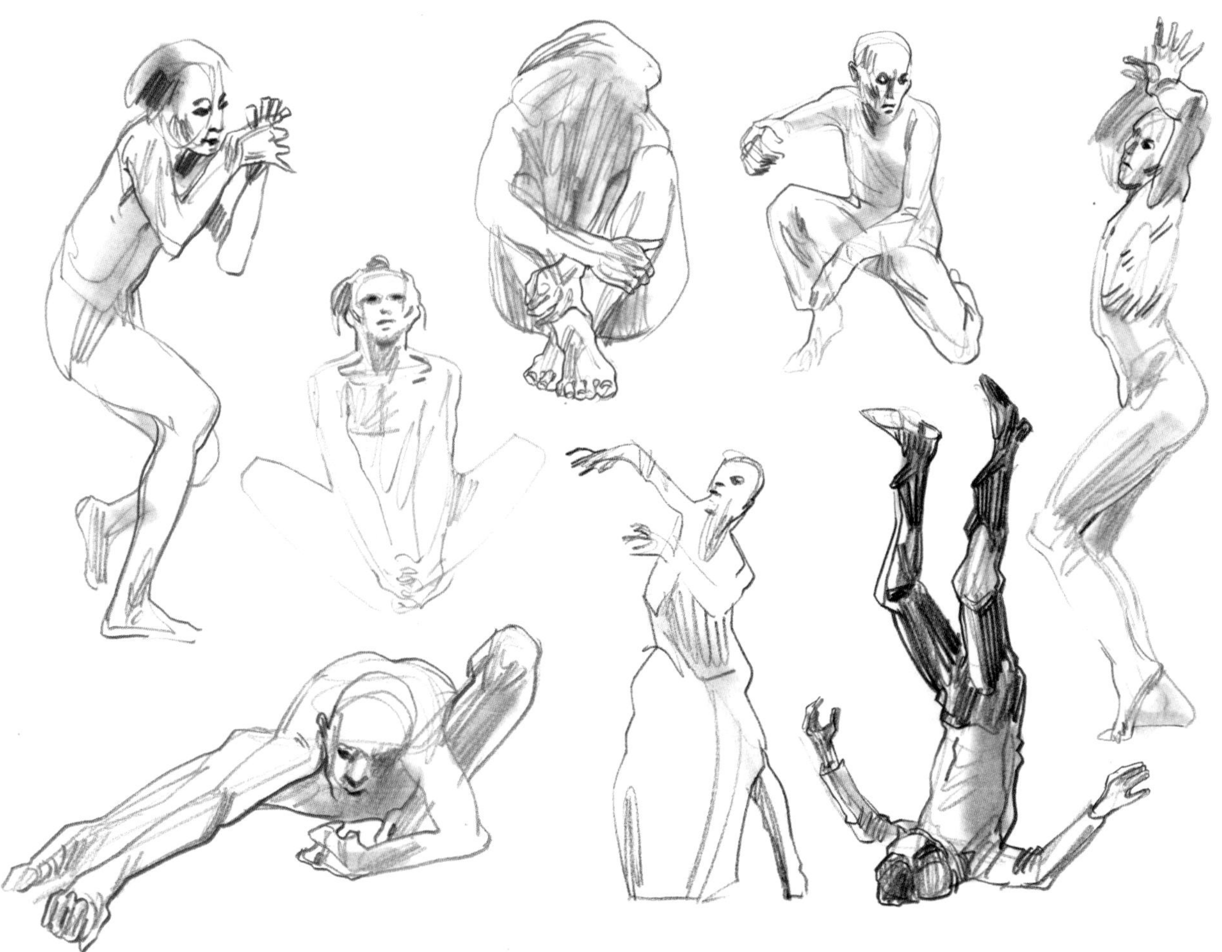

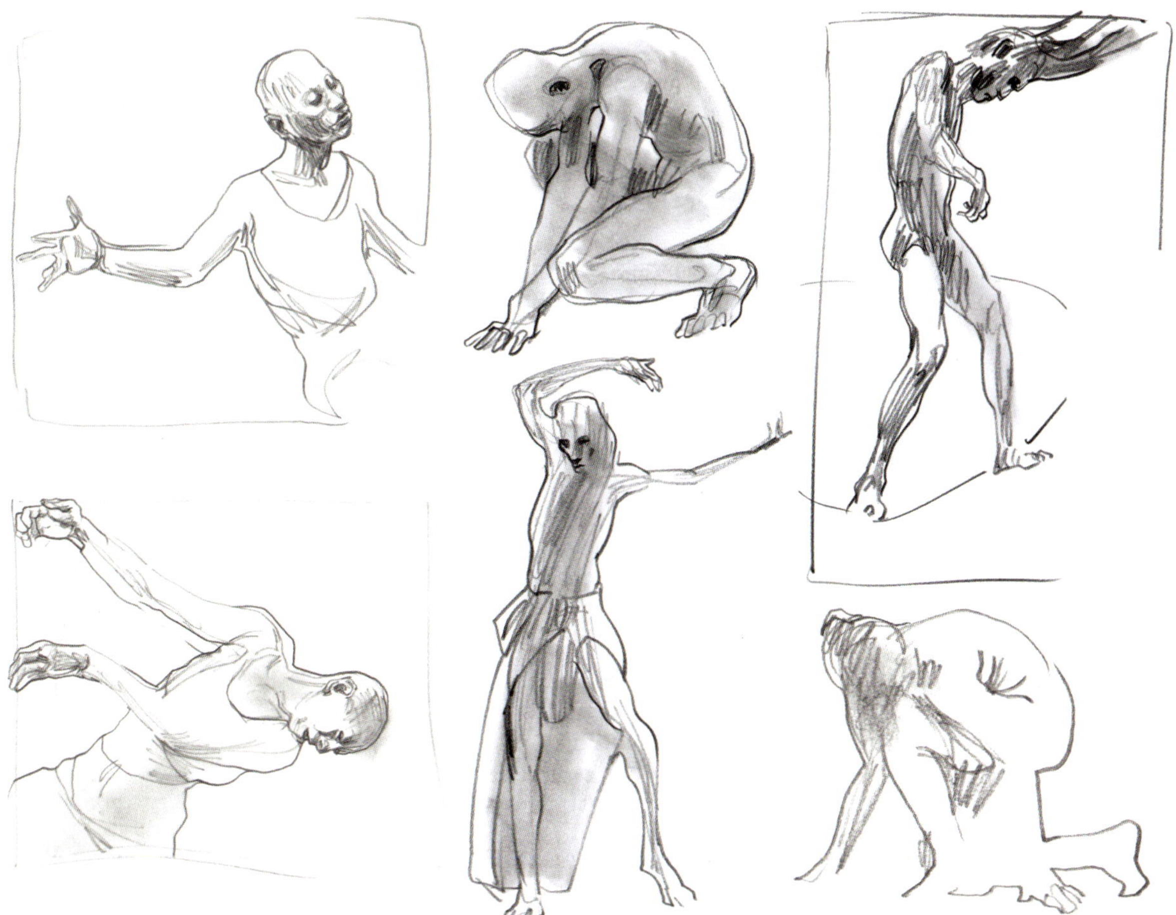

Drawing movement

When you see a fish, you don't think about its scales, you think about the speed of its movement, its sparkling and brilliant body, seen through the water.
—Constantin Brâncusi

Drawing the living implies representing movement, introducing the time that elapses into your image. This exercise requires a certain speed of execution, which can be seconded by your memory or imagination.

YOUR TURN

Choose the most practical support according to the conditions, outdoors or in your workspace: a small pocket notebook can do the trick. Prefer techniques that allow superimposition: graphite leads, crayons, greasy or dry pastels, etc.

In a café, draw people at the counter or sitting nearby. Draw your pet, fish in an aquarium, your loved ones—as long as they don't pose!

Feel free to continue drawing from memory, to recompose your image by using additional information: a school of fish will help you draw a single one in motion! You can also keep the same support as long as possible by overlaying your indications. You will thus keep up to date the passage of time, the history of all the poses, like chronophotography.

IF YOU HAVE THE TIME

• Take sheets of tracing paper with you. Draw by superimposing them and return to the previous layers if necessary. Design an image from this transparency effect.

Go and see

Étienne-Jules Marey (1830–1904), Les *chronophotographies*
Alexey Titarenko (born in 1962)
Claire Wendling (born in 1967), *The Desk* collection

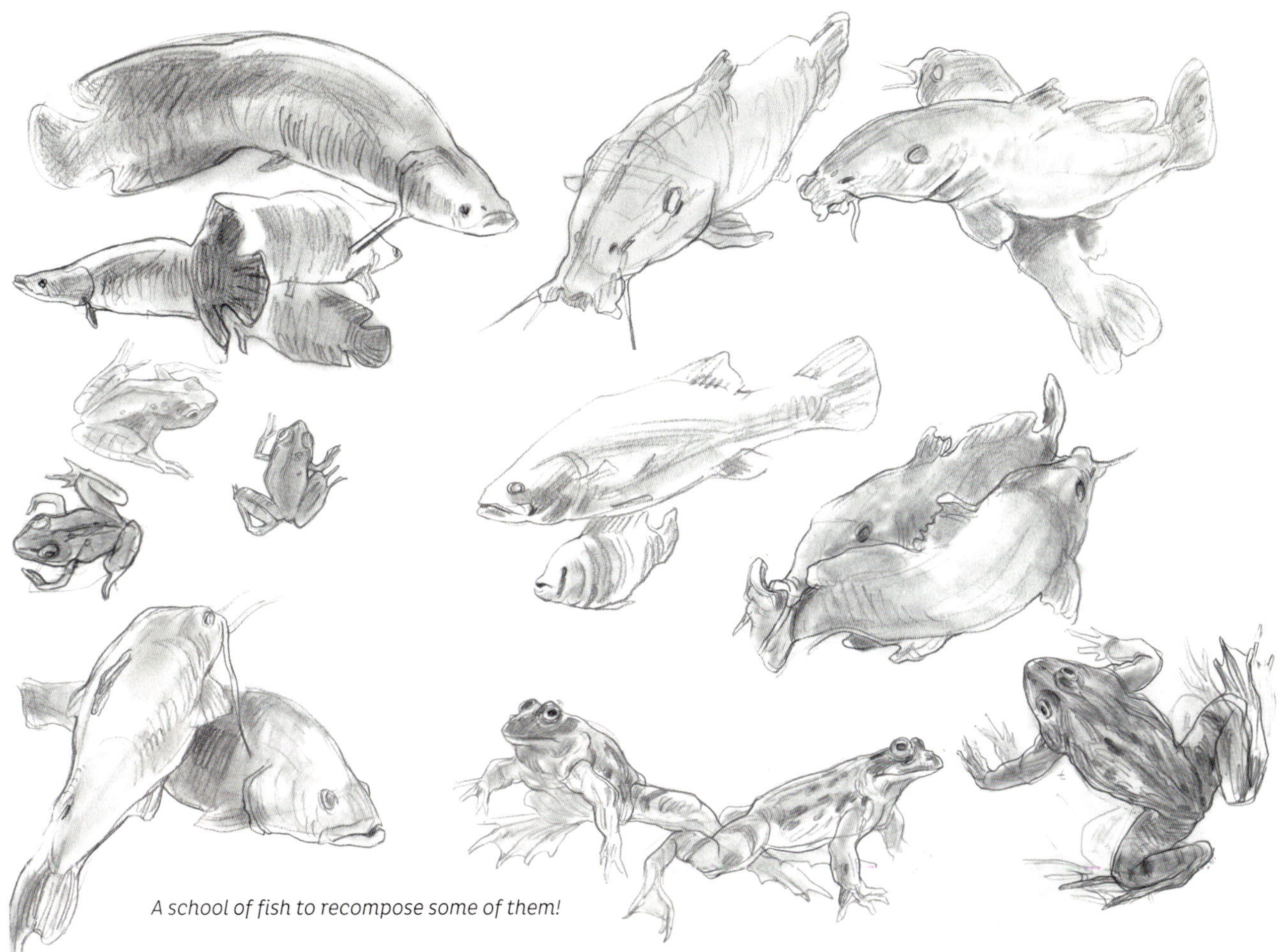

A school of fish to recompose some of them!

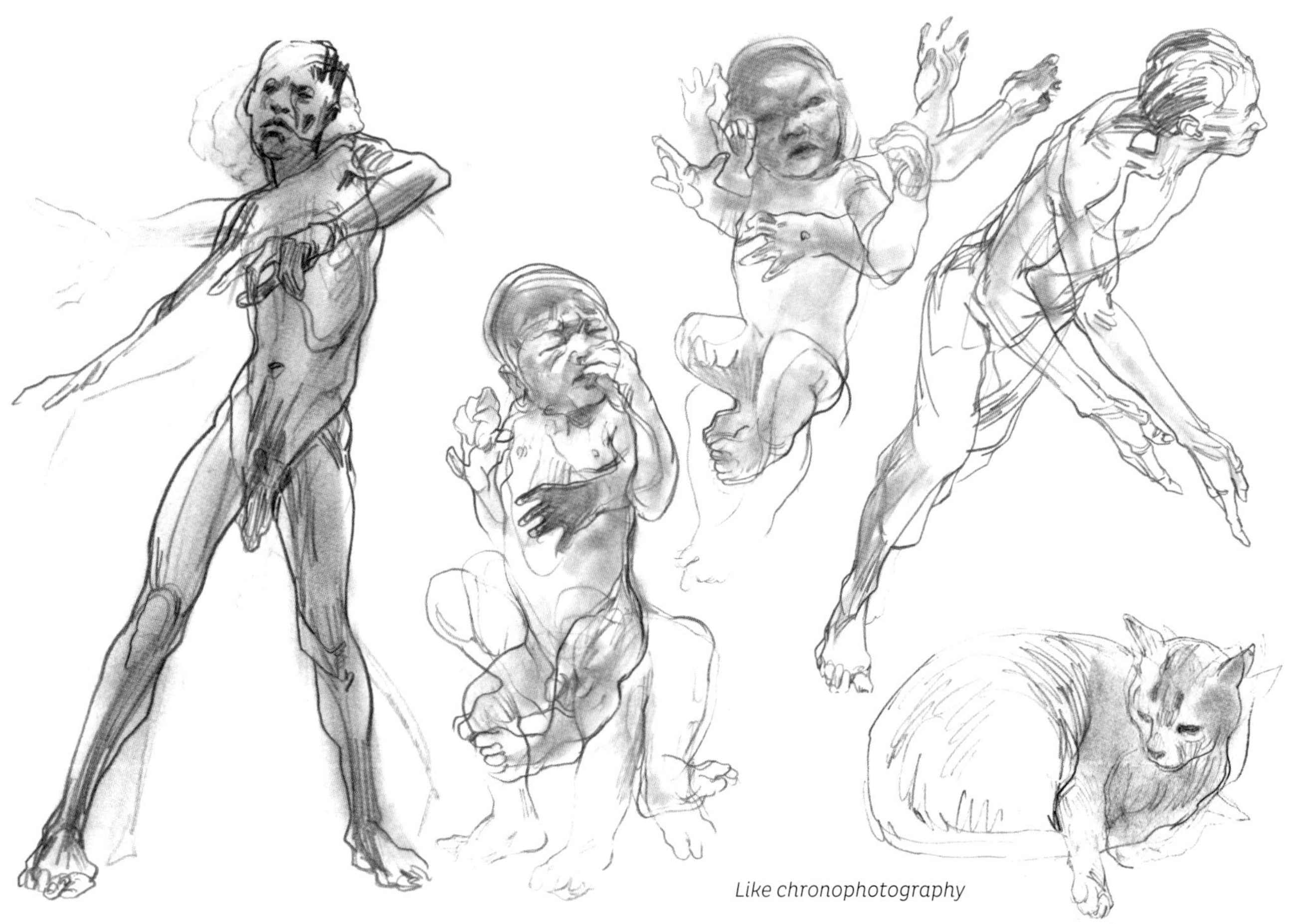

Like chronophotography

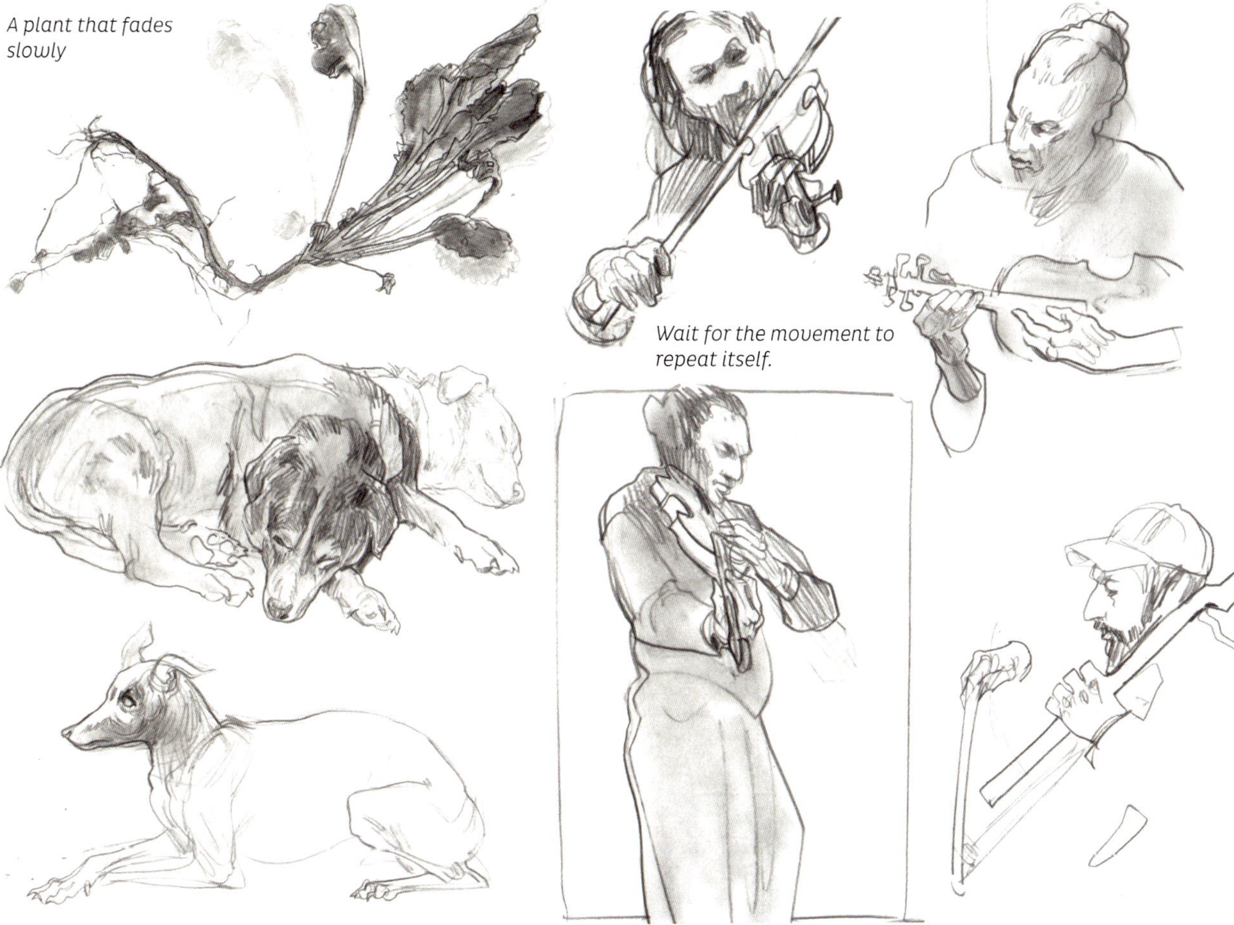

A plant that fades slowly

Wait for the movement to repeat itself.

Daily travel diary

Art is what makes life more interesting than art.
—Robert Filliou

A travel diary is a genre in itself. Many artists have made it their privileged "place" of expression. It includes the association of text and images, drawn, painted, or photographic. It is the space of mixed techniques, whose choice depends on mood, encounters, and variable comfort conditions. These notebooks reflect a period, travels, experiences . . . In all cases, it is a slice of life.

YOUR TURN

Use a notebook with a number of pages—about twenty, for example—adapted to the time you think you have. Don't use one that is too large to give yourself the satisfaction of filling each page. We recommend a practical format, such as A5.

Keep notes and drawings, of your daily life. Don't be afraid to consider the little things in life, the ordinary moments: that's the challenge! The idea is to recognize a creative potential and transform through the daily practice of drawing. A cup of coffee on the table, a sleeping cat, a pair of shoes, the view from your window, some photos or drawings of your workplace, a coffee break, some sketches in the street or on public transport, goodies from the market spread out on the table, the portrait of friends, self-portraits . . . In color or not, depending on your sensitivity.

IF YOU HAVE THE TIME

• A diary is also a small portable workshop, the place where you store all your research, experiments, and finds. This accumulated material can become a source of inspiration.

• Reuse one or more of these sketches, redrawing them in a larger format (A3 minimum). You will therefore have to expand it, reinvest it, and draw on your memory, without being afraid of transforming it.

Go and see

Titouan Lamazou (born in 1955)
Emmanuel Prost (born in 1968)
Alice Audebert (born in 1986)

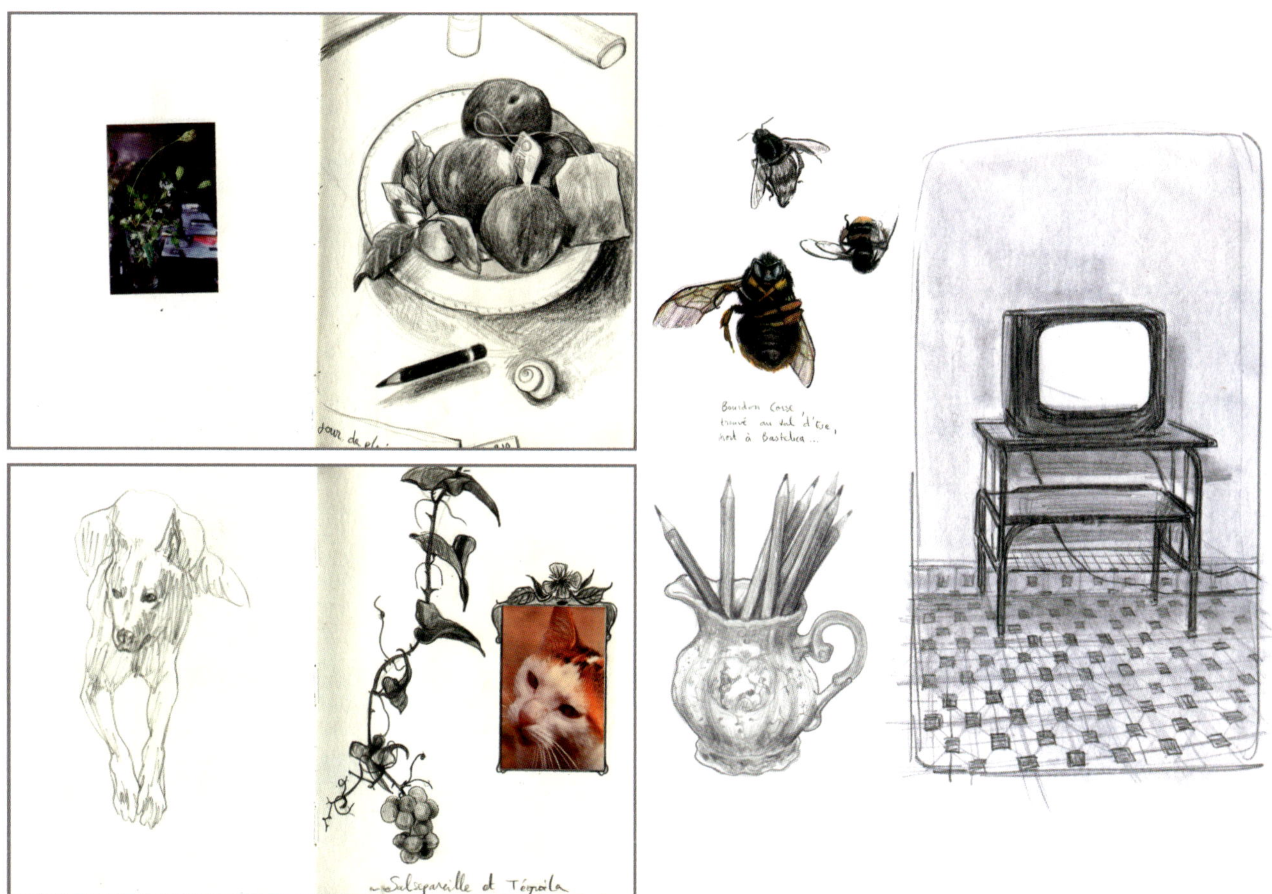
Bourdon Corse,
trouvé au val d'Ese,
mort à Bastelica...
Salsepareille et Téquila

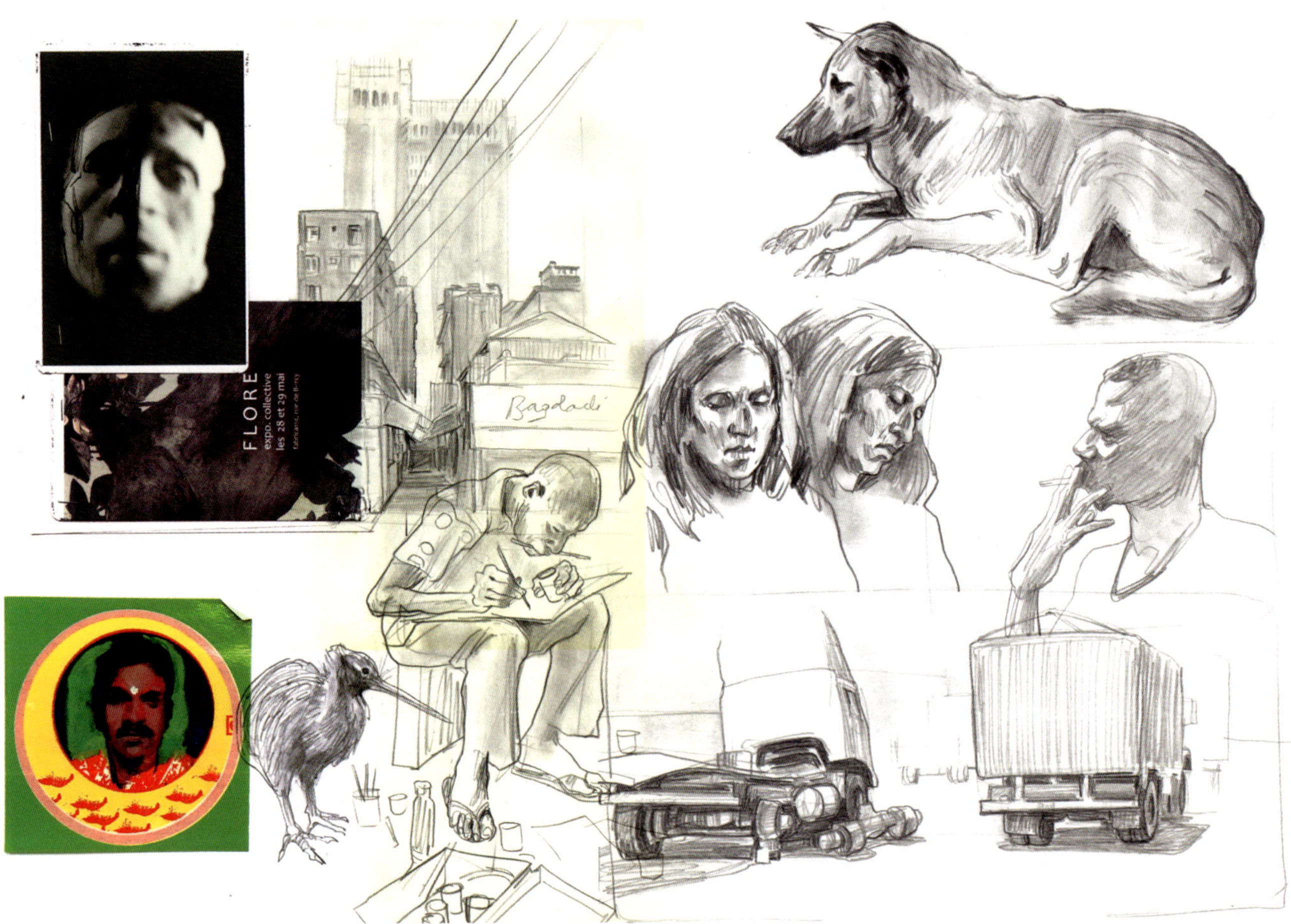
FLORE
expo. collective
les 28 et 29 mai
Bagdadi

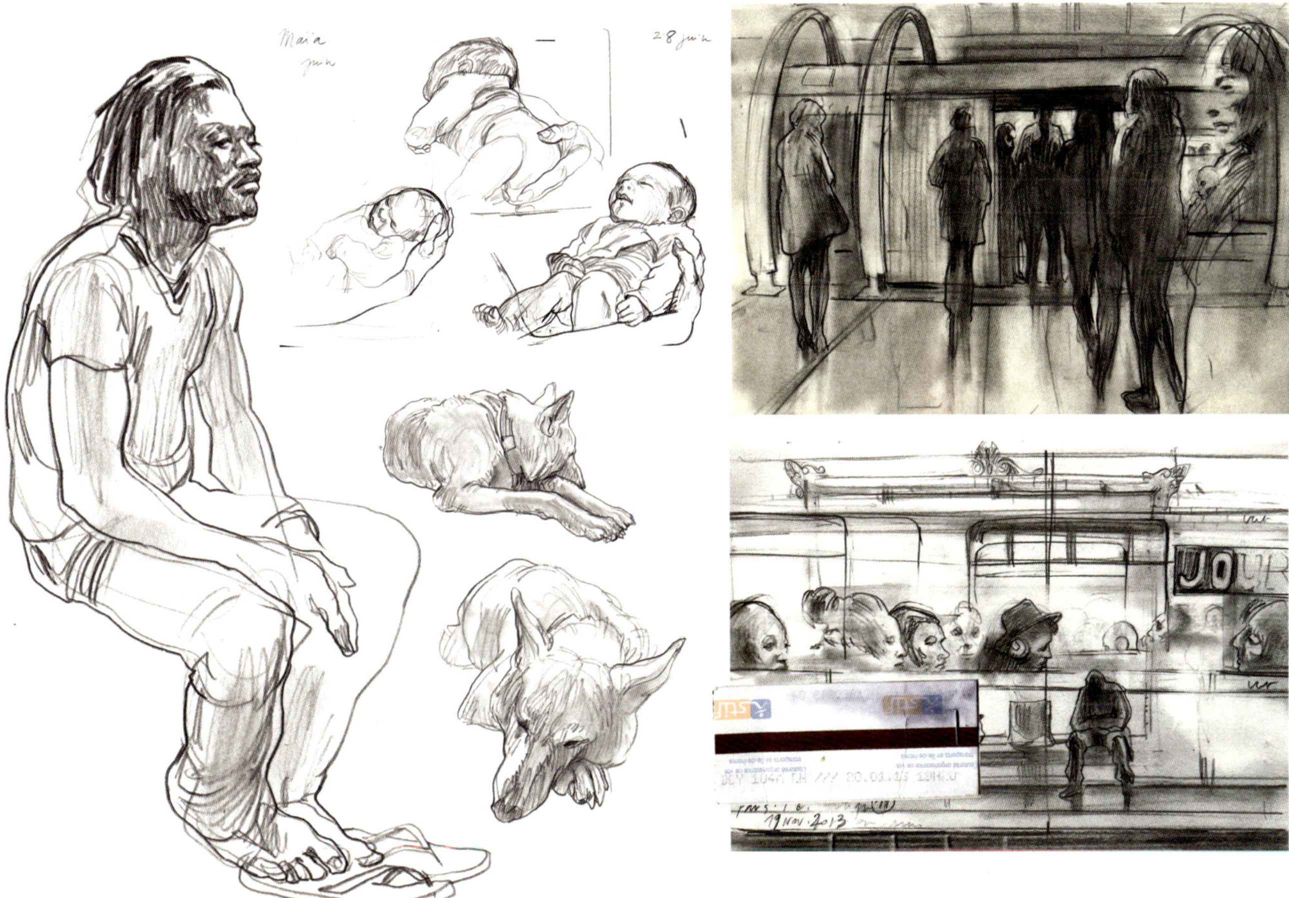
28 juin
19 NOV. 2013

Intention sketch

The desire to photograph, to see what we see. The fact that the picture reveals what's in your head.
—Sarah Moon

The idea this week is to work from the beginning, to define with the help of a small drawing, diagram, or "intention sketch" what touches us, challenges us, and motivates us for a more in-depth drawing.

It is a question of drawing a project with a minimum of indications, for a hypothetical longer, more elaborate drawing. A plan of action, in a way. Indeed, if we move away from a simple reproduction, we are quickly confronted with a multitude of possible biases. You will execute a drawing for yourself; it must be as close as possible to your vision of it.

YOUR TURN

This exercise may seem similar to that of week 35, but it is not the same thing! It is not just a simplification; it is to give an account, to show, to affirm a synthetic vision connected to your sensitivity, to your understanding of the motive.

All supports and techniques are possible and can be mixed.

Multiply the sketches in front of the same pattern: all these drawings will reflect different biases. Allow yourself two minutes per sketch. A photographic support can be stimulating without limiting your expression.

IF YOU HAVE THE TIME

• Find at least three different intent sketches for a given topic. Transform your model based on one of the previously developed sketches and deform it to take it where you want it.

Go and see

Constantin Brâncusi (1876–1957)
René Gruau (1909–2004)
Jean-Marc Reiser (1941–1983)

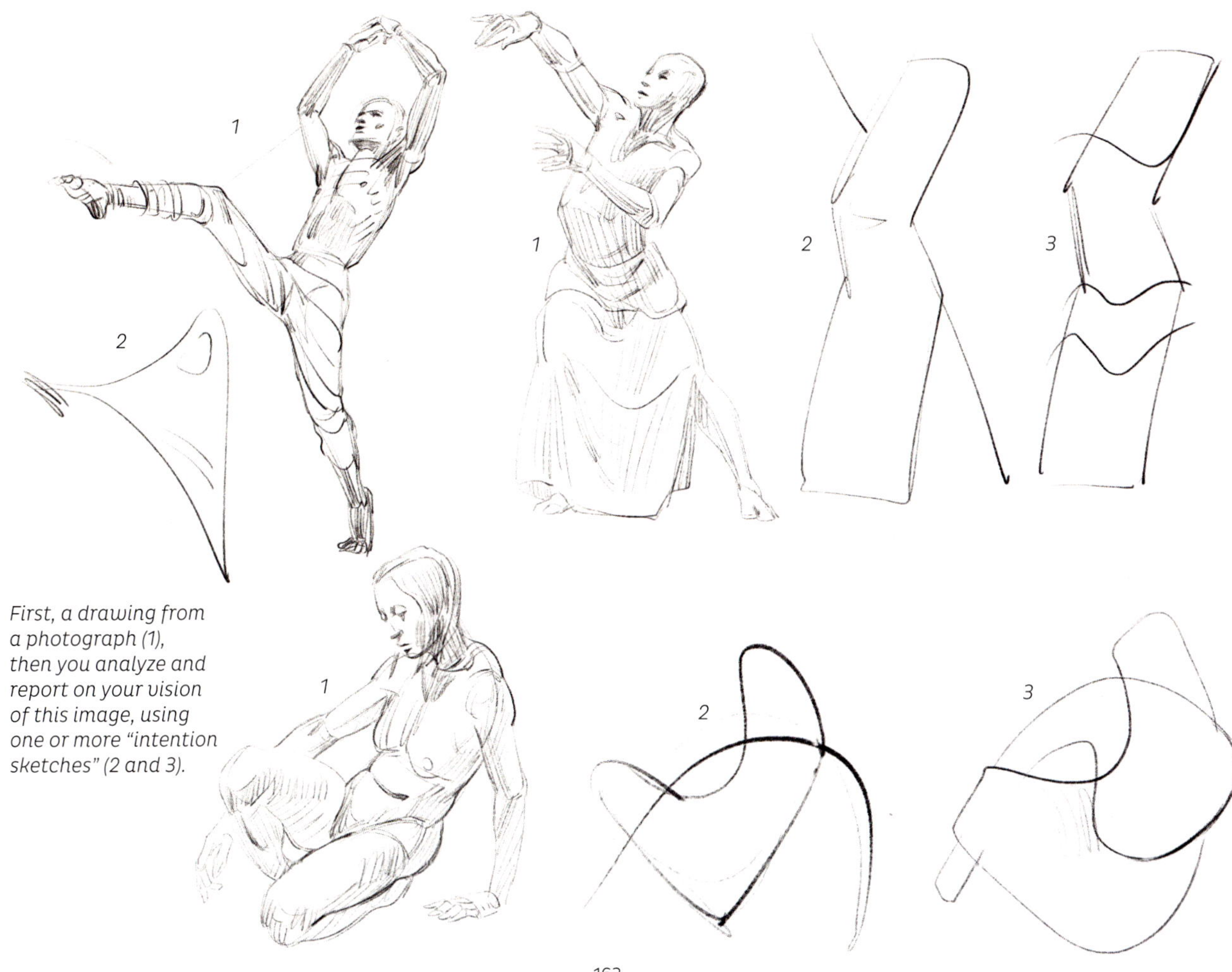

First, a drawing from a photograph (1), then you analyze and report on your vision of this image, using one or more "intention sketches" (2 and 3).

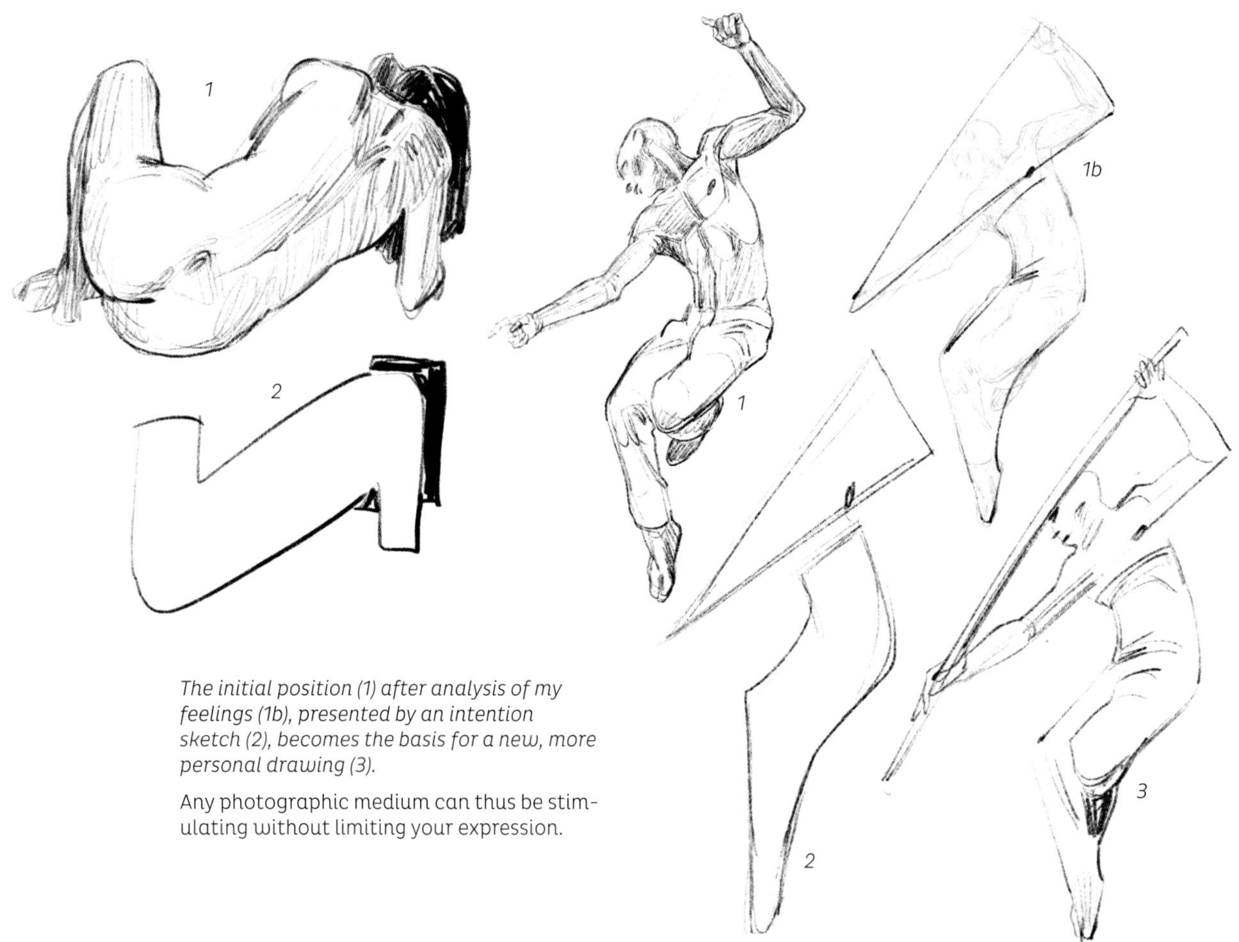

The initial position (1) after analysis of my feelings (1b), presented by an intention sketch (2), becomes the basis for a new, more personal drawing (3).

Any photographic medium can thus be stimulating without limiting your expression.

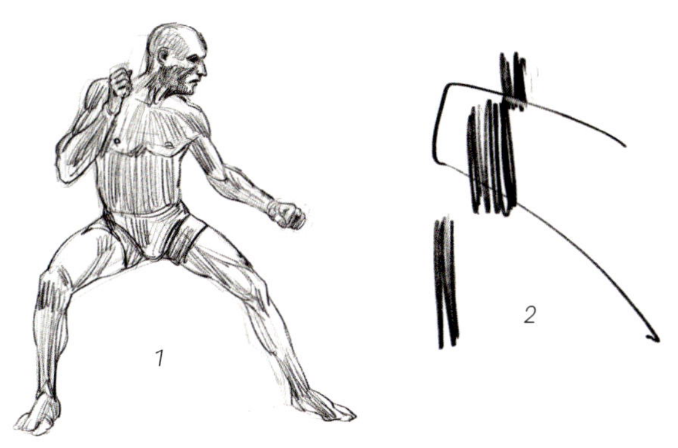

The initial position (1), followed by two intention sketches (2 and 3). One of them (3) supports the transformed proposal (4).

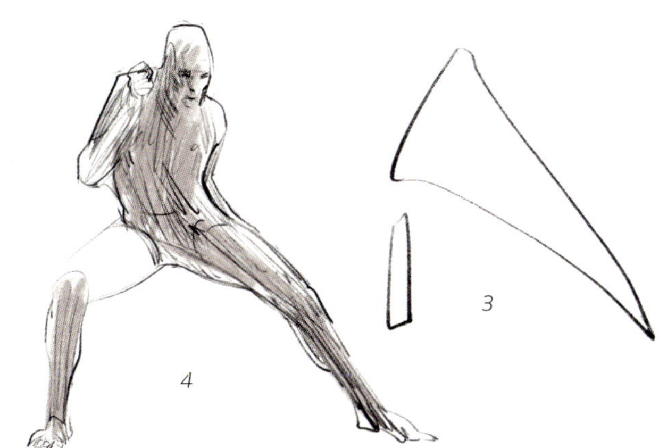

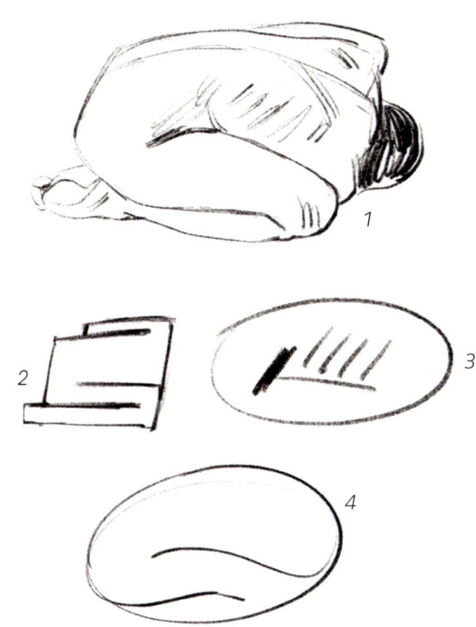

Initial installation (1) followed by three intention sketches (2, 3, and 4). The last one (4) is the sketch of the drawing below (5).

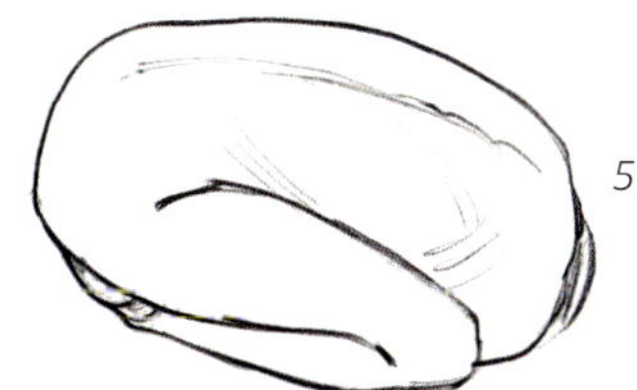

Inventories

Small things, trivialities of everyday life, insignificance of days, where the meaning rests abandoned. God lies in the details.
—Marie Depussé, *Dieu gît dans les détails*

To approach the theme of an inventory is to confront the diversity of what seems similar to us. Drawing things develops attention to details and particularities; an inventory will be an opportunity to show it.

YOUR TURN

Think of a "thing"—an object, a fruit or vegetable, a natural or manufactured element—that you like and that you have in several different copies at home. If you are a little bit of a collector, it will make it easier for you; if not, you can use pebbles, fruit and vegetables, toys. A minimum of ten models will allow you to compose a full page, in color or black and white, which will give you an overview of what brings them together while distinguishing them.

Use the tool that you think best suits your desires and your model; work by juxtaposing the objects until you fill your page with them. It is also a composition work where you will ensure that each element is properly "stored" or, on the contrary, that there is an assumed disorder on the page.

IF YOU HAVE THE TIME

- Expand your collection with other inventories.
- Make imaginary collections. Try to remember the shape of things without looking at them.

Go and see

Joëlle Jolivet (born in 1965), *Presque tout*
Rachel Pedder Smith (born in 1975)
Guillaume Trouillard (born in 1980), *Welcome*

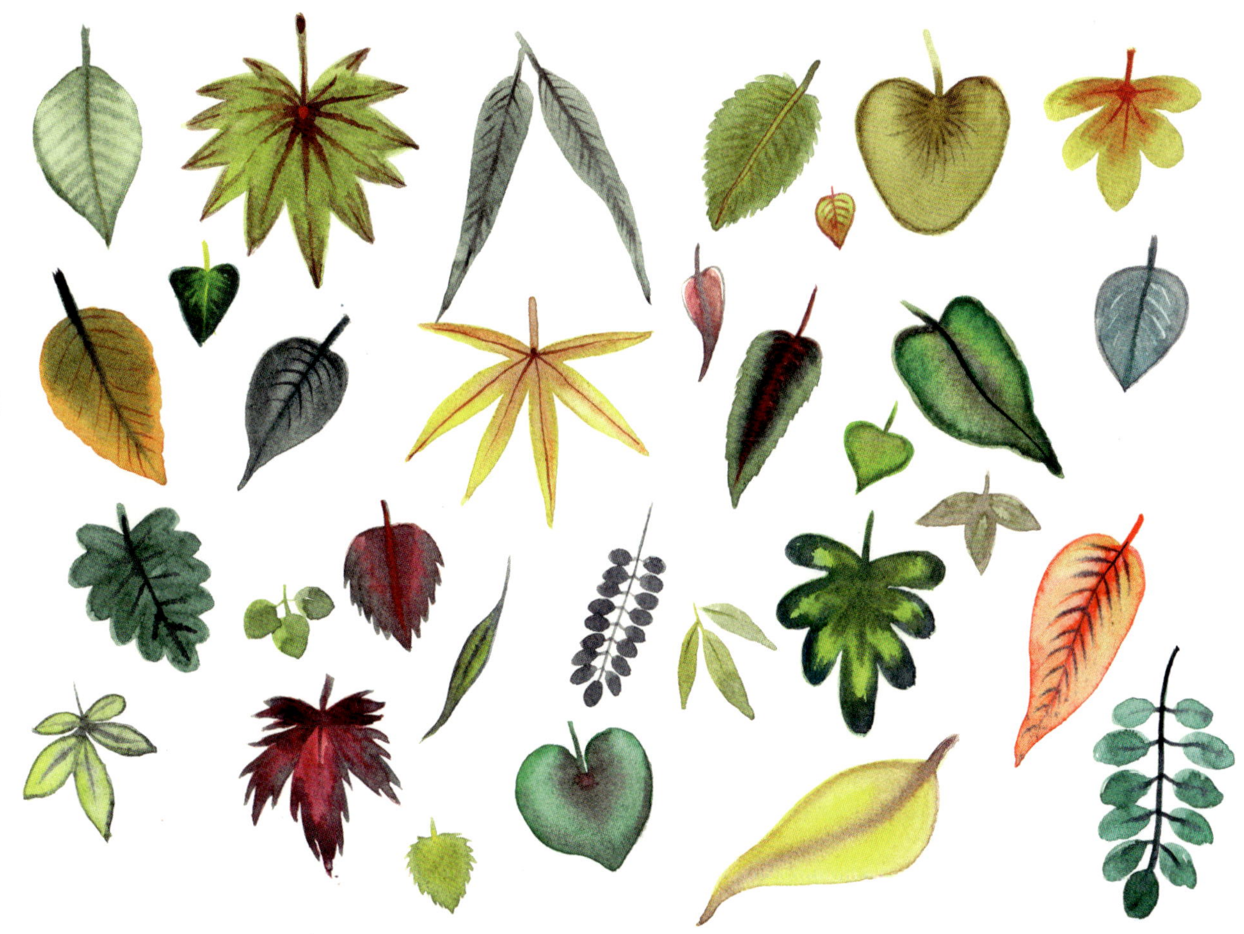

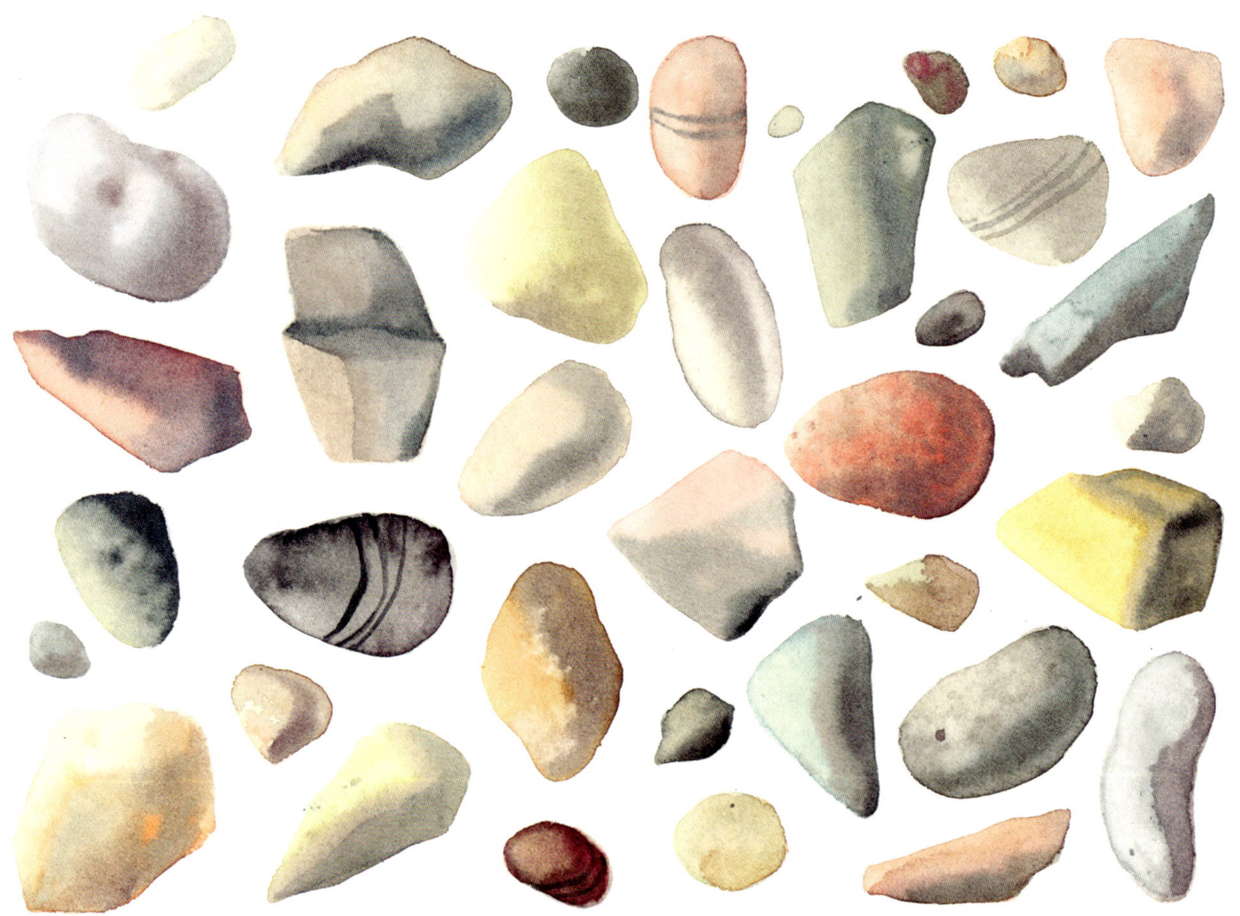

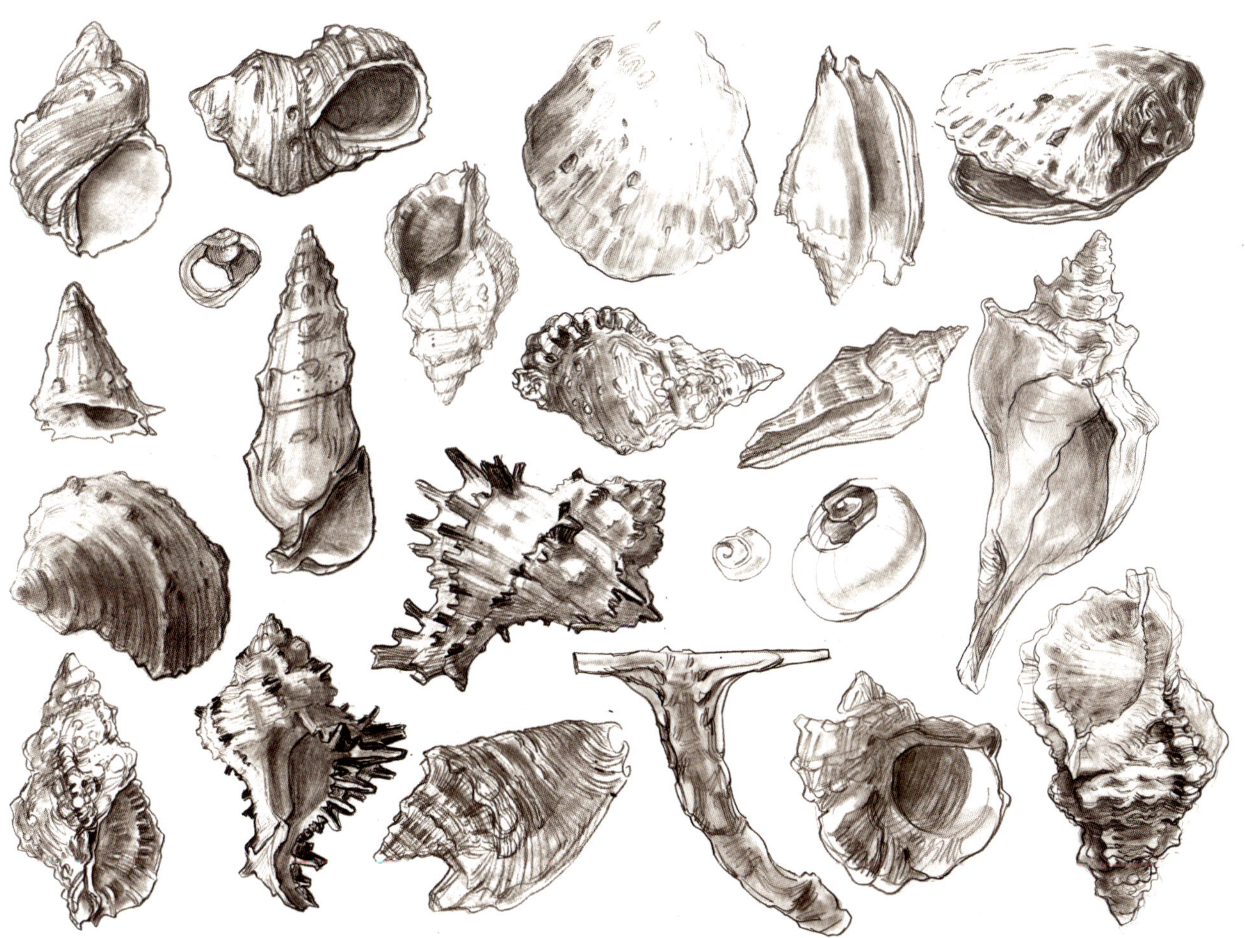

Characters

What art is first and foremost, and what it remains above all, is a game.
—Georges Bataille, *Lascaux or ou la naissance de l'art*

This exercise focuses on graphic expression. You will use your tool as a musician who gets numerous sounds and intensities of sound from just one instrument. These variations should be controlled and allow you to to conduct the eye of a hypothetical observer. You will play on these subtleties, graphic effects, and exaggerations in order to extract from your image a strong, obvious intention. A little like cartoonists, don't hesitate to "force the line."

YOUR TURN

Use A4 sheets (minimum) and as many different tools as possible (hard and soft, dry and greasy). Have a set of images of various animals (insects, mollusks, fish, birds, mammals, etc.). Preferably select strong, contrasting characters (feathers, hair, claws, beaks, etc.) and spectacular attitudes. Choose the most appropriate tool or tools for each animal.

Force the line; try to translate your feelings about this animal as if you had it in front of you, or, better yet, as if you had to physically imitate it.

IF YOU HAVE THE TIME

• Repeat the exercise, using photographs of actors. Portray the inner character of the persona played.

Go and see

André Franquin (1924–1997), the comic book *Idées noires*
Manu Larcenet (born in 1969), the comic book *Blast*
Kitty Crowther (born in 1970)

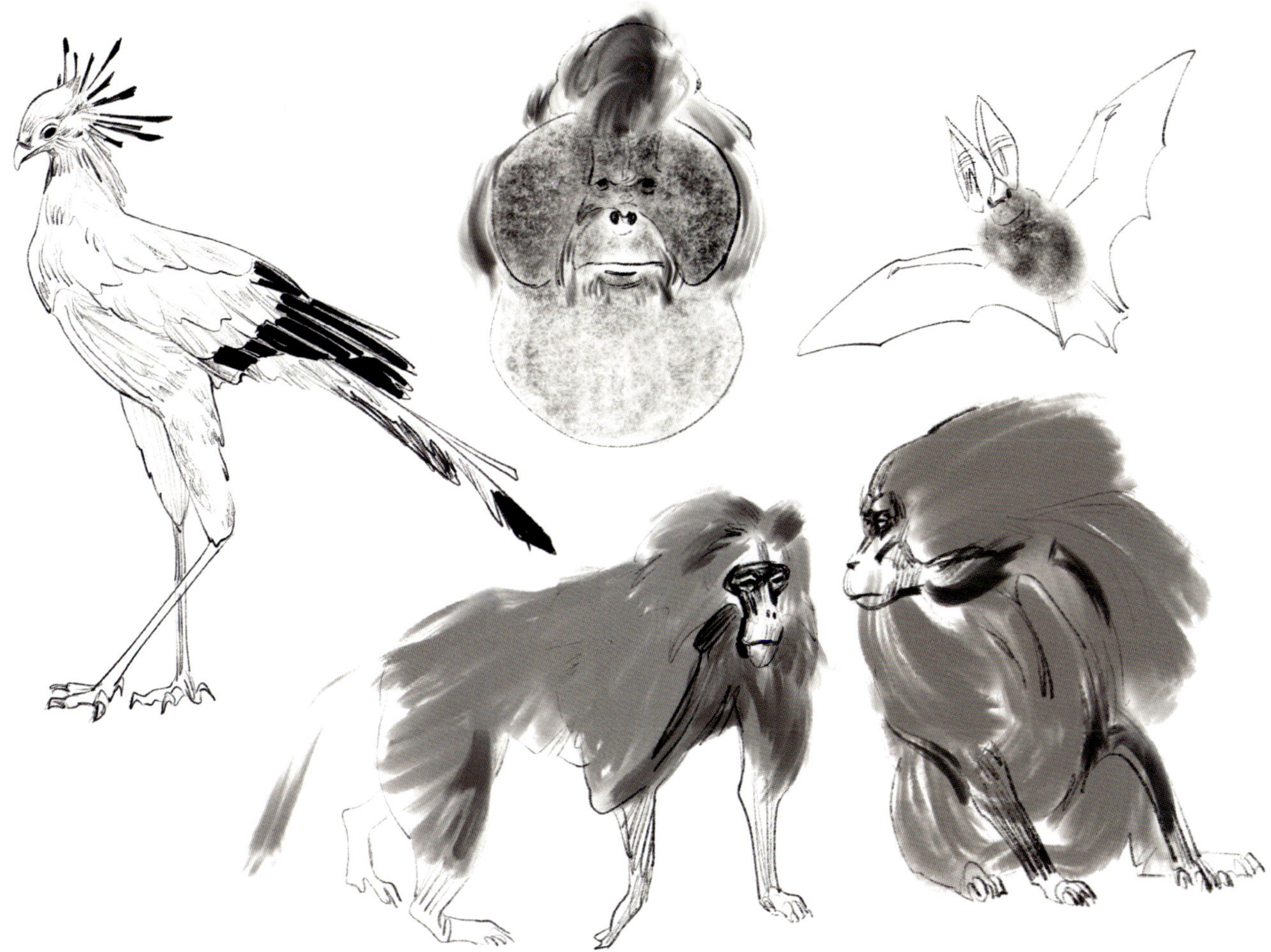

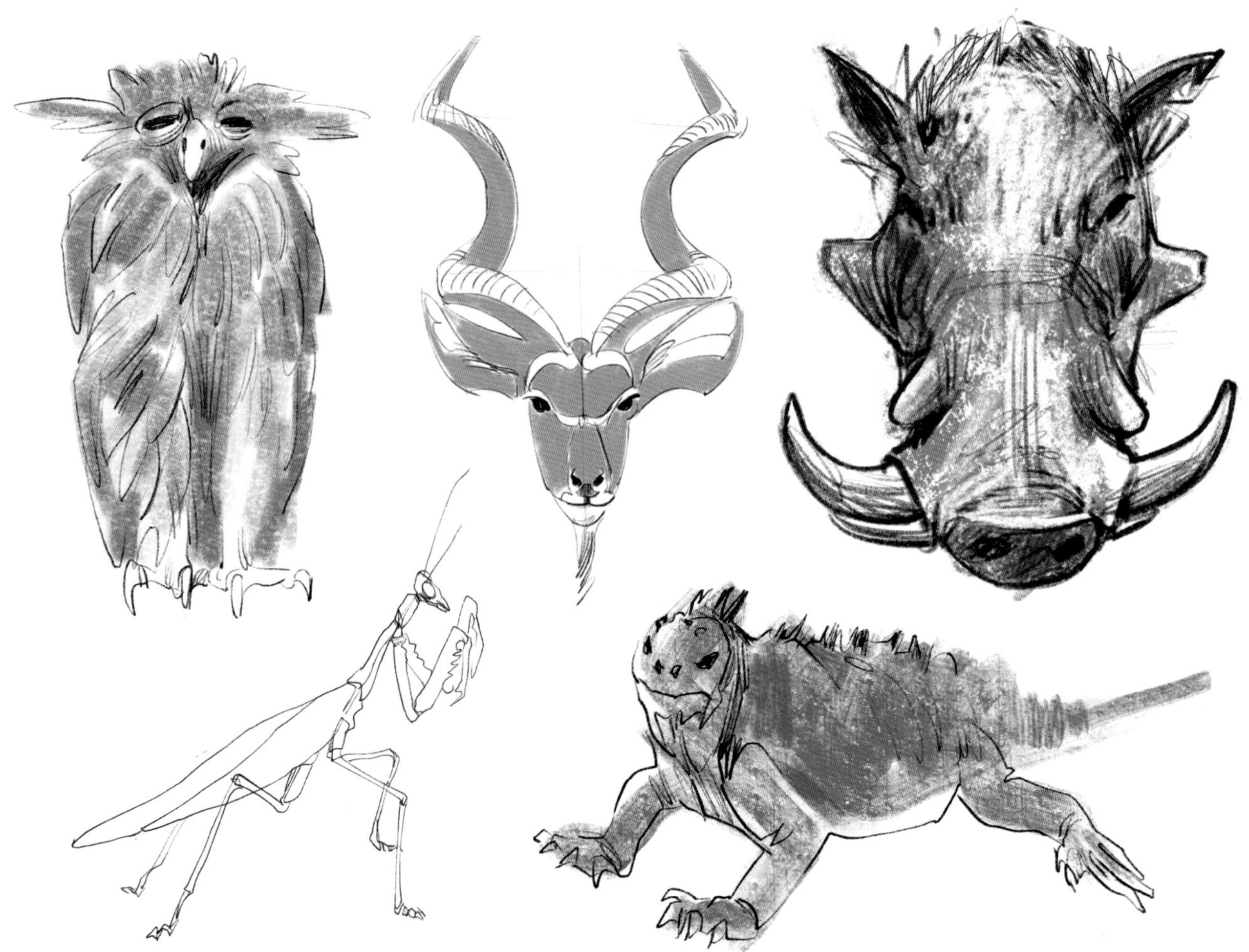

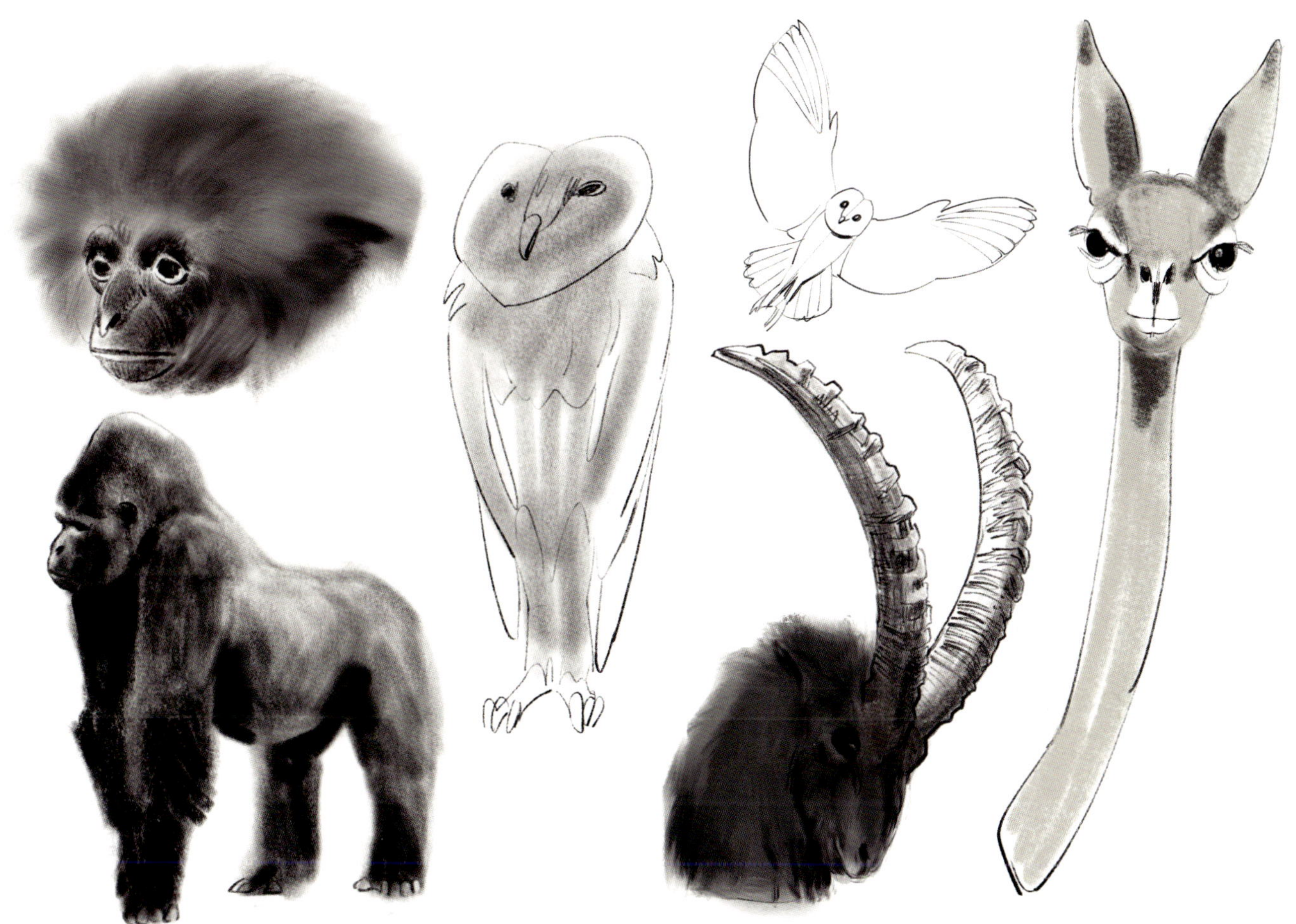

Imaginary creatures

Those who dream by day are cognizant of many things which escape those who dream only by night.
—Edgar Allan Poe, *Grotesque and Serious Stories*

Building on the previous week's experience, invent fantastic beings.

YOUR TURN

Choose a technique that will allow you to do big markings: paint, ink, charcoal . . .

Let chance play a role by placing a spot randomly on the paper. You can even avoid looking at your sheet when doing this: this will stop you from deciding what shape the blot will take. Now, observe this shape and try to distinguish a head (or two!). Once you have drawn it, it will be easier for you to imagine the rest of the body.

When you "see" your creature, all that remains is to make it visible to others. It is a question of making it emerge from the form by contrast. Add shadows and lights to evoke the texture of its body (hair? skin? scales?); give an expression and an attitude to this creature, initially born out of chance and what you could see in it.

IF YOU HAVE THE TIME

- Expand the family by giving your creatures brothers and sisters, grandparents, and children!
- Put all these little people in a setting that suits them.

Go and see

Didier Hamey (born in 1962)
Bobby Chiu (born in 1969)
Marie Boralevi (born in 1986)

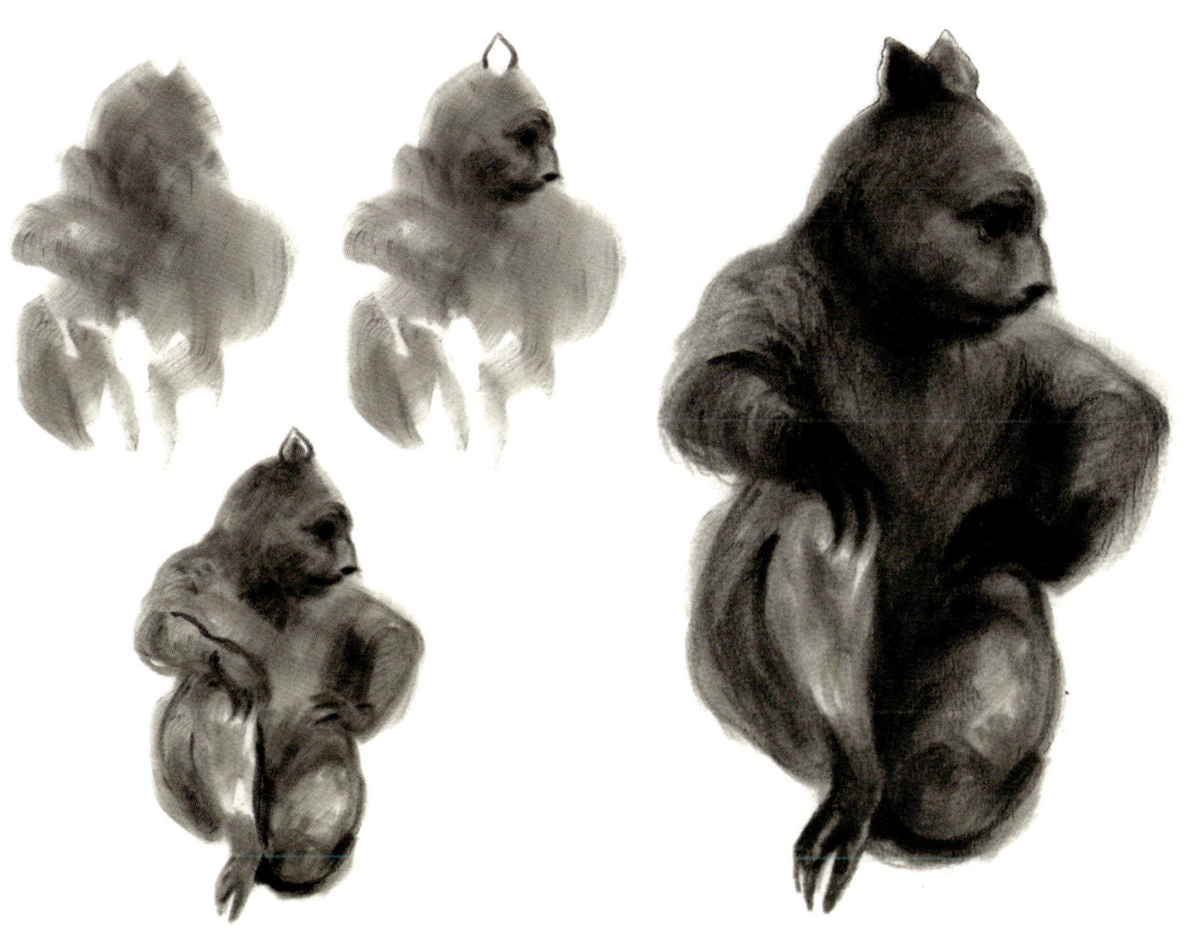

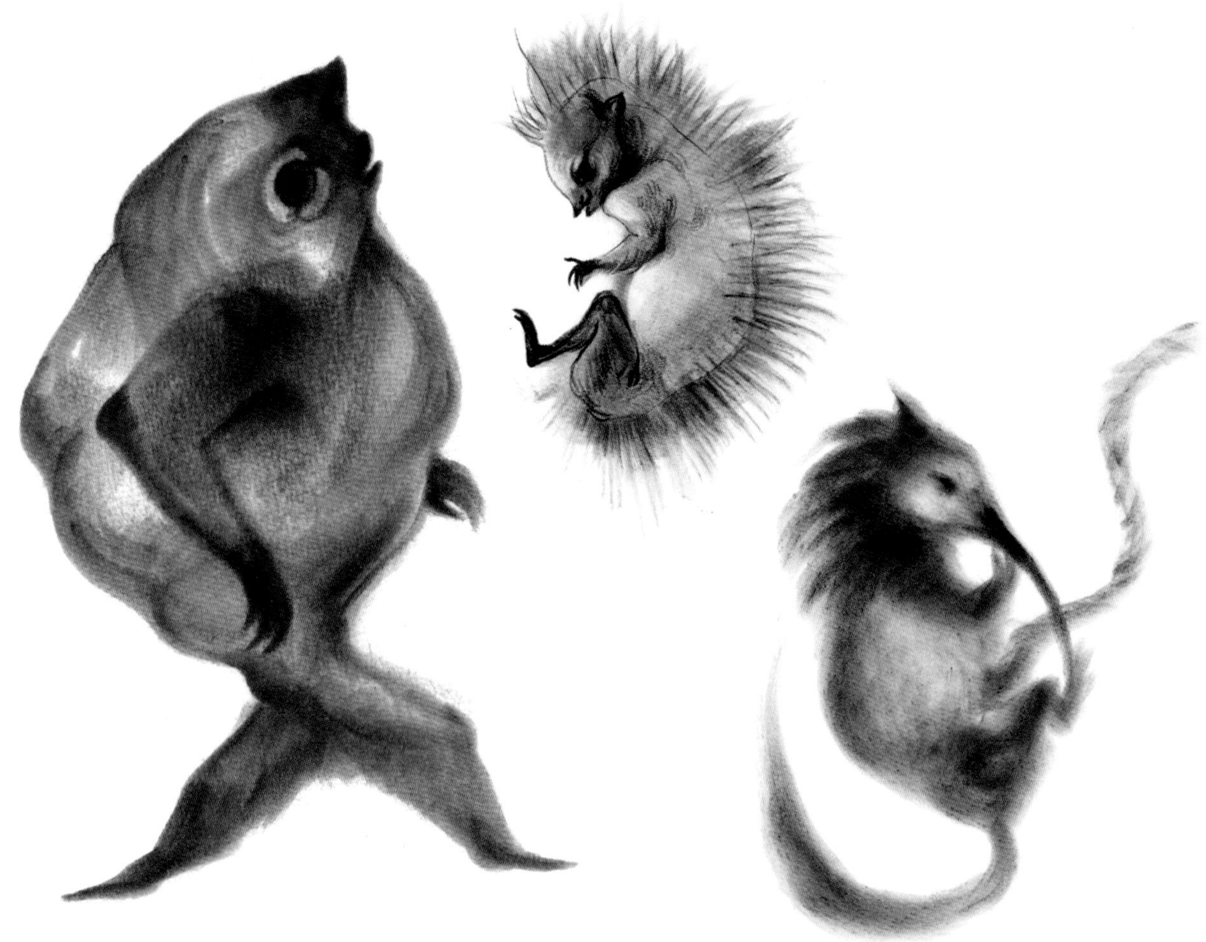

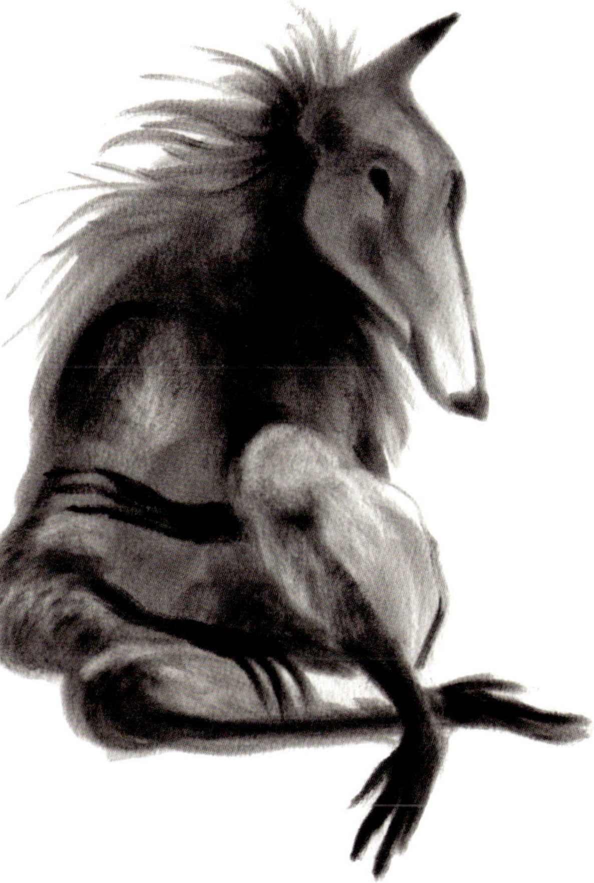

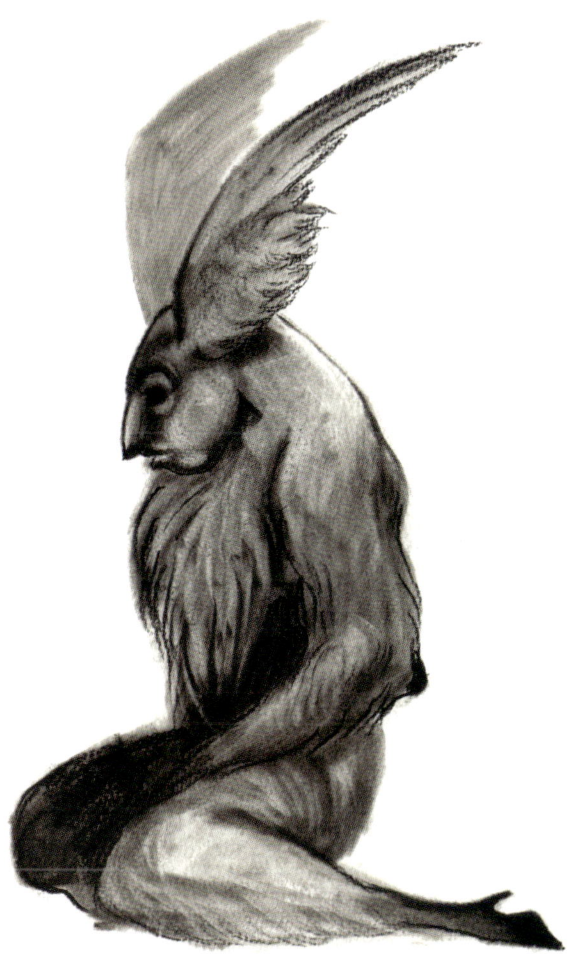

In the twilight

Every twilight is double, dawn and evening. This formidable chrysalis, which is called the universe, forever shudders to feel both the agony of the caterpillar and the awakening of the butterfly.
—Victor Hugo, *Philosophie, commencement d'un livre*

This particular time of day will be an excellent pretext to translate a psychological state into an image. It is an in-between time that generates all kinds of fantasies and emotions. Be inspired by Victor Hugo's sentence to feel its full depth.

We can portray semidarkness in black and white or in color. Twilight is also a particular contrast to translate: the tones are soft and dark at the same time. The lines fade, and it is only a question of undefined passages between one gray and another. In terms of color, blues are particularly important and intense and seem to color everything they touch.

YOUR TURN

You can use the tools of your choice.

Start with a twilight outing and take pictures. They will help you synthesize what you have before you.

Let yourself be touched by this atmosphere before making an image. Creation takes on its full scope when it draws its inspiration from its source in reality or in the memory of an experiment. We draw with what we see, what we think, and what we feel. Physical perceptions have a big role to play.

And you may have already noticed how much drawing increases our ability to see and feel, and vice versa.

IF YOU HAVE THE TIME

• Write a short story based on the image you have created, and continue it with other illustrations.

Go and see

Léon Spilliaert (1881–1946)
Anne Gorouben (born in 1959)
Aron Wiesenfeld (born in 1972)

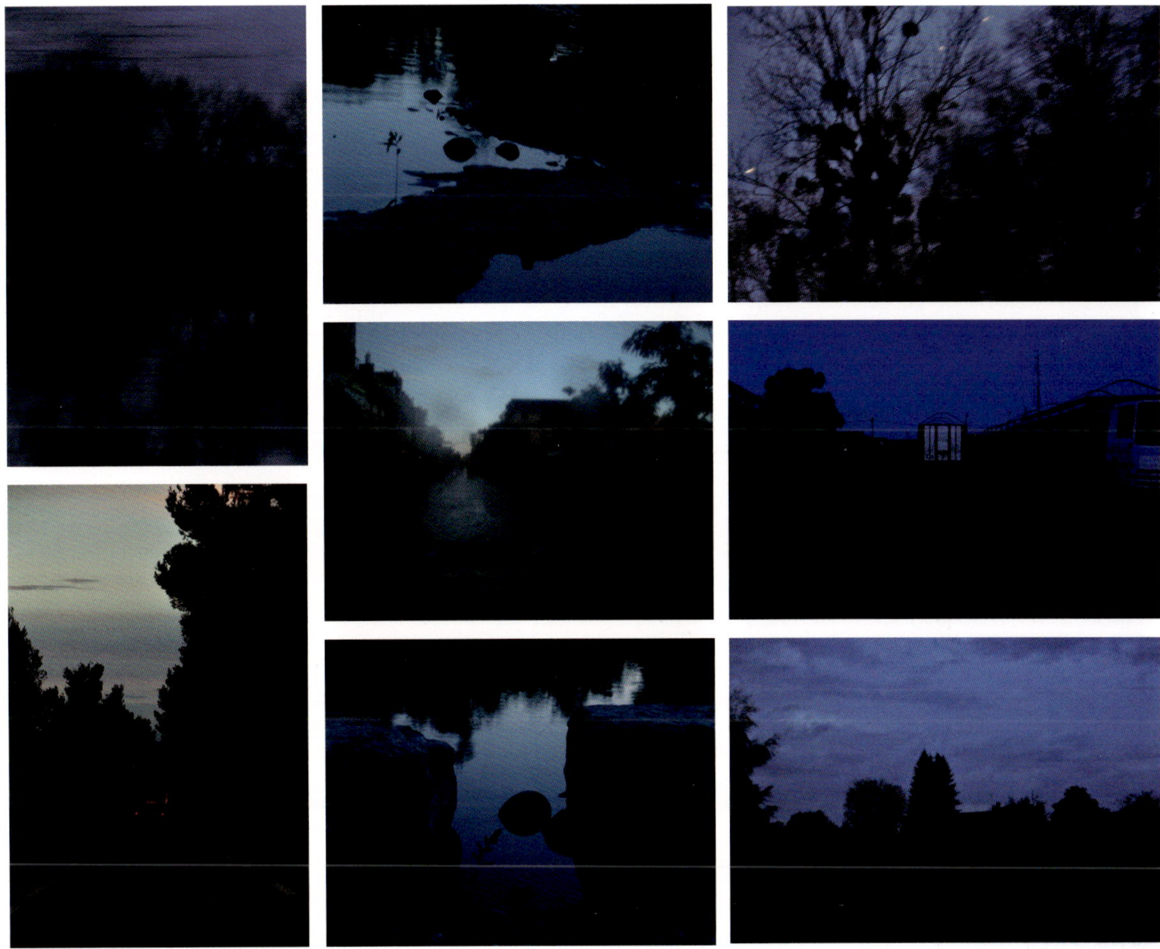

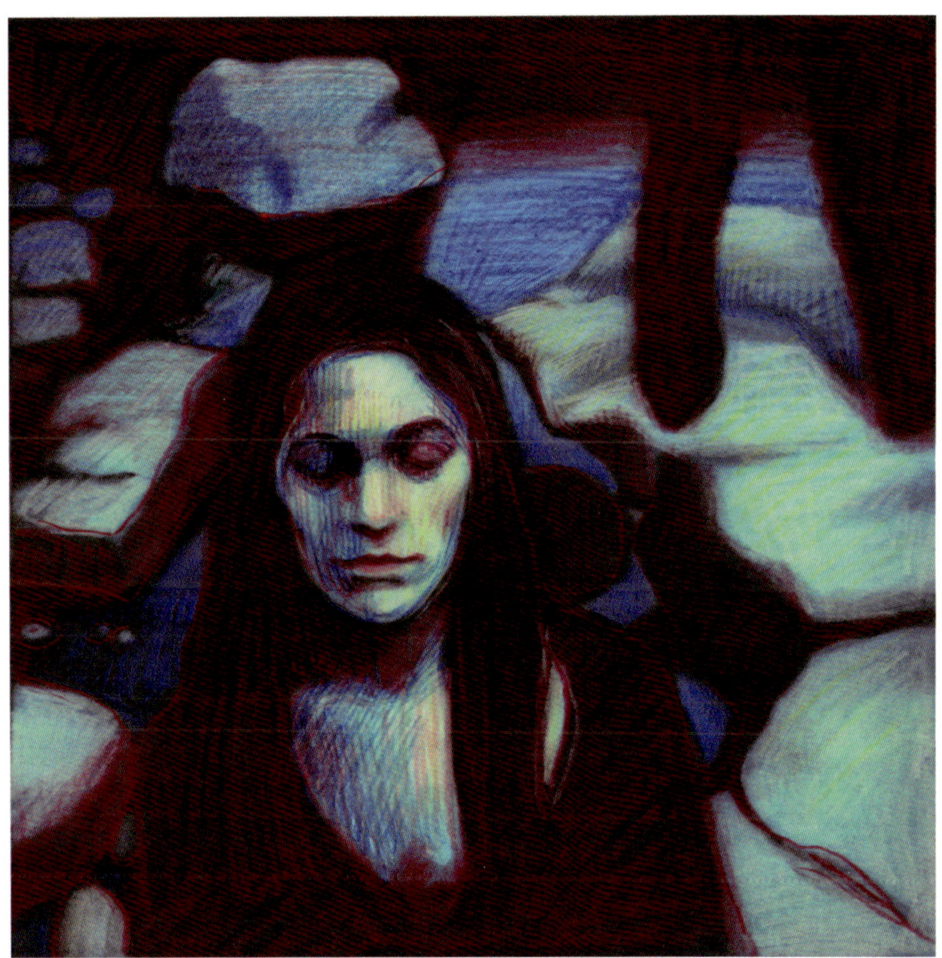

Maps

It is all very well to copy what one sees, but it is far better to draw what one now only sees in one's memory.
—Edgar Degas

To be useful, a map must be the schematic condensation of information, a perspective on the world. This week's exercise will work on the transformation of reality through our memory, our experience. It will testify, once again, to the necessary simplification in the face of the complexity of the world, partly offset by the multiple games of our imagination, a mixture of our knowledge, habits, experiences, intuitions, and prejudices. An image can testify to all of these phenomena at the same time.

YOUR TURN

Use a large format (raisin, demi-raisin) and the tools of your choice. Don't be afraid to mix techniques.

Represent the map of your daily space, encompassing the places that are most meaningful to you, your most frequent movements. Use text, colors, or collage if you wish. Don't be afraid of subjective scale relationships, the disproportions in distances, architectural elements or other landmarks. However, try to translate a certain reality.

Then map miniature spaces to the scale of an insect: the end of a path, the corner of a table.

IF YOU HAVE THE TIME

- Try other types of mapping: maps of time, emotions, relationships, etc.

Go and see

Lee Bontecou (born in 1931)
Sophie Ristelhueber (born in 1949), *Fait*, 1992
Mathias Poisson (born in 1978)

1. My daily travels in the city, represented from memory, without any concern for scale.

In the margin, the displacement line.

2. Light map, cutting my house into four levels and delimiting areas of natural light

3. Main daily trips in the same house. Three colors corresponding to three levels.

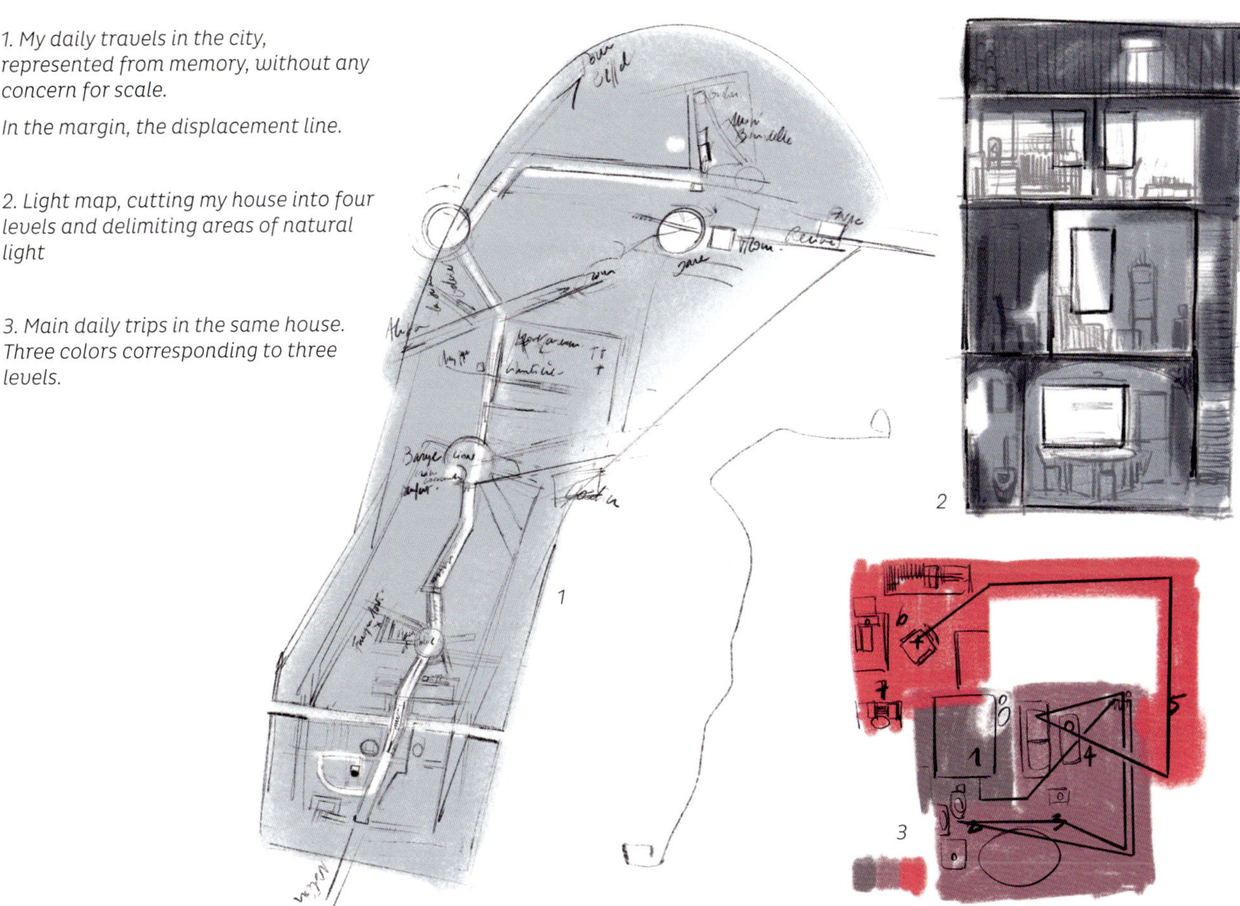

1 and 2. Plan of a natural rock layout after a river flood

3. Inverted map (south is at the top) of my travels, without concern for scale or geographical accuracy, made from memory

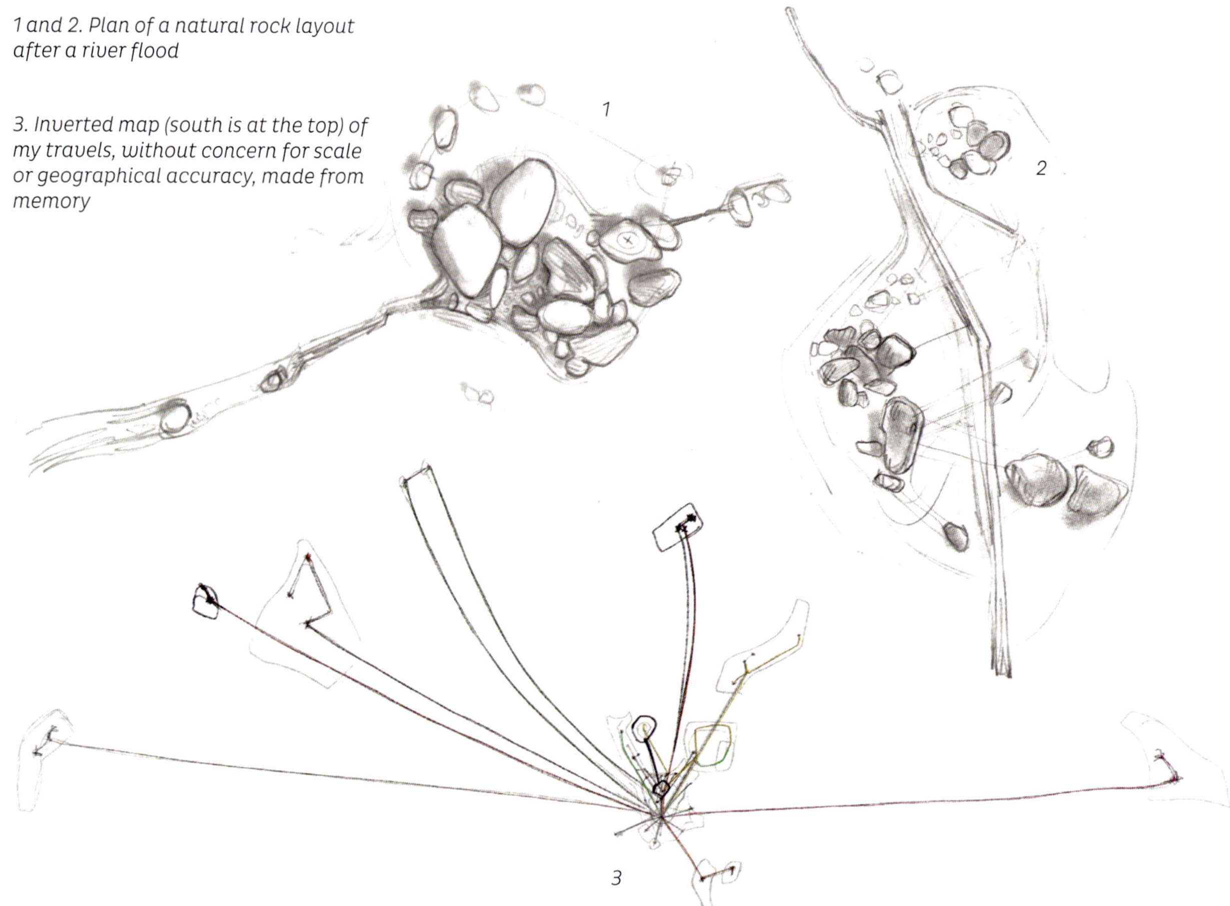

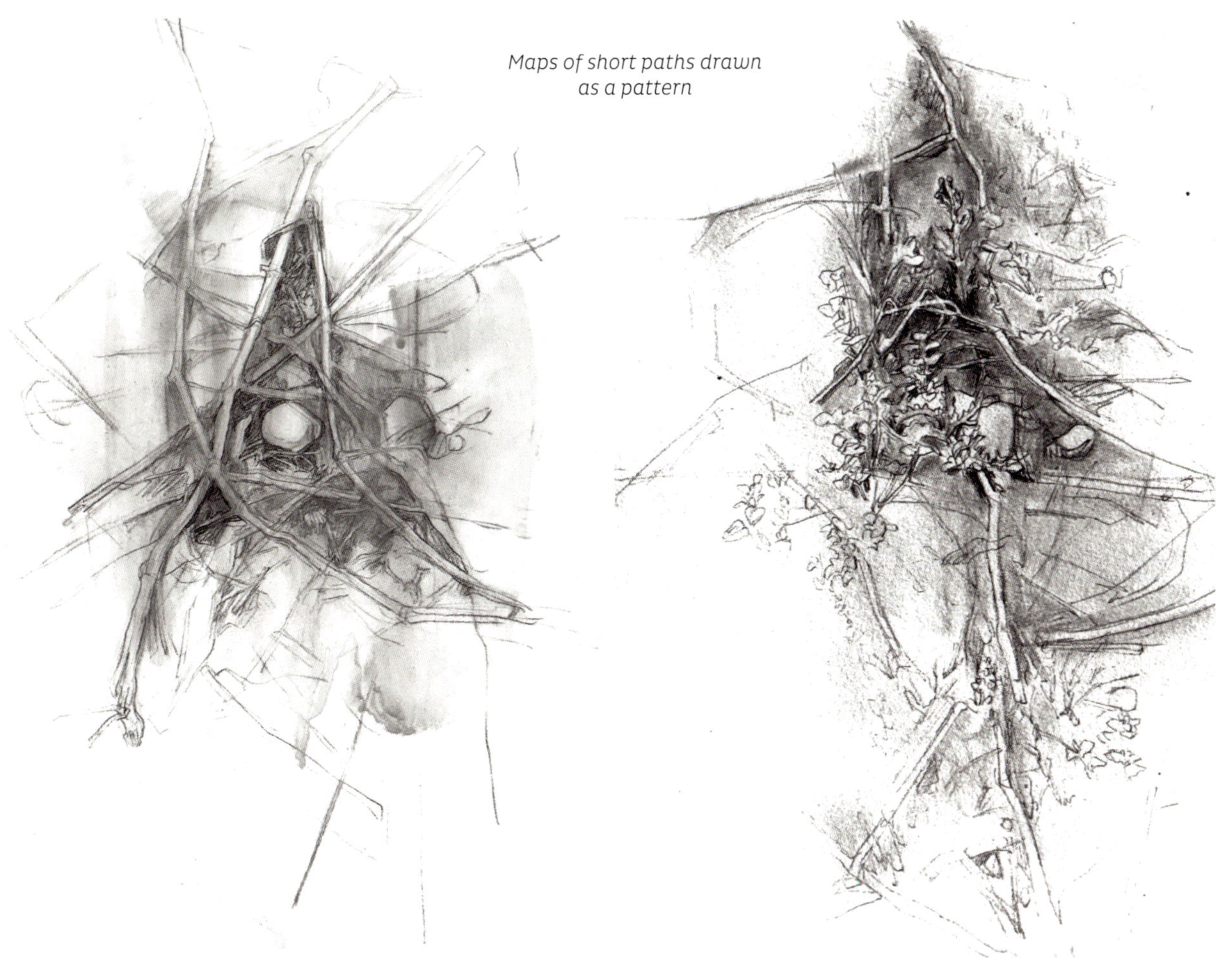

Maps of short paths drawn as a pattern

The color of time

Outside, take a model from creation, inside, follow the source of the soul.
—François Cheng, *Vide et plein*

This week, you will train yourself to notice the infinite variations in color and contrast of things over the days. You will see the full range of moods according to the time and color of the sky!

YOUR TURN

Put your pencils aside for a while and use a camera. The one on your mobile phone will do just fine: it's all about having a tool that helps you see. Choose a place that regularly crosses your path (e.g., the view from your window, on your way from home to the subway, around your workplace) and photograph it several times a day while keeping the same frame. A simple place is very suitable for this exercise: the simpler the subject, the more the change in light is obvious.

Select two images different from each other; after analyzing what distinguishes them and developing a chromatic range, reproduce them with a colored tool (crayons, watercolor, painting). Focus on color more than on the details. Your images can be almost abstract: the objective here is, above all, to fix in its memory different possible colors in the landscape.

Avoid black as much as possible. Look for which hue colors to use for dark tones and make them by mixing colors.

IF YOU HAVE THE TIME

- Put your photos on a page to compose a kaleidoscope.
- Remark the evolution of light during the day by classifying images from early morning to night.

Go and see

Katsushika Hokusai (1760–1849), *Thirty-Six Views of Mount Fuji*
Claude Monet (1840–1926), the Haystacks series and *Parliament of London*
Corinne Vionnet (contemporary)

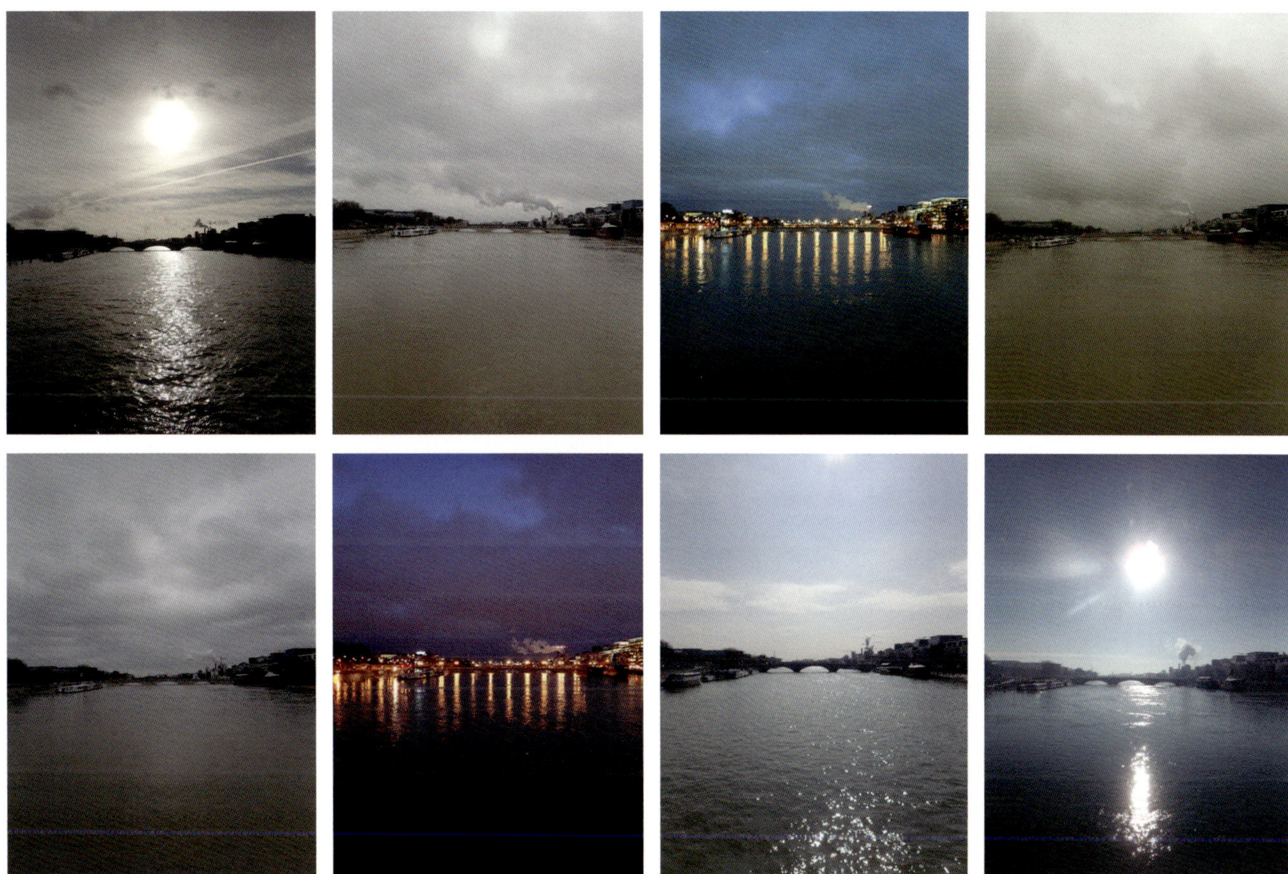

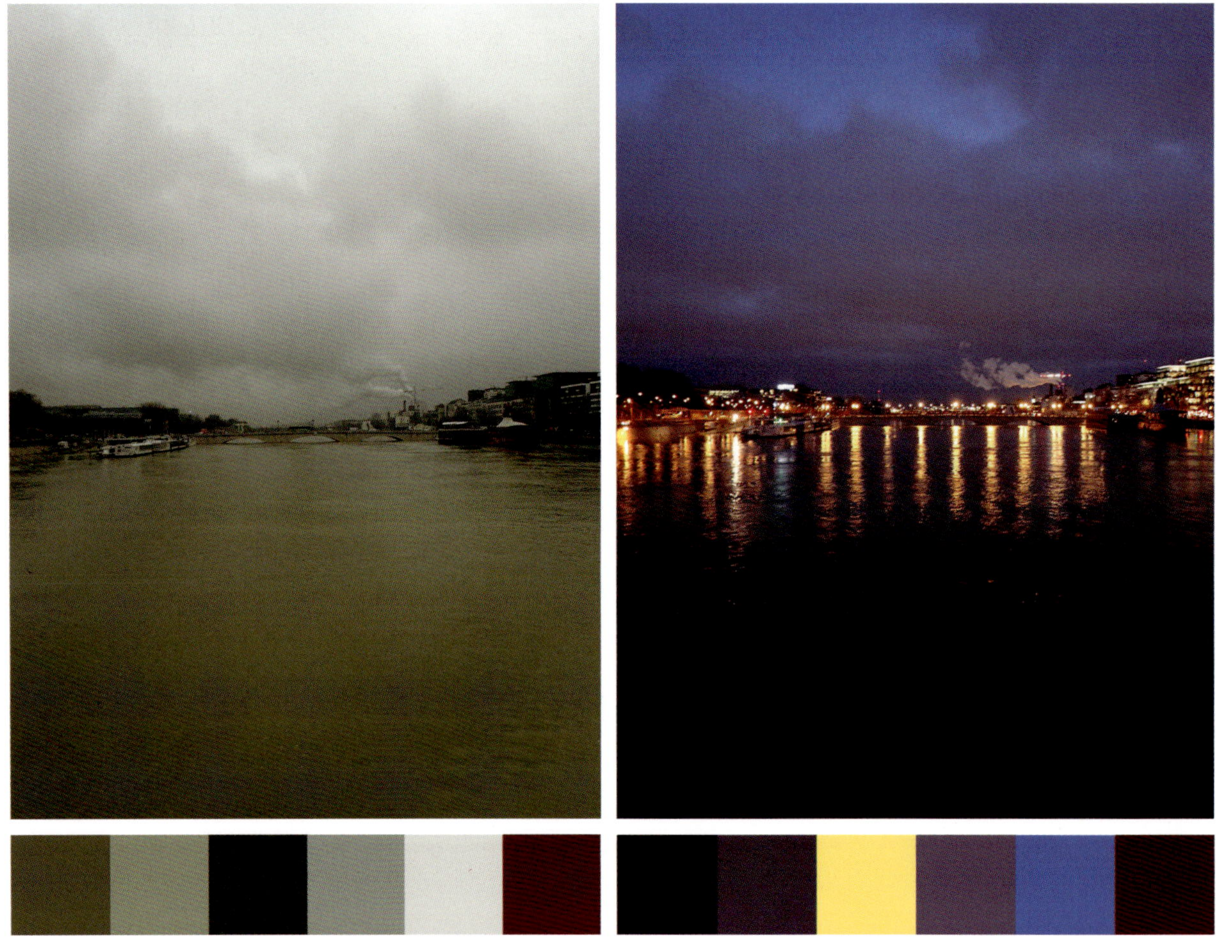

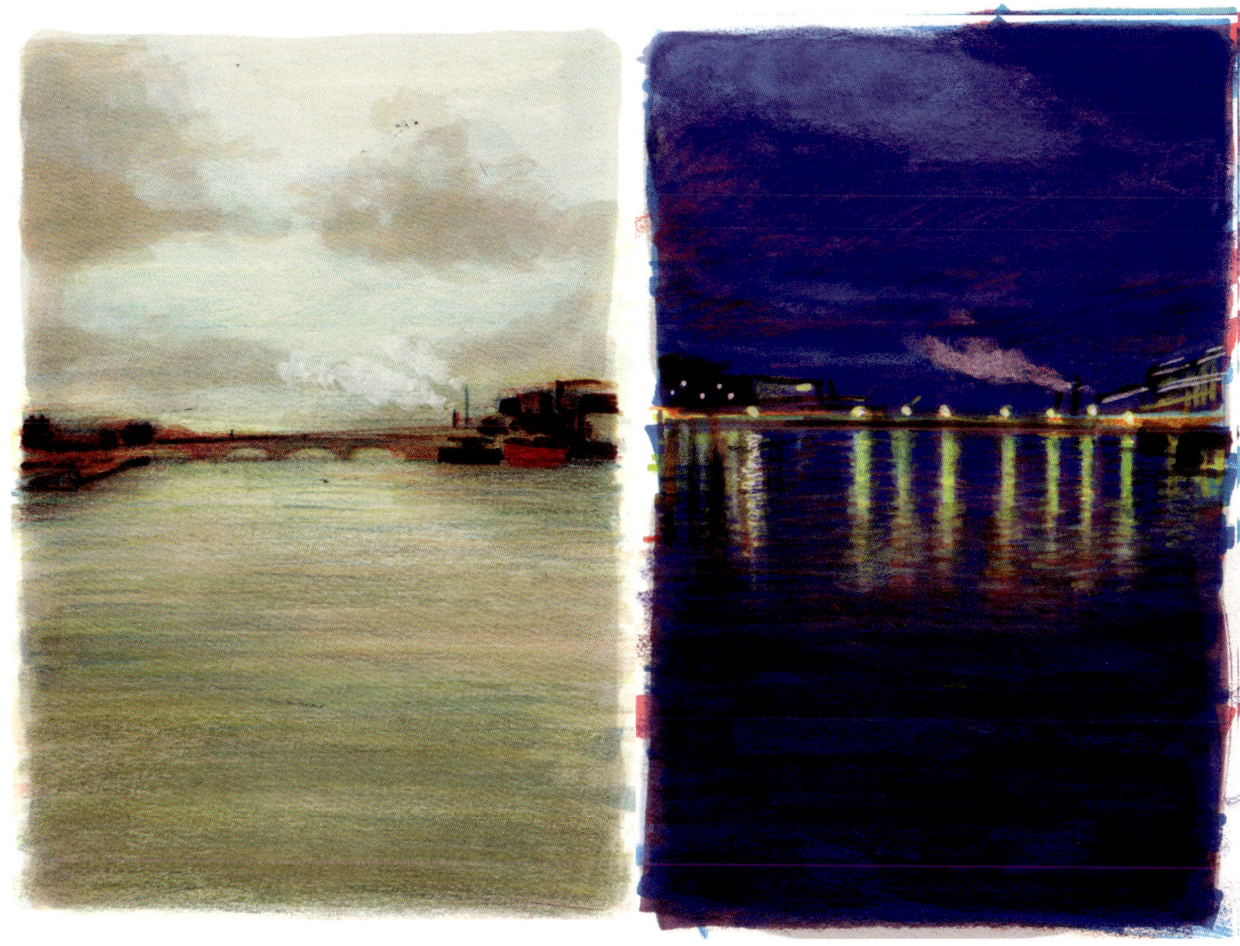

Inland landscapes

Allied to the beauty of a landscape, silence is a path to self, to reconciliation with the world. A moment of suspension of the time when a passage opens up that gives humans the possibility of finding their place again, of winning peace.
—David Le Breton, *Silence*

Focus on atmosphere and light. Navigate between abstraction and figuration while trying to represent landscapes. The challenge will be to find a balance between what you want to do and what the material will "say" on its own. You have understood that ink has its own life (see weeks 7 and 8): these water-based techniques invite us to accept the unexpected and appreciate its beauty.

YOUR TURN

Prepare several containers with different dilutions of colors, and one with clear water. Red, blue, and yellow will suffice and will allow you to obtain a wide palette by mixing or superimposing. You can use colored inks or watercolors. If you don't have watercolors, another diluted paint can do the trick. For paper and brushes, refer to week 7.

Start by cutting out small formats. Moisten the paper with clear water and then superimpose the colors, trying to create a depth effect. According to the atmospheric perspective (see week 19 for a definition), the first plane will be darker and warmer than the last plane. But anything is possible! Choose your colors intuitively.

Compare the reactions of the diluted colors when it they are applied to dry and wet paper. To obtain a stain with neat edges, wait until the underlay has dried; for a gradient, prefer a wet surface.

Note how the blur creates a photographic effect. Often, the less defined things are, the more realistic they seem to us.

IF YOU HAVE THE TIME

• Impose predefined constraints on yourself. Represent a storm, the rising sun, the setting sun, the night, summer, winter.

Go and see

Victor Hugo (1802–1885), *Les dessins*
Emil Nolde (1867–1956)
Gao Xingjian (born in 1940)

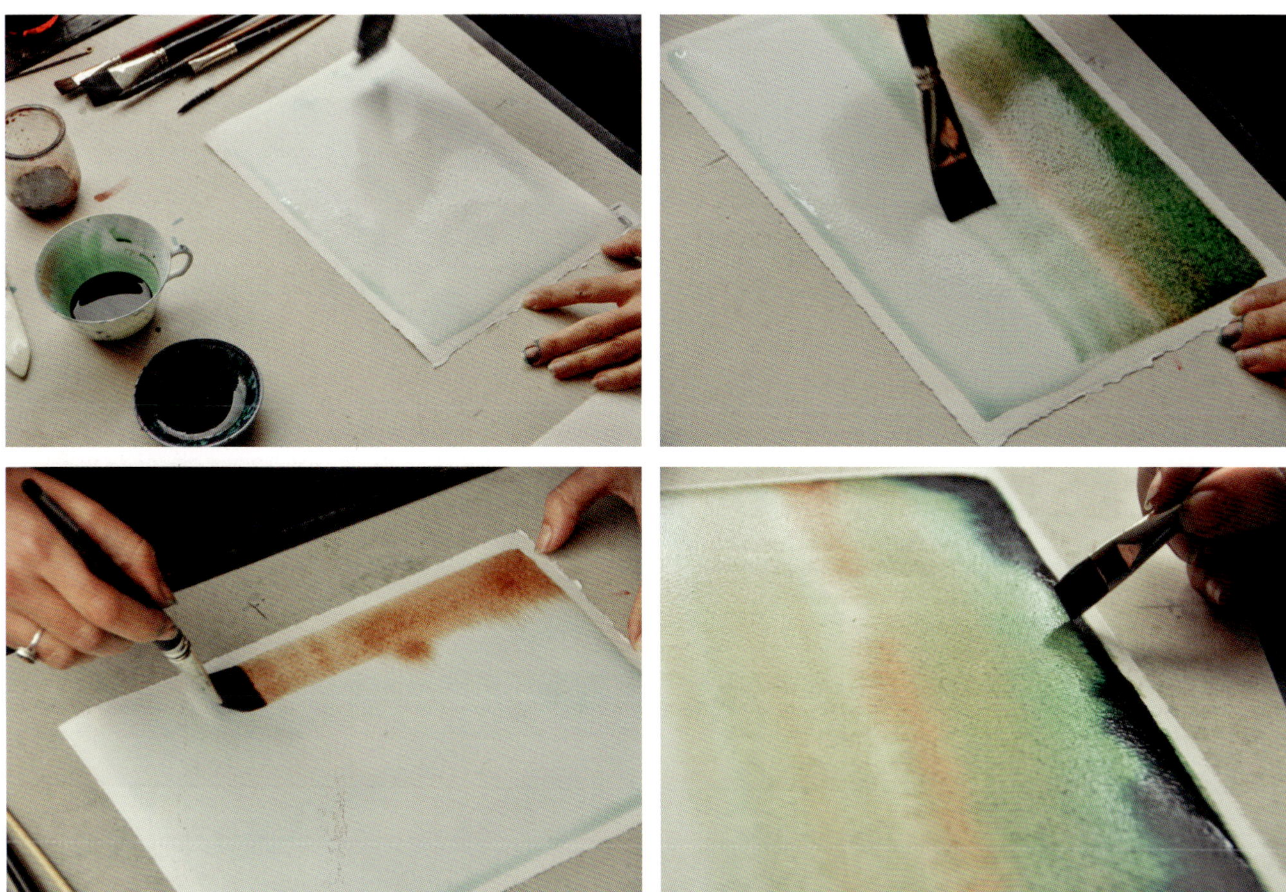

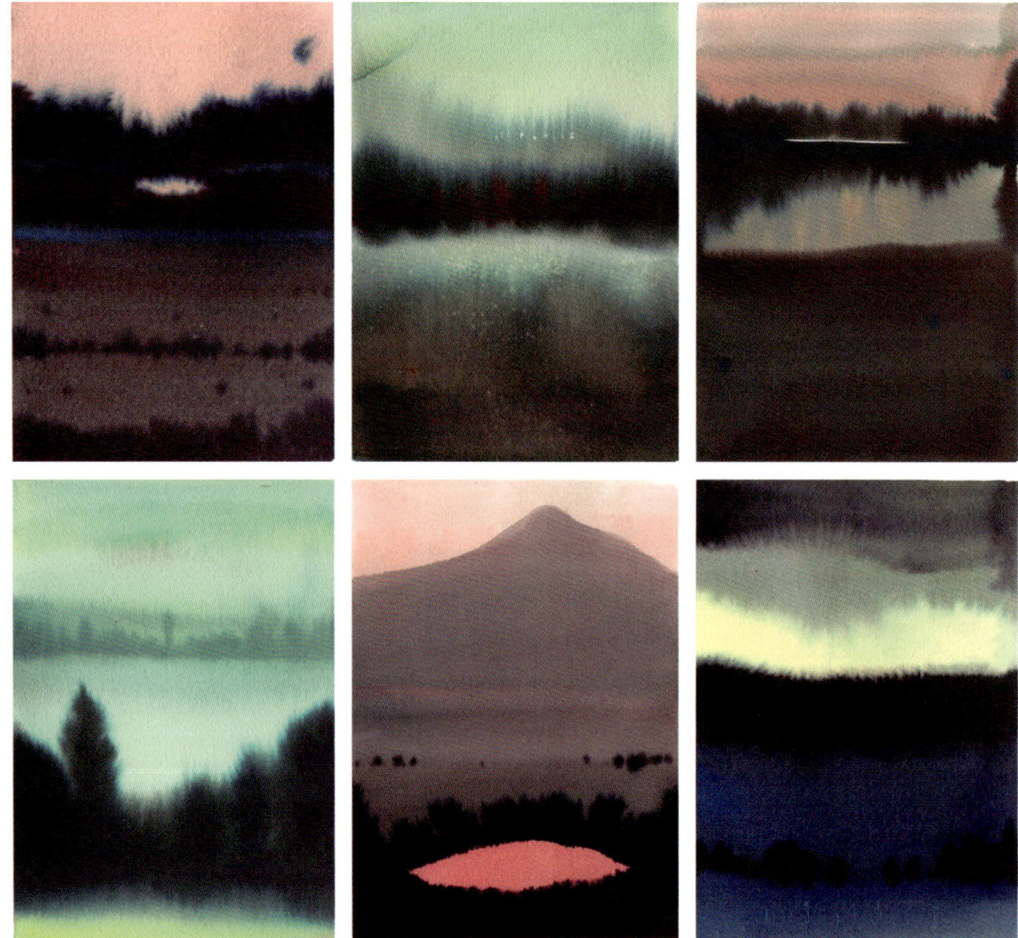

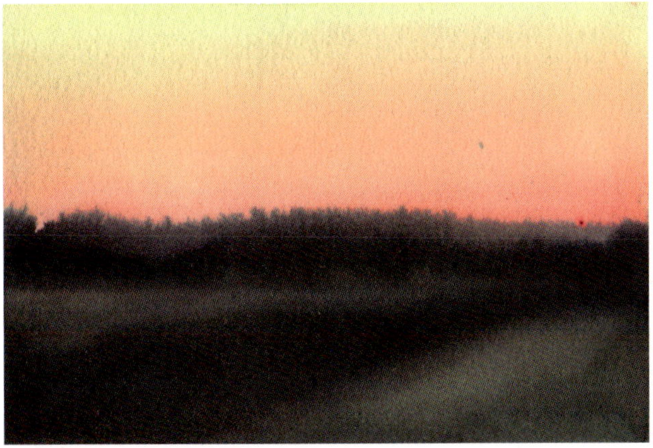

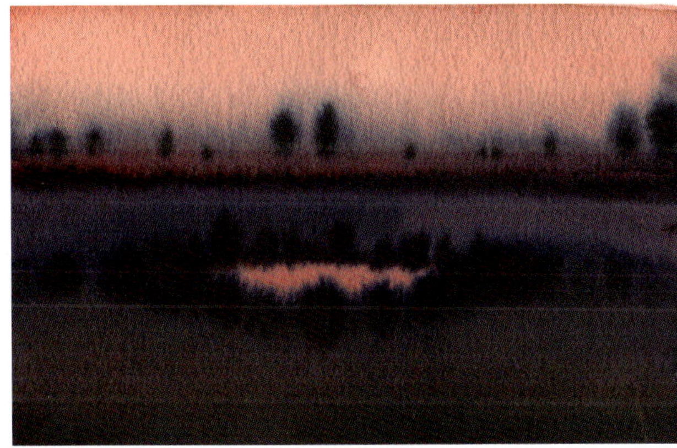

Family photos

All those moments that she had pinned like little pieces of eternity in her photo albums were moving, whispering.
—Sylvie Germain, *Le Livre des nuits*

It is always a good idea, when you want to connect to your creativity, to call upon the child you once were. Why don't you paint a portrait of yourself as a child?

YOUR TURN

Go through your family photos and find an image of yourself that pleases you. Take the time to feel what the photo is telling you. Mix the image you have in front of you with the memory that you keep of yourself as a child, to reinterpret this photo by completing it: change elements of the set, the characters around you, the colorful atmosphere, etc. Make it more compliant to the idea you have of your childhood today.

Use the technique of your choice. Start with two or three small, quick sketches: drawing is also a way of thinking. Then enlarge the part that seems closest to your feelings. If you don't have a lot of time to spare on it, a small drawing will be enough to begin with. Perhaps you will go back to it one day . . .

IF YOU HAVE THE TIME

- Write a short text on a childhood memory that you feel to be one of your foundations. This may involve your first memory of drawing, a first loss, a first love . . .
- Put this text in pictures in the form of a comic strip.

Go and see

Gerhard Richter (born in 1932), *Aunt Marianne*
Joanna Concejo (born in 1971)
Claire Tabouret (born in 1981)

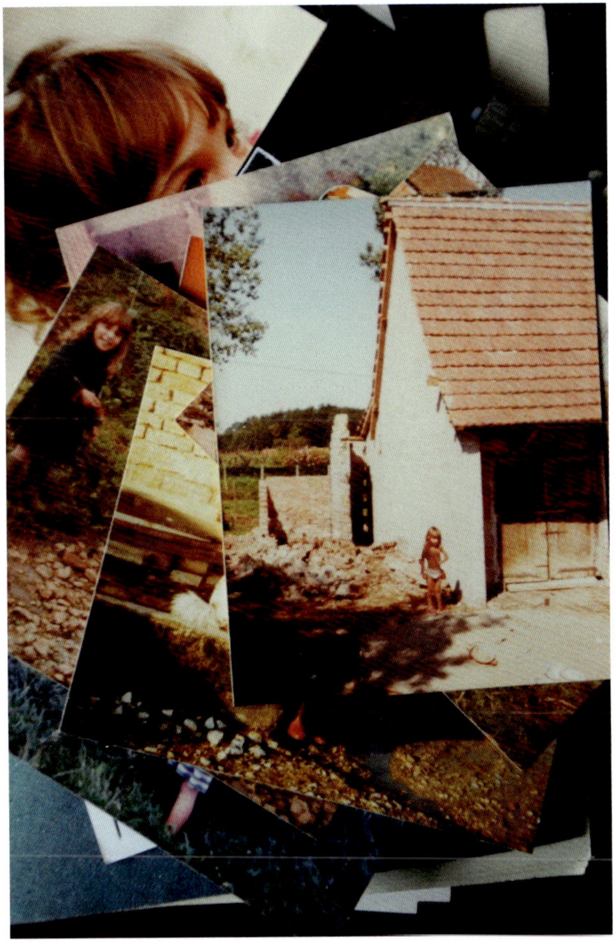

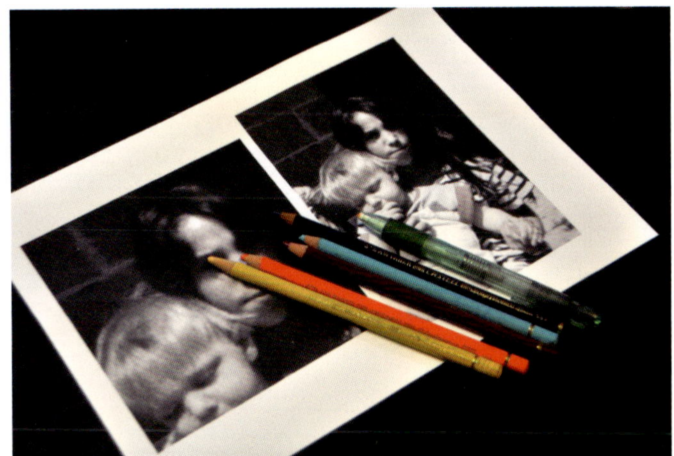

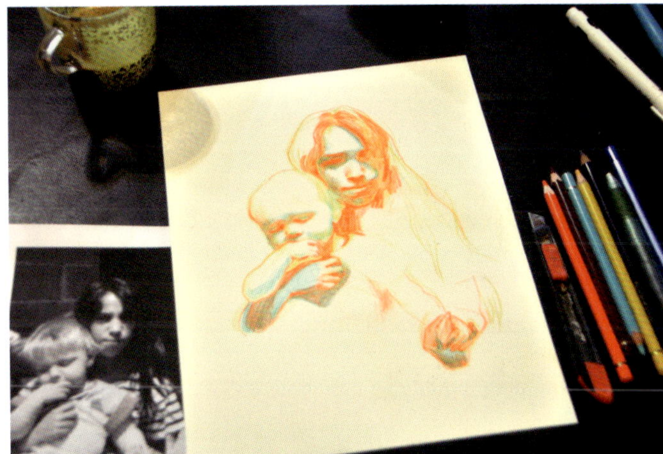

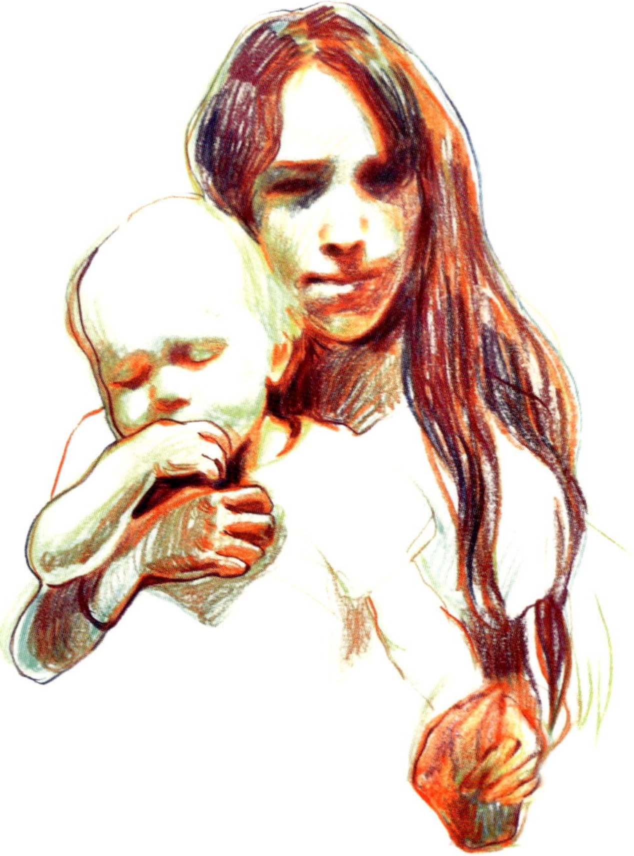

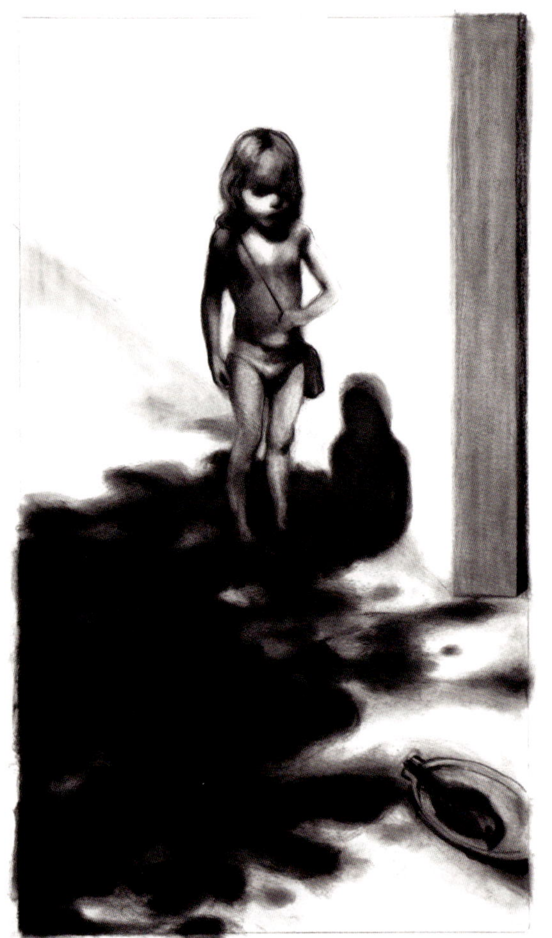

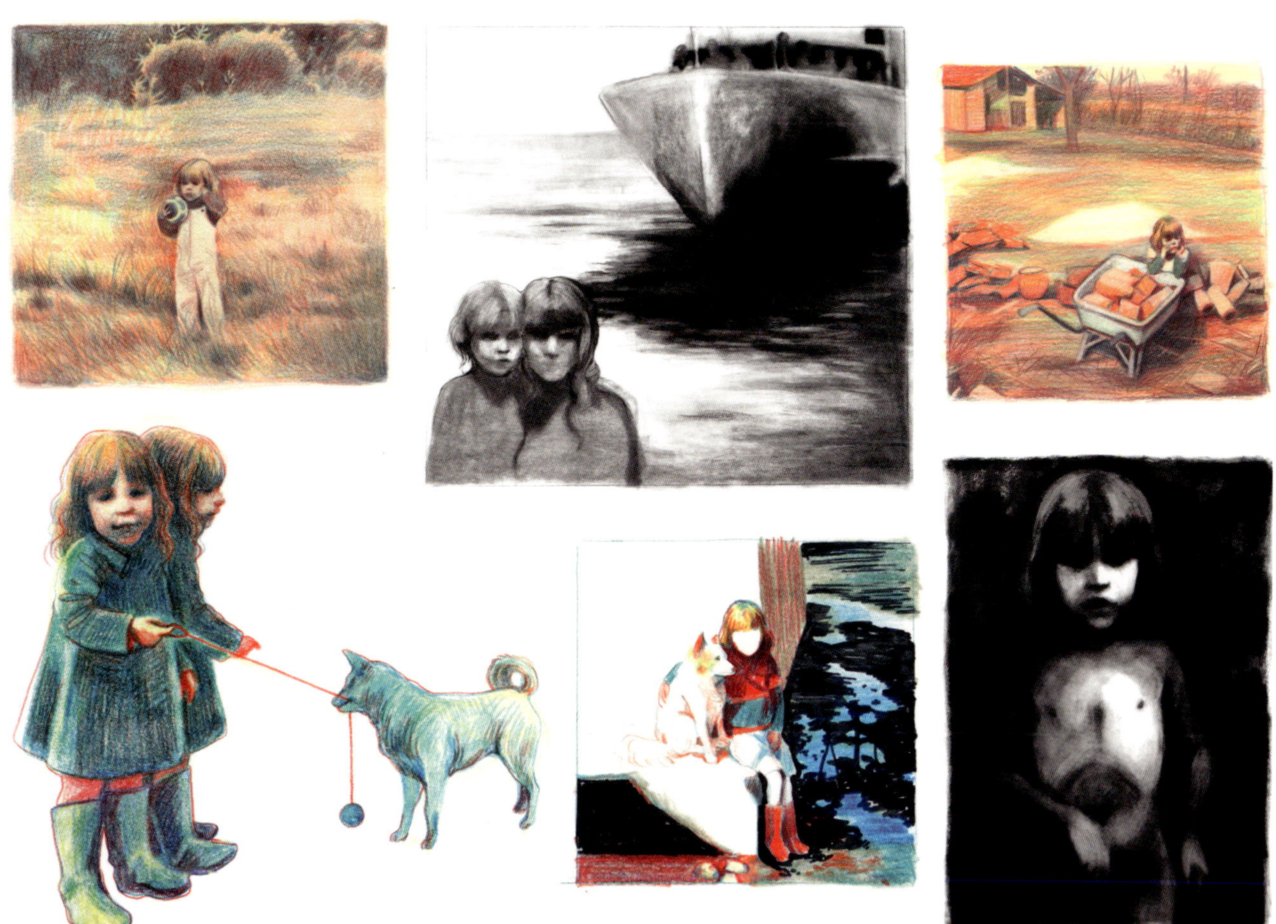

Drawing feelings

The public must receive works of art in their bellies. Where babies come from. This is where the primordial origin of a work lies.
—Bill Viola

Drawing can act as an emotional revealer. It has the incredible power to translate into images what our brains cannot put into words. And it can show everything, even what is impossible in reality!

YOUR TURN

Take your notebook with you every day and, with the tool of your choice, try to represent your intimate feelings. You will proceed a bit like automatic drawing, but with a feeling of departure and the will to make it visible.

You can draw without reference or by "sticking" together different observed pieces. The association of objects, characters, and natural elements can create a poetic language that will to take into account your feelings. Impregnate your design with the energy that you want to communicate. Your key must be in accordance with your intention. We are very talented as spectators, deciphering, without really being aware of it, the personality or the emotion in a line, in the same way that we know how to decipher the gestures or intonations of the voices of our interlocutors.

Don't try too hard to make a "beautiful" drawing; look for it instead to make a drawing that sounds right.

IF YOU HAVE THE TIME

- Start with one of these sketches to create a more complete drawing.
- Work on one of these color drawings again, asking yourself the question of emotions in relation to your color range.

Go and see

Odilon Redon (1840–1916)
Roland Topor (1938–1997)
Marion Fayolle (born in 1988)

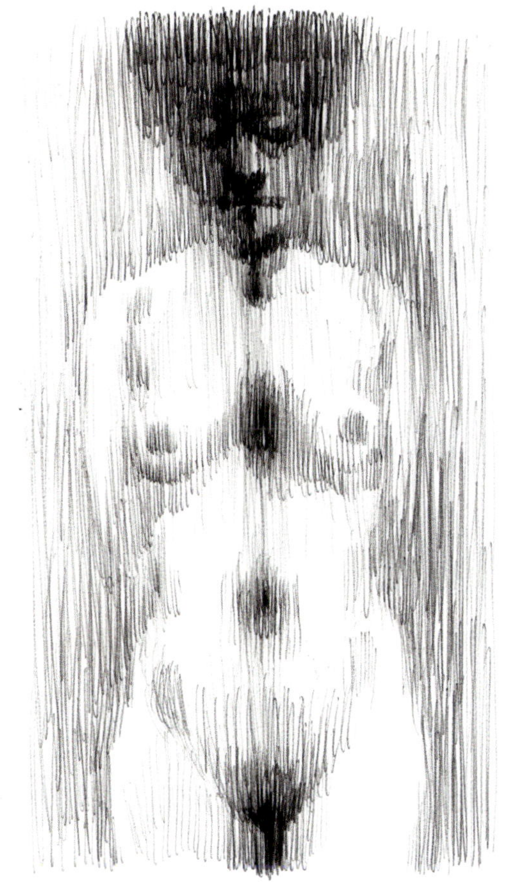

JOUR DE PLUIE 04/03/18

Rainy day

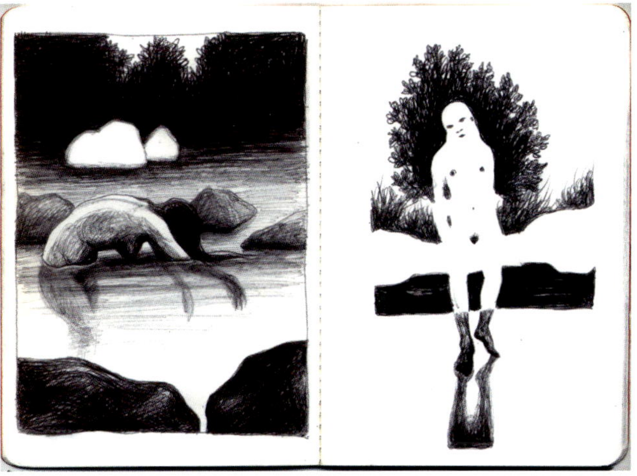

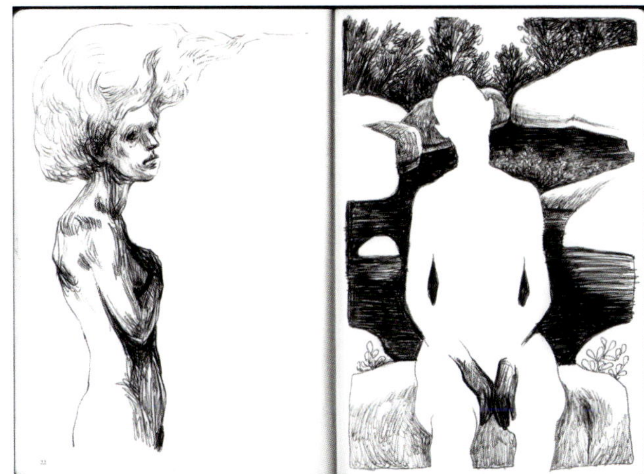

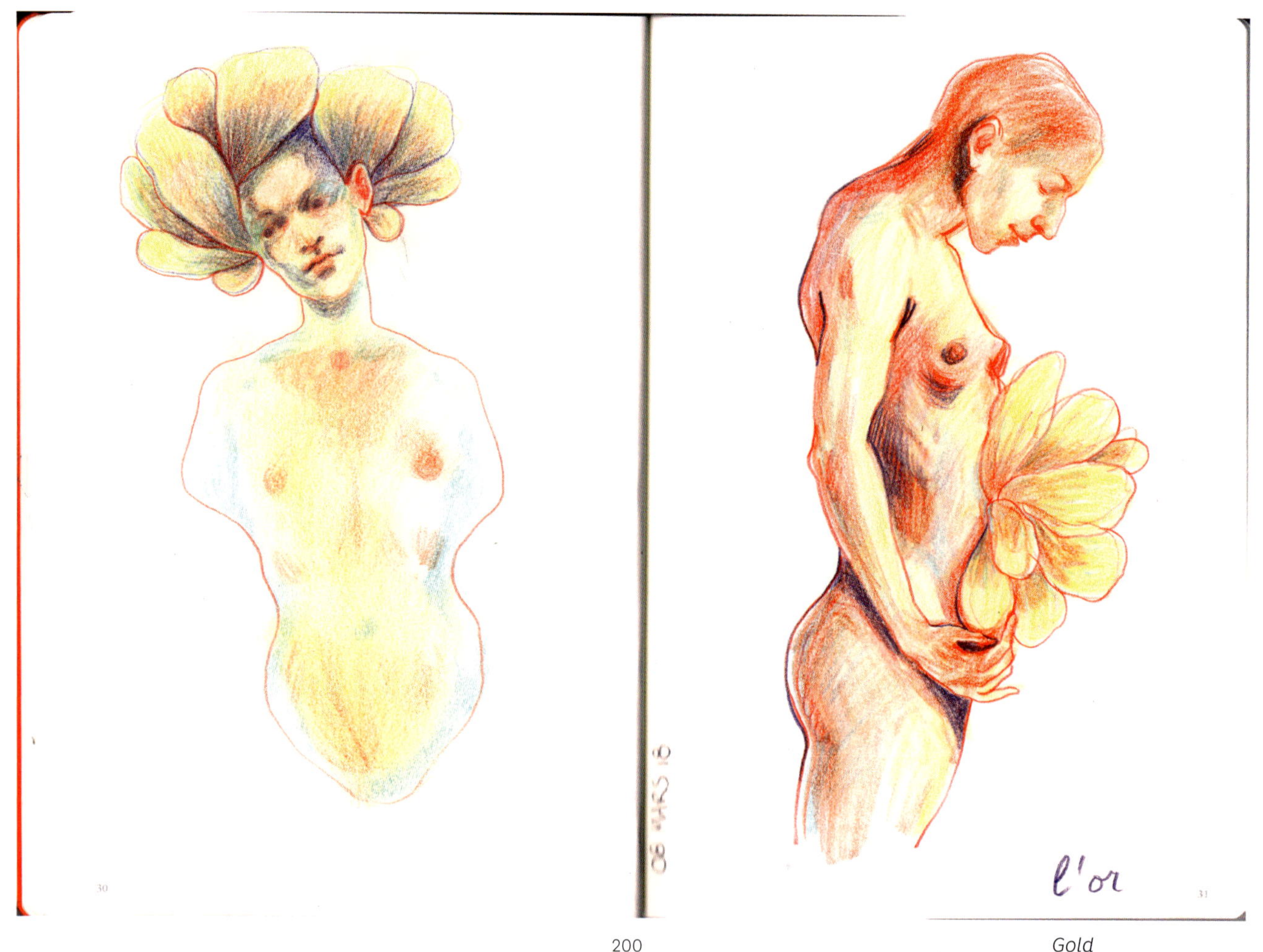

Gold

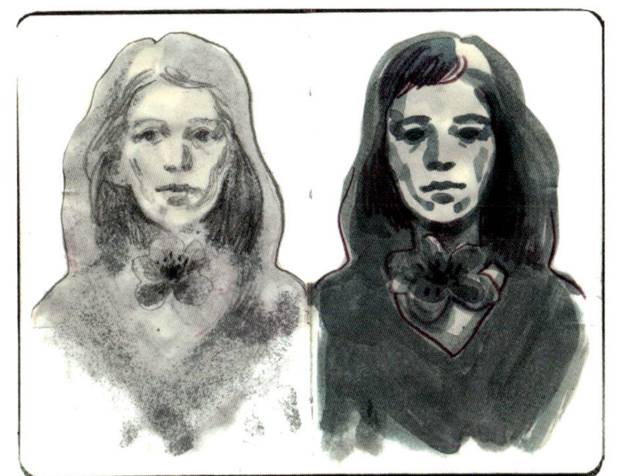

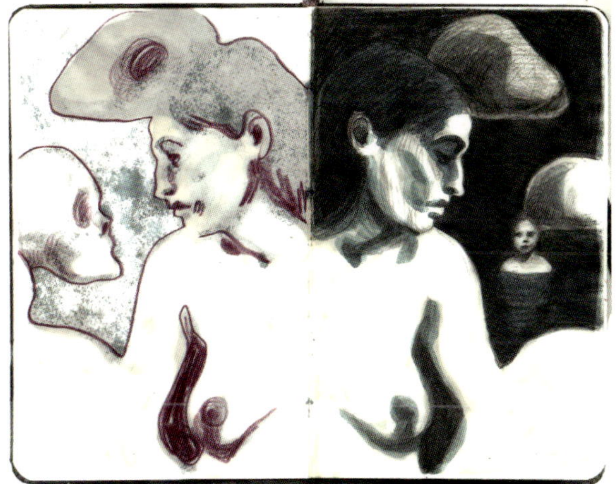

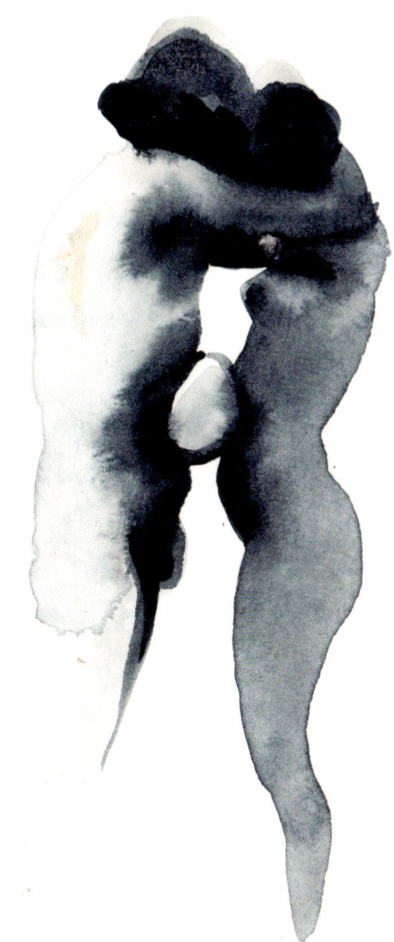

Repentances

Imperfection gives life; I love life.
—Niki de Saint-Phalle

The drawing is a trace, a print. It is a creative process, with its hesitations, its changes of point of view, and its moods. We can render the time it takes to develop an image visible.

YOUR TURN

Use a strong A3 support. Choose tools that you can mix if necessary. You can also use tracing-paper sheets.

The proposed examples are made by interposing a layer of gesso, thin and translucent, or white gouache between two steps.

Overlay all the steps of your drawing, using translucent layers, with surfaces that are carefully erased to preserve the previous steps, or layers. These are to archive each error, every hesitation. If your image is alive, place a new layer each time you change your posture; do the same if a puff of air displaces an element of your composition. The result will be an accumulation of superimposed translucent patterns, with strengths and mistakes accepted. It may look like the results of week 36. The movement here is that of time and the creative process.

IF YOU HAVE THE TIME

• Draw the same week on the same support by partially erasing each previous day, or by covering the support each day. Play on the transparencies, the traces.

Go and see

Antonin Artaud (1896–1948)
Barbara Kroll (born in 1960)
Stefano Ricci (born in 1966), the *Dépôt noir* collection

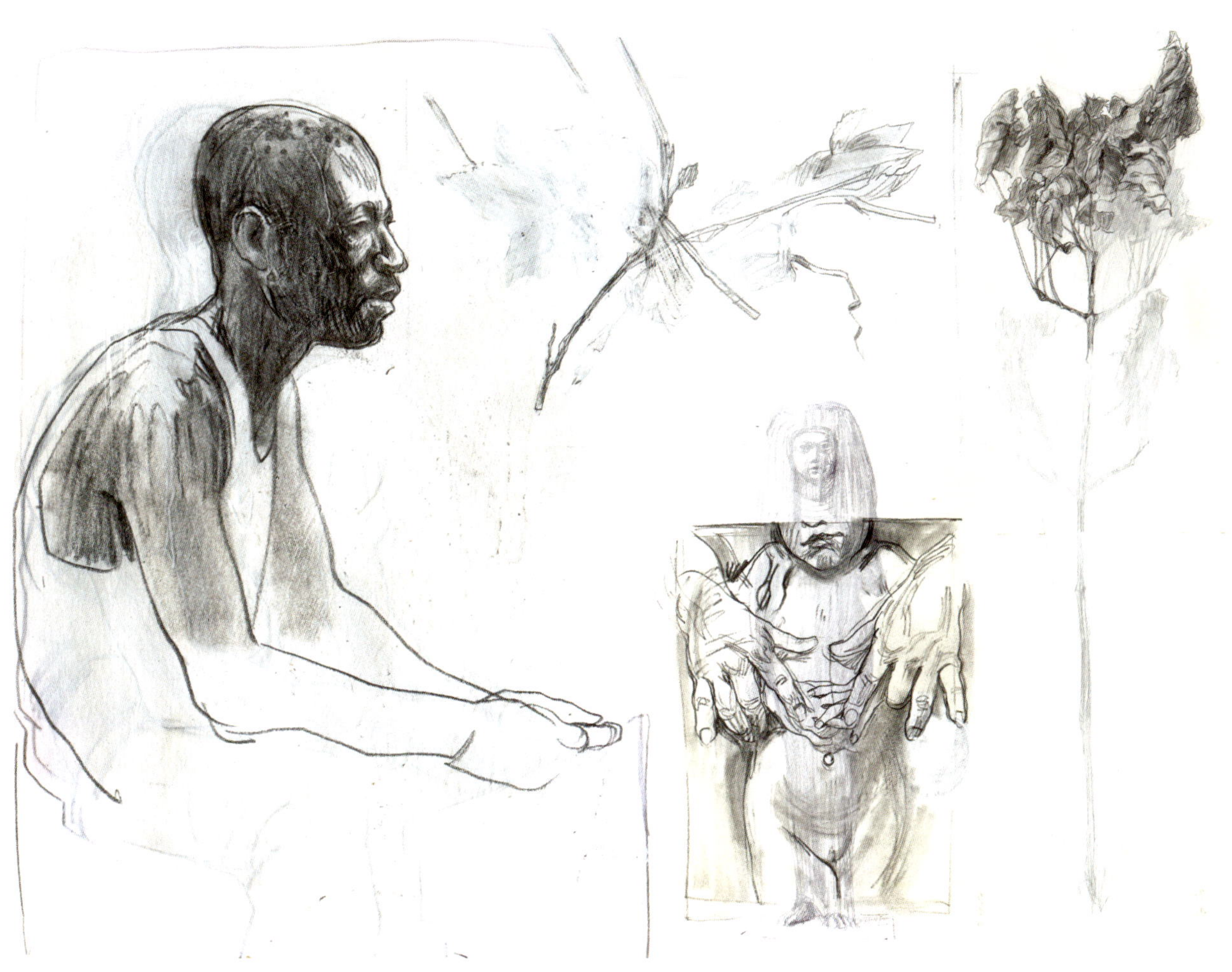

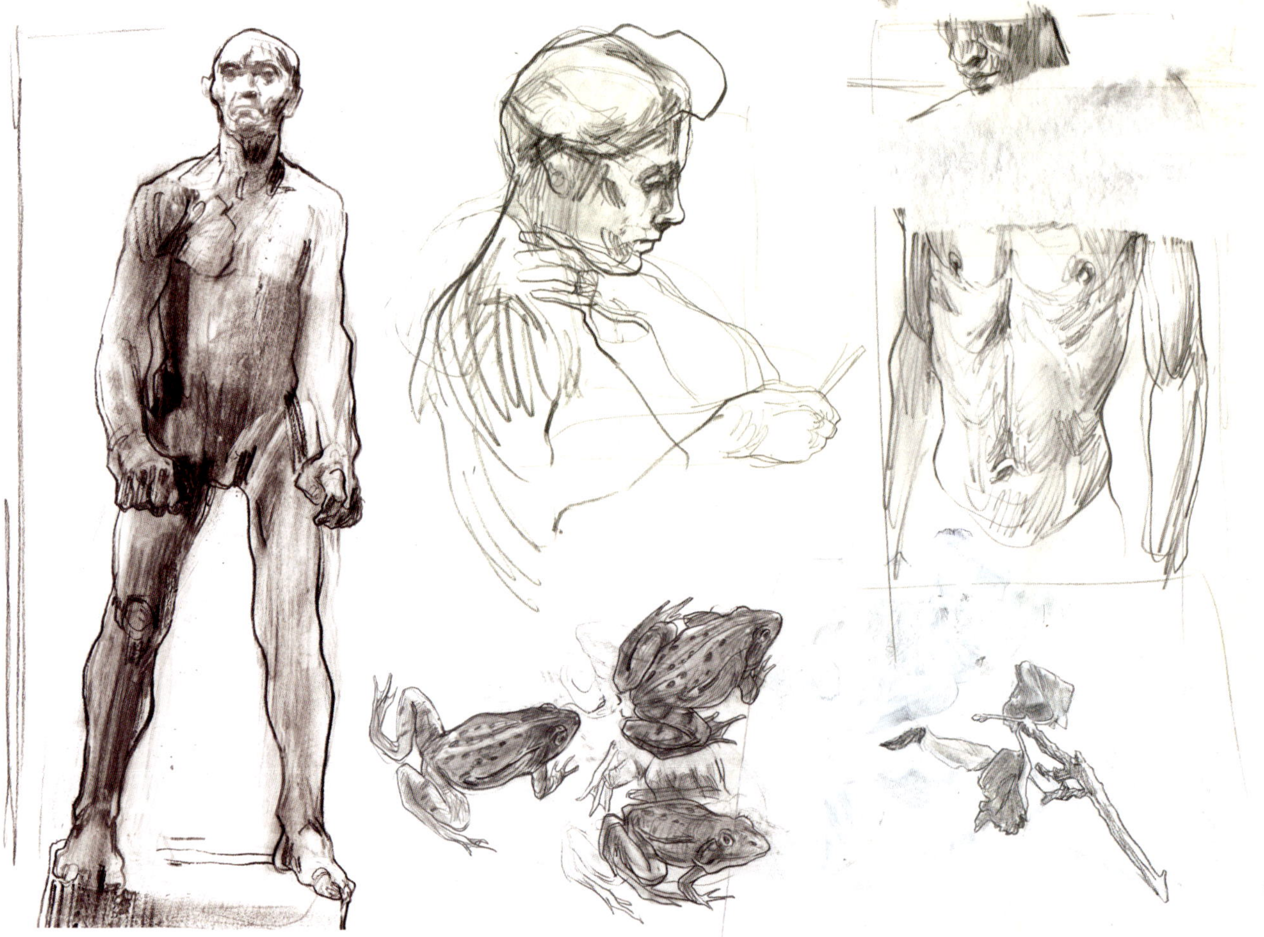

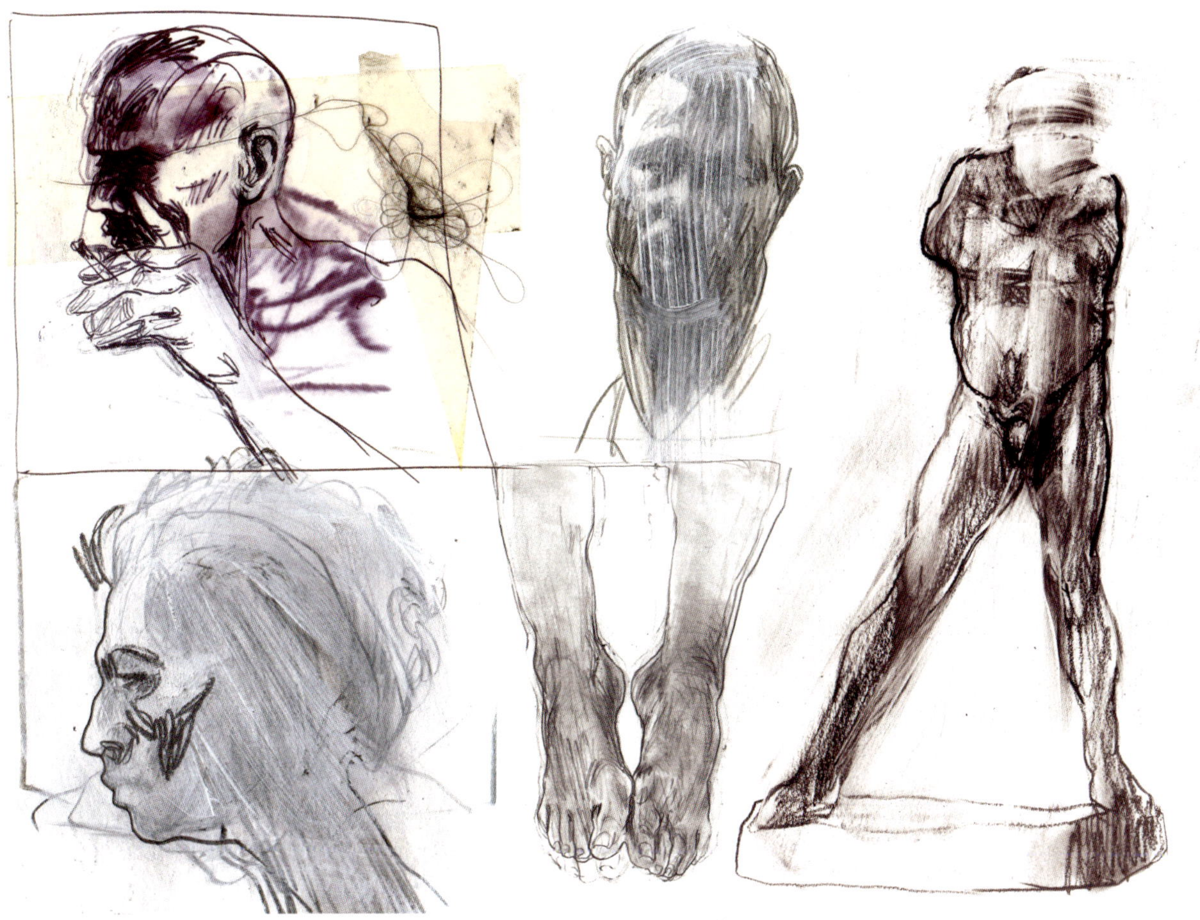

Redrawing space

Live bright, create a poem and go: increase the space of the earth.
—Adonis, *Memory of the Wind*

The desire naturally comes to many of us to make a mark on the landscape. From a hopscotch grid to graffiti, what great fun it is to draw on the ground or on a wall, and to leave a message to those who come after us!

YOUR TURN

This proposal starts with a walk! It is a question of considering an artistic intervention in a place of your choice.

Whether you are in town or in the country, go out for a walk and take a close look at what is around you. Take the time to observe, sit down, take breaks, take pictures . . .

Once you have chosen your little piece of the world, get involved spontaneously; if you don't dare, you can be satisfied with photo projects.

In a landscape, prefer an ephemeral intervention, with natural materials (charcoal, natural pigments, earth, watercolor) or what you find on the spot. The idea is to draw attention to the place and to pay tribute to it by respecting it.

IF YOU HAVE THE TIME

• Take a series of photos of your work at different times of the day to show how light shows it off.

Go and see

Georges Rousse (born in 1947)
Andy Goldsworthy (born in 1956)
Chiharu Shiota (born in 1972)

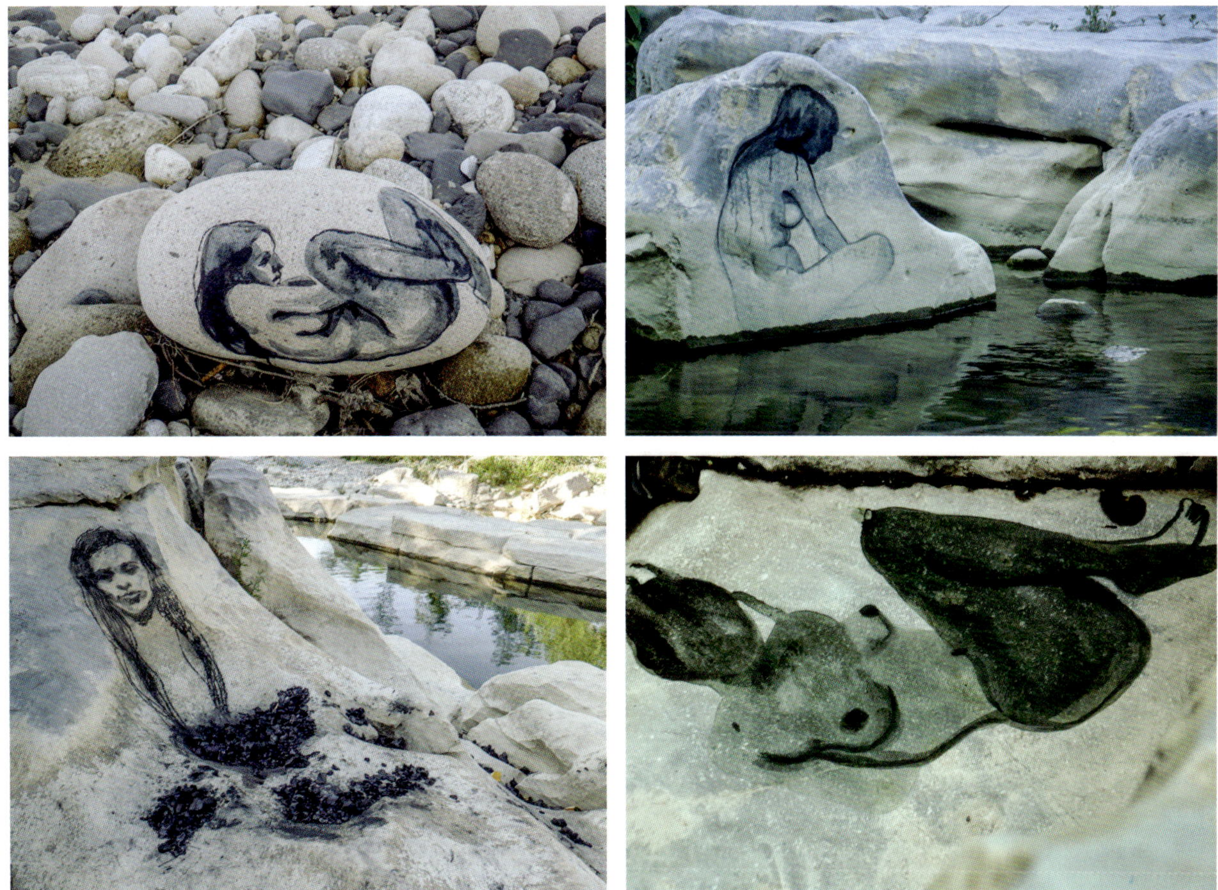

These figures were drawn on the rocks on the banks of a river in the Ardèche, in watercolor and charcoal (remains of a campfire).

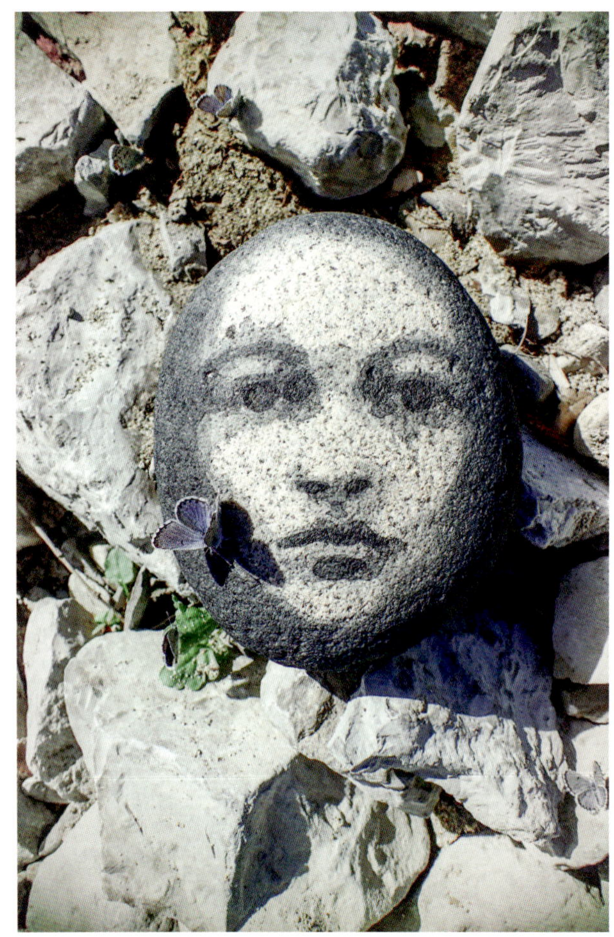

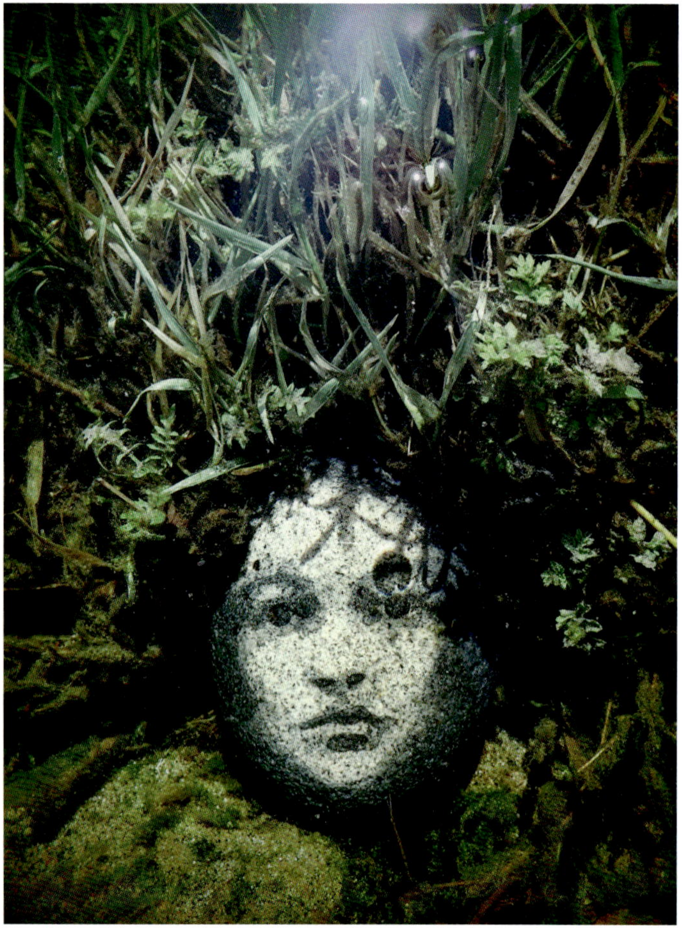

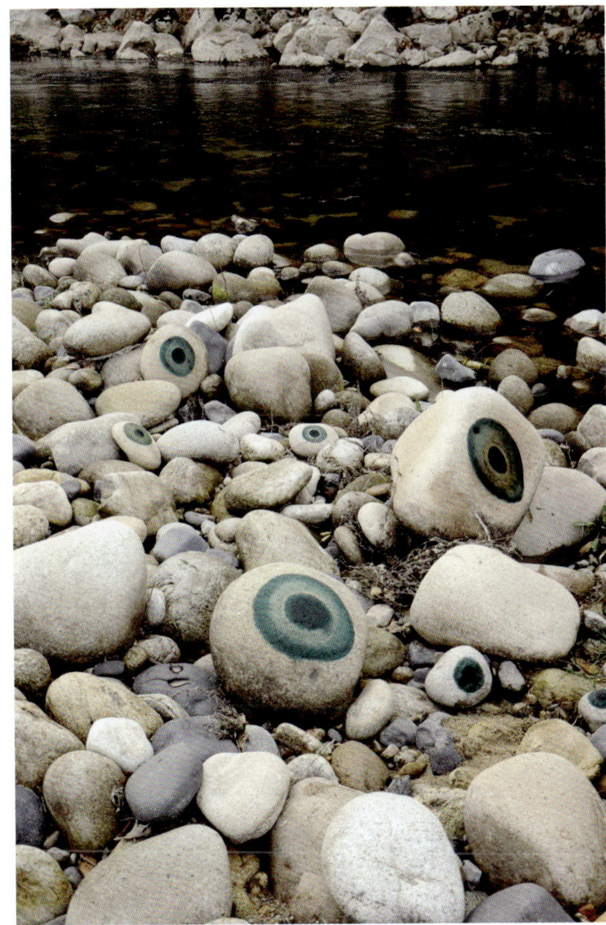

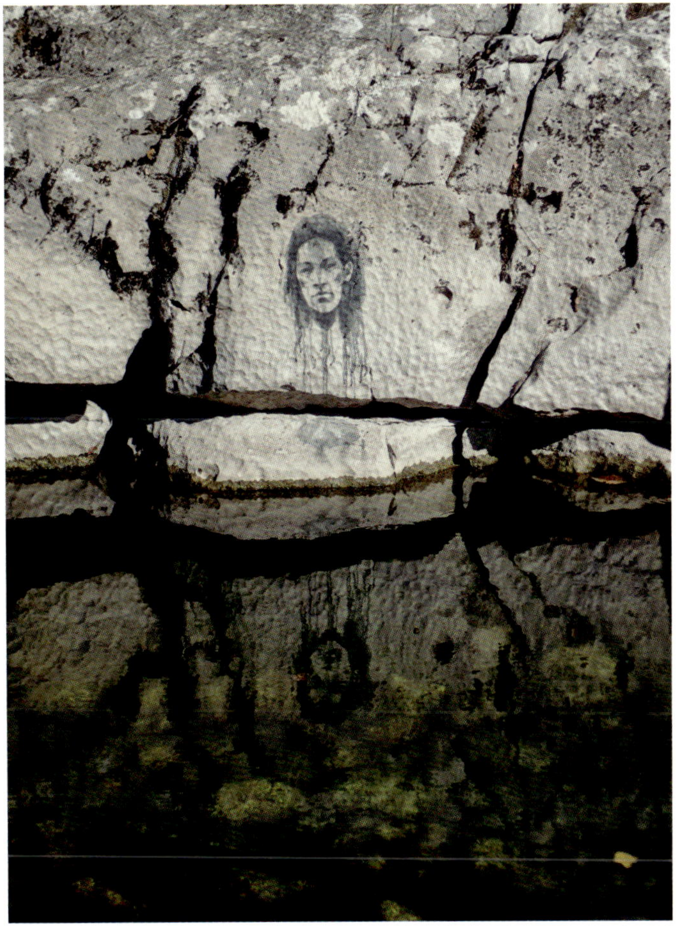

Supports

One sometimes finds what one is not looking for.
—Alexander Fleming, receiving the Nobel Prize

By focusing your attention on drawing media other than paper, this exercise may help you discover unexpected ways to use an already familiar technique. It is always good to remain open to experimentation. Serendipity is the friend of artists!

YOUR TURN

Start by looking around for what might be interesting to use. Newspapers and packaging papers can be very inspiring; raw cardboard used to work in white on gray/brown and fabric will reveal its weft if you draw on it with felt or ink. Maybe this is your chance to go out on a "recovery" expedition! Of course, you can also buy the materials that attract you.

Test different tools on these unconventional supports to determine the best interactions.

You now have a long-enough experience of drawing to work on your own subjects: experiment and enjoy!

IF YOU HAVE THE TIME

• Once you have identified a material that you particularly like and the tools that suit it, make the most of your discovery. Continue with a small series of drawings that will share this unique support.

Go and see

Ruan Hoffmann (born in 1971)
Brooks Shane Salzwedel (born in 1978)
Aurélie William Levaux (born in 1981)

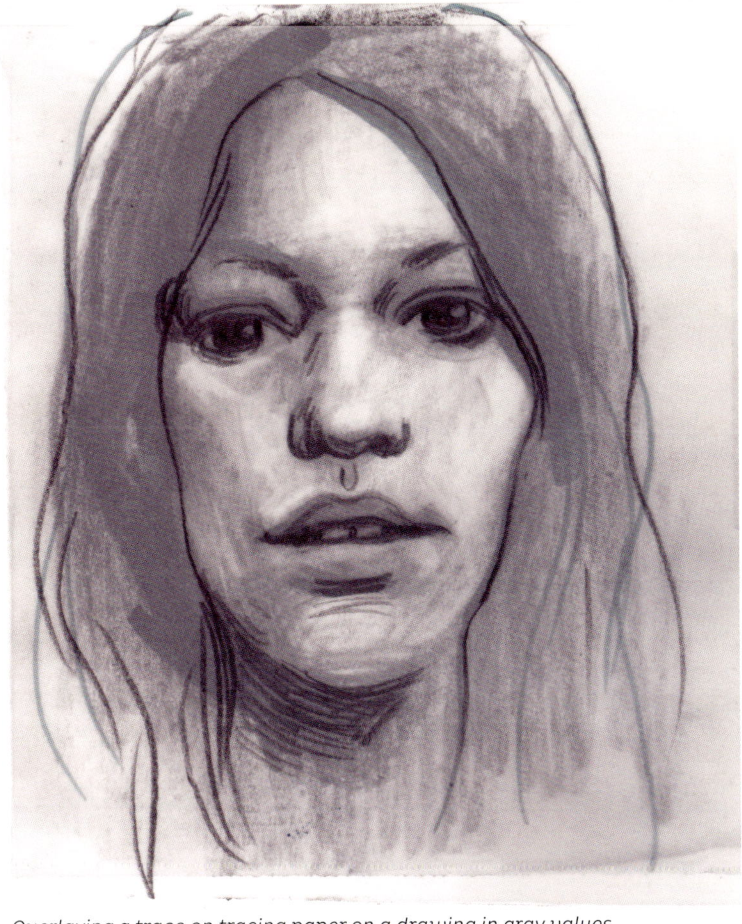

Overlaying a trace on tracing paper on a drawing in gray values

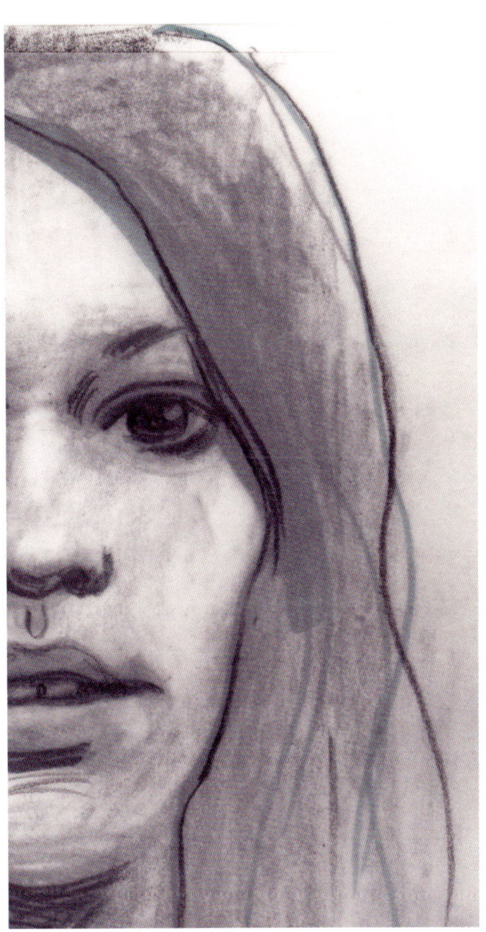

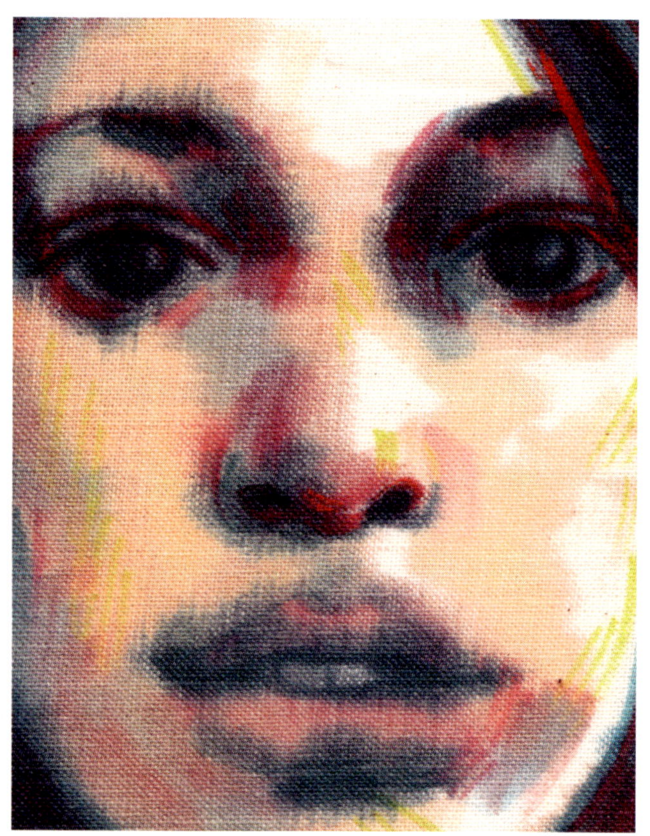

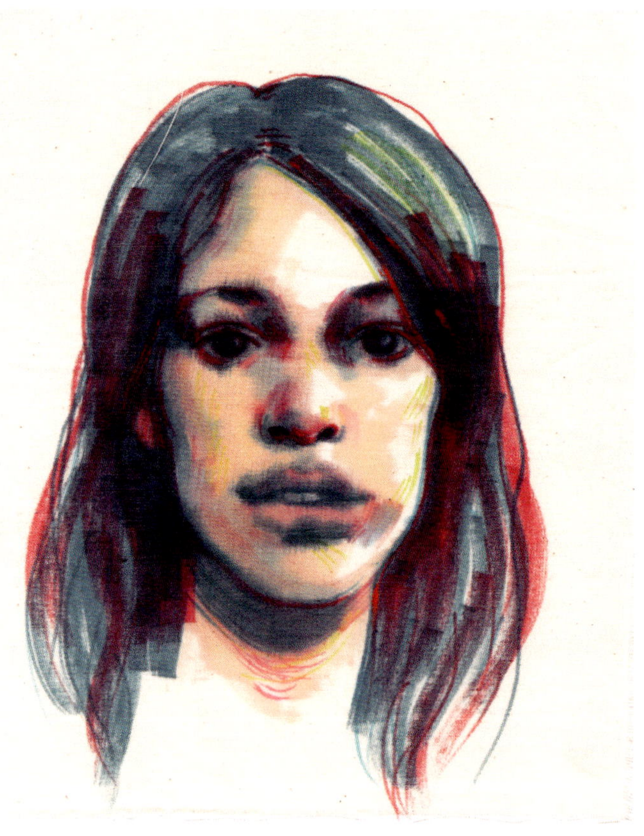

Alcohol-based felts on fabric

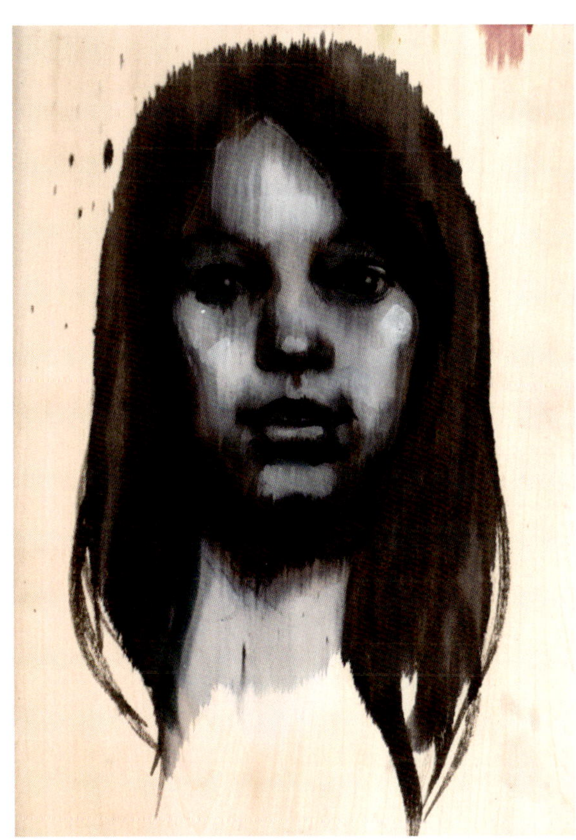

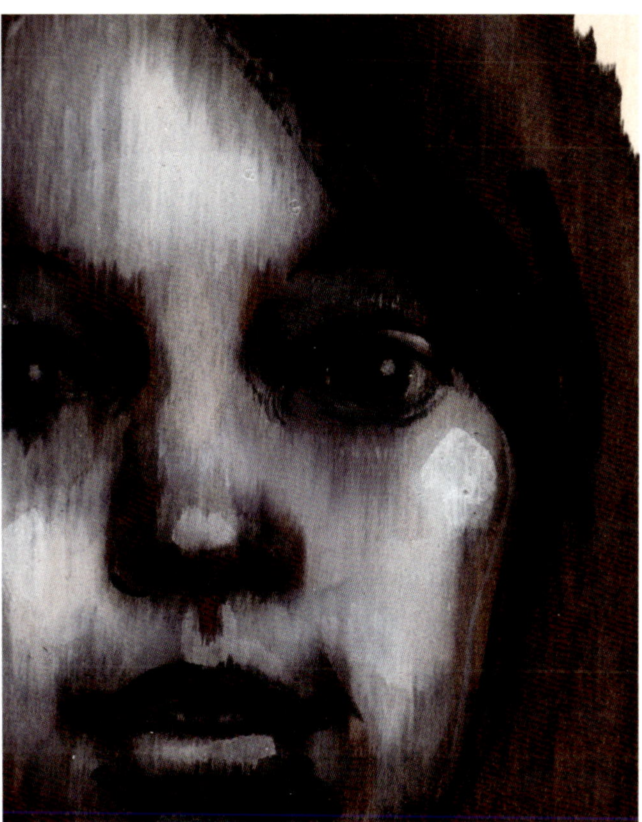

Black and white ink on plywood

Large format

Small fish will grow big.
—Jean de La Fontaine, *Le Petit Poisson* and *Le Pêcheur*

All formats are possible and justified. Miniatures create an intimacy with the work that is often highly appreciated; large formats are essential and encompass us. It would be interesting for you to experience it: drawing big is tracing with the amplitude of your whole body, and it changes the relationship to drawing a great deal.

YOUR TURN

From all your drawings this year, choose one that seems to deserve being bigger. Your tools will be much wider than the ones you used for smaller formats, in order to remain in a ratio of coherent proportions. It is possible to reinterpret a pencil drawing in paint: a black-and-white image can be transposed into color . . .

Take ownership of your production and choose a technique: you can use squaring (week 10) or start freehand to keep the gesture fresh.

The following images show that you can enlarge your design in several stages.

IF YOU HAVE THE TIME

- Make another large drawing that will be the counterpart of the first one in order to create a diptych, then a triptych, then a whole series on the same theme!

Go and see

Il Lee (born in 1952)
Ayako David-Kawauchi (born in 1963)
François Réau (born in 1978)

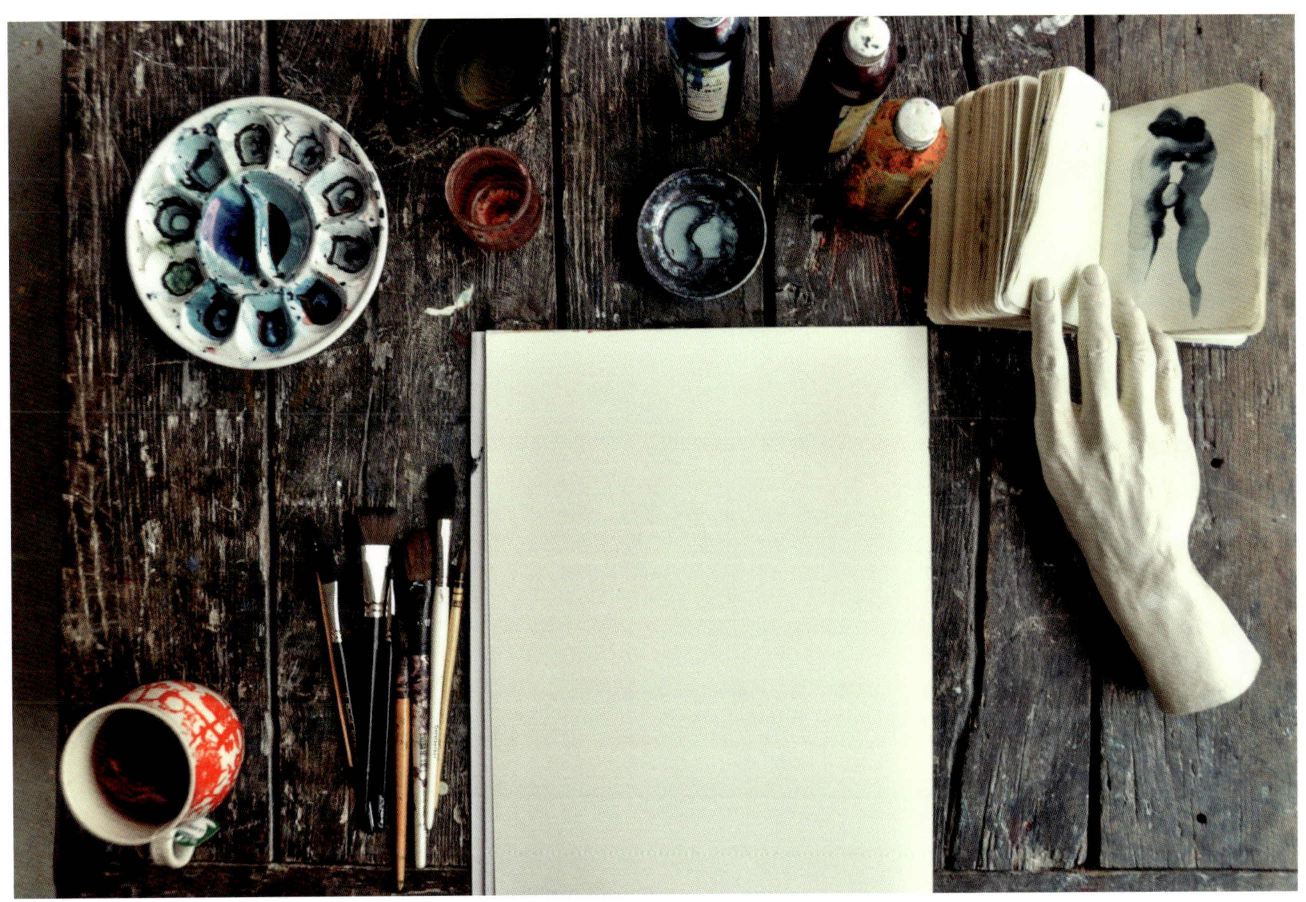

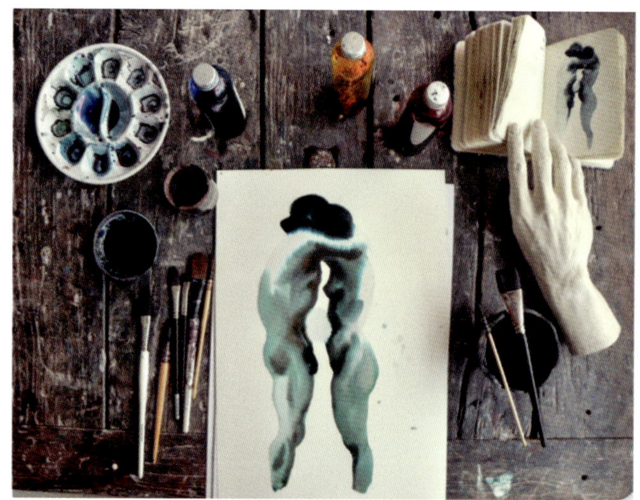

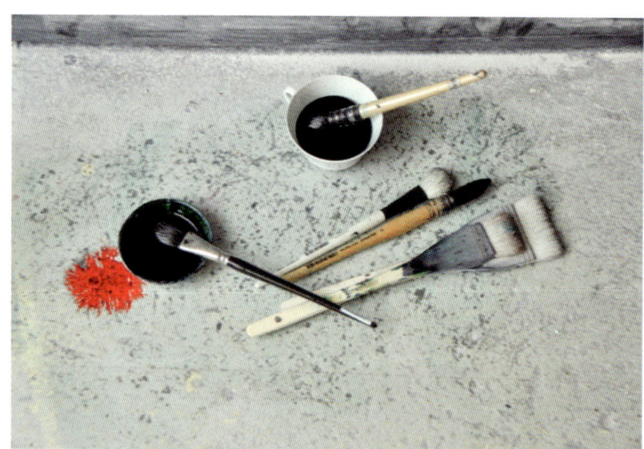

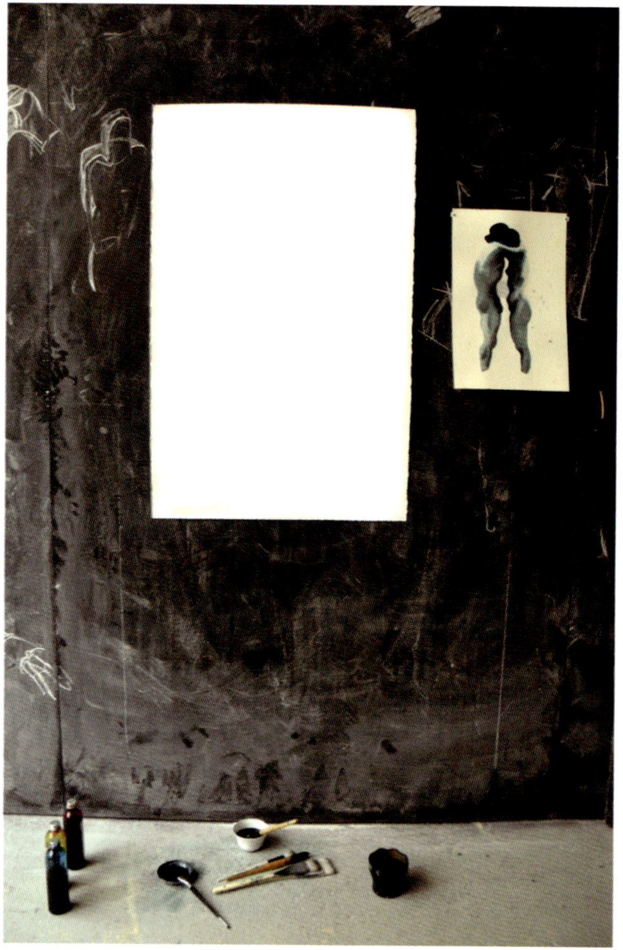

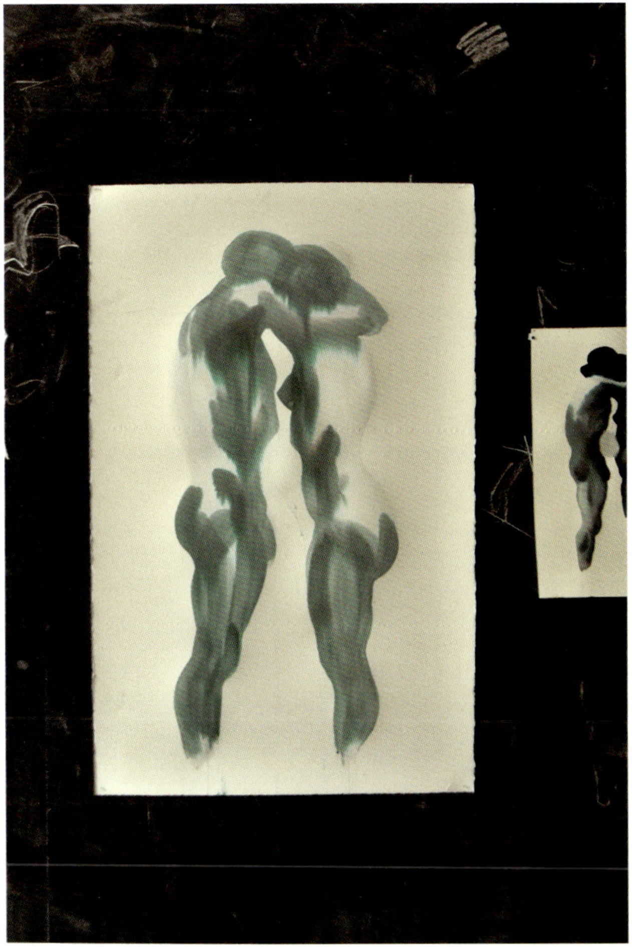

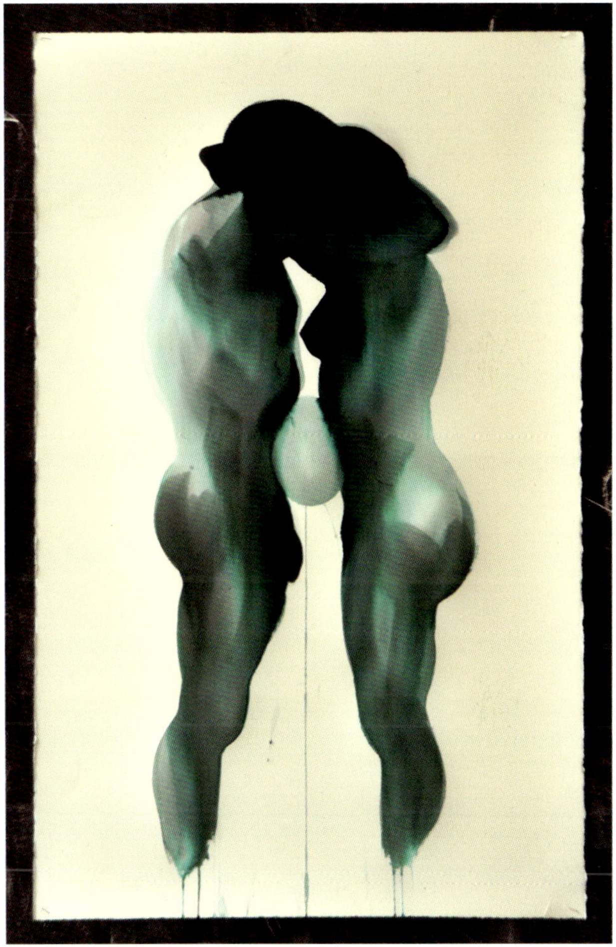

Final assessment

A year of drawing is a fuller year than the previous ones, right? The time spent observing the outside as well as the inside leaves traces in the memory but also in a concrete way: the accumulated drawings are the physical testimonies of the moments that saw them born.

Be lenient toward them: if they present clumsiness, they have the merit of existing above all. They show the steps taken, improve you, and reveal your view of life.

We advised you in week 1 not to show your images, in order to avoid being confronted with criticism too early. Perhaps you now feel strong enough in your practice to expose yourself to outside scrutiny. It's up to you to decide.

Anyway, this year of drawing should end with a little exhibition. Whether it is open to the public or not, be proud of it. You will see that the enhancement of your drawings is important and that several images put together will take on a meaning that you may not have noticed.

As in week 26, start by spreading out all your drawings around you. Admire the work done, and congratulate yourself!

Valuing your work does not necessarily mean framing your drawings. You can hang them without incurring any additional costs.

Why not visit some galleries (even virtually) to observe the way in which the works are displayed nowadays? From the most minimalist to the most abundant of frames, find what is appropriate for the spirit of your production.

Tell yourself that some drawings may not have a large attraction on their own, but that associated with others they will find their place. Select them according to what most resembles you and not based on technical success.

This exhibition will be the conclusion of a cycle. It's a small event that will open a new phase.

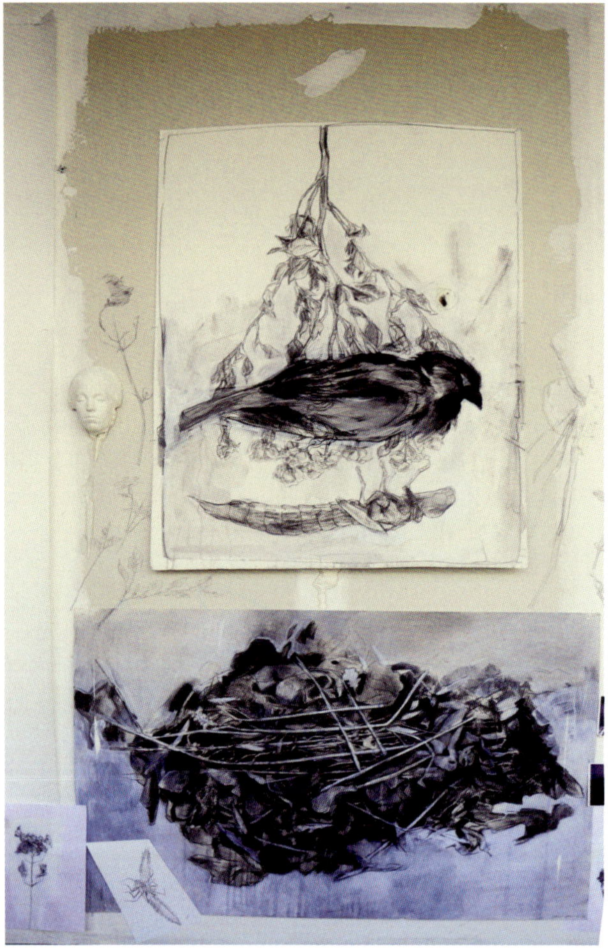

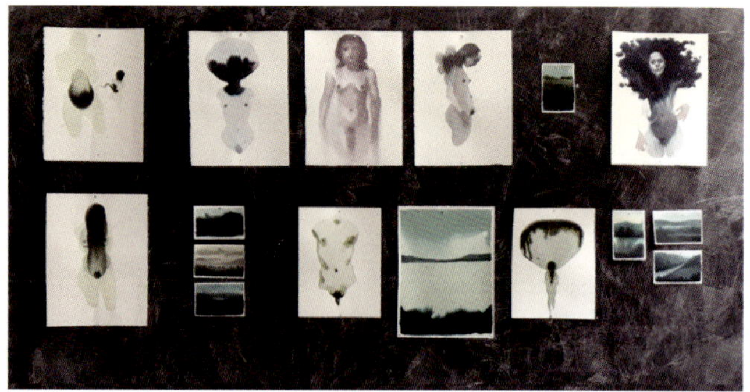

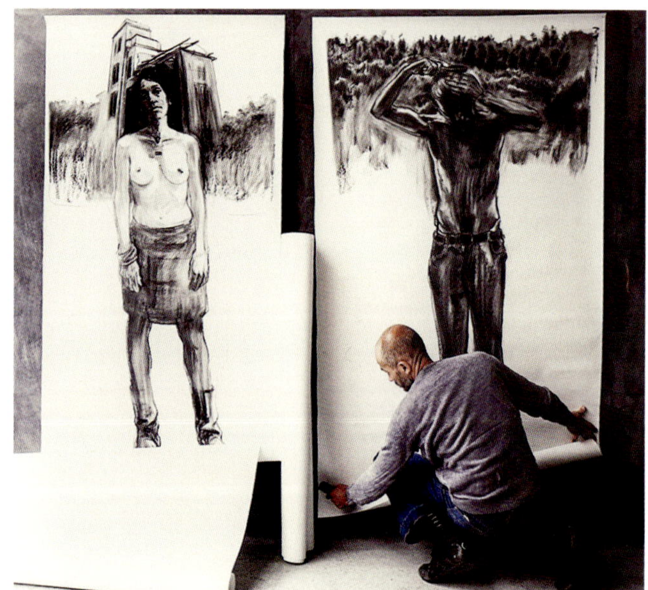

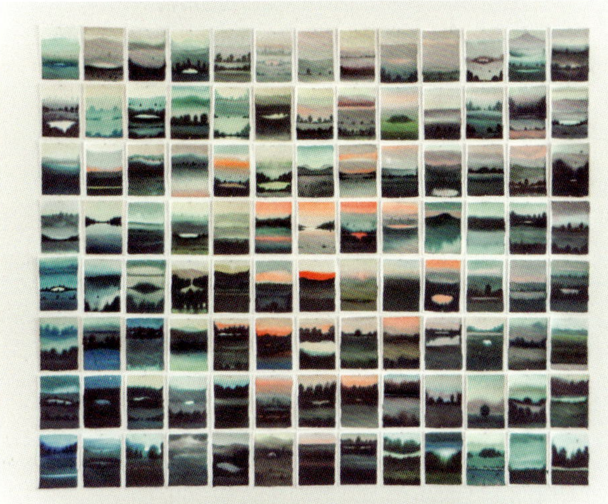

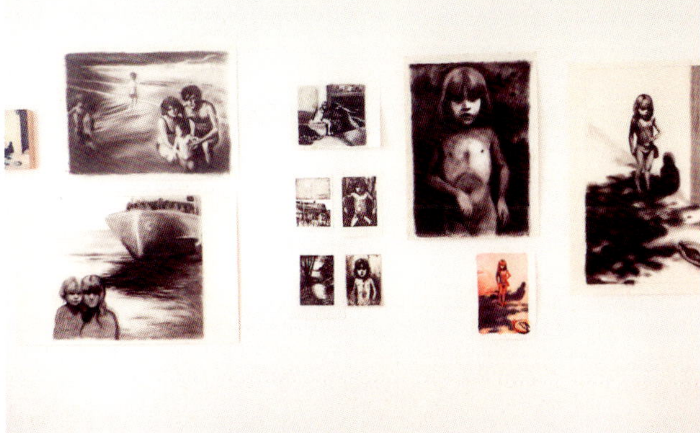

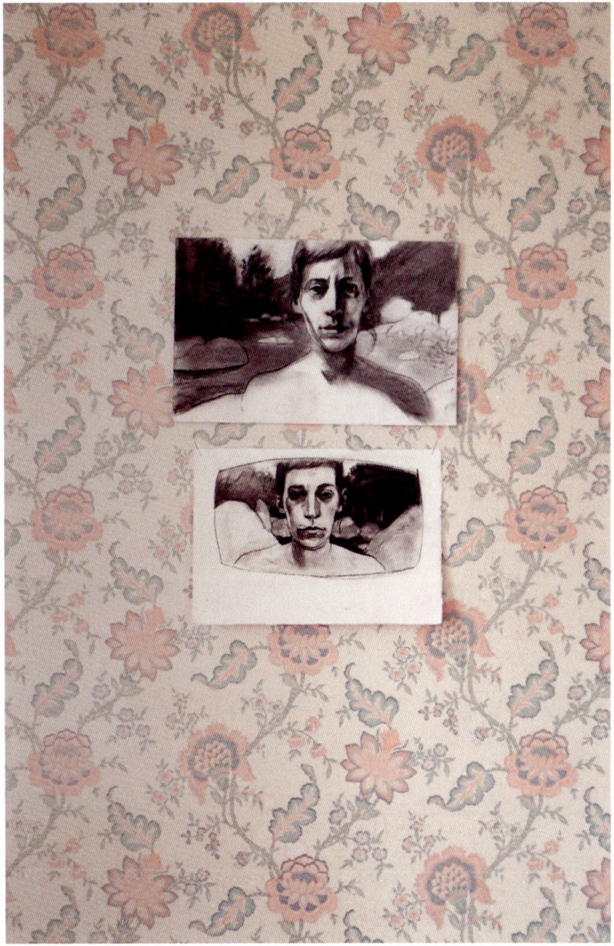

About the authors

Magali Cazo lives and works in France. Drawing has always been her main mode of expression, and today it's her main activity. After studying at the École Nationale Supérieure des Beaux-Arts de Lyon, she trained in several workshops in the city of Paris in living-model drawing, painting, engraving, lithography, morphology, and fresco. She teaches drawing and color at LISAA School of Art and Design (Paris).

the days of a.blogspot.com
cargocollective.com/magalicazo@magalicazo

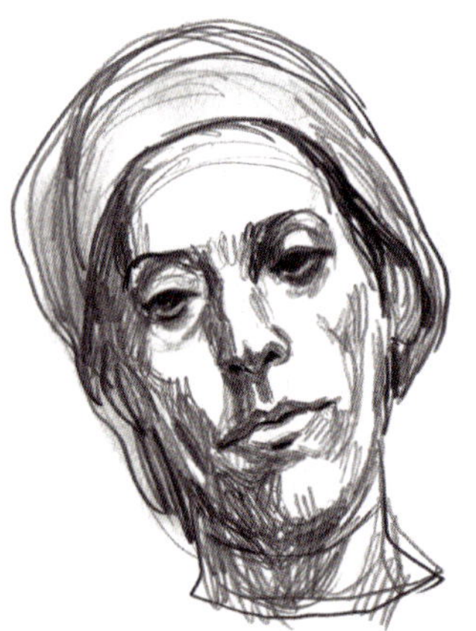

Michel Lauricella was trained at the École Nationale Supérieure des Beaux-arts de Paris. Teaching morphology for about 20 years, he has successively practiced at the Émile Cohl school (Lyon), at the Beaux-Arts workshops of the city of Paris, and at the Gobelins (Paris). He is currently a professor at LISAA (Paris) and at Fabrica 114 (Paris).

www.michellauricella.com
www.fabrica114.com

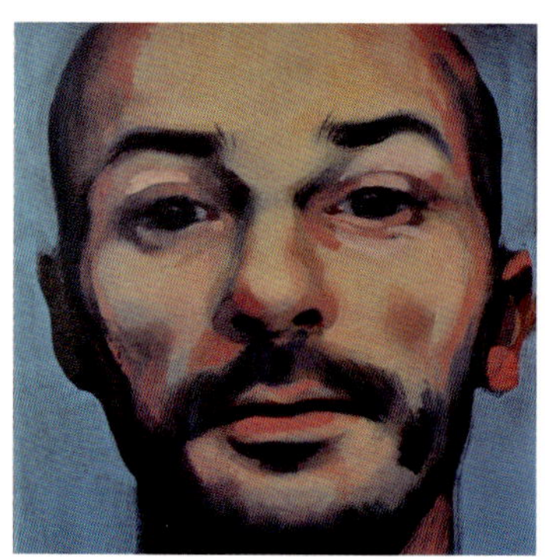

Resources

BIBLIOGRAPHY

- Juliette Aristides, *L'atelier de dessin* Paris: Oskar, 2011).
- Julia Cameron, *Unleash your Creativity* (I read, 2007).
- James Compton, Vegetal (Paris: Phaidon, 2016).
- Henri Cueco, *Le collectionneur de collections* (Paris: Seuil, 2005).
- Philippe Descola, *La fabrique des images* (Paris: Somogy, 2010).
- Bernard Duc, *L'art de la BD*, volume II (Grenoble, France: Glénat, 1983).
- Betty Edwards, *Drawing on the Right Side of the Brain* (Liège, Belgium: Mardaga, 2014).
- Ernst Hans Gombrich, *L'art et l'Illusion* (London: Phaidon, 2002).
- John Hessler, *Maps* (London: Phaidon, 2015).
- André Malraux, "Folio Tests," in *Le musée imaginaire* (Paris: Gallimard, 1996).
- Marcos Mateu-Mestre, *Framed Ink* (Culver City, CA: Design Studio Press, 2010).
- Marcos Mateu-Mestre, *Framed Perspective* (Culver City, CA: Design Studio Press, 2017).
- Ernest R. Norling, *Perspective Made Easy* (Mineola, NY: Dover, 1999).
- Annaïg Plassard and Nicolas Barberon, *De lignes en ligne* (Paris: Eyrolles, 2015).
- Scott Robertson, *How to Draw* (Culver City, CA: Design Studio Press, 2013).
- Sarah Simblet, *Carnets de dessin* (Rennes, France: Ouest-France, 2005).
- Sarah Simblet, *La botanique pour les artistes* (Paris: Eyrolles, 2012).
- Sarah Simblet, *Anatomy for the Artist* (Paris: Dessain and Tolra, 2014).
- Terryl Whitlatch, *The Science of Creature Design* (Culver City, CA: Design Studio Press, 2015).
- Thomas Wienc, *The Nude Drawing* (Paris: Dessain and Tolra, 2010).

YOUTUBE CHANNELS

- James Gurney
- Proko
- Coffee Sketch
- New Masters Academy
- Sketchbook Skool

INSPIRATION SITES

- paletton.com
- moviesincolor.com
- laboiteverte.fr
- boumbang.com
- grandpapier.org
- delignesenligne.com

Library of Congress Control Number: 2020943652

Originally published as *L'Atelier de poche: 52 semaines à dessiner*, © 2018 Éditions Eyrolles, Paris

Graphic design and layout: monsieurgerard.com

All illustrations are by authors, with the exception of photographs pages 16–17 :

1 © RMN copyright management / MCC/IMEC funds, photo © Centre Pompidou, MNAM-CCI, Dist. RMN-Grand Palais/Gisèle Freund, reproduction by Adam Rzepka; 2. Istituzione Bologna Musei/Museo Morandi's Archive (© Paolo Ferrari, Bologna); 3 © Estate Brassaï - RMN-Grand Palais, photo © RMN-Grand Palais/ Michèle Bellot; 4. Sarah Simblet; 5. Edmond Baudoin; 6. Amruta Patil; 7. Coco Fronsac (cocofronsac.com)

Type set in Kasandra Script/Chronicle Display/Pluto
ISBN: 978-0-7643-6185-2
Printed in China

Published by Schiffer Publishing, Ltd.
4880 Lower Valley Road
Atglen, PA 19310
Phone: (610) 593-1777; Fax: (610) 593-2002
E-mail: Info@schifferbooks.com
Web: www.schifferbooks.com